Cornerstone

Your Foundation for
Discovering Your Potential,
Learning Actively,
and Living
Well

FIFTH EDITION

Robert M. Sherfield
The Community College of Southern Nevada

Rhonda J. Montgomery
The University of Nevada, Las Vegas

Patricia J. Moody
The University of South Carolina

PEARSON

Prentice
Hall

Upper Saddle River, New Jersey
Columbus, Ohio

FROM ROBB: *To Matthew Karres*

FROM RHONDA: *To Chuck Delph, my father*

FROM PAT: *To Wallace W. Moody and our grandchildren, Jackson, Lauren, and Josh Moody*

Library of Congress Cataloging-in-Publication Data

Sherfield, Robert M.

Cornerstone: your foundation for discovering your potential, learning actively, and living well / Robert M. Sherfield, Rhonda J. Montgomery, Patricia G. Moody.—5th ed.

p. cm.

Includes bibliographical references and index.

ISBN 0-13-242811-3 (pbk., perforated)

1. College student orientation—United States. 2. Study skills—United States. 3. College students—United States—Life skills guides. I. Montgomery, Rhonda J. II. Moody, Patricia G. III. Title.

LB2343.32.S53 2008

378.1'98—dc22   2006027575

Vice President and Executive Publisher: Jeffery W. Johnston
Executive Editor: Sande Johnson
Development Editor: Jennifer Gessner
Editorial Assistant: Lynda Cramer
Production Editor: Alexandrina Benedicto Wolf
Production Coordination: Thistle Hill Publishing Services, LLC
Design Coordinator: Diane C. Lorenzo
Text and Cover Designer: Kristina D. Holmes
Production Manager: Pamela D. Bennett
Director of Marketing: David Gesell
Marketing Manager: Amy Judd
Marketing Coordinator: Brian Mounts

This book was set in Scala by Carlisle Publishing Services. It was printed and bound by R.R. Donnelley and Sons Company. The cover was printed by Phoenix Color Corp.

Pearson Education Ltd.
Pearson Education Singapore Pte. Ltd.
Pearson Education Canada, Ltd.
Pearson Education—Japan

Pearson Education Australia Pty. Limited
Pearson Education North Asia Ltd.
Pearson Educación de Mexico, S.A. de C.V.
Pearson Education Malaysia Pte. Ltd.

10 9 8 7 6 5 4 3 2 1
ISBN-13: 978-0-13-242811-8
ISBN-10: 0-13-242811-3

Contents

13 RELATE 284

A Celebration of People, Cultures, and Self

14 LIVE 306

Developing Your Plan for Wellness and Personal Responsibility

15 PLAN 326

Focusing on Your Professional Career and Living Well

About the Authors

ROBERT M. SHERFIELD, PH.D.

Robert Sherfield has been teaching public speaking, theatre, and student success and working with first-year orientation programs for over 25 years. A Professor at the Community College of Southern Nevada, he teaches student success, technical writing, public speaking, and drama. Robb is also an adjunct instructor in the College of Hotel Administration's Department of Tourism at The University of Nevada, Las Vegas.

An award-winning educator, Robb was named Educator of the Year at the Community College of Southern Nevada. He twice received the Distinguished Teacher of the Year Award from the University of South Carolina Union, and has received numerous other awards and nominations for outstanding classroom instruction and advisement.

Robb's extensive work with student success programs includes the design and implementation of these programs—including one program that was presented at the International Conference on the First-Year Experience in Newcastle upon Tyne, England. He has conducted faculty development keynotes and workshops at over 250 institutions of higher education across America. He has spoken in 42 states and several foreign countries.

He has also coauthored *Roadways to Success* (Prentice Hall, 2001), the trade book *365 Things I Learned in College* (Allyn & Bacon, 1996), *Capstone: Succeeding Beyond College* (Prentice Hall, 2001), *Case Studies for the First Year: An Odyssey into Critical Thinking and Problem Solving* (Prentice Hall, 2004), and *The Everything® Self-Esteem Book* (Adams Media, 2004).

Robb's interest in student success began with his own first year in college. Low SAT scores and a low high school ranking denied him entrance into college. With the help of a success program, Robb was granted entrance into college and went on to earn five college degrees, including a doctorate. He has always been interested in the social, academic, and cultural development of students and sees this book as his way to contribute to the positive development of first-year students across the nation.

Visit *www.robertsherfield.com*.

RHONDA J. MONTGOMERY, PH.D.

Rhonda J. Montgomery has been teaching, writing, and doing research in the area of first-year orientation programs for the past 24 years. She is an Associate Professor in the William F. Harrah College of Hotel Administration at the University of Nevada, Las Vegas, where she teaches in the Department of Tourism and Convention Administration.

An award-winning educator, Rhonda has been honored as Distinguished Educator of the Year at the University of South Carolina and has received several other awards for teaching and service. She is an active member of Phi Eta Sigma, a National Freshman Honorary Association, and has spoken at the National Conference on the Freshman Year Experience as well as at numerous other conferences around the country.

Her commitment to teaching and scholarship is evidenced by her prolific writing. She has also coauthored *Capstone: Succeeding Beyond College* (Prentice Hall, 2001) and *Case Studies for the First Year: An Odyssey in Critical Thinking and*

Problem Solving (Prentice Hall, 2004). She has also written in the area of hospitality management and written *Club Managers' Guide to Private Parties* (Wiley, 2001), *Meetings, Conventions, and Expositions: An Introduction to the Industry* (Wiley, 1998), as well as a chapter in *Contemporary Club Management* (Perdue, 2003), the trade book *365 Things I Learned in College* (Allyn & Bacon, 1996), as well as numerous articles in scholarly journals.

Patricia G. Moody, Ph.D.

Patricia G. Moody is Dean of the College of Hospitality, Retail and Sport Management at the University of South Carolina, where she has been a faculty member for over 30 years. An award-winning educator, Pat has been honored as Distinguished Educator of the Year at her college, Collegiate Teacher of the Year by the National Business Education Association, and was a top-five finalist for the Amoco Teaching Award at the University of South Carolina. She was a recipient of the prestigious John Robert Gregg Award, the highest honor in her field of over 100,000 educators.

Pat frequently speaks to multiple sections of first-year students, incorporating personal development content from her trademark speech "Fly Like an Eagle," as well as numerous strategies for building self-esteem and for achieving success in college. She also works with first-year classes on subjects such as goal setting, priority management, and diversity.

A nationally known motivational speaker, Pat has spoken in almost every state, has been invited to speak in several foreign countries, and frequently keynotes national and regional conventions. She has presented "Fly Like an Eagle" to thousands of people, from Olympic athletes to corporate executives to high school students. Her most recent presentation is "99 Ways to Motivate Students."

An avid sports fan, she follows Gamecock athletics and has chaired the University of South Carolina Athletics Advisory Committee. As the dean of her college, Dr. Moody has led several international trips to build relationships and establish joint research projects.

Acknowledgments

PROFESSIONAL ACKNOWLEDGMENTS

First, we would like to thank the following individuals at our respective institutions for their support:

At The Community College of Southern Nevada: Dr. Richard Carpenter, President; Dr. Michael Richards, Vice President for Academic Affairs; Dr. Carlos Campo, Dean of Arts and Letters; Professor Rose Hawkins, Chair, Department of English; and Dr. Kathy Baker, Assistant Chair, Department of English.

At The University of Nevada Las Vegas: Dr. Carol Harter, President; Dr. Stuart Mann, Dean, The W. F. Harrah College of Hotel Administration; and Professor Patti Shock, Department Chair, Tourism and Convention Administration.

At The University of South Carolina: Dr. Andrew A. Sorensen, President; and Dr. Mark Becker, Provost.

CONTRIBUTOR ACKNOWLEDGMENTS

Our sincere thanks to Paul Billings, Community College of Southern Nevada, for his contributions to the *At This Moment* assessments; Janet Lindner, Midlands Technical College, for developing the Companion Website; Linda Gannon, Community College of Southern Nevada, for her contributions to the Instructor's Manual, Test Bank, and PowerPoint presentations.

Our fondest gratitude to the following faculty and friends, who recommended students for *The Big Why:* Irma Camacho, El Paso Community College; Chloe Carson, Texas State University; Russell Davis, Houston Community College; Melanie Deffendall, Delgado Community College; Betty Fortune, Houston Community College; Tia Hamilton, Indiana University and Purdue University–Indianapolis; Janet Lindner, Midlands Technical College; Debra McCandrew, Florence-Darlington Technical College; Michael Osterbuhr, Butler Community College; Todd Phillips, East Central College; and Lya Redmond, The Art Institute of Philadelphia; and Darlla Roesler, Western Career College.

We offer our heartfelt thanks to our nominators and contributors to *From Ordinary to Extraordinary—True Stories of Personal Triumph:* Leo G. Borges, William (Bill) Clayton, Melanie Deffendall, Chuck Delph, Wendy Dileonardo, Tina Eliopulos, Dacia Jackson-Peters, Brian Kester, Antoinette Payne, Maureen Riopelle, Catherine Scheligh, and Chef Odette Smith-Ransome.

And thanks to our students who shared their real-life stories for *The Big Why:* Susan Marie Ault, Butler Community College; Oscar Bowser, Midlands Technical College; E. J. Grant, East Central College; La Dondo Johnson, Houston Community College; Paul Genovesse, The Community College of Southern Nevada; Joey Luna, California State University–Los Angeles; Monica Miller, Delgado Community College; Jackie Montgomery, The University of Nevada Las Vegas; Sheena Moses, Florence Darlington Technical College; Sakinah Pendergrass, The Art Institute of Philadelphia; Damion Saunders, Western Career College; Juanita Wilson, University of South Carolina; and Martin Zavala, Texas State University.

OUR WONDERFUL AND INSIGHTFUL REVIEWERS

For the Fifth Edition: Barbara Auris, Montgomery County Community College; Betty Fortune, Houston Community College; Joel V. McGee, Texas A&M University; Jan Norton, University of Wisconsin, Osh Kosh; and Todd Phillips, East Central College.

For Previous Editions: Fred Amador, Phoenix College; Kathy Bryan, Daytona Beach Community College; Dorothy Chase, Community College of Southern Nevada; JoAnn Credle, Northern Virginia Community College; Betty Fortune, Houston Community College; Doroteo Franco Jr., El Paso Community College; Cynthia Garrard, Massasoit Community College; Joel Jessen, Eastfield College; Peter Johnston, Massasoit Community College; Steve Konowalow, Community College of Southern Nevada; Janet Lindner, Midlands Technical College; Carmen McNeil, Solano College; Joan O'Connor, New York Institute of Technology; Mary Pepe, Valancia Community College; Bennie Perdue, Miami-Dade Community College; Ginny Peterson-Tennant, Miami Dade Community College; Anna E. Ward, Miami Dade Community College, Wistar M. Withers, Northern Virginia Community College, and Marie Zander, New York Institute of Technology. Joanne Bassett, Shelby State Community College; Sandra M. Bovain-Lowe, Cumberland Community College; Carol Brooks, GMI Engineering and Management Institute; Elaine H. Byrd, Utah Valley State College; Janet Cutshall, Sussex County Community College; Deborah Daiek, Wayne State University; David DeFrain, Central Missouri State University; Leslie L. Duckworth, Florida Community College at Jacksonville; Marnell Hayes, Lake City Community College; Elzora Holland, University of Michigan, Ann Arbor; Earlyn G. Jordan, Fayetteville State University; John Lowry-King, Eastern New Mexico University; Charlene Latimer; Michael Laven, University of Southwestern Louisiana; Judith Lynch, Kansas State University; Susan Magun-Jackson, The University of Memphis; Charles William Martin, California State University, San Bernardino; Jeffrey A. Miller; Ronald W. Johnsrud, Lake City Community College; Joseph R. Krzyzanowski, Albuquerque TVI; Ellen Oppenberg, Glendale Community College; Lee Pelton, Charles S. Mott Community College; Robert Rozzelle, Wichita State University; Penny Schempp, Western Iowa Community College; Betty Smith, University of Nebraska at Kearney; James Stepp, University of Maine at Presque Isle; Charles Washington, Indiana University—Purdue University; and Katherine A. Wenen-Nesbit, Chippewa Valley Technical College.

OUR CREATIVE AND SUPPORTIVE TEAM AT PEARSON/PRENTICE HALL

Without the support and encouragement of the following people at Prentice Hall, this book would not be possible. Our sincere thanks to Robin Baliszewski, Jeff Johnston, Sande Johnson, and Amy Judd. Your constant belief in us over the years has been a most precious gift. We are lucky to know you and are better people because of you. Thank you!

We also thank the following friends at Pearson/Prentice Hall for their support, dedication, and miraculous hard work: Jenny Gessner, Brenda Rock, Lynda Cramer, Walt Kirby, Debbie Ogilvie, Alan Hensley, Angie Smajstrla, Pam Jeffries, Barbara Donlon, Cathy Bennett, Meredith Chandler, Jeff McIlroy, Steve Foster, Matt Mesaros, and David Gesell.

Our goal in writing *Cornerstone* is to help you discover, build on, and use your academic, social, and personal strengths to enhance your performance. Another goal of *Cornerstone* is to provide you with concrete and useful tools that will help you identify and overcome areas where changes are necessary. We believe that in helping you identify and transform areas that have challenged you in the past, you can *discover your true potential, learn more actively, and live the life you deserve.* We wish you luck in your journey.

SQ3R AND 1941

You may be asking, "What does SQ3R mean and what could it and the year 1941 possibly have to do with me, my texts, this course, and my success?"

The answer: In 1941, Francis P. Robinson, educator and author, developed a reading and study method called SQ3R. It has been one of the most successful and widely used learning tools ever introduced. SQ3R stands for:

S = Scan (or Survey)

Q = Question

3 R = Read, Recite, Review

This simple yet highly effective mnemonic asks that before you actually read a chapter, you look over the contents, check out the figures, look at headings, and review any graphs or charts. This first step is called *Scanning*. Step two, *Question*, asks you to jot down questions that you will later answer about the chapter's content so you can master the material. These questions might come from charts or figures, but most commonly, they come from the chapter's section headings. Examine the following example.

POINT #2

Overcome Your Doubts and Fears

Success is a great motivator but fear can be, too. Fear probably motivates more people than anything else. Unfortunately, fear motivates most people to hold back, to doubt themselves and to accomplish much less than they could have without the fear. One of the biggest obstacles to reaching your potential may be your own personal fears.

From this heading, you might ask:

1. Why is it important to overcome my doubts and fears?
2. How can I go about overcoming my doubts and fears?
3. What consequences might arise if I do not work to overcome my doubts and fears?

After writing these three questions from the section heading above, you will read this section to identify the answers. The technique gives you more focus and purpose for your reading.

The three Rs, *Read, Recite,* and *Review,* ask you to read the chapter; recite major details, ideas, and topics from the chapter; and then go back and review the chapter to make sure you did not omit anything important.

SQ3R is thoroughly discussed in Chapter 4 in this text. The reason we introduce it here is because at the beginning of every chapter, you will see a feature called *Scan & Question*. This feature will help you use SQ3R to get the most out of your reading time and to assist you in mastering the chapter's material.

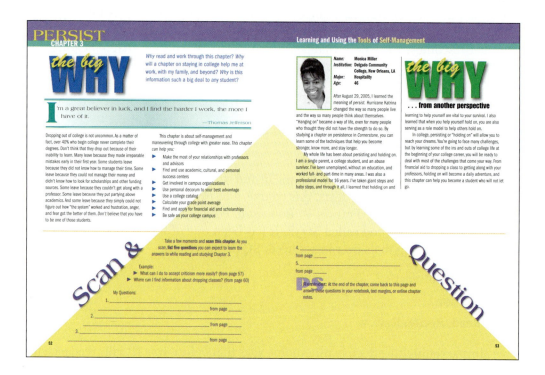

CORNERSTONE AND BLOOM'S TAXONOMY OF COGNITIVE LEARNING

A Strategy for Improving Your Study Skills, Reading Comprehension, Critical Thinking Abilities, and Problem-Solving Skills

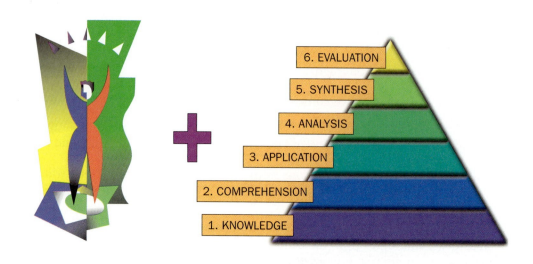

Bloom's Taxonomy (also called Levels of Thinking and Learning) explains the stages at which we all acquire information. These levels progress from simple learning and thinking (levels 1, 2, 3) to more complex learning and thinking (levels 4, 5, 6). Each chapter ends with an exercise called *Knowledge in Bloom*. This activity helps you process and apply the information from the chapter. Also, as you read through each chapter, you will be asked to reflect and respond to questions from each level. The level of learning and thinking is indicated on the pyramid.

For example, in Chapter 1, pages 6–7, you will find a checklist of skills that college can help you acquire. After reviewing the list, you will be asked the following question:

Which skill is most important to you? _____

Discuss how you think this skill will help you in your college classes, in your profession, and in your personal life. _____

_____

_____

_____

Bloom Level 2 question

As indicated by the pyramid, this is a level 2 question. Each chapter contains several pyramids.

IMPORTANT TERMS

Bloom, Benjamin: A scholar, editor, evaluation specialist, and professor of education at The University of Chicago. He edited the popular book *The Taxonomy of Educational Objectives,* from which Bloom's Taxonomy is taken.

Taxonomy: A way of classifying information into categories.

Cognitive Domain: The development of intellectual and/or mental skills such as the recall, recognition, perception, interpretation, and manipulation of information. Basically, the way we acquire knowledge.

SO, WHY USE BLOOM IN CORNERSTONE?

Bloom's Taxonomy is important to us because it helps us determine the level at which we understand important information. For example, it is important to be able to answer questions at level 1 such as:

▶ Abraham Lincoln was the _____ president of the United States.
▶ Abraham Lincoln's wife's name was _____ _____ Lincoln.

However, it is also important to be able to answer questions at levels 5 and 6, such as:

▶ Based on your knowledge of the Civil War era, predict what would have happened to the United States without the Emancipation Proclamation. Justify your answer.
▶ Summarize the main events that led to President Lincoln's assassination.

As you can clearly see, there is a great difference between these levels of learning. The higher the level, the more information and knowledge you need to be able to respond to the question or problem.

The chapter-end activity *Knowledge in Bloom,* will help you process and demonstrate your knowledge at different levels. This is important because you will have professors who **teach and test** at levels 1, 2, and 3 and those who **teach and test** at levels 4, 5, and 6. Learning to process and demonstrate your knowledge at every level can assist you in:

▶ Doing well in other classes by providing a foundation for effective studying/learning.

▶ Learning to solve problems more thoroughly.

▶ Predicting exam questions.

▶ Learning how to critically evaluate and assess ideas and issues.

▶ Learning to thoroughly and objectively research topics for papers and presentations.

▶ Testing your own reading comprehension.

Examine the Bloom's Taxonomy (Levels of Thinking and Learning) on page xv. You may need to refer to this chart throughout the text and the course. A quick reference chart is also included inside the front cover.

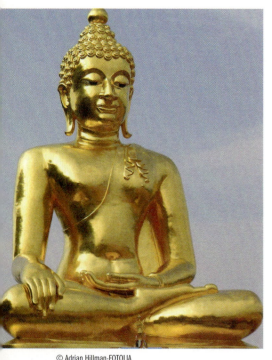

© Adrian Hillman-FOTOLIA

YOUR GOLDEN POTENTIAL

Have you ever thought of yourself as golden? More importantly, have you ever treated yourself as if you are golden? We wanted to begin your journey through *Cornerstone* with a true story about discovering your golden self.

In 1957, a massive statue of Buddha was being moved from a temple in Thailand that had been abandoned in the early 1930s. The Buddha stands over 15 feet tall and measures over 12 feet in diameter. A crane had to be used to move the massive statue, but when the crane began to lift the Buddha, the weight of it was so great that the statue began to crack. To make matters even worse, it began to rain. Concerned with the condition of the Buddha, the head monk decided to have the statue lowered so that it could be covered with a canvas until the rain stopped.

As nightfall came, the head monk peered under the canvas with a flashlight to see if the statue had begun to dry. As he moved the light around, he noticed something shining beneath one of the cracks and wondered if something was under the clay. As he hammered and chiseled away at the crack, he found that the clay Buddha was *not* made of clay after all. The monk found that the 15-foot statue was really made of pure, 18-carat gold.

Many scholars and historians believe that the Buddha was cast sometime in the mid-1200s. It is suggested that in the 1700s the Siamese monks knew that the Burmese army planned to attack them and, hoping to protect their statue, they covered it in eight inches of clay, which dried and hardened much like concrete. When the army attacked, all of the monks in the village were killed, leaving no one who knew the truth about the Buddha. The clay remained intact until the statue was moved on a rainy day in 1957.

BLOOM'S TAXONOMY
Examining the Levels of Thinking and Learning

Levels of thinking and learning (the more common term is italicized)	Skills you should have at this level (sometimes called action verbs or action questions)	Questions or activities you might anticipate or products you may have to generate
1—Knowledge *(Remember)* This level is based on simple recall of information. This type of knowledge usually comes from being told or basic reading. It is the "lowest" or most simple type of learning.	Write, list, label, name, state, define, describe, identify, recognize, recall, draw, select, locate, recite, quote, order, state, reproduce, match, tell, and the five standards (who, what, when, where, and how)	What is . . . , When did . . . , Why did . . . , Who were . . . , Describe the . . . , Which of the following . . . , Define the . . . **Example:** What are the six levels of learning in Bloom's Taxonomy?
2—Comprehension *(Understand)* This level determines your grasp or comprehension level of the information presented. It asks, "Do you understand the meaning?"	Summarize, describe, interpret, contrast, predict, associate, distinguish, estimate, differentiate, discuss, extend, convert, explain, generalize, give examples, rewrite, restate, classify, translate, paraphrase, illustrate, visualize, retell	How would you contrast . . . , Explain why the . . . , Summarize the main . . . , What facts show . . . , Predict the outcome of . . . , Restate the . . . **Example:** Explain why Bloom's Taxonomy is being used in *Cornerstone* and describe its importance.
3—Application *(Use)* This level asks you to "use" the information you have by solving, showing, or applying that information in "real-world" or workplace situations.	Apply, demonstrate, discover, modify, operate, predict, solve, draw, dramatize, model, sketch, paint, produce, prepare, make, calculate, record, compute, manipulate, modify, use, employ	How could you use . . . , How could you solve . . . , What approach would you take . . . , Why is ___ significant? **Example:** Prepare a plan to show how you could use Bloom's Taxonomy to get a better grade in your history class.
4—Analysis *(Examine)* This level asks you to "take apart" the information for clarification, classification, and prioritizing. It also asks you to recognize what is "not" said (i.e., hidden meanings and unstated assumptions). This level requires that you distinguish between facts and inferences.	Break down, distinguish, infer, arrange, prioritize, order, divide, categorize, appraise, test, examine, separate, deduce, choose, compare/contrast, detect, group, sequence, scrutinize, connect, outline, research, point out	How is ___ related to ___?, What conclusions can be drawn . . . , What is the relationship between . . . , Categorize the main . . . , Based on X, why is Y . . . **Example:** What assumptions can be made about the rest of the term if your history teacher's first two exams included 20 questions, all from level 6?
5—Synthesis *(Create / Generate)* This level asks you to integrate your previous knowledge with your new knowledge and come up with new ideas, plans, and solutions. It also asks you to be able to predict outcomes based on what you have learned. This level asks you to be innovative and creative.	Compose, combine, compile, create, design, generate, construct, revise, write, rewrite, tell, role play, formulate, invent, develop, modify, arrange, rearrange, prepare, assemble, set up, forecast, imagine, act, improvise, propose, substitute, integrate, incorporate	What would you predict . . . , How could you improve . . . , How could you test . . . , What alternative could you . . . , How would you design . . . , How would you create . . . **Example:** Write two possible test questions from each level of Bloom's Taxonomy from Chapter 1 of *Cornerstone*.
6—Evaluation *(Critique)* The highest level asks you to make personal judgments about the value of issues, ideas, policies, and evidence based on your complete understanding of the information and based on stated judging criteria.	Decide, rank, test, measure, recommend, defend, conclude, appraise, assess, judge, predict, rate, select, critique, justify, estimate, validate, measure, discriminate, probe, award, rank, reject, grade, convince, weigh, support	What is your opinion of . . . , How would you rate . . . , What judgment could you make . . . , Justify your opinion of . . . , Based on your research, convince the reader of your paper that . . . , What criteria would you use to assess the . . . **Example:** Assess how effective Bloom's Taxonomy was when used to study for your history exam. Recommend two ways to improve the use of Bloom's Taxnomy for the next test.

Today, the Golden Buddha, which was once covered with clay and abandoned, is said to be valued at almost two hundred million dollars.

Your Golden Opportunity

We all have incredible talents, skills, and experiences that are all too often covered or underdeveloped. We move through life hiding our brightness—our golden self. As you begin to read and work through *Cornerstone,* we want you to think about the strengths and talents that you already have and how you can polish and bring out their brilliance. We want you to chip away at the clay that may have been covering your true potential for years. We want you to explore who you really are, what you have to offer to the world, and how best to live up to your true golden potential. We also want you to think about the attitudes, beliefs, or behaviors that you may have to adjust to create your pathway to success.

In discovering your potential, we also invite you to:

Discover your open-mindedness.   A truly educated person learns to consider a person's character rather than the color of a person's skin, religion, sexual orientation, or ethnic background. As you become more open-minded, you will understand the need to learn before judging, to reason before reacting, and to delve deeper before condemning. As you discover your potential, strive hard to be more open-minded.

Discover your competence and ability to question.   You have already established a certain level of competence or you wouldn't be here. Now is the time to push yourself to learn more than you ever have before. Your future depends on the knowledge you gain today. As you move through the coming months and years, don't be afraid to ask questions of others, especially your professors. Questioning is the first step in becoming more competent and a more critical and logical thinker. Asking the right questions and listening will help you become a more active learner. You also have the opportunity to learn from your peers and their experiences.

Discover your need to be challenged.   The easy road will never lead to greatness or help you discover your true potential. Winston Churchill said, "It is from adversity that we gain greatness." When you are struggling, remember that you are getting stronger. You are preparing to be the person you were meant to be. As you register for classes, search for professors, volunteer for projects, and explore internships, choose those that will challenge and ultimately lead you to another level in the search of your true potential.

Discover your ability to balance.   No single thing will ever bring you joy, peace, or prosperity. Include family, friends, cultural events, social activities, work, and service to others in your daily life. Seek balance between work and play. Unless you have a sense of balance in your life, you will endlessly search for happiness. Harmony and balance help you reduce stress, have more time for what you love, and live well.

Discover your success and true potential.   You need to define exactly what success means to you so know what you are working toward. Whatever success is for you, pursue it with all of the passion and energy you have. Set your goals high and work hard to create a life you can ultimately look back on with pride, satisfaction, and joy. Create a life so that at the end of the road, you will be able to look back and say, "I did my best, I have no regrets."

Robb, Rhonda, Pat

INSTRUCTOR SUPPORT

Resources to simplify your life and engage your students.

Book Specific: Print

▶ Instructor's Manual with Test Bank   ISBN 0-13-229531-8
▶ PowerPoint Acetates   ISBN 0-13-223605-2

Technology

Easy access to online, book-specific teaching support is now just a click away!

Instructor Resource Center   Register. Redeem. Login. Three easy steps that open the door to a variety of print and media resources in downloadable, digital format, available to instructors exclusively through the Prentice Hall IRC. *www.prenhall.com*

Register today at www.prenhall.com to access instructor resources digitally.

Teaching an online course, offering a hybrid class, or simply introducing your students to technology, just got a whole lot easier!

OneKey Course Management   All you and your students need to succeed. OneKey is Prentice Hall's exclusive new resource for instructors and students providing access to the best online teaching and learning tools—24 hours a day, 7 days a week. OneKey means all your resources are in one place for maximum convenience, simplicity and success. Visit *www.prenhall.com/onekey* and scroll to Student Success through the gallery option for additional information.

Reinforce strong research skills, library usage, and combat plagiarism with this tool!

Prentice Hall's Research Navigator   Designed to help students with the research process, from identifying a topic to editing the final draft, it also offers guidance

on how to make time at the campus library more productive. RN includes four databases of credible and reliable source material to get your research process started: The EBSCO/Content Select, New York Times, Link Library, and The Financial Times. Visit *www.researchnavigator.com* for additional information.

Choose from a wide range of video resources for the classroom!

Prentice Hall Reference Library: Life Skills Pack   ISBN 0-13-127079-6 contains all 4 videos, or they may be requested individually as follows:

▶ Learning Styles and Self-Awareness, ISBN 0-13-028502-1

▶ Critical and Creative Thinking, ISBN 0-13-028504-8

▶ Relating to Others, ISBN 0-13-028511-0

▶ Personal Wellness, ISBN 0-13-028514-5

Prentice Hall Reference Library: Study Skills Pack   ISBN 0-13-127080-X contains all 6 videos, or they may be requested individually as follows:

▶ Reading Effectively, ISBN 0-13-028505-6

▶ Listening and Memory, ISBN 0-13-028506-4

▶ Note Taking and Research, ISBN 0-13-028508-0

▶ Writing Effectively, ISBN 0-13-028509-9

▶ Effective Test Taking, ISBN 0-13-028500-5

▶ Goal Setting and Time Management, ISBN 0-13-028503-X

Prentice Hall Reference Library: Career Skills Pack   ISBN 0-13-118529-2 contains all 3 videos, or they may be requested individually as follows:

▶ Skills for the 21st Century – Technology, ISBN 0-13-028512-9

▶ Skills for the 21st Century – Math and Science, ISBN 0-13-028513-7

▶ Managing Career and Money, ISBN 0-13-028516-1

Faculty Video Resources

▶ Teacher Training Video 1: Critical Thinking, ISBN 0-13-099432-4

▶ Teacher Training Video 2: Stress Management & Communication, ISBN 0-13-099578-9

▶ Teacher Training Video 3: Classroom Tips, ISBN 0-13-917205-X

▶ Student Advice Video, ISBN 0-13-233206-X

▶ Study Skills Video, ISBN 0-13-096095-0

▶ Building on Your Best Video, ISBN 0-20-526277-5

Current Issues Videos

▶ ABC News Video Series: Student Success, ISBN 0-13-031901-5

▶ ABC News Video, ISBN 0-13-152865-3

Faculty Development Series Workshops

▶ Sherfield: Cornerstone Workshop DVD, ISBN 0-13-171784-7

Active Learning Video   Video Cases on CD-ROM, ISBN 0-13-171063-X (Features six core issues within a peer setting, classroom setting, and expert commentator. Allows for real world application 24/7.)

T hrough partnership opportunities, we offer a variety of assessment options!

LASSI   The LASSI is a 10-scale, 80-item assessment of students' awareness about and use of learning and study strategies. Addressing skill, will and self-regulation, the focus is on both covert and overt thoughts, behaviors, attitudes, and beliefs that relate to successful learning and that can be altered through educational interventions. Available in paper, ISBN 0-13-172315-4, or online formats ISBN 0-13-172316-2 (Access Card).

Noel Levitz/RMS   This retention tool measures Academic Motivation, General Coping Ability, Receptivity to Support Services, plus Social Motivation. It helps identify at-risk students, the areas with which they struggle, and their receptiveness to support. Available in paper or online formats, as well as short and long versions. Paper Long Form A: 0-13-072258-8; Paper Form B: 0-13-079193-8; Online Forms A&B: 0-13-098158-3.

Robbins Self Assessment Library   This compilation teaches students to create a portfolio of skills. S.A.L. is a self-contained, interactive library of 49 behavioral questionnaires that help students discover new ideas about themselves, their attitudes, and their personal strengths and weaknesses. Available in paper, 0-13-173861-5; CD-ROM, 0-13-149804-5; and Online, 0-13-191445-6 (Access Card) formats.

Readiness for Education at a Distance Indicator (READI)   READI is a Web-based tool that assesses the overall likelihood for online learning success. READI generates an immediate score and a diagnostic interpretation of results, including recommendations for successful participation in online courses and potential remediation sources. Please visit *www.readi.info* for additional information. ISBN 0-13-188967-2.

T eaching tolerance and discussing diversity with your students can be challenging!

Responding to Hate at School   Published by the Southern Poverty Law Center, the Teaching Tolerance handbook is a step-by-step, easy-to-use guide designed to help administrators, counselors, and teachers react promptly and efficiently whenever hate, bias, and prejudice strike. ISBN 0-13-028458-0.

F or a terrific one-stop shop resource, utilize our Student Success Supersite!

Supersite (www.prenhall.com/success)   Students and professors alike may use the Supersite for activities, success stories, links, and more. To access PowerPoint slides, sample syllabi, articles and newsletters, supplemental information and more, instructors may go to the Faculty Lounge. Contact your local representative for ID and password information.

For a truly tailored solution that fosters campus connections and increases retention, talk with us about Custom Publishing.

Pearson Custom Publishing   We are the largest custom provider for print and media shaped to your course's needs. Please visit us at *www.pearsoncustom.com* to learn more.

STUDENT SUPPORT

Tools to help make the grade now, and excel in school later.

We offer an online study aid to help students fully understand each chapter's content, and assess their knowledge through practice quizzes and exercises.

Companion Website   Please visit the site for this text at *www.prenhall.com/sherfield*.

We recognize students may want a choice of how their text is delivered.

Where the Web meets textbooks for STUDENT SAVINGS.

SafariX eTextbooks Online   This joint venture between the industry's leading technical publishers, O'Reilly Media, Inc. and The Pearson Technology Group, provides an alternative to the traditional print version of the text. The entire book can be purchased in an online format for 50% off the cost. Now students have a choice! ISBN 0-13-156303-3.

Because students are pressed for time, we offer an alternative for studying on the go.

VangoNotes   Students are busy – we get it. With VangoNotes students can study "in between" all the other things they have to do to succeed in the classroom. These notes are flexible; just download and go. They're efficient; study in the car, at the gym or walking to class. Visit *www.prenhall.com/vangonotes* for additional information.

Hear it. Get it.

Time management is the number #1 challenge students face— we can help.

Prentice Hall Planner   A basic planner that includes a monthly and daily calendar, plus other materials to facilitate organization. $8\frac{1}{2} \times 11$.

Franklin Covey Planner   This specially designed, annual 4-color collegiate planner includes an academic planning/resources section, monthly planning (2 pages/month) and weekly planning (48 weeks; July start date). Spiral bound, 6×9.

Journaling activities promote self-discovery and self-awareness.

Student Reflection Journal   Through this vehicle, students are encouraged to track their progress and share their insights, thoughts, and concerns. $8^1/_2 \times 11$. 90 pages.

Our Student Success Supersite is a one-stop shop for students to learn about career paths, peer stories, and more!

Supersite (www.phenhall.com/success)   Students will benefit from sections such as Majors Exploration, Academic Skills, Career Path, Student Union, and more.

Learning to adapt to the diverse college community is essential to students' success.

10 Ways to Fight Hate   Produced by the Southern Poverty Law Center, the leading hate-crime and crime-watch organization in the United States, this guide walks students through 10 steps that they can take on their own campus or in their own neighborhood to fight hate every day. ISBN 0-13-028146-8.

The Student Orientation Series includes short booklets on specialized topics for facilitating greater understanding by students.

S.O.S. Guides   Connolly, *Learning Communities* ISBN 0-13-232243-9 and Watts, *Service Learning*, ISBN 0-13-232201-3, help students understand what these learning opportunities are, how to take advantage of them, and learn from their peers while doing so.

1

Change

© Getty Images

The greatest reward of an education is to be able to face the world with an open mind.

R. M. Sherfield

Why read and work through this chapter? *Why* will I ever be asked to use this stuff? *Why* will a chapter on change and goal setting help me in college, at work, with my family, and beyond? *Why* is this information such a big deal?

I have no clue as to how my story will end. But that's all right. When you set out on a journey and night covers the road, that's when you discover the stars.

—Nancy Willard

This chapter—indeed, this whole book and the course in which you are enrolled—is about helping you become the best college student, peer mentor, leader, citizen, and lifelong learner that you can possibly be. Quite simply, this chapter is included to help you identify your strengths and build on them, *and* to help you identify areas where you might need to change your actions or behaviors by setting realistic goals.

Learning to deal with *change* while setting and working toward your *goals* can be an essential key to your success in college and beyond. *This chapter can help you:*

► Adjust to life as a college student.
► Determine how college can help you beyond the classroom.

► Understand the demands and realities of your professors and institution.
► Comprehend the differences among high school, college, and career.
► Eliminate harmful roadblocks and negative attitudes.
► Create positive changes by setting and working toward realistic, measurable goals.

We hope this chapter will be an exciting introduction to a life filled with learning, growing, and new opportunities. Enjoy the ride. You'll never be the same!

Scan &

In Chapter 5, you will learn how to use the **SQ3R study method**. This mnemonic stands for **S**can, **Q**uestion, **R**ead, **R**ecite, and **R**eview. Scanning asks you to look over the chapter before reading it. Look at the headings, charts, photos, and call-out boxes. Questioning asks you to create study questions from the major headings. Take a few moments and **scan this chapter**. As you scan, **list five questions** you can expect to learn the answers to while reading and studying Chapter 1.

Example:
► What are the six basic truths about the culture of college? (from page 8)
► Why must goals be measurable? (from page 17)

My Questions:
1._____ from page _____

Name:	**Mark**
Institution:	**Spartanburg Methodist College, Spartanburg, SC**
Major:	**Associate of Arts— Theatre and Speech**
Age:	**18**

I am the son of textile workers. Both of my parents worked in a cotton mill for over 30 years. My hometown is in the rural South about 35 miles from the nearest metropolitan area. I attended a small high school and had never been a good student. Because of my poor academic performance through the years, full-time job, and family commitments, I decided to attend a community college and then transfer to a four-year college.

I finished high school with a D– average and my SAT scores and class rank were in the lowest 25th percentile. In fact, I was denied entrance to the community college. The college granted me provisional acceptance only if I enrolled in, and successfully completed, a summer preparatory program. I graduated high school on a Friday night and began my college studies the very next Monday morning in the prep program. I never realized what lay ahead.

My first class that semester was English. Professor Brannon walked in, handed out the syllabus, called the roll, and began to lecture. Lord Byron was the topic for the day.

the big WHY

. . . from another perspective

The class ended and after an hour's break, I headed across campus for history. Professor Wilkerson entered with a dust storm behind her. She went over the syllabus, and before we had a chance to blink, she was involved in the first lecture. "The cradle of civilization," she began, "was Mesopotamia." We all scurried to find notebooks and pens to begin taking notes. I could not believe I was already behind. "Who teaches on the first day?" I questioned.

One minute before class ended, she closed her book, looked directly at us, and said, "You are in history now. You elected to take this class and you will follow my rules. You are not to be late, you are to come to this class prepared, and you are to do your homework assignments. If you do what I ask you to do, you will learn more about Western civilization than you ever thought possible. If you don't keep up with me, you won't know if you are in Egypt, Mesopotamia, or pure hell! Class dismissed!"

(continued)

Question

2. _____
_____
from page _____
3. _____
from page _____
4. _____
from page _____
5. _____
from page _____

PS

Reminder: At the end of the chapter, come back to this page and answer these questions in your notebook, text margins, or online chapter notes.

Without a moment to spare, I ran to the other end of campus for my next class. I walked into the room in a panic, fearing I was late. To my surprise, the instructor was not yet in class. We waited almost 15 minutes before the professor entered. "You need to sign this roster and read Chapter 1 for Wednesday," he said. "You can pick up a syllabus on your way out." I was shocked. Was the class over?

On the 30-mile trip home, my mind was filled with new thoughts: *Lord Byron, Mesopotamia, professors who talked too fast, professors who did not talk at all, tuition, parking, the size of the library.* I knew that something was different, *something had changed in me.* I couldn't put my finger on it. It would be years later before I would realize that the change was not my classes, not my schedule, not the people, not the professors, but me; *I had changed.* In one day, I had tasted something intoxicating, something that was addictive. *I had tasted a new world.*

I had to go to work that afternoon at the mill, and even my job and my coworkers had changed. I had always known that I did not want to spend the rest of my life in the factory, but this day the feeling was stronger. My job was not enough, my family was not enough, the farm on which I had been raised was not enough anymore. *There was a new light for me, and I knew that because of one day in college, I would never be the same.* It was like tasting Godiva chocolate for the first time—Hershey's Kisses were no longer enough. It was like seeing the ocean for the first time and knowing that the millpond would never be the same. *I couldn't go back. What I knew before was simply not enough.*

My name is Robert *Mark* Sherfield, and 30 years later, as I coauthor your *Cornerstone* text, I am still addicted to that new world. College changed my life, and I am still changing—with every day, every new book I read, every new class I teach, every new person I meet, and every new place to which I travel, I am changing. I wish for you the same wonderful journey.

The college experience is different for every person.

© Stockdisc

COLLEGE AND YOU

The Partnership of a Lifetime!

Right now, you're one of almost four million first-year students enrolled in higher education in America. Some have enrolled to gain the skills and/or degree necessary to enter a great career field. Some are here for retraining, and some are here to complete a dream begun years ago. Some of your classmates may have recently lost a job and they are here to get skills and expertise that were not available 10 or 15 years ago. Regardless of your reason, you've made the first step and just like Mark in the opening story, your life will never be the same.

So, what can college do for you? The list will certainly vary depending on whom you ask, but basically, college can help you accomplish the following:

_____ Grow more self-sufficient and self-confident.
_____ Understand more about the world in which you live.
_____ Become a more involved citizen in social and political issues.
_____ Become more open-minded.
_____ Understand the value of thinking, analyzing, and problem solving.
_____ Develop your investigative and research skills.
_____ Develop commanding computer and information literacy skills.
_____ Manage your personal resources such as time and money.
_____ Become more proficient at written and oral communication.

_____   Grow more understanding and broad-minded about different cultures.
_____   Become a lifelong learner.
_____   Enter a career field that you enjoy.
_____   Become more financially independent.

Take a moment and place a check mark beside the statements that most accurately reflect the skills you hope to gain from attending college. If there are other skills that you desire to achieve from your college experience, list them here.

_____

_____

_____

Which skill is most important to you? _____

Discuss how you think this skill will help you in your college classes, in your profession, and in your personal life. _____

_____

_____

_____

Bloom Level 2 question

According to one of the leading research sources in higher education, _The Chronicle of Higher Education_ (August 26, 2005), first-year students had a variety of reasons for attending college such as: "To learn about things that interest me," "To get training for a specific career," and "To be able to get a better job." However, 70.1% of those polled stated that their reason for attending college was, "To be able to make more money" (p. 18).

Depending on how you approach college, especially your first semester, it will be one of the most exciting and important times of your life—regardless of your age, interests, past experiences, or reasons for attending. College can bring rewards of the mind, rewards of the soul, and yes, rewards of a more lucrative future.

According to the United States Census Bureau in the _Annual Social and Economic Supplement_ (issued in 2004), people with degrees in higher education earn considerably more than those who do not have a degree. For instance, men and women with a bachelor's degree average approximately $24,000 _more per year_ in earnings than those with only a high school education. Men and women with an associate's degree average approximately $20,000 more per year in earnings than those with only a high school education. For a complete look at the earning power of U.S. citizens over age 18, look at the Annual Earnings Chart in Figure 1.1.

> The real object of education is to give you resources that will endure as long as life endures.
>
> —S. Smith

By focusing on money in this section, we do not mean to suggest that the only reason for attending college is to make more money. As a matter of fact, we feel that it is a secondary reason. Many people without college degrees earn huge salaries each year. Yes, college may make that road easier, but college can also be a place where you make decisions about your values, your character, and your future. College can be a place where you make decisions about the changes that need to occur in your life.

The _Chronicle of Higher Education's_ annual report on first-year students does not list "I want to change" as one of the reasons for attending college. If you ask your

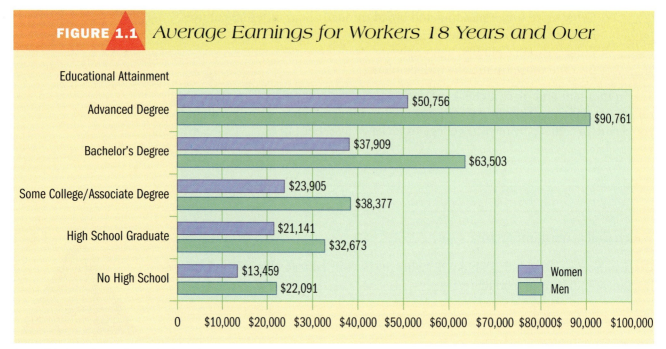

FIGURE 1.1 *Average Earnings for Workers 18 Years and Over*

Educational Attainment

- Advanced Degree — $50,756 / $90,761
- Bachelor's Degree — $37,909 / $63,503
- Some College/Associate Degree — $23,905 / $38,377
- High School Graduate — $21,141 / $32,673
- No High School — $13,459 / $22,091

Women / Men

0 $10,000 $20,000 $30,000 $40,000 $50,000 $60,000 $70,000 $80,000 $90,000 $100,000

Source: U.S. Census Bureau, *Current Population Survey, Annual Social and Economic Supplement* (June, 2004).

> **F**orget mistakes. Forget failures. Forget everything except what you're going to do now . . . and do it.
>
> —Will Durant

classmates, they will probably not give you this answer either. But *change* is one of the most important concepts and realities that you will face. It is one of the most common denominators for all college students and, effectively managed, it can be an exhilarating adventure.

You are going to experience changes in your attitudes, your values, your actions, and your intellectual character. You are going to notice changes in old relationships and even in the relationships with your family members. Many of the changes will be positive and rewarding. Sure, there will be a few changes that test your nature and temperament, but that is why this chapter is included in the book—to help you understand how to navigate difficult changes and create positive changes in your life by setting goals.

THE CULTURE OF COLLEGE

Six Basic Truths from Boot Camp 101

In your lifetime, you will experience many things that influence and alter your views, goals, and livelihood. These may include things such as travel, relationships, and personal victories or setbacks. However, few experiences will have a greater influence than your college experience. College can mean hopes realized, dreams fulfilled, and the breaking down of social and economic walls. To get the most from your college experience and to lay a path to success, it will be important to look at your expectations and the vast differences between high school, previous jobs, and the culture of college. This section will introduce you to some of the changes you can expect.

Where Are You . . .

AT THIS MOMENT

Before reading any further, take a moment and assess where you are at this moment with your knowledge and application of change and goal setting. Read each statement carefully and then respond accordingly.

1. I am excited about college and all of the changes and challenges it offers.   YES ☐   NO ☐

2. I look forward to meeting and interacting with my professors.   YES ☐   NO ☐

3. I think that I am going to enjoy reading about, hearing, and discussing opinions, issues, and situations that are very different from my own perspective.   YES ☐   NO ☐

4. I am excited that college is going to be more demanding than high school.   YES ☐   NO ☐

5. I know that college offers me more freedom and I am sure that I will make wise use of my free time.   YES ☐   NO ☐

6. I know how to set realistic goals to bring about positive change in my life.   YES ☐   NO ☐

7. In my past, I have always been able to deal with major life changes with relative ease.   YES ☐   NO ☐

If you answered "yes" to most of the questions (five or more), you are well on your way to enjoying and benefiting from your first term in college. You understand the value of change and goal setting and are probably good at both. *If you answered "no"* to most of the questions, you may need to talk to your advisor, friends, family, or other trusted individuals about your initial college experience and how best to proceed. You may need to do more research on goal setting and how to bring about positive change in your life.

Basic truth #1: College is a two-way street. Perhaps the first thing that you will notice about college is that you have to give in order to receive. Not only do you have expectations of your institution and professors, but your institution and professors have expectations — great expectations—of you. To be successful you will need to accept substantially more responsibility for your education than you may have in the past. By attending your college of choice, you have agreed to become a part of its community, values, and policies. You now have the responsibility to stand by its code of academic and moral conduct, and you have the responsibility to give your very best to every class and organization in which you are involved. And you have a responsibility to *yourself* to approach this new world with an open mind and curious enthusiasm. In return, your institution will be responsible in helping you reach your fullest potential and live the life you desire.

So, what are your thoughts at the moment? Respond to the following questions honestly and personally.

Regardless of your background or reasons for attending college, the experience of change is something you'll share with everyone. Will you be able to open yourself up to new people and new situations?

© Corbis

1. My toughest professor this term is Mr./Mrs./Ms./Dr. _____
   Thus far, I've learned that she or he expects me to _____

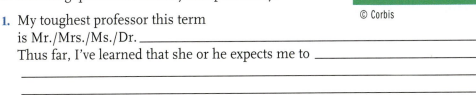

2. To meet this expectation, how will my academic habits have to change?

_____

_____

3. To meet this expectation, how will my personal habits have to change?

_____

_____

_____

4. By meeting this expectation, what will I gain?

_____

_____

_____

> The will to win, the desire to succeed, the urge to reach your full potential . . . these are the keys that will unlock your personal excellence.
>
> —Eddie Robinson

Basic truth #2: Freedom is seldom free. Maybe you're one of those people who works best when you have one thing after another to accomplish with little time to get it all done. If so, you're not alone. Many people do their best when they are busy and have a limited amount of time. One of the first changes you will notice about college is the *degree of freedom* you are given. Yes, freedom! There are no tardy notes to be sent to the principal's office, no hall passes, no mandates from the state regarding attendance, and usually no parent telling you to get up and get ready for school. You may have only one or two classes in a day. "Great!" you say, and maybe you're right. This freedom can be wonderful, but it can also be dangerous. This is sometimes called the **Freedom Trap.** Understanding your work and study habits, planning your time wisely, and planning time for joy and entertainment can help you handle your freedom. Chapter 4 will help you learn how to set priorities.

Have you met someone thus far in the term who can help you if you feel yourself getting behind or procrastinating too much?

_____

_____

Bloom Level 4 question

Examine your current class and work schedule. Based on the times you are in class, the hours that you work, and your family commitments, what is going to be the most effective time of the day (or night) for you to study and avoid the "Freedom Trap"? Why?

_____

_____

_____

_____

Basic truth #3: You're in charge here. Another change coming your way involves the workload for your courses and the choices *you* will make regarding your schedule and classes. As you plan, consider that the workload is likely to be greater than what you are used to. You may be assigned a significant amount of reading as homework. Although you may have only two classes in one day, the rule of thumb is that for every hour spent in class, a minimum of 2 hours should be spent in review and preparation for the next class. Quick math: If you are taking 5 classes and are in class for 15 hours per week, you need to spend 30 hours studying; this makes a 45-hour week—5 hours more than a normal workweek for most people! "Not I," you may say, and you may be right. It all depends on how wisely you use your time and how difficult the work is. Think about your schedule before you register to make sure that you have enough time to deal with the demands of the courses you have selected. Many professors now post their syllabi on the Web, thus enabling you to review their course requirements before you schedule their classes. Talk to friends, residence hall assistants, and returning students about your schedule so that you can make informed decisions. Yes, you're in charge here—make it count.

Considering your work schedule, family commitments, time for friends, and your study habits, how many classes or hours would be realistic for you next term? Why?

_____

_____

Understanding and using technology can help you research, write, and communicate.

Patrick White/Merrill

Basic truth #4: .com will be one of your best friends. College professors embrace and use the power of technology. Your high school will probably have introduced you to many different computing concepts and applications. However, if you are returning to college after a few years in the workforce or if your high school did not have a strong computer emphasis, consider taking every opportunity to learn as much about computers and technology as possible. You may be asked to submit assignments electronically, conduct research on the Internet, use a CD-ROM with one of your textbooks, create your own Web site, respond to interactive simulations, download a podcast, or design your own statistical program for a research project. If you do not know how to type, this is the first order of business. Enroll in a keyboarding class or a continuing education class in typing. You'll thank yourself for this essential skill.

If you're uncomfortable with technology or don't know how to type, where can you go on your campus for assistance?_____

_____

_____

Basic truth #5: An open mind and patience can be two of your best teachers.
Good news! If you came from a small high school, town, community, or state where everyone is fairly homogeneous, you've got an exciting time ahead of you. If you went to school in a metropolitan area such as New York, Atlanta, Los Angeles, Boston, Chicago, Dallas, or Washington, D.C., you may be used to a diverse student body. Regardless of your background, you may meet students, peers, professors, and classmates whose views, values, customs, language, sexual orientation, race, ethnicity, and origin are 100 percent different from yours. You may encounter people who are atheistic and people who are ultra-religious; people who are pro-life and people who are pro-choice; people who are against the death penalty and people who support capital punishment; people who abhor interracial relationships and people to whom race does not matter. If you come from a region or family in which these positions are not openly expressed, give others a chance—listen to different viewpoints, try to walk in their shoes for a moment, and strive to approach others with respect. Remember, at the end of the day, it does not cost you anything to give someone else your attention for a few moments. The choice of what you do with the information garnered is always up to you. Chapter 13 is dedicated to understanding relationships and diversity.

If you are really interested in a new culture, religion, idea, concept, or person representing one of these areas, where could you learn more? _____

_____

_____

Basic truth #6: This is not high school. It sounds so simple, but this is perhaps the most universal and important truth discussed here: College is very different from high school and the world of work and perhaps one of the most unique places you'll ever encounter. Expectations in four different areas are outlined in Figure 1.2. Review each area carefully and consider your past experiences as you study the differences.

> In human life there is a constant change of fortune; and it is unreasonable to expect an exemption from this common fate.
>
> —Plutarch

LOOKING FORWARD

Creating Positive Habits, Attitudes, and Behaviors

We hope that after reading and reflecting thus far, you have identified some of your major strengths and talents. You may also have identified several areas where changes might be necessary. So that you have a clearer understanding of both, take a few moments and jot down your personal strengths and areas of transition.

My Greatest Strengths/Talents	Things I Need to Change in My Life
_____	_____
_____	_____
_____	_____
_____	_____
_____	_____

Now, choose one of the things that you have identified as needing to change in your life. _____

After reviewing your strengths and talents, determine how you can use them to help you bring this change about in your life. (Example: If you listed *courageous* as being one of your strengths, how can your personal courage help you deal with one of the items you need to change?)

_____

_____

_____

_____

ELIMINATING ROADBLOCKS

What to Do If Your Emotions, Fears, and Self-Talk Try to Derail You

Try as you might, sometimes harmful emotions, fear of the unknown, and that nagging little voice inside your head (negative self-talk) can cause you problems. Negative self-talk usually appears when you are afraid, uneasy, hurt, angry, depressed, or lonely. Most people experience some degree of negative self-talk during their lives.

FIGURE 1.2	*A Guide to Understanding Expectations*

	HIGH SCHOOL	COLLEGE	WORK
PUNCTUALITY AND ATTENDANCE	Expectations: • State law requires a certain number of days you must attend • The hours in the day are managed for you • There may be some leeway in project dates Penalties: • You may get detention • You may not graduate • You may be considered a truant • Your grades may suffer	Expectations: • Attendance and participation in class are strictly enforced by many professors • Most professors will not give you an extension on due dates • You decide your own schedule and plan your own day Penalties: • You may not be admitted to class if you are late • You may fail the assignment if it is late • Repeated tardiness is sometimes counted as an absence • Most professors do not take late assignments	Expectations: • You are expected to be at work and on time on a daily basis Penalties: • Your salary and promotions may depend on your daily attendance and punctuality • You will most likely be fired for abusing either
TEAMWORK AND PARTICIPATION	Expectations: • Most teamwork is assigned and carried out in class • You may be able to choose teams with your friends • Your grade may reflect your participation Penalties: • If you don't participate, you may get a poor grade • You may jeopardize the grade of the entire team	Expectations: • Many professors require teamwork and cooperative learning teams or learning communities • Your grade will depend on your participation • Your grade may depend on your entire team's performance • You will probably have to work on the project outside of class Penalties: • Lack of participation and cooperation will probably cost you a good grade • Your team members will likely report you to the professor if you do not participate and their grades suffer as a result	Expectations: • You will be expected to participate fully in any assigned task • You will be expected to rely on coworkers to help solve problems and increase profits • You will be required to attend and participate in meetings and sharing sessions • You will be required to participate in formal teams and possess the ability to work with a diverse workforce Penalties: • You will be "tagged" as a non-team player • Your lack of participation and teamwork will cost you raises and promotions • You will most likely be terminated

FIGURE 1.2 *continued*

	HIGH SCHOOL	COLLEGE	WORK
PERSONAL RESPONSIBILITY AND ATTITUDE	Expectations: • Teachers may coach you and try to motivate you • You are required by law to be in high school regardless of your attitude or responsibility level Penalties: • You may be reprimanded for certain attitudes • If your attitude prevents you from participating, you may fail the class	Expectations: • You are responsible for your own learning • Professors will assist you, but there is little "hand holding" or personal coaching for motivation • College did not choose you, you chose it and you will be expected to hold this attitude toward your work Penalties: • You may fail the class if your attitude and motivation prevent you from participating	Expectations: • You are hired to do certain tasks and the company or institution fully expects this of you • You are expected to be positive and self-motivated • You are expected to model good behavior and uphold the company's work standards Penalties: • You will be passed over for promotions and raises • You may be reprimanded • You may be terminated
ETHICS AND CREDIBILITY	Expectations: • You are expected to turn in your own work • You are expected to avoid plagiarism • You are expected to write your own papers • Poor ethical decisions in high school may result in detention or suspension Penalties: • You may get detention or suspension • You will probably fail the project	Expectations: • You are expected to turn in your own work • You are expected to avoid plagiarism • You are expected to write your own papers • You are expected to conduct research and complete projects based on college and societal standards Penalties: • Poor ethical decisions may land you in front of a student ethics committee or a faculty ethics committee, or result in expulsion from the college • You will fail the project • You will fail the class • You may face deportation if your visa is dependent on your student status	Expectations: • You will be required to carry out your job in accordance with company policies, laws, and moral standards • You will be expected to use adult vision and standards Penalties: • Poor ethical decisions may cause you to be severely reprimanded, terminated, or in some cases could even result in a prison sentence

When you experience change, your body, mind, and soul typically go through a process of physical and emotional change as well. Learning to recognize these symptoms in order to control them can help you control the stress that can accompany change.

Many people report the following when they encounter a major life change:

▶ Nervousness

▶ Stress

▶ A sense of being on the edge

▶ Fear

▶ Fatigue

▶ Guilt

▶ Homesickness

▶ Denial

▶ Anger

▶ Depression

Y ou gain strength, experience, and confidence by every experience where you stop to look fear in the face. You must do the thing you think you cannot.

—Eleanor Roosevelt

These feelings are normal when you go through a powerful change, *but remember, they are temporary.* If any of these feelings become overwhelming or life-threatening, seek counseling, talk to your friends, go to your advisor, or speak with your parents, spouse, partner, or professors. These people are your support group; use them. No one is going to look down on you or criticize you for feeling depressed or edgy—they've experienced some of the same feelings you're feeling now.

Beyond your emotions, pay close attention to your negative "self-talk." You'll know it is within you if you begin to experience thoughts such as these:

▶ The "I can't" syndrome

▶ Apathy, or the "I don't care" syndrome

▶ Closed-mindedness

▶ Unfounded anxiety

▶ Fear of taking chances

▶ Loss of motivation

▶ The "let someone else deal with it" syndrome

To rid yourself of this voice, you have to admit that it is talking to you and, sometimes, you have to tell it to "shut up." Yes, that's right; you have to make a conscious effort to literally say to this voice, "*Stop!* You are not going to rob me of any more of my life. You are not going to convince me that I'm incapable, unable, or unwilling." The next time this voice begins to invade your life, immediately combat it by saying five positive things about yourself, your abilities, and your talents. This is the best way to slay the "dragon" of negative self-talk. Without your permission, this voice cannot live.

One of the most important things to remember about negative self-talk is that you are not alone. Almost everyone experiences the dragon during stressful times. Just because these

YES YOU CAN !

IDEAS FOR Success

Consider the following strategies for adjusting to change in the days to come:

▶ Approach change with an open mind.

▶ If you haven't done so, take an afternoon and explore all the resources on your campus such as the library, the academic support center, the counseling and advising office, etc.

▶ Don't be afraid to ask people in your class or your professors questions about things that are confusing or unclear.

▶ So you won't fall behind, adjust your study habits to accommodate more rigorous assignments.

▶ Join a club, organization, or study group so you can start building a network of friends.

▶ If you are not technologically savvy, find out if there are any resources that can help you catch up.

thoughts are in your head does not mean that you have to accept them as reality. You can begin eliminating them any time you choose.

Fortunately, not all reactions to change will be negative. You may also begin to experience some of the following positive emotions and self-talk:

▶ A renewed sense of excitement

▶ Heightened awareness

▶ A more dynamic energy level

▶ Increased sensitivity to others

▶ Greater optimism

▶ A feeling of belonging

▶ Happiness

BUILDING A NEW YOU

Bringing About Change Through Goal Setting

Positive change can be brought about in several ways, but the most effective way is through goal setting and having a "change plan." Simply allowing others or the world to force changes on you or not knowing how to deal with the changes over which you have no control can be detrimental to your success. The relationship between successful change and goal setting is a powerful one in that it gives you tools to control your own life. This section will help you learn more about setting and evaluating your goals.

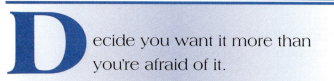

Decide you want it more than you're afraid of it.

—Bill Cosby

Beginning the Goal-Setting Process

Think about what you really *want* or what you *need* to change in your life. More importantly, think about why you want this thing and what it is going to mean to your life. By thinking about what you want, the changes that need to be made, and where you want to be, goals become easier.

Goal setting itself is relatively easy—it is the personal *commitment* that requires detailed attention, hard work, and unbridled passion. Many people make goals, and to succeed in meeting them they define their goals in concrete, measurable terms; they work toward them daily; they have a specific, clear plan of how to attain them; and they know when they want the goal to be reached. The most vital steps toward reaching your goal are making a personal commitment to yourself that you believe in it and then committing all of your available resources toward the completion of that goal.

As you begin to think about your life, your future, and your goals, think about setting a goal in at least two of the following categories:

▶ Personal or self-improvement   ▶ Academic   ▶ Family

▶ Community service   ▶ Social   ▶ Health

▶ Financial   ▶ Spiritual   ▶ Career

Characteristics of Attainable Goals

The following characteristics will help you in your quest to bring about change through effective goal setting. Goals should be:

▶ **Reasonable**—Your goal should be a challenge for you, but also within reach of your abilities.

▶ **Believable**—To achieve a goal, you must really believe it is within your capacity to reach it.

▶ **Measurable**—Your goal needs to be concrete and measurable in some way. Avoid such phrases as "earn a lot" or "lose some weight."

▶ **Adaptable**—Your goals may need to be adapted to the changing circumstances of your life.

▶ **Controllable**—Your goals should be within your own control; they should not depend on the whims or opinions of anyone else.

▶ **Desirable**—To attain a difficult goal, you must want it very badly. You should never work toward something just because someone else wants it.

Have you thought much about your own goals?

© Stockdisc

How to Write Your Goals to Bring About Positive Change

"I will pass my next math test with a B or better" is an example of a short-term goal. *"I will purchase my first home by the time I am _____ years old"* is probably a long-term goal. During your college years, more of your goals may be short-term than long-term, but you can certainly begin setting both. Goals can be lofty and soaring, but great goals can also be as simple as *"I will spend two hours at the park with my children tomorrow afternoon."*

Well-written, meaningful, and effective goals include these features:

▶ A goal statement with a target date

▶ Action steps

▶ A narrative statement

▶ An "I deserve it" statement

▶ A personal signature

The *goal statement* should be specific and measurable; that is, it should entail some tangible evidence of its achievement and it should have a *target date*, a timeline for accomplishing your goal. Your goal statement *must* use an action verb. An example of a goal statement with an action verb and target date is *"I will lose 10 pounds in six weeks"* or *"I am going to join a campus club by the fifth week of this term."* This is a much more powerful statement than "I am thinking about joining a club" or "I want to have a new car."

> **S**uccess is focusing the full power of all that you are and all that you have to offer on what you have a burning desire to achieve.
>
> —W. Peterson

After you write the goal statement, you'll need to create *specific action steps* that explain exactly what you are going to do to reach your goal. There is no certain number of steps; it all depends on your goal and your personal commitment. An example of action steps for weight loss might be: (1) join the campus health center, (2) meet with a personal trainer on campus, (3) set an appointment with a nutrition counselor in the health center, (4) begin walking 1 mile per day, and so on.

The next step is to write a *narrative statement* about what your goal accomplishment will mean to you and how your life will change when you achieve this goal. For example, if your goal is to lose 50 pounds, paint a "verbal picture" of how your life is going to look once this goal has been reached. Your verbal picture may include statements such as "I'll be able to wear nicer clothes," "I'll feel better," "I'll be able to ride

My Personal Goal

To help you get started, use this goal-setting sheet as template for this and future goals.

Name _____

Goal Statement (with action verb and target date)   _____
_____
_____

Action Steps (concrete things you plan to do to reach your goal)
1. _____
2. _____
3. _____
4. _____

Narrative Statement (how your life will look when you reach your goal)   _____
_____
_____
_____
_____
_____
_____

I deserve this goal because:
1. _____
_____
2. _____
_____

I hereby make this commitment to myself.

_____   _____
Signature   Date

my bicycle again," or "My self-esteem will be stronger." If your goals don't offer you significant rewards, you are not likely to stick to your plan.

Next, write down two reasons why you deserve this goal. This is called your *"I deserve it" statement*. It may seem simple, but this is a complex question. Many people do not follow through on their goals because deep down, they don't feel they deserve them. The narrative statement helps you understand how your life will look once the goal is met, but your "I deserve it" statement asks you to consider *why* you deserve this goal. Considering the goal of losing 50 pounds, your "I deserve it" statement might read, *"I deserve to lose 50 pounds because I deserve to be healthy. I deserve to live a long life to be with my partner and my children. I deserve to look good."*

Finally, *sign your goal statement*. This is an imperative step in that your signature shows that you are making a personal commitment to see this goal to fruition. This is your name. Use it with pride. The date helps you keep a timeline for the goal.

When you have accomplished your goal, you will find that the feeling is somewhat addictive. The feeling that you get from reaching an important milestone in your life is incredible, and many people begin the goal-setting process again. Successful people never get to a target and sit down; they are always "becoming." They reach one goal and begin dreaming, planning, and preparing for the next accomplishment. Goal setting and follow-through are major components of your personal staying power as a college student, and indeed a successful person. Goal setting is also a powerful tool to help you build healthy self-esteem, "crack the clay," and discover your golden potential. Chapter 2 will help you look more deeply at your life and how to enhance your self-concept.

Library of Congress

Abraham Lincoln was raised in great poverty, lost the love of his life when he was 26, suffered a nervous breakdown at age 27, failed in business twice, lost eight elections, and suffered the death of a child all before he became our president and changed the course of our nation.

YOUR GOAL EVALUATION PLAN

Now that you have set your goal(s) and begun the work, consider the following questions as a way to evaluate your goal.

- ▶ Do I want to achieve this goal enough to pay the price and to stick with it?
- ▶ What is the personal payoff to me if I achieve this goal? What is the payoff to society and the good of other people?
- ▶ Who will notice if I achieve this goal? Does that matter to me?
- ▶ How realistic is this goal? Is it over my head at this stage of my development?
- ▶ Do I need to reduce my expectations so I won't be disillusioned in the beginning, and then increase the difficulty of my goal only after I have conquered the first steps?
- ▶ Can I control all the factors necessary to achieve this goal?
- ▶ Is this goal specific and measurable?
- ▶ Does this goal contribute to my overall development? Is this goal allowing me to spend my time in the way that is best for me right now?
- ▶ How will I feel when I reach this goal?
- ▶ Will the people who love me be proud that I accomplished this goal?

Think About It
Chapter Reflection

The transition from one place to another is seldom easy, even when the change is what you want. Entering college has given you the opportunity to assume new roles, develop new friendships, meet new people, work under different circumstances, and perhaps adjust your lifestyle. It has also given you the opportunity to reflect on your strengths and consider areas where you might need to change. These changes form the very essence of the college experience; they create wonderful new possibilities and help you discover who you really are and what you have to offer the world.

As you reflect on this chapter, keep the following points in mind:

▶ Evaluate your reason(s) for attending college and what it means to your life.
▶ Devise a plan to avoid the "Freedom Trap."
▶ Use goal setting to help direct changes in your life.
▶ Don't just let change happen. Get involved in your own life and learning.
▶ Focus on the positive by eliminating your negative self-talk.
▶ Keep your sense of humor.
▶ Talk to friends and family. Share your experience.
▶ Be courageous by facing your fears.
▶ Be objective.

A possibility was born the day you were born, and it will live as long as you live.

—R. Burak

Knowledge in Bloom

Utilizes levels 1–6 of the taxonomy

Each chapter-end assessment is based on *Bloom's Taxonomy of Learning*. See the inside front cover for a quick review.

Bringing Positive Change in Your Life

Explanation: After reading and reflecting thus far, you may have identified several changes that you need to make to your personal or academic life. Also, changes may have been thrust upon you by choices you or those around you have made. The following model provides a method for bringing positive changes into your life.

Process: Based on Bloom's Taxonomy, the Change Implementation Model asks you to consider questions and recommend actions at each level of learning. The chart moves from less difficult questions (levels 1, 2, 3) to more challenging questions (levels 4, 5, 6). To begin the change process in your life, follow the five steps in this chapter-end activity.

Step 1: Review the steps of the Change Implementation Model based on Bloom's Taxonomy.

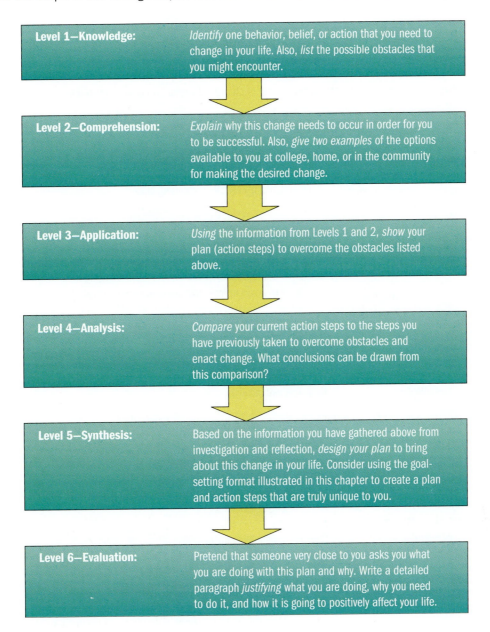

Level 1—Knowledge: *Identify* one behavior, belief, or action that you need to change in your life. Also, *list* the possible obstacles that you might encounter.

Level 2—Comprehension: *Explain* why this change needs to occur in order for you to be successful. Also, *give two examples* of the options available to you at college, home, or in the community for making the desired change.

Level 3—Application: *Using* the information from Levels 1 and 2, *show* your plan (action steps) to overcome the obstacles listed above.

Level 4—Analysis: *Compare* your current action steps to the steps you have previously taken to overcome obstacles and enact change. What conclusions can be drawn from this comparison?

Level 5—Synthesis: Based on the information you have gathered above from investigation and reflection, *design your plan* to bring about this change in your life. Consider using the goal-setting format illustrated in this chapter to create a plan and action steps that are truly unique to you.

Level 6—Evaluation: Pretend that someone very close to you asks you what you are doing with this plan and why. Write a detailed paragraph *justifying* what you are doing, why you need to do it, and how it is going to positively affect your life.

Step 2: After studying the Change Implementation Model above, read the following fictional scenario in which you encounter difficulty in Accounting 101.

You enter your Accounting 101 class eager to take the first course in your major field. You are shocked to find that the professor begins lecturing on the first day. Not only is the material difficult to understand, but so is the professor, whose first language is not English.

For homework, the professor assigns two chapters to read per class, but the lectures are not based on material found in the text. You try to study as you had in high school but now you feel overwhelmed and isolated. The material is much harder.

After three weeks and a failed first test, you notice that the students who passed the test had formed study groups, something that you once thought only the brightest students practiced.

Using the Change Implementation Model, you decide to make positive changes in your study habits. As an example, your plans for change are shown in Figure 1.3.

Step 3: Review how you might use the Change Implementation Model to enact changes to save your grade in Accounting 101. Figure 1.3 is an example.

FIGURE 1.3   *Using the Change Implementation Model*

Level 1—Knowledge *Identify* one behavior, belief, or action that you need to change in your life. Also, *list* the possible obstacles that you might encounter.	If I could, I would change my study habits in accounting and become stronger in my math skills. Obstacles: fear of change, shyness, pride, time constraints.
Level 2—Comprehension *Explain* why this change needs to occur in order for you to be successful. Also, *give two examples* of the options available to you at college, home, or in the community for making the desired change.	Why I need change: Weak math skills causing me to fail accounting Campus: Tutoring center and math lab; professor's office hours Community: Aunt works in accounting office
Level 3—Application *Using* the information form Levels 1 and 2, *show* your plan (action steps) to overcome the obstacles listed above.	Step 1— I will join a study group. I will make an appointment for tutoring in the math lab. Step 2— I will talk to my advisor about services available. Step 3— I will plan at least five hours per week to study for my accounting class.
Level 4—Analysis *Compare* your current action steps to the steps you have previously taken to overcome obstacles and enact change. What conclusions can be drawn from this comparison?	Past: I took notes in class, looked over them before a test. New: Join study group, go to tutoring center and math lab. New: Talk with advisor. Conclusion: In taking personal responsibility for my education, taking calculated risks to bring about change, and asking for help, I'm more likely to pass accounting.
Level 5—Synthesis Based on the information you have gathered above from investigation and reflection, *design your plan* to bring about this change in your life. Consider using the goal-setting format illustrated in this chapter to create a plan and action steps that are truly unique to you.	Goal: I *will* get involved with a study group, schedule a tutor, and spend at least five hours per week studying for accounting. I will do this by the end of this week. Action Steps: Step 1— I will join a study group. I will make an appointment for tutoring in the math lab. Step 2— I will talk to my advisor about services available. Step 3— I will plan at least five hours per week to study for my accounting class. Step 4— I will talk to supervisor at work and design a plan to ensure I have at least five hours per week to devote to my accounting class. Narrative Statement: Basically, by getting involved and not trying to go this alone, I will begin to enjoy college more and do better in my classes. I *deserve* this goal because I have the courage to ask for help and the intelligence to put my pride aside and seek assistance. I *deserve* to learn this material so that I can successfully run my own business.
Level 6—Evaluation Pretend that someone very close to you asks you what you are doing with this plan and why. Write a detailed paragraph justifying what you are doing, why you need to do it, and how it is going to positively affect your life.	I am working so hard to pass accounting because I want this degree and I want the knowledge of how to run my own business. If I don't change my habits, I will not pass accounting and I will not have this degree. Without this degree, I will most likely have to work in low-paying jobs for the rest of my life. By asking for help, spending more time studying, and spending more time around people who have some of the same interests, I can develop the skills to graduate, start my own business, and help my family out financially.

Step 4: After studying the Change Implementation Model example in Figure 1.3, focus on a few things that you might want to change about your own academic life. Answer "I would change . . . " for at least four of the areas below.

AREA	I would change:
Study habits	_____
Motivational level	_____
Attitude	_____
Time management abilities	_____
Money management abilities	_____
Relationship skills	_____
Reading and/or writing abilities	_____
Math abilities	_____
Speaking abilities	_____
Career decisions	_____

Step 5: Now, choose *one* of the major changes you wish to incorporate into your life from the list in Step 4. Using the Change Implementation Model, devise a strategy to effect this change.

Level 1—Knowledge *Identify* one behavior, belief, or action that you need to change in your life. Also, *list* the possible obstacles that you might encounter.	
Level 2—Comprehension *Explain* why this change needs to occur in order for you to be successful. Also, *give two examples* of the options available to you at college, home, or in the community for making the desired change.	
Level 3—Application *Using* the information form Levels 1 and 2, *show* your plan (action steps) to overcome the obstacles listed above.	
Level 4—Analysis *Compare* your current action steps to the steps you have previously taken to overcome obstacles and enact change. What conclusions can be drawn from this comparison?	
Level 5—Synthesis Based on the information you have gathered above from investigation and reflection, *design your plan* to bring about this change in your life. Consider using the goal-setting format illustrated in this chapter to create a plan and action steps that are truly unique to you.	
Level 6—Evaluation Pretend that someone very close to you asks you what you are doing with this plan and why. Write a detailed paragraph justifying what you are doing, why you need to do it, and how it is going to positively affect your life.	

Preparing for Success

Refer back to pages 4–5 of this chapter and answer the questions you developed from scanning this chapter's headings. You should also be able to answer the following questions if they were not on your list:

1. Why is change important to growth? _____

   _____

2. What is a narrative statement? _____

   _____

3. How can goal setting help you achieve your educational dreams? _____

   _____

4. Why is open-mindedness important in your college education? _____

   _____

2

Engage

To be successful you need to find something to hold on to, something to motivate you, something to inspire you.

Tony Dorsett

the big WHY

Why will I ever be asked to use this stuff? *Why* will a chapter on personal motivation and academic energy help me in college, at work, with my family, and beyond? *Why* is self-engagement such a big deal?

> **I**f you want to achieve worthwhile things in life, you must become a worthwhile person in your own self-development.
>
> —Brian Tracy

Success is built on motivation and self-engagement—the ability to immerse yourself in your own life, your own goals, your own beliefs, values, judgments, purpose, and behaviors. Engagement means that you have made a commitment to give your best to the endeavors you have chosen to undertake. You can read about motivation, study how others became motivated, and even emulate those whom you perceive as motivated, but the only person, place, or thing that can ever give you *internal motivation* is you.

Developing energy and a passion for learning and personal development can be a critical tool for expanding your internal motivation and drive. *This chapter can help you:*

► Grasp the relationship between self-discovery and motivation.

► Grasp the relationship between motivation and personal/professional success.

► Examine your values, beliefs, and what makes you "tick."

► Move beyond your comfort zone.

► Overcome adversity and setbacks of the past.

► Evaluate your self-image and work to build healthier self-esteem.

► Understand the impact of your attitude on motivation and self-esteem.

We hope the information in this chapter will help you find the means necessary to become more involved in your own learning and your personal development.

Scan &

Take a few moments and **scan this chapter**. As you scan, **list five questions** you can expect to learn the answers to while reading and studying Chapter 2.

Example:
► How can adversity be overcome? (from page 36)
► What are the five characteristics of self-esteem? (from page 45)

My Questions:

1. _____
   _____ from page _____

2. _____
   _____ from page _____

3. _____
   _____ from page _____

Name:	Juanita Wilson
Institution:	University of South Carolina, Columbia, SC
Major:	Biology/Biotechnology
Age:	23

Why would anyone want to read a chapter on motivation and self-esteem development? In my opinion, self-esteem is the vehicle of life and motivation is the fuel to get you there. Without a sense of who you are and where you are going, you will most certainly be lost. Without the tools to learn how to become a more motivated individual, you sit still most of your life. Reading and learning more about self-motivation and self-improvement are essential to your college life—and beyond.

I am the "queen" of goal setting and self-motivation. I grew up in London, lived in Guam and Italy, and finally settled in America. Since I was five years old, I knew that I would have a profession in the sciences—somehow—some way! From my earliest years, I remember my parents saying, "You've got to have a plan." So, for as long as I can remember, I've had a plan.

the big WHY

. . . from another perspective

It was very hard to move from abroad to the States. It was an emotionally trying time and I felt like I was in a whirlwind. I had to make new friends, adapt to a new culture, and change my way of living. To make matters worse, I had a mean high school advisor who was no help at all. I knew that if I was going to make it in this world, I would have to learn how to motivate myself and draw on the support of my family and those who cared about me.

By studying a chapter on motivation and self-esteem, you can begin to understand more about yourself, what makes you "tick," how to avoid people who bring you down, and most importantly, how to develop the attitude of a winner.

4. _____

_____

from page _____

5. _____

_____

from page _____

Question

PS Reminder: At the end of the chapter, come back to this page and answer these questions in your notebook, text margins, or online chapter notes.

THE POWER AND PASSION OF MOTIVATION

Two Perspectives to Consider

Motivation can change your life! Read that statement again: *Motivation can change your life!* Ask any successful businessperson. Ask your favorite athlete or actor. Ask your classmates who pass every exam, project, or paper with an A. It is their burning desire—their aspiration to succeed, to live a motivated life, and to reach their goals—that changed their lives and got them to where they are today. Motivation is a force that can transform your attitude, alter the course of your performance, intensify your actions, and illuminate your future. Motivation can help you live a life that reflects your true potential.

If you have a need or desire to change your motivation level or attitude toward personal and academic success, there are steps you can take to help you with this goal. Some of the steps described in this chapter will be easy and others will greatly challenge you, but taken seriously, each step can assist you in discovering who you really are and what you want in life, and help you find the motivation you need to change.

There are two types of motivation: external and internal. *External motivation* is the weaker of the two because, as the word suggests, there are *external* forces or people causing you to do something. You do not own it. External motivators may be things or people such as your parents, spouse, or partner pushing you to complete your degree; your work supervisor telling you to do "*x, y, or z*" or you will be fired; or even your professors giving you an exam to make sure you have read Chapter 2. You may do the things asked, but the reason for doing them is external.

Internal motivation is yours. It is *energy* inside of you—pushing you to go after what *you* want. Internal motivation is a strong and driving force because you own it. There are no external forces or people telling you that you must do it—it comes from **your desire** *to be something, to have something, or to attain a goal that is near and dear to you.* Successful people live in the world of internal motivation or find ways to convert external motivation into internal motivation.

> **The** moment you begin to do what you really want to do, your life becomes a totally different kind of life.
>
> —B. Fuller

A simple example of this conversion may be that your current degree requires you to take classes even though you cannot understand their value or purpose. You may ask yourself, "Why would a theatre major have to take two classes in college math?" The class is hard, math is not your thing, the chapters are frustrating and difficult to read, and math has little to do with your interests, career goals, or overall life plan. The challenge for you is to find an internal reason to move forward—a rationale for how math is going to help you, now and in the future. This is called *internalizing*.

By converting this external motivation (a requirement for your degree) into internal motivation (something that can help you), the math class will become easier because you have found a way to link it to your success, your goals, your money, your health, your family, or your overall life plan.

By internalizing, you see that good math skills can help you land a work-study job in the theatre scene shop. You find that good math skills can help you create an effective personal budget plan and help you save money. You find that the more you learn about the logic and process of math, the easier it is to solve problems and think more critically, thus helping you perform better in other classes. By silencing your

Where Are You . . .

Before reading any further, take a moment and assess where you are at this moment with your knowledge and application of motivation and self-esteem development. Read each statement carefully and then respond accordingly.

1. My self-esteem is very healthy and I have no problem identifying my positive attributes. YES NO

2. When things go wrong in my life, I take full responsibility for my actions or beliefs that caused the issue. YES NO

3. I am a very motivated person and seldom put things off until the last minute. YES NO

4. When I am frustrated, I dig in my heels and get the job done. I don't give up easily. YES NO

5. I am generally not afraid of failure and I try new things frequently. YES NO

6. I know how to avoid contaminated people in my life. YES NO

7. I do not let my past setbacks and adversities hold me back. YES NO

8. I know how to develop the motivation I need to reach a goal. YES NO

9. I have written and posted my personal mission statement. YES NO

If you answered "yes" to most of the questions (six or more), you know how important a positive attitude is to your success. You understand the value of self-engagement and feel good about yourself. *If you answered "no"* to most of the questions, you will need to examine why your motivation level is low, why you have unhealthy self-esteem, and how your attitude affects both. You may need to speak with your advisor or counselor to find assistance on campus or in the community to help you focus on your motivation level and develop a healthier attitude.

negative self-talk about math, you are able to internalize the rewards of the class and own the outcome. You have made a conversion.

The remainder of this chapter will give you the framework to convert external motivators into internal motivators and help you become a more engaged person. The advice and strategies are included to assist you to discover what you actually want out of life and focus on what type of person you want to be. Also, our intention is to help you make the connection among self-discovery, clarifying your values, strengthening your character, and intensifying your motivation. This connection will help you convert external motivation into internal motivation.

THE CORNERSTONES OF PERSONAL AND PROFESSIONAL SUCCESS

A Ten-Point Plan for Discovering Your Potential and Increasing Your Motivation

"I am a winner."
"I fail at everything I do."

"I am a dedicated person."
"I don't really care about anything."

"I am a giving person."
"Life is about looking out for number one—me!"

"I am proud of my name."
"What's in a name?"

How are the friends you're making in college influencing your decisions?

© BananaStock Ltd.

As you can see by the two different perspectives above, your attitude and perspective on how you approach life, relationships, problems, and goals can mean the difference between being a motivated, inspired, and successful person or a weary, doubtful, and unsuccessful person.

As you scanned this chapter and its section headings earlier, you may have asked yourself: What does my *comfort zone* or *contaminated people* or *character* have to do with my motivation? The answer is simple. *Everything.* The reason we have included this ten-point plan in this chapter is to help you see that by focusing on you—becoming a person who knows where you're going, what you want, and what you have to offer—your motivation, passion, and energy for learning and growing will flourish. By knowing more about yourself, you can establish a clearer vision of your true golden potential.

POINT #1

Surround Yourself with Positive, Upbeat, Happy People

You've probably sat next to him or her in one of your classes or seen him or her at work—the person who always seems to be happy, motivated, bubbling with personality, organized, and ready for whatever comes his or her way. They greet people as they enter the room, they respond in class, they volunteer for projects, and they have a presence about them that is positive and lively. You may even look at him or her out of the corner of your eye and ask, "What is that person on?"

Positive, upbeat, and motivated people are easy to spot. You can basically see their attitude in the way they walk, the way they carry themselves, the way they approach people, and the way they treat others.

> Successful people are the ones who can lay a firm foundation with the bricks others have thrown at them.
>
> —David Brinkley

As a new college student, you have a clean slate where friends are concerned. Choose your friends carefully. Seek out people who have ambition, good work habits, positive attitudes, and high ethical standards. Look for those who study hard, enjoy learning, are goal oriented, and don't mind taking a stand when they believe strongly in something. Find friends who will work out with you, go to the library with you, attend plays and concerts with you, and be certain to look for friends who know how to develop and work by a schedule that allows time for fun and joy.

Befriend people who have interests and hobbies that are new to you. Step outside your comfort zone and add people to your circle of friends who are from a different culture, are of a different religion, or who have lived in a different geographic region.

Be wary, however, of the others. The ones you need to avoid. Whiners. Degraders. Attackers. Manipulators. Pessimists. Back-stabbers. Abusers. Cowards. Two-faced racists, sexists, ageists, homophobic ethnocentrists. These people carry around an aura so negative that it can almost be seen in a dark cloud above them. They degrade others because they do not like themselves. They find fault with everything because their own lives are a mess. They do nothing and then attack you for being motivated and trying to improve your life. We call them *contaminated people.*

Examine the following two lists. As you read through the lists, consider the people with whom you associate. Are the majority of your friends, family, peers, and work associates positive or contaminated?

POSITIVE PEOPLE ARE THOSE WHO . . .	CONTAMINATED PEOPLE ARE THOSE WHO . . .
Bring out the best in you	Bring out the worst in you
Find the good in bad situations	Find the bad in every situation
Are gracious and understanding	Are rude and uncaring
Build people up	Sabotage people, even loved ones
Support your dreams	Criticize your hopes and plans
Make you feel comfortable and happy	Make you feel uneasy, nervous, and irritable
Tell you the truth and offer constructive criticism	Are two-faced and always use harsh language to "put you in your place"
Are open-minded and fair	Are narrow and ethnocentric
Are patient	Are quick to anger
Are giving	Are jealous and smothering
Love to learn from others	Know everything already

As you think about these lists and the people in your life, ask yourself, "Do I surround myself with more positive or more contaminated people?" As you consider your friends, family, classmates, and work associates, compare and contrast one positive person with one contaminated person in your life.

Positive Person _____

His/Her Attributes _____

_____

_____

Contaminated Person _____

His/Her Attributes _____

_____

_____

Compare and Contrast _____

_____

_____

_____

_____

Bloom Level 4 question

What effect does each person have on you, your attitude, and your motivation?

Positive Person	**Contaminated Person**
_____	_____
_____	_____
_____	_____
_____	_____

POINT #2

Overcome Your Doubts and Fears

Success is a great motivator, but fear can be, too. Fear probably motivates more people than anything else. Unfortunately, fear motivates most people to hold back, to doubt themselves, and to accomplish much less than they could have without fear.

One of the biggest obstacles to reaching your potential may be your own personal fears. If you are afraid, you are not alone; everyone has fears. Isn't it interesting, though, that *our fears are learned*? As a baby, you had only two fears: a fear of falling and a fear of loud noises. As you got older, you added to your list of fears. And, if you are like most people, you let your fears dominate parts of your life, saying things to yourself like: "What if I try and fail?" "What if people laugh at me for thinking I can do this?" or "What if someone finds out that this is my dream?"

You have two choices where fear is concerned. You can let fear dominate your life, or you can focus on those things you really want to accomplish, put your fears behind you, and *go for it*. The people who are most successful in their fields admit they have fears, but they also confess that they work daily to overcome them because their desire to achieve and experience success is greater than their fear.

Dr. Robert Schuller, minister, motivational speaker, and author, once asked, *"What would you attempt to do if you could not fail?"* This is an important question for anyone, especially those trying to increase their motivation level. Work through this idea by answering the following questions truthfully. We have adapted and expanded this question for the purpose of this exercise.

1. What would you do attempt to do or what would your college major be if you could not fail?_____

   _____

   _____

2. Beyond the answers "I'm afraid" or "I fear," *why* are you not doing this thing?_____

   _____

   _____

   _____

3. What has not doing this thing cost you? In other words, how have you suffered or what damages have been done to your life because you have not done this thing?_____

   _____

   _____

   _____

4. On a scale of 1 to 10 (10 being the strongest), how often do you dream about or think about doing this thing?

1   2   3   4   5   6   7   8   9   10

5. If you did this thing and were successful at it, how would your life change? Be specific. _____
_____
_____
_____
_____
_____
_____

Bloom Level 6 question

6. List five action steps that you could begin to take today (by yourself or with another person) that could put you on the road to begin doing this thing.

▶ _____
▶ _____
▶ _____
▶ _____
▶ _____

Consider using a goal sheet like the one in Chapter 1 to develop an entire goal strategy to bring this thing to fruition in your life.

POINT #3

Move Out of Your Comfort Zone

It sounds cozy, doesn't it? *Comfort zone.* Do not let the term fool you. A comfort zone is not necessarily a happy and comfortable place. It is simply a place where you are familiar with your surroundings and don't have to work too hard. Yes, it is where you feel confident of your abilities, but it is also a place where your growth stops. *It can be a prison.* Successful people who have won personal and professional victories know that enlarging your comfort zone helps in cultivating your ambition, reaching your potential, and creating opportunities for positive growth.

An expanded comfort zone means that you are more comfortable in more places in the world. It means that you can enjoy people and events to a greater degree. It also means that you can enjoy life more completely, learn things from travel, and express your feelings and thoughts without embarrassment. It means that you have greater opportunities than those who refuse to expand their comfort zone.

If you are interested in taking control of your life, stretching your comfort zone is the perfect place to start. By expanding the area where you feel comfortable and safe, you begin to feel comfortable and safe in many more places—around many more people, doing many more things. This feeling gives you more control of your own life.

> Not taking risks can help you avoid suffering, disappointment, fear, and sorrow. It can also help you avoid learning, changing, growing, loving, or really living.
> —R. Sherfield

Think about it for a moment. Deciding to go to college probably caused you some level of discomfort and raised some fears: *"What if I can't make good grades?" "What if I flunk out?" "What if I don't fit in?" "What if I can't keep up with classmates just out of high school?" "What if I can't do my job, go to school, and manage a family at the same time?"* The mere fact that you are here is a step outside your comfort zone—a very important step that can change your life dramatically. Be very proud of this monumental achievement.

To move past your comfort zone, consider the following tips:

▶ Make a personal commitment to take one calculated risk per week.

▶ Ask a friend or classmate to join you in your endeavors.

▶ Start with small, short-term goals and work toward larger goals.

▶ Put courage in front of comfort.

▶ Tell yourself, "I am capable." "I am willing." "I am able." "I am as good as the next person." "I *can* do this."

▶ Focus on new opportunities and forget about past negative experiences.

▶ Make decisions that are creative and uncommon.

▶ Think about how expanding your comfort zone can help your academic work, career, and/or future goals.

▶ Try to imagine your life if you do not move beyond your current comfort zone.

POINT #4

Put Adversity and Failure into Perspective

YES YOU CAN!

IDEAS FOR Success

Consider the following strategies for dealing with failure and adversity:

▶ Accept the fact the *everyone* experiences adversity and failure. You are not alone.

▶ Make a commitment to yourself that you will not walk away when things get tough.

▶ Identify the reasons that you have experienced adversity or failure.

▶ Determine if a certain person or people in your life contributed to this failure.

▶ Be honest and truthful with yourself and determine what role, if any, you played in bringing about this adversity or failure.

▶ If you played a role in your own failure, devise a plan or set a goal to eliminate the behavior that caused the problem.

▶ Develop the mind-set that every new minute brings new hope. You can start over at any moment you choose.

Being motivated means learning to deal with failure. Have you ever given up on something too quickly, or gotten discouraged and quit? That feeling is quite different from completing a goal and getting an adrenaline rush from success. Can you think of a time when you were unfair to yourself because you didn't stay with something long enough? Completing a goal feels much different from giving up. Have you ever stopped doing something you really loved because somebody laughed at you or teased you about it? Doing what brings you joy in the face of adversity gives you a feeling much different from caving in to peer pressure. Overcoming failure and learning from mistakes make victory much more rewarding. Motivated people know that losing and making mistakes are necessary aspects of winning: The difference between winning and losing is the ability to get up, stand tall, and try again.

Reflect on your life thus far and you will probably discover that your greatest strength and deepest courage were developed during adverse times. Difficult situations make you tougher and more capable of developing your potential. They make you a fighter—a warrior against failure. Overcoming adversity is an essential part of success in college, career, and life. Think of a time in your life when you faced difficulties but persisted and became stronger as a result. Perhaps you failed a course, didn't make an athletic team, had a serious illness, broke up with a longtime boyfriend or girlfriend, or experienced a divorce. You may have been fired from a job or passed over for a promotion, or experienced the death of a person very close to you. These are the events of life; most are inescapable. Motivated and successful people reflect on these events, put them into perspective, learn from them, and move on.

POINT #5

Develop a Winning, Optimistic Attitude

Your attitude is exclusively yours. It belongs to you. You own it. Good or bad, happy or sad, optimistic or pessimistic, it is yours and you are responsible for it. However, your attitude is greatly influenced by situations in your life and by the people with whom you associate. Developing a winning, optimistic attitude can be hard, yet extremely rewarding, work. Motivated and successful people have learned that one's attitude is the mirror of one's soul.

Optimism has many benefits beyond helping you develop a winning attitude. Researchers have found that people who are optimistic live longer, are more motivated, survive cancer treatment at a greater rate, have longer, more satisfying relationships, and are mentally healthier than pessimists. This would suggest that developing and maintaining a winning, optimistic attitude can help you have a longer and more satisfying life. *It would also suggest that by thinking positively, you increase your motivation level.*

Listen to yourself for a few days. Are you more of an optimist or a pessimist? Do you hear yourself whining, complaining, griping, and finding fault with everything and everybody around you? Do you blame others for things that are wrong in your life? Do you blame your bad grades on your professors? Is someone else responsible for your unhappiness?

The greatest discovery of my generation is that we can alter the course of our lives simply by altering our attitude.

—William James, psychologist

If these thoughts or comments are in your head, you are suffering from the *"I CAN'T"* syndrome (**I**rritated, **C**ontaminated, **A**ngry, **N**egative **T**houghts). This pessimistic condition can negatively influence every aspect of your life, from your self-esteem to your motivation level, academic performance, relationships, and livelihood.

If you want to eliminate *"I CAN'T"* from your life, consider the following tips:

- ▶ Work every day to find the good in people, places, and things.
- ▶ Discover what is holding you back and what you need to push you forward.
- ▶ Visualize your success—visualize yourself actually being who and what you want to be.
- ▶ Locate, observe, and associate with positive, optimistic people and things in your life.
- ▶ Make a list of people who support you and help you feel positive—then make a point to be around them more.

You are likely to achieve goals that relate to your own personal value system and that are truly important to you.

© Corbis

▸ Take responsibility for your own actions and their consequences.

▸ Find out what resources are available on your campus to help you develop a more positive outlook.

▸ Force yourself to find five positive things a day for which to be thankful.

Basically, a winning attitude comes from eliminating negative thoughts, actions, and behaviors, listening to yourself, evaluating what you hold dear, putting fears and adversity into perspective, and seeing yourself as motivated and successful.

POINT #6

Identify and Clarify What You Value in Life

If you have been highly motivated to accomplish a goal in the past, this achievement was probably tied to something you valued a great deal. Most of what you do in life centers on what is truly important to you. This is why it is important to identify and then clarify what you value in your life—what matters to you.

> Our souls are not hungry for fame, comfort, wealth, or power. These rewards create almost as many problems as they solve. Our souls are hungry for meaning, for the sense that we have figured out a way to live so that our lives matter.
>
> —H. Kushner

Values, self-esteem, motivation, and goal setting are all mixed up together, making it difficult to separate one from the other. *The things you work to accomplish* are directly connected to those things, ideas, and concepts that you value. Therefore, your *attitude* and *actions* are tied to your *values*. If you value an attitude or belief, your actions will be centered on this ideal. If you love to spend time with your friends and this is valuable to you, you will make the time for this on a daily basis. Why? Because your friendships are a fundamental part of your value system. You like something, so you are motivated by it and you do it. It is that simple. *Our values influence our actions.*

You were not born with your basic values. Your values were learned over the years and were shaped to a great extent by your parents, the school you attended, the community where you grew up, and the culture that nourished you. Because of your unique, personal background, you have developed a set of unique, personal values. To make sound decisions, set appropriate goals that are right for you, and manage your priorities accordingly, you must identify those things in your life that you esteem.

Many of our values lie in our unconscious mind. They were put there by things we've heard, items we've read, music we've listened to, TV shows we've watched, and by what we may have seen others do. We may not even know that we value something until it is threatened or removed. Until you clarify what it is that *you* really value, you may be working toward goals or pursuing career choices that someone else values, not you. By having vague or poorly clarified values, you may be working toward something, believing something, or acting in a way that is not really who you are. This can cause you to wander aimlessly and become frustrated, eventually destroying your motivation level. *Values bring direction to your life and help you stay motivated.*

Following is a wide and varied list of items. Read over them carefully and circle the ones you value in others and in you. Be careful and selective. Do not just randomly circle words. As a criterion for each word you circle, ask yourself, "Can I defend why I value this in my life?" and "Is this truly something I value or something I was told to value and never questioned why?" If you value something and it is not on the list, add it to the spaces at the bottom.

Honesty	Affection	Punctuality	Respect
Frankness	Open-mindedness	Reliability	Trustworthiness
Sincerity	Wit/humor	Spontaneity	Devotion
Frugality	Justice	Creativity	Caring
Spirituality	Friendliness	Energy	Intellect
Attentiveness	Conversation	Money	Security
Fine dining	Beauty	Devotion	Enthusiasm
Positivism	Commitment	Foresightedness	Creativity
Organization	Learning	Listening	Giving
Control	Comfort	Knowledge	Success
Athletic ability	Thoughtfulness	Independence	Courage
Safety	Fun	Excitement	Partying
Love	Friendship	Writing	Speaking
Reading	Family	Dependability	Teamwork
Time alone	Time with friends	Phone calls	Walks
Exercise	Problem solving	Empowerment	Integrity
Service to others	Modesty	Strength	Tolerance
Imagination	Self-esteem	Food	Power
Winning	Goals	Risk taking	Change
Self-improvement	Forgiveness	Fairness	Optimism
Successful career	Motivation	Trust	Direction in life
Working	Hobbies	Books	Mentoring
Stability	_____	_____	_____
_____	_____	_____	_____
_____	_____	_____	_____
_____	_____	_____	_____

Now that you have circled or written what you value, choose the five that you value the most. In other words, if you were only allowed to value five things in life, what five would you list below?

In the space to the right of each value, rank them from 1 to 5 (1 being the most important to you, your life, your relationships, your actions, your education, and your career).

List   **Rank**

_____   _____

_____   _____

_____   _____

_____   _____

_____   _____

Look at your *number one* choice and answer the following questions.

Where did this value originate?_____

_____

_____

Bloom Level 6 question

Defend why this is the one thing in life you value more than anything else.

_____

_____

_____

How does this one value motivate you?_____

_____

_____

_____

POINT #7

Take Pride in Your Name and Personal Character

At the end of the day, the end of the month, the end of your career, and the end of your life, your name and your character are all that you have. Taking pride in developing your character and protecting your good name can be two powerful, motivational forces.

"My name?" you may ask. "What does my name have to do with anything?"

> Your character is determined by how you treat people who can do you no good and how you treat people who can't fight back.
>
> —Abigail Van Buren

Imagine for a moment that you are working with a group of students on a project for your psychology class. The project is to receive a major grade and you and your group will present your findings to a group of 300 psychology students at a campus forum. Your group works hard, develops an effective research tool to gather information, and builds a product of which everyone is exceptionally proud. When you present the project, your group receives a standing ovation and earns an A. The name of each individual group member is read aloud as you stand to be recognized. Your name and project are also posted in a showcase. You are proud. Your hard work paid off. Your name now carries weight in the psychology department, with your peers, and among the psychology faculty. It feels good.

Conversely, imagine your group slacks off; the project is poorly prepared and poorly received by the audience and your professor. Your name is associated with this project and your name and grade is posted with every other group's. Your group is the only group to receive an F. It doesn't feel good.

Your name and your character are tied together in that one overlaps the other. If you have pride in your name, you will act in ways and treat others in ways that bring credit to your name. If you are constantly acting in a way that reflects your strong, reputable character, people will recognize this by your name. Your name carries weight when people respect you, your actions, and your work.

Basically, it comes down to this: Every time you make a choice, every time you complete a project, every time you encounter another person, you define your character and your name. Both are exclusively yours and you are responsible for their well-being.

If you are truly concerned about building strong character and having credit to your name, this will be a force that motivates you. By taking your character and name into account when you submit projects, encounter people, and work in your profession, you are constantly motivated to do your very best to protect (or build) them both. You are motivated to ensure that your name and character are not damaged by giving less than you are capable of giving.

BILL CLAYTON
ACE Certified Personal Trainer/Post-Rehabilitation Specialist
Owner/Operator, Clayton Personal Fitness, Las Vegas, NV

"*I was . . .*" Those are powerful words. For example, *I was* the manager of the gardening department of a major retail chain. *I was* an employee in a shop that prints and mails inserts and flyers. *I was* a rock band drummer for several bands. *I was* a crystal meth addict. Yes . . . *I was!*

It seems strange to write that now, but the term "I was . . ." is impossible to erase. My friends and clients often ask me how I managed to go from the life of a meth addict to a personal trainer. The journey was a strange one and often difficult.

I began playing the drums when I was six years old and by the time I was eight, I had my first garage band. Writing and playing music were my only passions. They were my life. After high school, I worked many odd jobs, but my love of performing never waned.

In my twenties, I had a band that steadily played gigs and I was living the life of a rocker. We traveled. We sang. We partied. We traveled some more and we partied some more . . . and more. Before I really realized what was happening with me, I had become addicted to meth. It was my life. I hung around people who used with me and they became my family.

I met Kathy, the woman I would eventually marry, while performing with my band. She and I hit it off even though she knew of my addiction. One evening after we were married, Kathy and I were talking and she mentioned that she would like to have children one day. I wanted children, too. At that moment, the strangest thing came to my mind. I thought, "If she gets pregnant, I'll stop doing meth." How could I be so messed up that I would work to abolish my addiction for a child not yet born, *but* I would not consider trying to stop *just for me?* That was my wake-up call. I knew I had to change my life. I was 29 years old.

I was one of the lucky ones. I was able to stop "cold turkey" on my own. I know that others are not so lucky. I began to look at my life and tried to determine what I wanted to do. I had to seriously evaluate every aspect of who and what I was. I knew that I had to set goals to get my life back on track.

I had been in a life-threatening motorcycle accident years earlier and remembered the great care I received from my physical therapist. So I began to look at PT programs and that is when I found the personal trainer program at our local college. Something about this was very attractive to me. Again, I was lucky. I happened to find my passion and my life's vocation without much struggle.

Today, after working through my addiction, surviving a divorce, and mourning the death of my mom, I can say without a doubt that I am one of the luckiest people on earth. Because I was willing to change and stay committed to finding a better life, I found my true soul mate; I own my own gym; hold certifications from every major fitness and rehabilitation organization in America; and count each day as a true gift.

Who can you think of in your personal life or in the national spotlight that has a reputable character and is thought highly of when people hear his or her name?_____

_____

Why is this person's character and name in good standing?_____

_____

_____

_____

What qualities does he or she possess that you admire?_____

_____

_____

Choose one and describe how you can bring this quality to fruition in your life. _____

_____

_____

_____

POINT #8

Clear Up the Past Through Forgiveness

"Forgive and forget." You've probably heard that old saying since you were a child. It is, however, easier said than done. It takes a strong, dedicated person to do either. Some would even suggest that the "forget" part is impossible even if the "forgive" part takes place. Dragging around either can be a drain on your self-esteem, your attitude, your behavior toward others, and your level of motivation.

Try to picture it this way. You have been training to compete in a five-mile race. You hired a personal trainer, you've been going to the gym every day, you run each evening, and you have bought all of the proper equipment and paid your entrance fee for the race. On the day of the race, you arrive at the assigned starting location ready, anxious, and excited. There are many other runners there and you see them stretching and warming up.

> To forgive is the highest, most beautiful form of love. In return, you will receive untold peace and happiness.
>
> —Robert Muller

You join the crowd, complete your stretches, and then, out of nowhere, the organizer of the race comes toward you with a huge backpack—the kind you see mountain hikers carry when they plan to spend a week in the woods. The organizer tells you that you must wear the backpack in order to compete. Upon further inspection, you determine that the backpack weighs over 50 pounds. You did not practice with that extra 50 pounds and when you put on the backpack, you can feel the weight bearing heavily on your ankles and lower back.

Before you know it, the gun fires and the race is on. Like the other runners, you begin. You are the only one carrying a backpack. Each step on the pavement is painful. You feel sluggish. You can't concentrate on the race because all you can think about is the backpack. It begins to hurt. You fall behind. You can see all the other runners progressing in front of you.

This analogy is what carrying around a grudge—and anger—and frustration feels like: a 50-pound bag of weight on your back. It bogs you down, keeping you from performing at your truest golden potential. Forgiving and forgetting is the only way to rid yourself of this extra weight. Without forgiveness, the weight is crushing. Without forgetting, the race is lost.

By clearing up your past through true forgiveness, your motivation level will increase and so will the way you feel about yourself. You actually feel lighter and freer by letting go of that negative weight.

Some of the positive benefit of forgiveness can be:

- A paramount sense of relief
- The ability to face the day free of frustration, guilt, and anger
- A renewed sense of joy
- Greater inner peace
- A release of pent-up stress and tension
- Healthier self-esteem
- Improved motivation

POINT #9

Develop a Strong, Personal Guiding Statement

You're wearing a T-shirt to class. It is not your normal, run-of-the-mill T-shirt, however. You designed this T-shirt for everyone to see and read. It is white with bright red letters. On the front of the T-shirt is written your personal guiding statement—the words by which you live. The words that govern your life. What will your T-shirt say? Perhaps you will use the golden rule, "Do unto others. . . ." It might be an adaptation of the Nike® slogan, "Just Do It," or it might be something more profound, such as, "I live my life to serve others and to try to make others' lives better."

> Success is a state of mind. If you want success, start thinking of yourself as a success.
>
> —Anonymous

Whatever your guiding statement, it must be yours. It can't be your parents' or your professor's or your best friend's statement. It must be based on something you value and it must be strong enough to motivate you in hard, tough times. Your guiding statement must be so powerful that it will literally "guide" you when you are ethically challenged, broke, alone, angry, hurt, sad, or feeing vindictive. It is a statement that will guide you in relationships with family, friends, and spouses, partners, or would-be love interests.

As you've been reading, have you thought of your statement? If you already have a statement, be proud. However, if you do not, you are not alone. This is a very difficult question and most likely you've never been asked to develop a guiding statement before. It may take you some time to write your statement, and this section will help you.

One of the best places to start working on your guiding statement is to look back at those things you circled as valuable to you on page 39 of this chapter. If you value something, it may appear in your guiding statement.

For example, if you circled the words *Respect, Giving,* and *Optimism* as being among those you value, this is a basis for your statement. A guiding statement based on these words might be:

"I will live my life as a positive, upbeat, motivated person who respects others and enjoys giving to others on a daily basis."

If your circled words included *Integrity, Truth,* and *Fairness,* your statement might be:

"My integrity is the most important thing in my life and I will never act in any way that compromises or tarnishes my integrity. I will be truthful, fair, and honest in all my endeavors."

As you can see, if one of these statements was your guiding statement, and you truly lived your life by that statement, your actions would be in alignment with your values. This is the purpose of a guiding statement.

In the following space, transfer the most important words from the value list on page 39 and then work to develop your guiding statement.

My most important values are:

_____

_____

_____

_____

_____

Draft of my guiding statement (Take your time and be sincere. You will need this statement later in the chapter.)_____

_____

_____

_____

POINT #10

Make a Commitment to Strengthen Your Self-Esteem

If you were asked to name the areas of your life that are impacted by self-esteem, what would you say? The correct answer is, "Everything." Every area of your life is affected by your self-esteem.

Self-esteem and self-understanding are two of the most important components of your personal makeup. To be truly motivated, you have to know yourself and love yourself. There are many highly accomplished people who never truly know themselves and never recognize their personal worth or potential. Many people who are in therapy are there simply because they cannot accept the fact that they are OK. Self-esteem is a powerful force in your life and is the source of your joy, your productivity, and your ability to have meaningful relationships with others.

Self-esteem is so important, it is even connected to your mental and physical health. Unhealthy self-esteem and a lack of self-understanding are connected to loneliness and depression. "Self-esteem is the armor that protects us from the dragons of life: drugs, alcohol, delinquency and unhealthy relationships" (McKay and Fanning, 2000).

You might think of self-esteem as a photograph of yourself that you keep locked in your mind. It is a collective product—the culmination of everyone with whom you have associated, everywhere you've traveled, and all of the experiences you have had.

William James, the first major psychologist to study self-esteem, defined it as "the sum total of all a person can call their own: the Material Me (all that you have), the Social Me (recognition and acceptance from others), and the Spiritual Me (your innermost thoughts and desires)."

Stanley Coopersmith, noted psychologist and developer of the most widely used self-esteem inventory in America, defined self-esteem as "a personal judgment of worthiness." Psychologist and author Nathaniel Branden defines self-esteem as "confidence in our ability to cope with the basic challenges of life." And finally, psychologist Charles Cooley calls it "the looking glass." In everyday terms, perhaps we can define healthy self-esteem as "I know who I am, I accept who I am, I am OK, and I'm going to make it."

Self-esteem has five basic characteristics:

- A sense of security (I am safe and have the basics of life: food, water, etc.)
- A sense of identity (I know who I am and where I'm going)
- A sense of belonging (I know how to love and I am loved)
- A sense of purpose (I know why I'm here and what I am going to do with my life)
- A sense of personal competence (I have the ability to achieve my goals and grow)

These characteristics are considered key to a person's ability to approach life with motivation, confidence, self-direction, and the desire to achieve outstanding accomplishments.

LOVING YOU MORE

Improving Your Self-Esteem

You may be wondering what the point of all this is. "Why should I be worried about my self-esteem when I already have concerns about grades, work, laundry, family, relationships, groceries, and a million other things? Who has time for all this extra stuff?" The reason you need to be concerned about your self-esteem is that your grades, work, social life, family ties—*everything*—are tied to your self-esteem. The way you feel about yourself and the way you face life on a daily basis are guided by the image you hold of yourself. Also, the image you hold of yourself determines your level of motivation and commitment.

Ten Ways to Enhance Your Self-Esteem

Take control of your own life. If you let other people rule your life, you will always have unhealthy self-esteem. Part of growing up is taking control of your life and making your own decisions. Get involved in the decisions that shape your life. Seize control—don't let life just happen to you!

Adopt the idea that you are responsible for you. The day you take responsibility for yourself and what happens to you is the day you start to develop healthier self-esteem. When you can admit your mistakes and celebrate your successes knowing you did it your way, loving and respecting yourself become much easier.

Refuse to allow friends and family to tear you down. You may have family or friends who belittle you, criticize your decisions, and refuse to let you make your own decisions. Combat their negativity by admitting your mistakes and shortcomings to yourself and by making up your mind that you are going to overcome them. By doing this, you are taking their negative power away. If you freely admit that math is not your strength, then no one can make you feel small or inadequate by telling you (or others) that you stink at math.

DID YOU KNOW?

Tim McGraw, recording artist and country music sensation, has recorded almost a dozen CDs, has 23 number one hits, and has sold 32 million CDs to date. However, his first series of singles failed so badly that he was told to give up his dream of becoming a country recording artist. One producer even told him, "You'll never make it, son."

Control what you say to yourself. Self-talk is important to your self-esteem and to your ability to motivate yourself positively. Your brain is like a powerful computer and it continually sends messages to you. If these self-talk messages are negative, they will have a detrimental impact on your self-esteem and on your ability to live up to your potential. Surrounding yourself with positive, upbeat, motivated, happy people makes it more difficult for negative self-talk to emerge.

Take calculated risks. Many people find risk taking very hard, but it is one of the best ways to raise your self-esteem level. If you are going to grow to your fullest potential, you will have to learn to take some calculated risks and step out of your comfort zone. While you should never take foolhardy risks that might endanger your life, you must constantly be willing to push yourself.

Your relationships with others depend on how well you have developed your own self-esteem.

© Corbis

Stop comparing yourself to other people. You may never be able to beat some people at certain things. Does it really matter? You only have to "beat yourself" to get better. If you constantly tell yourself that you "are not as handsome as Bill" or "as smart as Mary" or "as athletic as Jack," you will begin to believe these statements, and your motivation will suffer. Everyone has certain strengths and talents to offer to the world. Yours are no smaller or less effective than the person's next door.

Develop a victory wall or victory file. People often take their accomplishments and hide them in a drawer or closet. Put your certificates, letters of praise, trophies, and awards out where you can see them on a daily basis. Keep a file of great cartoons, letters of support, or friendly cards so that you can refer to them from time to time. You'll be amazed at what a victory file or wall can do for your attitude.

Keep your promises and be loyal to friends, family, and yourself. If you have ever had someone break a promise to you, you know how it feels to have your loyalty betrayed. The most outstanding feature of one's character is one's ability to be loyal, keep promises, and do what one has agreed to do. Few things can make you feel better about yourself than being loyal and keeping your word.

Win with grace—lose with class. Everyone loves a winner, but everyone also loves a person who can lose with class and dignity. On the other hand, no one loves a bragging winner or a moaning loser. If you are engaged in sports, debate, acting, art shows, or academic competitions, you will encounter winning and losing. Remember, whether you win or lose, if you're involved and active, you're already in the top 10 percent of the population.

Be a giver. Author, speaker, and teacher Leo Buscaglia states, "You want to make yourself the most brilliant, the most talented, the most fabulous person that you can possibly be so that you can give it all away. The only reason we have anything is to be able to give it away." By giving to other people, you begin to live on a level where kindness, selflessness, and others' needs gently collide. Medical research has shown that those who give to others and help others experience an increased level of adrenaline, thus making them feel better, too. By giving selflessly to others, your self-esteem will flourish. Whatever you want in this life, give it away and it will come back to you.

> All that you give to the lives of others will come back into your own.
>
> —Annie Laura Ginn

Think About It
Chapter Reflection

Motivation can change your life. Healthy self-esteem can change your life. *You* can change your life. This chapter has been about self-discovery and defining what you value, what role your attitude plays in your motivation, and how to surround yourself with positive, optimistic people. By focusing on you and determining what is important to your college studies, your career, your relationships, and your personal life, you can develop a vision of your future. If you can see your future, *really see it*, then you are more likely to be motivated to achieve it. Remember, we are motivated by what we value. As you continue on in the semester and work toward personal and professional motivation, consider the following ideas:

▶ Convert external motivators into internal motivation.

▶ Use the power of positive thinking and surround yourself with positive people.

▶ Step outside your comfort zone.

▶ Use your values to drive your life-statement.

▶ Clear up your past by forgiving those who may have hurt you.

▶ Do one thing every day to strengthen your self-esteem.

▶ Turn negative thoughts into positive energy.

▶ Don't give in to defeat.

▶ View adversity as a stepping-stone to strength.

▶ Picture yourself as optimistic and motivated.

Good luck to you as you begin developing the motivation and positive attitude you need to be successful in your studies and beyond.

> The thing always happens that you believe in; and the belief in a thing makes it happen.
>
> —Frank Lloyd Wright

Knowledge in  Bloom

Utilizes levels 3 and 6 of the taxonomy

Using and Evaluating Your Guiding Statement

Process: Now that you have developed your guiding statement, consider how it can be used to guide you in the following situations.

Guiding statement as written on page 44 of this chapter:

_____
_____
_____

How Will Your Guiding Statement Help . . .

If you have a disagreement with your supervisor at work? _____

_____

_____

_____

_____

If your class paper or project receives a failing grade from your professor?_____

_____

_____

_____

If you are having a disagreement with someone for whom you care deeply (friend, spouse, partner, parent, work associate, etc.)?_____

_____

_____

_____

_____

If you see that someone is struggling and having a hard time "making it"?

_____

_____

_____

_____

_____

_____

Now that you have had a chance to apply your guiding statement to several situations, on a scale of 1 to 10 (1 being not effective at all and 10 being very effective), how would you rate its effectiveness to you and to those involved? Why? Discuss. _____

_____

_____

_____

_____

_____

Preparing for Success

Refer back to pages 28–29 of this chapter and answer the questions you developed from scanning this chapter's headings. You should also be able to answer the following questions if they were not on your list:

1. Explain how self-esteem plays a role in your motivation. _____

   _____

2. How can the "I CAN'T" syndrome affect your classroom performance? _____

   _____

3. What is a comfort zone and how can you expand yours? _____

   _____

4. Define the word *character* and discuss how it plays a role in your motivation level. _____

   _____

3

Persist

I know the price of **success:** dedication, **hard work,** and constant devotion to the **things** you want to see **happen.**

Frank Lloyd Wright

> **I**'m a great believer in luck, and I find the harder I work, the more I have of it.
>
> —Thomas Jefferson

Dropping out of college is not uncommon. As a matter of fact, over 40% who begin college never complete their degrees. Don't think that they drop out because of their inability to learn. Many leave because they made irreparable mistakes early in their first year. Some students leave because they did not know how to manage their time. Some leave because they could not manage their money and didn't know how to look for scholarships and other funding sources. Some leave because they couldn't get along with a professor. Some leave because they put partying above academics. And some leave because they simply could not figure out how "the system" worked and frustration, anger, and fear got the better of them. *Don't* believe that you have to be one of those students.

This chapter is about self-management and maneuvering through college with greater ease. *This chapter can help you:*

► Make the most of your relationships with professors and advisors
► Find and use academic, cultural, and personal success centers
► Get involved in campus organizations
► Use personal decorum to your best advantage
► Use a college catalog
► Calculate your grade point average
► Find and apply for financial aid and scholarships
► Be safe on your college campus

Scan &

Take a few moments and **scan this chapter**. As you scan, **list five questions** you can expect to learn the answers to while reading and studying Chapter 3.

Example:
► What can I do to accept criticism more easily? (from page 57)
► Where can I find information about dropping classes? (from page 60)

My Questions:

1. _____
_____ from page _____

2. _____
_____ from page _____

3. _____
_____ from page _____

Name: **Monica Miller**
Institution: **Delgado Community College, New Orleans, LA**
Major: **Hospitality**
Age: **46**

... from another perspective

After August 29, 2005, I learned the meaning of *persist.* Hurricane Katrina changed the way so many people live and the way so many people think about themselves. "Hanging on" became a way of life, even for many people who thought they did not have the strength to do so. By studying a chapter on persistence in *Cornerstone,* you can learn some of the techniques that help you become stronger, know more, and stay longer.

My whole life has been about persisting and holding on. I am a single parent, a college student, and an abuse survivor. I've been unemployed, without an education, and worked full- and part-time in many areas. I was also a professional model for 16 years. I've taken giant steps and baby steps, and through it all, I learned that holding on and learning to help yourself are vital to your survival. I also learned that when you help yourself hold on, you are also serving as a role model to help others hold on.

In college, persisting or "holding on" will allow you to reach your dreams. You're going to face many challenges, but by learning some of the ins and outs of college life at the beginning of your college career, you will be ready to deal with most of the challenges that come your way. From financial aid to dropping a class to getting along with your professors, holding on will become a daily adventure, and this chapter can help you become a student who will not let go.

4. _____

_____

from page _____

5. _____

_____

from page _____

Question

PS Reminder: At the end of the chapter, come back to this page and answer these questions in your notebook, text margins, or online chapter notes.

TO BE SUCCESSFUL, YOU HAVE TO LAST

Persistence in College

Before everything else, getting ready is the secret to success.

—Henry Ford

Have you ever faced adversity and unlikely odds while attempting to do something? Most everyone has. If you refused to let that adversity hold you back and you continued with the project at hand, then you know how it feels to be a winner. You know how it feels to reach a goal when the odds are not in your favor. You know the value of persistence.

Conversely, have you ever given up on something in the past and regretted it later? Do you ever think back and ask yourself, "What would my life be like if only I had done X or Y?" Have you ever made a decision or acted in a way that cost you dearly? If you have, then you know how difficult it can be to begin new projects or face the future without motivation.

Persistence. The word itself means that you are going to stay—that you have found a way to stick it out, found a way to make it count, and found a way *to not give up*. That is what this chapter is all about—giving you the tools to discover how

Where Are You . . .   AT THIS MOMENT

Before reading any further, take a moment and assess where you are at this moment with your knowledge about self-management and persistence. Read each statement carefully and then respond accordingly.

1. I am comfortable talking with my professors and advisors.   YES NO
2. I enjoy participating in college activities and clubs.   YES NO
3. I know where to find many types of financial aid and scholarships.   YES NO
4. I know how to calculate my grade point average (GPA).   YES NO
5. If I must stop attending a class, I know what steps to take to avoid ruining my GPA.   YES NO
6. I know the best way to approach my professor if I fail a paper or project.   YES NO
7. I understand about how to transfer my classes to another college.   YES NO
8. I have met my advisor and know where his or her office is located.   YES NO

If you answered "yes" to most of the questions (six or more), you have a firm understanding of some of the most important aspects of your college's policies and procedures. You know how to approach your professors and advisor and you have an understanding of the services available to you at your college. If you answered "no" to most of the questions, you will need to begin practicing the art of self-management. Your will need to get a copy of your college's catalog and read it carefully. You need to introduce yourself to your professors and advisor, and you may need to speak with your peers to find out what on-campus services are available and helpful.

your college works and what you will need to do to be successful. Self-management is about taking initiative and not waiting for someone to tell you how "it" works and not waiting until something goes wrong. Self-management is about investigating and researching ways to be successful at your college from this day forward.

By discovering how your college professors think and conduct classes, what support services and activities are available, how your personal decorum can affect your success, and knowing the importance of advising, preplanning for finances and classes, and a host of other topics, you will be less likely to make mistakes that force other students to drop out.

WHAT YOU NEED TO KNOW UP FRONT

College Policies and Procedures

The policies and procedures of colleges vary, but it is your responsibility to know what you can expect from your institution and what your institution expects from you. These policies can be found in the college catalog (traditional and online) or student handbook or schedule of classes, depending on your college.

Some Universal College Policies

▶ Students must meet certain residence requirements for a degree (even if you transfer into the college).

▶ All students are subject to the Federal Privacy Act of 1974 (this ensures your privacy, even from your parents).

> The very first step toward success in any endeavor is to become interested in it.
>
> —William Osler

▶ Most institutions require placement tests (these are different from admission tests). They are used to assign you to the appropriate English, math, foreign language, reading, and/or vocabulary classes.

▶ Most colleges adhere to a strict drop/add date. Always check your schedule of classes for this information.

▶ Most colleges have an attendance policy for classroom instruction.

▶ Most colleges have a strict refund policy.

▶ Many colleges will not allow you to take more than a certain number of credit hours per semester (18 semester hours is usually the upper limit).

▶ Most colleges in America have an academic dishonesty policy (this is discussed further in Chapter 10).

▶ Most colleges have a standing drug and alcohol policy.

Colleges put these types of policies into place to ensure that all students are treated fairly and equitably. Some of the policies are also mandated by the federal government in order for the college to receive federal funding. By reviewing your college's catalog, you can familiarize yourself with your institution's specific guidelines.

NUTTY OR NURTURING?

The College Professor

The college teaching profession is like no other profession on earth. There are certain rights and privileges that come with this profession that are not granted to any other career; however, there are also demands that no other profession faces.

Unlike high school teachers, college professors are charged with much more than just classroom instruction. Many are required to do research, write articles and books, attend and present at academic conferences, advise students, and keep current in their ever-changing fields of study.

Many of your college professors attended college for seven to 12 years preparing to teach you. College professors, for the most part, must have at least a master's degree in their field, but many are required to have a doctorate. A professor who has obtained a bachelor's, a master's, and a doctorate may have spent as many as 12 or more years in higher education.

The Freedom to Teach and Learn

Professors are granted something called academic freedom. Most high school teachers do not have this privilege. Academic freedom means that a professor has the right to teach controversial issues, topics, subjects, pieces of literature, scientific theories, religious tenets, and political points of view *without* the threat of termination. However, this does not mean that a faculty member has the right to push a personal agenda. Teaching information that is related to the course is different from spending an hour talking about one's own political or religious ideology.

You might not have been able to read Lillian Hellman's *The Children's Hour* in your high school drama class because of its homosexual overtones, but you would be able to study it uncensored in a college literature or drama class. This is the right of the college professor—to teach and guide in an unobstructed atmosphere free from parental, administrative, trustee, religious, political, or public pressure.

Because of academic freedom, you too have the right to speak your mind on issues ranging from politics to religion to social ills to controversial health and science matters. You can even disagree with your professors. If you choose to do so, be certain that you do so respectfully and in an assertive manner, not an aggressive one.

F? What Do You Mean, an F?

There will be times when you are disappointed with a grade that *you earn* from a professor. And yes, you do *earn* an A or an F; professors *do not give* A's or F's. What do you do? Threaten? Sue? Become argumentative? Those techniques usually cost you more than they benefit you.

First, remember that the grade assigned by a professor is usually impervious. This means that seldom is the grade changeable. If you made a less than satisfactory grade, there are several things you need to do. First, be truthful with yourself and examine the amount of time you spent on the project. Did you really give it your best? Next, review the requirements for the assignment. Did you miss something? Did you take an improper or completely wrong focus? Did you omit some aspect of the project? Did you turn the project in late?

DID YOU KNOW?

Nelson Mandela was raised in great poverty. Throughout his life, he suffered abuse and discrimination. He was asked to leave college because of his beliefs and protests. He endured a five-year trial for treason and later spent 27 years in prison for his outspoken opinions. He was released in 1990. In 1994, at the age of 76, he became the first black president of South Africa.

Next, consider the following questions, because they can contribute to your total understanding of material, projects, and expectations.

▶ Did you attend class regularly?

▶ Did you come to class prepared and ready for discussion?

▶ Did you ask questions in class for clarification?

▶ Did you meet with the professor during office hours?

▶ Did you seek outside assistance in places such as the writing center or math lab?

▶ Did you ask your peers for assistance or join a peer study or focus group?

These activities can make the difference between the success or failure of a project or a class.

If you are truly concerned about the grade, talk to the professor about the assignment. Ask him or her what is considered to be the most apparent problem with your assignment, and ask how you might improve your studying or preparing for the *next* assignment.

Above all, don't get into a verbal argument over the grade. In 99% of the cases, this will not help. Also, make sure that *the professor is your first point of contact*. Unless you have spoken with him or her *first* and exhausted all options with him or her, approaching the department chair, the dean, the vice president, or the president will more than likely result in your being sent directly back to the professor.

Accepting Criticism

If you receive a grade or comment that is less than you desired, think about the following tips for accepting criticism:

▶ Try to remember that the comment, criticism, or grade is about a paper or project, *not about you personally.*

▶ Don't panic—staying composed can help you think and act appropriately.

▶ If you are confused about the criticism, ask the professor to explain his or her comment in greater detail.

▶ Listen before you respond—don't attack the person offering the criticism.

▶ Be open-minded—ask for help in making the project or paper more appropriate next time.

▶ Don't make excuses.

▶ *Valid, constructive* criticism can help you grow—take the advice and make it work for you next time.

Classroom Challenges

When the professor doesn't show. At times during your college career, a professor will not show up for class. This will be rare, but it will happen. Sometimes, a note on the board or door will explain the circumstances of the professor's absence. If there is no note, assume that the professor is late. Do not leave class just because the professor is not there on time. You should normally wait at least 15 minutes for a professor. Use common sense and wait long enough to see whether the professor is just late or is truly not going to show up for the class.

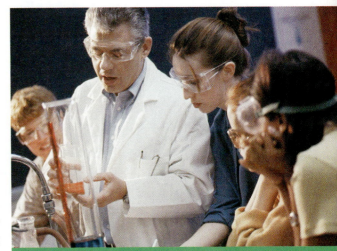

Large lecture classes often have a lab component in which instruction is much more focused.

©EyeWire, Inc.

YES YOU CAN !

Consider the following strategies for making the most of your relationships with your professors:

▶ Make an effort to get to know your professors outside the classroom if possible.

▶ Come to class prepared, bringing your best to the table each class session.

▶ Answer questions and *ask* questions in class.

▶ Ask for help if you see things getting difficult.

▶ Never make excuses; talk and act like an adult.

▶ Volunteer for projects and co-curricular opportunities.

▶ *Never* ask, "Are we doing anything important today?"

▶ Be respectful, and it will most likely be returned.

You might consider circulating a roster for students to sign before they leave so that you all have proof that you attended the class. You can present the list to the professor if there is a question about attendance.

Consult your college catalog or your class syllabus for details regarding a policy for waiting when a professor does not arrive.

When professors don't speak English well. Yes, you will have professors who do not speak English well. Universities often hire professors from around the world because of their expertise in their subjects. You may be shocked to find that it is difficult to understand a professor's dialect or pronunciation. If you have a professor with a foreign accent, remember these hints:

▶ Sit near the front of the room.
▶ Watch the professor's mouth when you can.
▶ Follow the professor's nonverbal communication patterns.
▶ Use a tape recorder if allowed.
▶ Read the material beforehand so that you will have a general understanding of what is being discussed.
▶ Ask questions when you do not understand the material.

SOMETHING FOR EVERYONE

Success Centers and Student Services on Campus

Most colleges offer you assistance for academic, social, cultural, spiritual, and physical enrichment outside the classroom. Your tuition or student activities fee may fund many of the centers on your campus. You've paid for them; you should take full advantage of their services.

Computer Labs offer students the opportunity to use e-mail, Internet services, and other online applications usually free of charge. These centers are also usually staffed with trained professionals who can help you with problematic programming issues.

Writing Centers are staffed with professionals who are trained to assist you with your writing skills. They will not rewrite your paper for you, but they can give you advice on how to strengthen your project, properly document information, and add to the overall quality of your work. This can really help your grade in the classes where writing is important.

Math Centers are staffed with professionals and usually student tutors. They are in place to help you with complex math problems, one-on-one or group tutoring, and study sessions. Traditionally, math is the single most difficult course for first-year students—even for those students who did well in high school math. Make use of this service before your first test or homework project. Even if you just drop by to confirm that what you've done is correct, it could save you grief later on.

Tutoring or Mastery Learning Centers are usually staffed by student tutors and offer assistance in almost any subject matter. Many colleges offer this service free of charge (or for a very nominal fee), whereas an outside tutor may charge upward of $30 to $45 per hour.

Language Labs are in place to help you if you are taking a foreign language or sign language. There may be "live" tutors to assist you or, more traditionally, there are computer-based tutorials that drill you in the respective language.

Libraries are not for the dead! As a matter of fact, your college library can be the hub of your learning experience, from printed materials to Internet usage to computer-assisted tutorials. Your library and librarians are vital to helping you succeed in your classes.

Unlike academic success services, student success services usually concentrate on the social, personal, career, and spiritual success of students. Some of these services include the following:

Veteran affairs

Reentry or adult learning centers

Health services

International student services

Minority student services

Career services

Mental/emotional health services

Student activities

Disabled student services. If you have a documented disability, colleges and universities across America are required by law to offer you "reasonable accommodations" to ensure your success (Americans with Disabilities Act, Sec. 504). Some of these accommodations are the following:

- ▸ Handicapped parking
- ▸ Special testing centers
- ▸ Extended time on tests and timed projects
- ▸ Textbook translations and conversions
- ▸ Interpreters
- ▸ Note-taking services
- ▸ TTY/TDD services
- ▸ Closed captioning

THE GOLDEN RULE— OR JUST A CROCK?

Classroom Etiquette and Personal Decorum

You may be surprised, but the way you act in (and out) of class can mean as much to your success as what you know. No one can make you do things or act in ways that you do not want. The following tips are provided from years of research and actual conversations with thousands of professors teaching across America. You must be the one who chooses whether or not to use this advice.

- ▸ Bring your materials to class daily: texts, notebooks, pens, calculators, and syllabi.

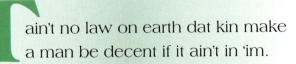

Tain't no law on earth dat kin make a man be decent if it ain't in 'im.

—Zora Neale Hurston, *Sweat*

- Come to class prepared: Read your text and handouts, do the assigned work at home, bring questions to be discussed.

- Turn in papers, projects, and assignments on time. Many professors do not accept late work.

- Participate in class. Ask questions, bring current events to the discussion, and contribute with personal experiences.

- Visit professors during office hours. The time before and after class may not be the most appropriate time for you or the professor. Your professor may have "back-to-back" classes and may be unable to assist you.

- If you are late for class, enter quietly. *Do not* walk in front of the professor. Don't let the door slam. Don't talk on your way in. Take the seat nearest the door. Make every effort not to be late to class.

- Wait for the professor to dismiss class before you begin to pack your bags to leave. You may miss important information or you may cause someone else to miss important information.

- Never carry on a conversation with another student while the professor or another student is talking.

- Do not sleep in class. If you are having problems staying awake, you should consider dropping the class and taking it at another time next semester.

- If for any reason you must leave during class, do so quietly and quickly. It is customary to inform the professor that you will be leaving early before class begins.

- If you make an appointment with a professor, keep it. If you must cancel, a courtesy call is in order.

- If you don't know how to address your professor; that is, by Mr., Mrs., Miss, Ms., or Dr., ask which he or she prefers, or simply call him or her "Professor _____."

- You should not wear sunglasses, oversized hats, strong cologne or perfume, skates, or earphones to class.

- Turn off your iPod. Even if your iPod is off, take your earbuds out of your ears. Leaving them in is a sign of disrespect.

- Be respectful of other students. Profanity and obscene language may offend some people. You can have strong, conflicting views without being offensive.

- Turn off your cell phone or beeper. If you have a home or work situation that requires that you "stay connected," put the device on vibrate.

- If you act like an adult (which you are), you'll be treated as one.

Remember that respect for others on your part will afford you the opportunity to establish relationships that you might otherwise never have had.

GOTTA GET OUT OF HERE!

Dropping Classes, Dropping Out, Stopping Out

Sometimes, students have to drop a class or their entire schedule because of family problems, medical reasons, work, or other reasons. We mention this because some students simply leave college, thinking that if they do not come back, their classes will automatically be dropped and everything will be fine. Later, when they return or transfer to another college, they are horrified to see five F's on their transcript. Never assume that your classes have been dropped from your records. At most colleges, classes are not automatically dropped. You must take care of this process. To make matters worse, some colleges never remove grades from your transcript, even if you repeat the course several times and make an A every time. If you leave your classes without taking care of the paperwork, your grade of F can stay with you and be calculated in your grade point average (GPA) for the rest of your college years.

WHERE IS IT WRITTEN?

Your College Catalog

Every college in the nation has a different catalog. Your college catalog is one of the most important publications you will read during your college years. It describes the rules, regulations, policies, procedures, and requirements of the college and your academic degree. It is imperative for you to keep the college catalog that was issued during your first year because college degree requirements can change from year to year. Most colleges require that you graduate under the rules and requirements stated in the catalog under which you entered the college. This policy is sometimes referred to as the *grandfather clause*.

The college catalog includes information about adding and dropping classes, auditing, probation, plagiarism, attendance, honors, course descriptions, graduation requirements, faculty credentials, and college accreditation, and usually includes a campus map. It is an important tool.

LET ME GIVE YOU A PIECE OF ADVICE

The Academic Advisor/Counselor

Your academic advisor can be of enormous assistance to you throughout your college career. They are usually assigned to you although a few colleges allow students to select their own advisor. Your advisor will help you select courses for the completion of your degree. However, you are the person most responsible for registering for classes that will count toward graduation. You should know as much as your advisor about your degree.

If you do not know why you have to take certain courses or in what sequence courses should be taken, don't leave your advisor's office until you find out. Lack of understanding of your course sequence, your college catalog, or the requirements for graduation could mean the difference between a four-year degree, a five-year degree, or no college degree at all.

Academic advisors are not psychological counselors. They are assigned to assist students in completing their academic programs of study. They may offer advice on personal or career matters, but they are not trained to assist

Your academic advisor is one of the most important people you will meet at college.

©Corbis

> The single most important influence in the life of a person is another person who is worthy of emulation.
>
> —Paul Shafer

with psychological and emotional matters. However, if you are having problems not related to your academic studies, your academic advisor may be able to direct you to the professional on campus who can best help you address certain issues and problems. Your academic advisor may be the first person to contact in times of crisis.

Making the Most of Your Student-Advisor Relationship

▶ Locate your advisor as soon as you arrive on campus and introduce yourself. Begin your relationship on a positive note.

▶ Stop by to say hello if you see your advisor in his or her office. Don't stay for a long time without an appointment, but a brief hello can help you build your relationship.

▶ Prepare a list of questions before you go to your advisor. This will help ensure that you have all the answers you need when you leave.

▶ Call your advisor if you have a problem that can be dealt with over the phone.

▶ Don't go to your advisor unprepared. You should have an idea of which classes you would like to take or need to take for the upcoming semester.

MOVING ON!

Transfer Issues

Many students enroll with the notion that they will one day transfer to another institution, perhaps after a semester, a year, or after earning a two-year degree.

First, your "Survival Guide for Transfer" is the college catalog; not only the catalog from your current institution, but also the catalog from the institution to which you plan to transfer. They are both helpful, but you need to be as mindful of the receiving college's requirements and policies as those of your current college.

You also need to be aware that most colleges *will not* accept grades below a C (2.0) from another institution. Also, you will find that your future college *does not* transfer your GPA. When you transfer to your future college, your GPA will start anew. This can be a double-edged sword. If you have a 4.0 at your current college, sadly, you must start again at the future college. However, if you had a 2.0, you get to start again at your future college. GPAs are explained later in this chapter.

Finally, and maybe *most* importantly, you need to speak with an informed, qualified *transfer* advisor or counselor before registering for any course or degree if you plan to transfer. Your relationship with your advisor or counselor holds as much importance as your relationship with your professors and peers.

DOES 1 + 1 REALLY EQUAL 2?

How to Calculate Your Grade Point Average

The GPA is the numerical grading system used by almost every college in the nation. GPAs determine if a student is eligible for continued enrollment, financial aid, or honors. Most colleges operate under a 4.0 system. This means that:

Each A earned is worth 4 quality points

Each B is worth 3 points

Each C is worth 2 points

Each D is worth 1 point

Each F is worth 0 points

For each course, the number of quality points earned is multiplied by the number of credit hours carried by the course. For example, if you are taking

English 101 for 3 semester hours of credit

Speech 101 for 3 semester hours of credit

History 201 for 3 semester hours of credit

Psychology 101 for 3 semester hours of credit

Spanish 112 for 4 semester hours of credit

then you would be enrolled for 16 hours of academic credit. Your calculation would look like this:

	GRADE	SEMESTER CREDIT		QUALITY POINTS		TOTAL POINTS
ENG 101	A	3 hours	×	4	=	12 points
SPC 101	C	3 hours	×	2	=	6 points
HIS 201	B	3 hours	×	3	=	9 points
PSY 101	D	3 hours	×	1	=	3 points
SPN 112	B	4 hours	×	3	=	12 points
		16 hours				42 total points

42 total points divided by 16 semester hours equals a GPA of 2.62 (or C+ average).

Lowering a GPA is very easy, but raising one is not as easy. Examine how just one grade can affect your GPA. In the following example, the Spanish grade has been lowered from a B to an F.

	GRADE	SEMESTER CREDIT		QUALITY POINTS		TOTAL POINTS
ENG 101	A	3 hours	×	4	=	12 points
SPC 101	C	3 hours	×	2	=	6 points
HIS 201	B	3 hours	×	3	=	9 points
PSY 101	D	3 hours	×	1	=	3 points
SPN 112	F	4 hours	×	0	=	0 points
		16 hours				30 total points

30 total points divided by 16 semester hours equals a GPA of 1.87 (or D+ average).

ON THE GO AND GOING ONLINE

Succeeding in Distance Education Courses

Distance learning classes can be great for students who may live far from campus, have transportation issues, work full-time, or have families and small children. These courses have flexible hours and few, if any, class meetings. Most online classes allow you to work at your own pace, but most still have stringent deadlines for submitting assignments.

Do not let anyone try to tell you that these courses are easier than regular classroom offerings; they are not. Distance-learning courses are usually more difficult for the average student. Some colleges reserve distance-learning courses for students with GPAs of 3.0 or higher. You need to be a self-starter and highly motivated to complete and do well in these courses. Take the distance education readiness assessment on page 65 to determine if an online class is right for you.

If you decide to take an online class, consider the following advice:

▶ If at all possible, review the course material before you register. This may help you in making the decision to enroll. Often, professors' syllabi are accessible online.

▶ Begin before the beginning! If at all possible, obtain the distance-learning materials (or at least the text) before the semester begins.

▶ Make an appointment to meet the professor as soon as possible. Some colleges will schedule a meeting for you. If it is not possible to meet, at least phone the professor and introduce yourself.

▶ Develop a schedule for completing each assignment and stick to it! Don't let time slip away from you. This is the biggest problem with online classes.

▶ Keep a copy of all work mailed, e-mailed, or delivered to the professor.

▶ Always mail, e-mail, or deliver your assignment on time—early if possible.

▶ Try to find someone who is registered for the same course so that you can work together or at least have a phone number to call if you run into a problem.

▶ Take full advantage of any online orientation or training sessions.

▶ Participate in class and in your groups (if you are assigned a group).

▶ If you have computer failure, have a backup plan.

▶ Log in *every day* even if you do not have an assignment due.

▶ Alert your professor immediately if your have family, computer, or personal problems that would prevent you from completing an assignment on time.

▶ Work ahead if possible.

▶ Find out where to go or whom to call on campus should you encounter technical problems with the learning platform or getting online.

After taking the Readiness Assessment and reading over the advice and suggestions above, do you plan to take an online class?   **YES   NO   MAYBE**
Why or why not? _____
_____
_____
_____

Bloom Level 5 question

Develop an action plan (based on Chapter 1's goal-setting strategies) to ensure your success in an online class. _____
_____
_____
_____
_____
_____
_____
_____
_____
_____

Distance Education Readiness Assessment

Please answer each question truthfully to determine your readiness for online learning.

1. Do you own your own computer? `YES` `NO`

2. Is your computer relatively new (enough memory, CD-ROM, graphics card, wireless Internet, etc.)? `YES` `NO`

3. Can you type? `YES` `NO`

4. Are you comfortable using a computer and Web technology? `YES` `NO`

5. Do you have the technical requirements for online learning (Internet access; Internet browser; Adobe, Word, or compatible program; PowerPoint)? `YES` `NO`

6. Are you highly organized? `YES` `NO`

7. Are you a good manager of time? `YES` `NO`

8. Are you highly motivated, a self-starter? `YES` `NO`

9. If you work full- or part-time, do you feel you have at least 6–8 hours per week to spend working with each of your online classes? `YES` `NO`

10. If you have family issues that require a great deal of your time, do you have family support? `YES` `NO`

11. Do you have "down time" to spend working on your online classes? `YES` `NO`

12. Can you get to campus if necessary? `YES` `NO`

13. Do you feel comfortable chatting online with unknown persons? `YES` `NO`

14. Do you think you can "relate" to others in an online relationship? `YES` `NO`

15. Do you consider yourself a good reader with high-level comprehension? `YES` `NO`

16. Can you concentrate on your work even with online distractions (e-mail, friends, etc.)? `YES` `NO`

17. Do you feel comfortable calling your professor during his or her office hours if you need to do so? `YES` `NO`

18. Do you think you will be able to take notes during an online chat or class session? `YES` `NO`

19. Are you comfortable with online terminology such as URL, listserv, Portal, Streaming Video, etc.? `YES` `NO`

20. Are you excited about taking an online class? `YES` `NO`

If you answered "no" to more than five of these questions, you should reconsider taking an online class at this time. To prepare for future classes, you may also want to spend time researching and becoming more familiar with the questions that you marked "no." You can also speak with your advisor or professor about your potential for success in his or her course. Your campus probably offers an online orientation from which you might benefit.

PLAYING IT SAFE

Protecting Yourself on Campus

Each year, colleges and universities around the nation are required to report and publish the number of crimes committed on campus. These crimes include homicide, rape, forcible sex offenses, assaults, robberies, and burglaries. The statistics may be found in your student handbook, class schedule, or college catalog.

The following tips are provided to assist you in protecting yourself against simple or violent crimes (Business and Legal Reports, Inc., 1995).

▶ Allow campus security to escort you to your car or residence hall if you are taking a night class.
▶ Walk in groups at night or in poorly lit places.
▶ Don't bring valuables to campus.
▶ Wherever you live: lock your doors and windows when you are sleeping, don't prop your door open, pull the blinds or curtains in the evenings, never give your key to anyone, and never invite strangers into your residence.
▶ Protect your belongings by taking out a renter's insurance policy.
▶ When walking around campus, walk confidently and not like a victim.
▶ Lock your car doors and always have your keys ready when you approach your car.
▶ Park in well-lit areas close to buildings.
▶ Lock valuables in your trunk.
▶ Never carry a lot of money with you.
▶ Use an ATM that is outside, well lit, and in a populated area.
▶ Never leave your book bag unattended.
▶ Always lock your bicycle to something that can't be moved.
▶ If you are robbed, never fight back; let them have what they want.
▶ *Never* go anywhere with a person who attacks you; try every means possible to get away.
▶ Lock your car doors immediately upon entering the car.
▶ If someone is following you, try to "lose" them by making unexpected turns or go inside a safe place and alert someone.
▶ Always date in groups until you get to know new people.
▶ Let someone know where you are going and with whom.
▶ Be very careful where you use alcohol—it can cloud your judgment.

WON'T YOU STAY FOR A WHILE?

Persisting in College

It is estimated that each year, nearly 40% of the people who begin their college career do not enroll for a second year. The national college dropout rate for public two-year colleges is 48%. The average college dropout rate for public four-year colleges is 32% (ACT, Inc., 2000).

The age-old "scare tactic" for first-year students, "Look to your left, look to your right—one of those people will not graduate with you," is not far from the truth. But the good news (actually, the great news) is that you do not have to become a statistic. You do not have to drop out of classes or college. You have the power to earn your degree. Sure, you may have some catching up to do or face a few challenges, but the beauty of college is that if you want help, you can get help.

Here you will find some powerful, helpful tips for persisting in college. Using only a few of them can increase your chances of obtaining your degree. Using all of them virtually assures it!

> **S**triving for success without hard work is like trying to harvest where you have not planted.
>
> —David Bly

- ▶ Visit your advisor or counselor frequently and establish a relationship with him or her. Take his or her advice. Ask him or her questions. Use him or her as a mentor.

- ▶ Register for the classes in which you place. It is unwise to register for Math 110 if you placed in Math 090 or English 101 if you placed in English 095. It will only cost you money, heartache, time, and possibly a low GPA.

- ▶ Make use of every academic service that you need that the college offers, from tutoring sessions to writing centers; these are essential tools for your success.

- ▶ Work hard to learn and understand your learning style. This can help you in every class in which you enroll. Chapter 4 will assist you with this endeavor.

- ▶ Work hard to develop a sense of community. Get to know a few people on campus such as a special faculty member, a secretary, another student, or anyone that you can turn to for help.

- ▶ Join a club or organization. Research proves that students who are connected to the campus through activities drop out less.

- ▶ After reading Chapter 1, "Change," concentrate on setting realistic, achievable goals. Visualize your goals. Write them down. Find a picture that represents your goal and post it so that you can see your goal every day.

- ▶ Work hard to develop and maintain a sense of self-esteem and self-respect. The better you feel about yourself, the more likely you are to reach your goals.

- ▶ Learn to budget your time as wisely as you budget your money. You've made a commitment to college and it will take a commitment of time to bring your degree to fruition.

- ▶ If you have trouble with a professor, don't let it fester. Make an appointment to speak with the professor and work through the problem.

- ▶ If you get bored in class or feel that the class is not going to benefit you, remember that it is a required class and you will always have a few boring classes during your college career. Stick to it and it will be over soon.

- ▶ If you feel your professor doesn't care, it may be true. Some don't. This is where you have to apply the art of self-management.

- ▶ Find some type of strong, internal motivation to sustain you through the tough times—and there will be tough times.

- ▶ Focus on the future. Yes, you're taking six classes while your friends are off partying, but in a few years, you'll have something that no party could ever offer, and something that no one can ever take away . . . your very own college degree.

- ▶ Choose optimism. Approach each day with a positive and upbeat attitude, even if it is Tuesday and you have your two hardest classes. Today is the day you're going to have a breakthrough!

▶ Move beyond mediocrity. Everyone can be average. If college were easy, everybody would have a college degree. You will need to learn to bring your best to the table for each class.

▶ Focus on your career choice. Can you do what you want to do without a college degree? That is perhaps the most important question when it comes to persistence. Can you have what you want, do what you want, be who you want to be without this degree?

As professors, we wish our students every success imaginable. Use us as resources, contact us, ask us questions, trust us, visit us, and allow us to help you help yourself.

Think About It
Chapter Reflection

College is an exciting and wonderful place. You're meeting new people, being exposed to innovative ideas, and learning new concepts. There has never been a time when the old saying "knowledge is power" is more true. By participating in your own learning, engaging in the art of self-management, and taking the initiative to learn about your institution, you are avoiding potential mistakes that could cost you your education. Good for you!

Simply taking the time to familiarize yourself with the workings of your college can eliminate many of the hassles that first-year students face. By doing this, you can enjoy your experience with more energy, excitement, and optimism. As you continue on in the semester and work toward self-management, consider the following ideas:

▶ Determine if you have the *time* to take an online class.
▶ Use *personal decorum* in and out of the classroom.
▶ Establish a *relationship* with your professors.
▶ Speak with your *advisor or counselor* frequently.
▶ Know the *rules and policies* of your college.
▶ Seek *academic assistance* when needed.
▶ Join a *campus club* and get involved.
▶ Apply for *financial aid* early and often.
▶ Make use of *student services*.

Practicing self-management can help you not only in your classes, but as you enter the world of work. Strive to become a person who is accountable and responsible for his or her own life and learning.

There is no secret to success. It is the result of preparation, hard work, and learning from failure.

—General Colin Powell

Knowledge in Bloom

Utilizes level 1 of the taxonomy

Each chapter-end assessment is based on *Bloom's Taxonomy of Learning*. See the inside front cover for a quick review.

Discovering Your Campus Resources

Explanation: Now that you have discovered more about your campus, professors, and available services, complete the following Identification and Scavenger Hunt.

Question	Answer	Location	Phone #
If you happen to fail a math test, where could you go on your campus to find assistance?			
If you are having trouble writing a paper, where could you go on your campus to get assistance before you turn in the paper to your professor?			
Where can you go to find out the names and meeting times of clubs and organizations on your campus?			
If you need to speak to someone about a personal health issue, where could you go on your campus to get help?			
If you are having difficulty coping with the stress of college and are feeling depressed, where could you go on your campus to get help?			
You have been assigned the strange project of identifying the sculptor *and* material from which "The Thinker" was cast. Where could you go for help? *Be specific and find the answer to the question.*			
You discover that someone broke into your car while you were in class. Where should you go at this point?			
You are not really sure about your major in college or what you want to do for a career. What office on your campus can help you?			
You read in the schedule of classes that you must have your advisor's signature to register for next semester. Who is the person and where is he or she located?			
You're thinking of taking an online class. Where is the first place you could go on your campus to speak with someone about the technical requirements?			
If you want to read more about the penalties for academic dishonesty (cheating) on your campus, where could you look?			

Preparing for Success

Refer to pages 52–53 of this chapter and answer the questions you developed from scanning this chapter's headings. You should also be able to answer the following questions if they were not on your list:

1. List three tips for succeeding in a class where the professor and you do not have the same first language. _____
   _____

2. Why is personal decorum important in a college classroom? _____
   _____

3. Discuss two ways that you can keep yourself safe on campus. _____
   _____

4. Why are college professors so different from teachers in high school? _____
   _____

4

Prioritize

Plan your progress **carefully**; hour by hour, day by day, month by month. Maintained enthusiasm is the wellspring of your **power**.

Paul Meyer

the big **WHY**

Why read and work through a chapter on stress and time? *Why* will a chapter on managing time and stress help me in college, at work, with my family, and beyond? *Why* is controlling stress and managing my time so important?

If you really want to know what you value in life, look at your checkbook and your calendar.

—Herb Kelleher

Time and stress—partners in crime or helpful allies? You cannot get more of one, but you can certainly have more than your share of the other. In reality, one can define and drive the other. The more effectively you manage your time, the less stress you will have in your life. Time, of course, is not the only thing in your life that can cause stress. It can be brought on by relationships, work, family issues, and money, to name a few. However, by learning to more effectively manage your time, you can reduce this one factor that contributes to the stress level in your life. *This chapter can help you:*

▶ Learn to make an effective "to do" list.
▶ Utilize a priority check-off system for your "to do" list.
▶ Understand the cycle of procrastination.
▶ Overcome procrastination.
▶ Manage your time more effectively to reduce stress.
▶ Identify the major stressors in your life.
▶ Understand the effects of stress on your body and memory.

By learning to manage your time and reduce your level of stress, you can concentrate on the important aspects of your education and become a more productive student.

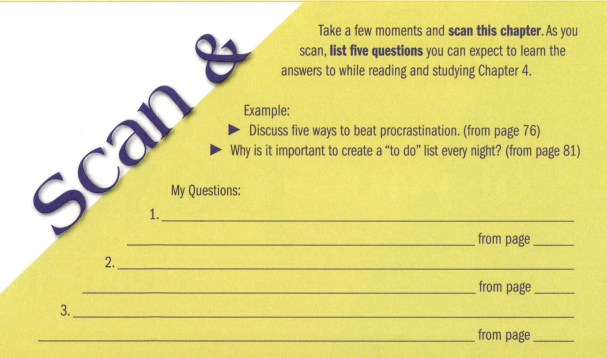

Scan &

Take a few moments and **scan this chapter**. As you scan, **list five questions** you can expect to learn the answers to while reading and studying Chapter 4.

Example:
▶ Discuss five ways to beat procrastination. (from page 76)
▶ Why is it important to create a "to do" list every night? (from page 81)

My Questions:

1. _____
   _____ from page _____

2. _____
   _____ from page _____

3. _____
   _____ from page _____

▶ Look at completing the project in terms of your *long-range goals* and your overall life plan.

▶ *Don't get involved* in too many organizations, accept too many commitments, or overextend yourself.

▶ *Just do it!* Force yourself to jump into the task.

▶ Start on the difficult, *most boring tasks first.*

▶ Find a *quiet place to study* and concentrate.

▶ Weed out your personal belongings and living space. Organization helps you manage your time and *get to work.*

▶ *Prepare to be successful* by getting ready the evening before.

▶ Take time to do the *things you love*—creating a healthy balance in your life.

Think of something that you have been putting off in one of the major areas of your life: academic, financial, household, and so on. Using three to four of the tips above, develop a plan for getting this important task done this afternoon. That's right—*this afternoon.* List at least five action steps to cross this project off your "to do" list.

_____

_____

_____

_____

_____

_____

Bloom Level 5 question

Evaluating How You Spend Your Time

Knowing Where Time Goes Means Getting to Enjoy More of It

So how do you find out where your time goes? The same way that you find out where your money goes—you track it. Every 15 minutes for one week, you will record exactly how you spent that time. This exercise may seem a little tedious at first, but if you will complete the process over a period of a week, you will have a much better concept of where your time is being used. Yes, that's right—for a week, you need to keep a written record of how much time you spend sleeping, studying, eating, working, getting to class and back, cooking, caring for children, watching television, doing yard work, going to movies, attending athletic events, hanging out, doing laundry, whatever.

Take your plan with you and keep track of your activities during the day. To make things simple, round off tasks to 15-minute intervals. For example, if you start walking to the cafeteria at 7:08, you might want to mark off the time block that begins with 7:00. If you finish eating and return to your home at 7:49, you can mark off the 7:45 and 8:00 blocks. You will also want to note the activity so you can evaluate how you spent your time. Study the example that is provided for you in Figure 4.2

On pages 79–80, you will find a daily time log for you to use for this exercise. Remember to take this page with you and record how you are spending your time during the day. As you progress through the week, try to improve the use of your time. When you finish this exercise, review how you spent your time.

FIGURE 4.2 *How You Really Spend Your Time*

7:00	get up & shower	7:00			
	X	7:15			12:15
		7:30	Walked to Union		12:30
	Breakfast	7:45	1:00	Ate lunch	12:45
8:00		8:00			1:00
		8:15			1:15
	Read paper	8:30			1:30
	Walked to class	8:45	Talked w/ Joe		1:45
9:00	English 101	9:00	2:00		2:00
		9:15	Went to book		2:15
		9:30	store		2:30
		9:45	Walked to		2:45
10:00		10:00	3:00	my room	3:00
		10:15	Called Ron		3:15
		10:30			3:30
	Walked to class	10:45			3:45
11:00	History 210	11:00	4:00	Watched	4:00
		11:15		Friends	4:15
		11:30			4:30
		11:45		Walked to	4:45
12:00		12:00	5:00	library	5:00
					5:15

WHAT KIND OF PERSON ARE YOU, ANYWAY?

Day People vs. Night People

Are you a "morning person" or an "evening person"? Discovering your body's clock can be of great assistance to you. If you are a morning person trying to study at night, or a night person trying to study in the morning, you may not be using your body's clock to your best advantage. Although knowing your prime "body time" is important to your concentration and motivation, it is not the only thing that can adversely affect your concentration level and study efforts. Other factors hurt you, *cause procrastination*, and add to the difficulty of working against your body's cycle:

▶ Complexity of the material you are studying

▶ Interest level in the material you are studying

▶ Noise or interference by others

▶ Hunger or thirst

▶ Sleep deprivation

▶ Your social environment

▶ Your study environment (too hot, too cold, too close to distractions, etc.)

▶ Ambiguity (not really knowing what needs to be done)

▶ Lack of information needed to complete the task

FIGURE 4.3 Daily Time Sheets

Monday		Tuesday		Wednesday	
6:00	6:00	6:00	6:00	6:00	6:00
	6:15		6:15		6:15
	6:30		6:30		6:30
	6:45		6:45		6:45
7:00	7:00	7:00	7:00	7:00	7:00
	7:15		7:15		7:15
	7:30		7:30		7:30
	7:45		7:45		7:45
8:00	8:00	8:00	8:00	8:00	8:00
	8:15		8:15		8:15
	8:30		8:30		8:30
	8:45		8:45		8:45
9:00	9:00	9:00	9:00	9:00	9:00
	9:15		9:15		9:15
	9:30		9:30		9:30
	9:45		9:45		9:45
10:00	10:00	10:00	10:00	10:00	10:00
	10:15		10:15		10:15
	10:30		10:30		10:30
	10:45		10:45		10:45
11:00	11:00	11:00	11:00	11:00	11:00
	11:15		11:15		11:15
	11:30		11:30		11:30
	11:45		11:45		11:45
12:00	12:00	12:00	12:00	12:00	12:00
	12:15		12:15		12:15
	12:30		12:30		12:30
	12:45		12:45		12:45
1:00	1:00	1:00	1:00	1:00	1:00
	1:15		1:15		1:15
	1:30		1:30		1:30
	1:45		1:45		1:45
2:00	2:00	2:00	2:00	2:00	2:00
	2:15		2:15		2:15
	2:30		2:30		2:30
	2:45		2:45		2:45
3:00	3:00	3:00	3:00	3:00	3:00
	3:15		3:15		3:15
	3:30		3:30		3:30
	3:45		3:45		3:45
4:00	4:00	4:00	4:00	4:00	4:00
	4:15		4:15		4:15
	4:30		4:30		4:30
	4:45		4:45		4:45
5:00	5:00	5:00	5:00	5:00	5:00
	5:15		5:15		5:15
	5:30		5:30		5:30
	5:45		5:45		5:45
6:00	6:00	6:00	6:00	6:00	6:00
	6:15		6:15		6:15
	6:30		6:30		6:30
	6:45		6:45		6:45
7:00	7:00	7:00	7:00	7:00	7:00
	7:15		7:15		7:15
	7:30		7:30		7:30
	7:45		7:45		7:45
8:00	8:00	8:00	8:00	8:00	8:00
	8:15		8:15		8:15
	8:30		8:30		8:30
	8:45		8:45		8:45
9:00	9:00	9:00	9:00	9:00	9:00
	9:15		9:15		9:15
	9:30		9:30		9:30
	9:45		9:45		9:45
10:00	10:00	10:00	10:00	10:00	10:00
	10:15		10:15		10:15
	10:30		10:30		10:30
	10:45		10:45		10:45
11:00	11:00	11:00	11:00	11:00	11:00
	11:15		11:15		11:15
	11:30		11:30		11:30
	11:45		11:45		11:45
12:00	12:00	12:00	12:00	12:00	12:00

FIGURE 4.3 *continued*

Thursday		Friday		Saturday		Sunday	
6:00	6:00	6:00	6:00	6:00	6:00	6:00	6:00
	6:15		6:15		6:15		6:15
	6:30		6:30		6:30		6:30
	6:45		6:45		6:45		6:45
7:00	7:00	7:00	7:00	7:00	7:00	7:00	7:00
	7:15		7:15		7:15		7:15
	7:30		7:30		7:30		7:30
	7:45		7:45		7:45		7:45
8:00	8:00	8:00	8:00	8:00	8:00	8:00	8:00
	8:15		8:15		8:15		8:15
	8:30		8:30		8:30		8:30
	8:45		8:45		8:45		8:45
9:00	9:00	9:00	9:00	9:00	9:00	9:00	9:00
	9:15		9:15		9:15		9:15
	9:30		9:30		9:30		9:30
	9:45		9:45		9:45		9:45
10:00	10:00	10:00	10:00	10:00	10:00	10:00	10:00
	10:15		10:15		10:15		10:15
	10:30		10:30		10:30		10:30
	10:45		10:45		10:45		10:45
11:00	11:00	11:00	11:00	11:00	11:00	11:00	11:00
	11:15		11:15		11:15		11:15
	11:30		11:30		11:30		11:30
	11:45		11:45		11:45		11:45
12:00	12:00	12:00	12:00	12:00	12:00	12:00	12:00
	12:15		12:15		12:15		12:15
	12:30		12:30		12:30		12:30
	12:45		12:45		12:45		12:45
1:00	1:00	1:00	1:00	1:00	1:00	1:00	1:00
	1:15		1:15		1:15		1:15
	1:30		1:30		1:30		1:30
	1:45		1:45		1:45		1:45
2:00	2:00	2:00	2:00	2:00	2:00	2:00	2:00
	2:15		2:15		2:15		2:15
	2:30		2:30		2:30		2:30
	2:45		2:45		2:45		2:45
3:00	3:00	3:00	3:00	3:00	3:00	3:00	3:00
	3:15		3:15		3:15		3:15
	3:30		3:30		3:30		3:30
	3:45		3:45		3:45		3:45
4:00	4:00	4:00	4:00	4:00	4:00	4:00	4:00
	4:15		4:15		4:15		4:15
	4:30		4:30		4:30		4:30
	4:45		4:45		4:45		4:45
5:00	5:00	5:00	5:00	5:00	5:00	5:00	5:00
	5:15		5:15		5:15		5:15
	5:30		5:30		5:30		5:30
	5:45		5:45		5:45		5:45
6:00	6:00	6:00	6:00	6:00	6:00	6:00	6:00
	6:15		6:15		6:15		6:15
	6:30		6:30		6:30		6:30
	6:45		6:45		6:45		6:45
7:00	7:00	7:00	7:00	7:00	7:00	7:00	7:00
	7:15		7:15		7:15		7:15
	7:30		7:30		7:30		7:30
	7:45		7:45		7:45		7:45
8:00	8:00	8:00	8:00	8:00	8:00	8:00	8:00
	8:15		8:15		8:15		8:15
	8:30		8:30		8:30		8:30
	8:45		8:45		8:45		8:45
9:00	9:00	9:00	9:00	9:00	9:00	9:00	9:00
	9:15		9:15		9:15		9:15
	9:30		9:30		9:30		9:30
	9:45		9:45		9:45		9:45
10:00	10:00	10:00	10:00	10:00	10:00	10:00	10:00
	10:15		10:15		10:15		10:15
	10:30		10:30		10:30		10:30
	10:45		10:45		10:45		10:45
11:00	11:00	11:00	11:00	11:00	11:00	11:00	11:00
	11:15		11:15		11:15		11:15
	11:30		11:30		11:30		11:30
	11:45		11:45		11:45		11:45
12:00	12:00	12:00	12:00	12:00	12:00	12:00	12:00

To determine your best working time, place a check by the questions that pertain to your attitude:

1. _____ Are you lethargic in the morning until you have been up for an hour or so?
2. _____ Do you try to schedule your classes after 10 A.M. so you can sleep later?
3. _____ Do you feel down around 5 P.M. but feel ready to go again around 8 P.M.?
4. _____ Have you pulled successful all-nighters in the past?
5. _____ Do you wake up early and spring right out of bed?
6. _____ Do you have a hard time being productive during the late afternoon hours?
7. _____ Is it impossible for you to concentrate after 10 P.M.?
8. _____ Are you one of those rare college students who love 8 A.M. classes?

If you answered yes to questions 1 through 4, or to most of them, you are a night person; if you answered yes to questions 5 through 8, or to most of them, you are a morning person. Being a morning person does not mean that you can never get anything done at night, but it does mean that your most productive time is morning. If you are a morning person, you should tackle difficult, complex problems early in the morning when you are at your peak. If you are a night person, you should wait a few hours after getting up in the morning before you tackle difficult tasks.

© Lynn Goldsmith/Corbis

DID YOU KNOW?

Tina Turner, born and raised Anna Mae Bullock in Nutbush, TN, was abandoned by her migrant worker parents. She was raised by her grandmother and worked in the cotton fields as a child. She endured a rough and very abusive marriage. She was repeatedly beaten and raped by her husband, Ike. During their divorce hearings, she had to defend the right to even keep her name. She went on to record many number one hits such as "Private Dancer" and "What's Love Got to Do With It?" She has won seven Grammy® awards, has a star on the Hollywood Walk of Fame, is listed in the Rock and Roll Hall of Fame, and a motion picture was made about her starring Angela Bassett.

PLANNING AND PREPARING

The Secret to Priority Management

In the past, you may have said to yourself, "I don't have time to plan." "I don't like to be fenced in and tied to a rigid schedule." "I have so many duties that planning never works." Scheduling does not have to be a tedious chore or something you dread. Scheduling can be your lifeline to more free time.

To manage your time successfully, you need to spend some time planning. To plan successfully, you need a calendar that has at least a week-at-a-glance or month-at-a-glance section as well as sections for daily notes and appointments. If you have not bought a calendar, you can download one from the Internet or create one using Word or other computer programs.

Planning and Organizing for School

Each evening, you should take a few minutes (and literally, that is all it will take), sit in a quiet place, and make a list of all that needs to be done tomorrow. Successful time management comes from *planning the night before!* Let's say your list includes

Research speech project
Study, finance test on Friday
Read Chapter 13 for chemistry
Meet with chemistry study group
Attend English class at 8:00 am
Attend mgt. class at 10:00 am

Exercise
Buy birthday card for Mom
Wash the car
Take shirts to dry cleaner
Buy groceries
Call Janice about weekend

Now, you have created a list of tasks that you will face tomorrow. Next, separate this list into three categories:

Must Do
Read Chapter 13 for chem
Study for finance test on Fri.
Exercise
English class @ 8:00
Mgt. class @ 10:00
Meet w/chem study gp.

Need to Do
Research speech project
Buy birthday card for Mom
Shirts to cleaner
Buy groceries

Fun Stuff
Wash the car
Call Janice re. wkend

Don't get too excited yet. Your time-management plan is not finished. The most important part is still ahead of you. Now, you will need to rank the items in order of their importance. You will put a 1 by the most important, a 2 by the next most important, and so on, in each category.

Must Do
1 Read Chapter 13 for chem
2 Study for finance test on Fri.
3 Exercise
1 English class 8:00
1 Mgt. class 10:00
2 Meet w/chem study gp.

Need to Do
1 Research speech project
2 Buy birthday card for Mom
3 Shirts to cleaner
2 Buy groceries

Fun Stuff
2 Wash the car
1 Janice re. wkend

Now, you have created a *plan* to actually get these tasks done! Not only have you created your list, but now you have divided it into important categories, ranked them, and you have made a written commitment to these tasks.

Now, look at how these tasks are placed into a daily calendar (see Figure 4.4). You would schedule category 1 first (Must Do), category 2 next (Need to Do), and category 3 (Fun Stuff) next. Remember, *never* keep more than one calendar. Always carry it with you and always schedule your tasks immediately so that you won't forget them. For an example of a weekly calendar, see Figure 4.5 on page 84.

Planning and Organizing for Work

▶ Organize your materials at work as they are organized at home. If you have a desk in both places, keep your supplies in the same place in both desks. Simplify your life by following similar patterns at work and at home.

▶ Write directions down! Keep a notebook for repetitive tasks. Keep a calendar and be on time to meetings.

▶ Learn to do paperwork immediately rather than let it build up. File—don't pile!

▶ Never let your work responsibilities slide because you are studying on the job. Employers always notice.

▶ Leave the office for lunch, breaks, and short walks.

▶ When you are given projects that require working with others, plan carefully to do your work well and on time.

▶ Keep a Rolodex file or use a Palm Pilot or your iPod for important phone numbers and addresses that you use frequently.

▶ Perform difficult, unpleasant tasks as soon as you can so you don't have them hanging over your head.

FIGURE 4.4   *Daily Calendar*

DAY Monday

Time	Task	Priority	Complete?
6:00			Yes __ No
6:30			Yes __ No
7:00	Study for finance		Yes __ No
7:30	↓		Yes __ No
8:00	English 101		Yes __ No
8:30			Yes __ No
9:00	↓		Yes __ No
9:30	Read Pg. 1–10 of Chem. Chapter		Yes __ No
10:00	Management 210		Yes __ No
10:30			Yes __ No
11:00	↓		Yes __ No
11:30	Finish Reading Chem. Chapter		Yes __ No
12:00			Yes __ No
12:30	↓		Yes __ No
1:00	Meet w/ Chemistry group (take lunch)		Yes __ No
1:30			Yes __ No
2:00			Yes __ No
2:30	↓		Yes __ No
3:00	Exercise at Golds		Yes __ No
3:30			Yes __ No
4:00	↓		Yes __ No
4:30	go th grocery store & get B/day card		Yes __ No
5:00	& drop off shirts		Yes __ No
5:30			Yes __ No
6:00			Yes __ No
6:30	Dinner		Yes __ No
7:00	↓		Yes __ No
7:30	Internet Research for speech		Yes __ No
8:00			Yes __ No
8:30	↓		Yes __ No
9:00	call Janice @ w/end		Yes __ No
9:30			Yes __ No

▶ When you plan your work schedule, allow for unexpected problems that might interfere with the schedule.

▶ Practice detached concern—care about your work but avoid taking it home with you.

Planning and Organizing for Home (Traditional Students)

▶ Organize as effectively at home as you do at work.

▶ If you have roommates, divide the chores. Insist on everyone doing his or her share.

FIGURE 4.5 *Weekly Calendar*

Week of: _____

	Mon	Tues	Wed	Thur	Fri	Sat	Sun
6–7 AM							
7–8 AM		Study		Study			
8–9 AM	Eng 101		Eng 101		Eng 101		Study
9–10 AM						Work	
10–11 AM	Mgt 210	Exercise	Mgt 210	Exercise	Mgt 210		
11–12 AM							
12 (noon)–1 PM	Study	Math 110	Study	Math 110	Study		Exercise
1–2 PM	Chem group		Chem group		Chem group		
2–3 PM		Study		Study			
3–4 PM	Exercise	Phil 101	Exercise	Phil 101	Exercise		
4–5 PM							
5–6 PM						Free Time	
6–7 PM	Dinner		Dinner				
7–8 PM		Work		Work	Work		
8–9 PM	Study		Study				
9–10 PM							
10–11 PM							
11 PM–12 (midnight)							

▶ Plan a rotation schedule for major household chores and stick to it—do laundry on Mondays and Thursdays; clean bathrooms on Saturdays; iron on Wednesdays; and so on.

▶ Organize your closet and your dresser drawers. Get rid of clothes you don't wear.

▶ Put a sign by your telephone that reads "Time" to remind yourself not to waste it on the phone.

▶ If you can't study in your room because of drop-in visitors or loud roommates, go to the library.

- If you drive to class or work, fill up your tank ahead of time so you won't be late.
- Keep yourself physically fit with a regular exercise plan and nutritious meals.
- Get out of the house. Take a walk. Visit a friend.

Planning and Organizing for Home (Nontraditional Students)

If you are a nontraditional student and have children, teach them to be organized so they don't waste your time searching for their shoes, books, and assignments. Teach family members responsibility! You can't work, go to school, and hold everybody's hand all the time. Give each of your children a drawer in a filing cabinet. Show them how to organize their work. You will be preparing them to be successful.

Nontraditional students face special challenges and choices.

© Image 100 Ltd.

- If you are a perfectionist and want everything in your home to be perfect, get over it!
- Get rid of the clutter in your garage, basement, closets, kitchen, bathroom, etc.
- Establish a time for study hall in your home. Children do their homework, and you do yours.
- If you have a family, insist that all of you organize clothes in advance for school or work for several days.
- Put a message board in a convenient place for everyone to use.
- If your children are old enough to drive, have them run errands at the cleaners, post office, and grocery store.
- Carpool with other parents in your neighborhood.
- Delegate, delegate, delegate! You are not Superwoman or Superman. Tell your family you need help. Children can feed pets, make their own beds, fold clothes, vacuum, sweep, iron, and cut the grass if they are old enough.

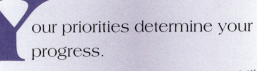

Your priorities determine your progress.

—Mike Tully

- Schedule at least one hour alone with each of your children each week. Make this a happy, special time—a fun break!
- Make meals happy, relaxed times when each person's successes are shared and celebrated. Discuss current events.
- Plan special times with your spouse or partner if you have one so that he or she does not get fed up with your going to school.
- Tell your family and friends when you have to study; ask them to respect you by not calling or dropping by at this time.
- Post a family calendar where everyone can see it. Put all special events on it— for example, Janie's recital, Mike's baseball game, Jasmine's company party.
- Put fun days on this calendar so that your entire family has something to look forward to.

TOMORROW? WHAT DO YOU MEAN, IT'S DUE TOMORROW?

The Relationship between Poor Time Management and Monumental Stress

There are probably as many stressors in this world as there are people alive. For some people, loud music causes stress. For others, a hectic day at the office with people demanding things and equipment breaking down causes stress. For others, that loud music and a busy day at the office is just what the doctor ordered. One thing is for sure, however: Poor planning and "running out of time" are on most people's list of major stressors.

Most stress does not just happen to us. We allow it to happen by not planning our day or week. We allow our "to do" list to get out of hand, and before we know it, there is more on the list than can be done in a month. Because of poor planning and procrastination, we become anxious and nervous about not getting it all done. By planning and doing, we can actually lower our stress level and improve our general health and our memory.

Medical research has shown that exposure to stress over a long period of time can be damaging to your body. Stress can also have an effect on your memory. When you are stressed, your brain releases cortisol, which affects the neurons in your brain. Over time, cortisol can be toxic and damage parts of the hippocampus—the part of the brain that deals with memory and learning. Therefore, learning to control stress through managing your time more effectively can be key to better memory.

Stress—What Is It, Anyway?

The word *stress* is derived from the Latin word *strictus,* meaning "to draw tight." Stress is your body's response to people and events in your life; it is the mental and physical wear and tear on your body as a result of everyday life. Stress is inevitable, and it is not in itself bad. It is your response to stress that determines whether it is good stress (eustress) or bad stress (distress). The same event can provoke eustress or distress, depending on the person experiencing the event; just as "one person's trash is another's treasure" (as you know if you shop at secondhand stores), so one person's eustress may be another person's distress.

The primary difference between eustress and distress is in your body's response. It is impossible to exist in a totally stress-free environment; in fact, some stress is important to your health and well-being. Only when the stress gets out of hand does your body become distressed. The following are some physical signs of distress:

Headaches	Muscular tension and pain
Fatigue	Abdominal pain and diarrhea
Dry mouth	Hypertension and chest pain
Impotence	Heartburn and indigestion
Cough	Menstrual disorders
Insomnia	Loss of appetite
Depression	Suicidal tendencies

MAUREEN RIOPELLE
Founder, Mary's Circle of Hope—The Mary Maguire Foundation
Milford, OH

Things could not have been better! I was a star basketball player recruited by over 100 colleges and was the #1 pick by the University of Iowa. My dream of going to college, becoming an Olympic athlete, and later a sportscaster was so close I could see it all happening. But life has a funny way of turning on a dime.

I had suffered knee problems for many years and most doctors attributed it to "growing pains." I continued to play sports in high school despite the pain. By the time I got to the University of Iowa, I finally saw a specialist and the diagnosis came that my knee cartilage was completely gone. I had lost over 35% of the range of motion.

After surgery on my knees, my body began to reject the treatment. I had massive infections and after more tests, another surgery was scheduled. It was then determined that my body was actually forming another "bone" in my knee— basically, a hardening of the tissues to the point of bone density. I was told that I would have to have surgery every two years to repair the damage and that I only had a 50/50 chance of ever walking again.

In a relatively brief period of time, I went from a college basketball standout and Olympic hopeful to losing my scholarship, dropping out of college, and facing the rest of my life in a wheelchair. I had five surgeries in seven months and I spent that summer in a wheelchair and on crutches, but within a year, I was walking on my own again.

I attribute my recovery to my drive and determination. I am the most stubborn person you'll ever meet. When I was told that I would not walk, run, or play basketball again, I took it as a *personal challenge* to prove everyone wrong: *"I'll show you."* I eventually went back to college, graduating with a 4.0 GPA. After graduation, I began working, and life was moving along. Little did I know that within a few short years, I would have to call upon that teenager again who years earlier had told herself, *"I'll show you."*

One morning I found a lump in my breast and immediately scheduled a mammogram. After the test, I was told that everything was fine. But there was a little voice in my head that said, "You need to ask someone else. Get a second opinion." This little voice saved my life. I did, indeed, have breast cancer and it had even spread to my lymph nodes. My determination and strong will to live and beat the odds became my salvation once again. After surgery and treatment, there are no signs of cancer.

Both of these experiences, while trying and frightening, have led me to my real calling in life— founding Mary's Circle of Hope—The Mary Maguire Foundation: a nonprofit organization dedicated solely to the support of women cancer survivors. We help provide financial assistance for therapy, postoperative treatment, health-related retreats and workshops, and services when the medical profession leaves off. Being able to help others thrive in the face of adversity has become my passion and focus in life. Visit us at www.marymaguirefoundation.org.

Three Types of Stressors in Your Life

TYPE	CAUSE	REDUCTION
Situational	Change in physical environment	Change your residence or environment to suit your needs.
	Change in social environment	Find a quiet place to relax and study. Arrange your classes to suit your individual needs.
Psychological	Unrealistic expectations	Surround yourself with positive people.
	Homesickness	Surround yourself with people who support you.
	Fear	Talk to professors, counselors, family, and friends.
Biological	Hormonal changes	Develop a healthy eating plan.
	Weight loss/gain	Develop an exercise plan.
	Change in physical activities	Increase your daily activity.

YES YOU CAN!

IDEAS FOR Success

Consider the following strategies for dealing with stress in your life:

▶ Adjust your attitude—look at problems, and life in general, through different eyes.

▶ Maintain a positive attitude.

▶ Use relaxation techniques such as visualization, listening to music, and practicing yoga.

▶ Let minor hassles and annoyances go. Ask yourself, "Is this situation worth a heart attack, stroke, or high blood pressure?"

▶ Don't be afraid to take a break. Managing your time can help you take more relaxation breaks.

▶ Practice "seat aerobics" such as inhaling and exhaling, stretching, and neck rolls.

▶ Do everything possible to get enough rest and sleep.

▶ Address one issue at a time and then move on to the next one. Don't try to face everything at once.

▶ Ask yourself: In 10 years, will this really make a difference?

▶ Learn to say "No."

Take the following stress assessment to determine the level of distress you are currently experiencing in your life. Check the items that reflect your behavior at home, work, school, or in a social setting.

❍ **1.** Your stomach tightens when you think about your schoolwork and all that you have to do.

❍ **2.** You are not able to sleep at night.

❍ **3.** You race from place to place trying to get everything done that is required of you.

❍ **4.** Small things make you angry.

❍ **5.** At the end of the day, you are frustrated that you did not accomplish all that you needed to do.

❍ **6.** You get tired throughout the day.

❍ **7.** You need some type of drug, alcohol, or tobacco to get through the day.

❍ **8.** You often find it hard to be around people.

❍ **9.** You don't take care of yourself physically or mentally.

❍ **10.** You tend to keep everything inside.

❍ **11.** You overreact.

❍ **12.** You fail to find the humor in many situations others see as funny.

❍ **13.** You do not eat properly.

❍ **14.** Everything upsets you.

❍ **15.** You are impatient and get angry when you have to wait for things.

❍ **16.** You don't trust others.

❍ **17.** You feel that most people move too slowly for you.

❍ **18.** You feel guilty when you take time for yourself or your friends.

❍ **19.** You interrupt people so that you can tell them your side of the story.

❍ **20.** You experience memory loss.

Total Number of Checkmarks

0–5　= Low, manageable stress

6–10　= Moderate stress

11+　　= High stress; could cause medical or emotional problems

Think About It
Chapter Reflection

Managing your time and reducing your levels of stress are two skills that you will need for the rest of your life. By learning to avoid procrastinating and taking the time to enhance the quality of your life, you are actually increasing your staying power as a college student. Further, as you enter the world of work, both of these skills will be necessary for your success. Technological advances, fewer people doing more work, and pressure to perform at unprecedented levels can put your life in a tailspin, but with the ability to plan your time and reduce your own stress level, you are making a contribution to your own success.

As you continue this term in college and work toward managing your time and stress level, consider the following ideas:

▶ Make a to-do list every evening to plan for the next day.

▶ Always include time for friends, joy, and adventure in your schedule.

▶ Avoid procrastination by practicing the "just do it" mentality.

▶ Work hard to lose the superhuman and perfectionist attitudes.

▶ Delegate everything you can.

▶ Plan your day and week to avoid becoming too stressed.

▶ To reduce stress, take a few moments to relax in private.

▶ When stress is overwhelming, take time to decompress.

Good luck to you as you develop your plan for managing your time and stress.

I wanted a perfect ending. Now I've learned, the hard way, that some poems don't rhyme, and some stories don't have a clear beginning, middle and end. Life is about knowing, having to change, taking the moment and making the best of it without knowing what is going to happen next.

—Gilda Radner

Knowledge in Bloom

Each chapter-end assessment is based on *Bloom's Taxonomy of Learning*. See the inside front cover for a quick review.

Utilizes levels 4, 5, and 6 of the taxonomy

Reducing Stress in Your Everyday Life

Take a moment and examine your academic and personal life right now. You probably have many things going on and may feel as if you're torn in many directions.

If you had to list the one major stress in your life at this moment, what would it be? _____

_____

_____

Why is this a major cause of stress in your life? _____

_____

_____

_____

Are there other people or things contributing to this stress? In other words, is someone or something making the matter worse? If so, who or what? _____

_____

_____

In Chapter 1, you learned to write a narrative statement. This is the statement that "paints a verbal picture" of how your life is going to look once a goal is reached. Reflect for a moment and then write a paragraph predicting how your life would change if this major source of stress was gone from your life. Be realistic and optimistic.

_____

_____

_____

_____

_____

_____

_____

_____

As you know, accomplishing anything requires action. Now that you have a picture of how your life would look if this stress were gone, develop a plan from beginning to end to eliminate this stressor from your life.

Step 1 _____

_____

Step 2 _____

_____

Step 3 _____

_____

Step 4 _____

_____

Step 5 _____

_____

Preparing for Success

Refer to pages 72–73 of this chapter and answer the questions you developed from scanning this chapter's headings. You should also be able to answer the following questions if they were not on your list:

1. What is cortisol and how does it affect memory? _____

_____

2. What is one of the major problems of procrastinating? _____

_____

3. Discuss five ways to manage your time better at home. _____

_____

4. Why is planning so important? _____

_____

5

Read

© Getty Images

The difference between the right word and the almost right word is the difference between lightning and the lightning bug.

Mark Twain

Why do you think I can't read? *Why* will a chapter on reading and comprehension help me in college, at work, with my family, and beyond? *Why* is this information such a big deal since I'm already in college?

nly you can improve your reading skills, and reading is a skill—just like driving a car.

—Dorothy Seyler

Why would professors put a chapter in a college textbook about reading? "I can read," you might say. "I've been reading since I was four years old." The answer is quite simple. There is a monumental difference between knowing and reading the words on a page and being able to comprehend, interpret, analyze, evaluate, and remember those written words. Herein lies the problem: Just because you have hands, this does not make you a mechanic. Just because you have a voice does not make you a singer, and just because you can read words does not mean that you comprehend what the author intended. *This chapter can help you*:

▶ Read a page or section and *remember* what you have just read

▶ Determine your reading speed and comprehension level
▶ Discover if you are more of an active or passive reader
▶ Learn to use a dictionary more effectively
▶ Develop a more powerful vocabulary
▶ Locate and understand the main points of paragraphs and chapter sections
▶ Understand and use the SQ3R method of reading
▶ Apply the strategies of Bloom's Taxonomy to increase comprehension

By learning to read more effectively *and* by learning how to increase your comprehension, you will quickly become more successful in every college class you take.

Scan &

Take a few moments and **scan this chapter**. As you scan, **list five questions** you can expect to learn the answers to while reading and studying Chapter 5.

Example:
▶ What is a logodaedalian? (from page 100)
▶ How can fixation help increase reading speed? (from page 103)

My Questions:

1. _____
_____ from page _____

2. _____
_____ from page _____

3. _____
_____ from page _____

Name: **Susan Marie Ault**
Institution: **Butler Community College, Eldorado, KS**
Major: **Music Education**
Age: **20**

I was not the best high school student and reading has never been something I overly enjoyed or something I excelled at. There are times that I have struggled with reading comprehension and faced the task of having to read and understand four or five chapters per week *per class*. I took a summer class in general psychology and was amazed at the length of the chapters, the difficulty of the material, and the number of new words and terms I encountered. Reading has never played a more important part in my life than it does now in college.

I find that my college professors require much more reading than my high school teachers and that my college professors use the material from our textbooks more frequently for quizzes and exams.

Another area where reading comprehension and speed is important is in online classes. A few of my classmates told me that online classes were easier. Well, I quickly found that they are not easier and they require much more time

the big WHY

. . . from another perspective

because of the reading component. Also, in an online class, you have fewer opportunities to discuss the material with the professor or classmates, so understanding the material you've read is even more important.

This chapter in *Cornerstone* will help you, as it helped me, learn how to calculate the amount of time you need to spend reading a chapter, how to properly highlight information and take notes while reading, and how to self-test your understanding of the material.

The most important thing I learned from the chapter was that by looking up words I did not understand, pulling out the key terms and ideas, rereading the material, and taking notes while reading, my comprehension increased in both my traditional and online classes. I think it will help you, too.

Question

4. _____
_____
from page _____

5. _____
_____
from page _____

PS **Reminder:** At the end of the chapter, come back to this page and answer these questions in your notebook, text margins, or online chapter notes.

IS READING FUNDAMENTAL OR JUST PURE TORTURE?

The Answer Can Change Your Life

> It is impossible for people to learn what they think they already know.
>
> —Epictetus

Quick question: "What are the top two academic problems faced by college students today?" According to faculty members, assessments, national tests, and yes, even your peers around the nation, the two greatest problems students face today are college math classes and reading comprehension—and some of the math difficulty can even be attributed to poor reading skills.

How many times have you read to the bottom of a page or completed a section in a textbook and said to yourself, *"I don't know anything about what I just read, much less remember it"*? All of us have done this at one time or another. The strategies outlined in this chapter will help you eliminate this common occurrence from your study time. By applying these strategies, you will be able to read a page, a section, or an entire chapter so that when you reach the end, you will *comprehend and remember* what you just read.

As you begin to explore the methods in this chapter, you may say to yourself, "How much time do the authors of this book think I have?" Yes, it is true. The methods do take some time, but if they are properly used, you will never get to the bottom of a page again and not know what you've read. Think of it this way: Would you rather read it four or five times and *not* remember what you read or *one* time and know it? That is the beauty of practicing SQ3R.

Finally! A Six-Pack That Can Actually Help You
The ingredients for successful reading:

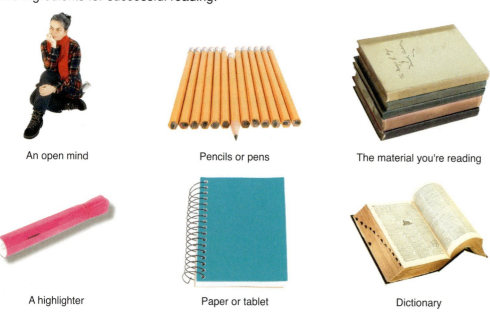

An open mind   Pencils or pens   The material you're reading

A highlighter   Paper or tablet   Dictionary

It may seem elementary, but without the tools shown here, you can't improve your reading comprehension, analysis, or speed. Enough said!

FIGURE 5.4 *Sample Note-taking Methods*

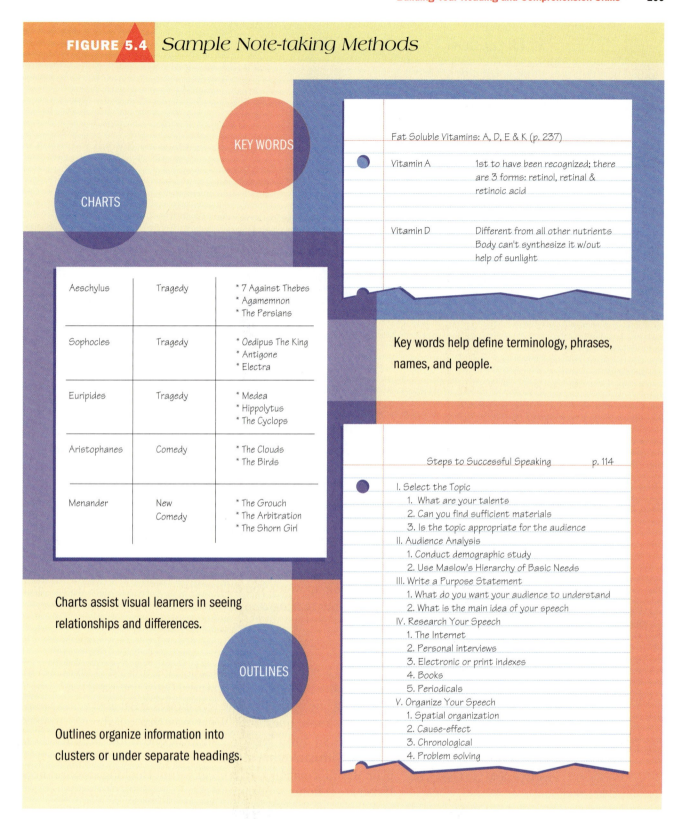

KEY WORDS

Fat Soluble Vitamins: A, D, E & K (p. 237)

Vitamin A — 1st to have been recognized; there are 3 forms: retinol, retinal & retinoic acid

Vitamin D — Different from all other nutrients Body can't synthesize it w/out help of sunlight

Key words help define terminology, phrases, names, and people.

CHARTS

Aeschylus	Tragedy	* 7 Against Thebes * Agamemnon * The Persians
Sophocles	Tragedy	* Oedipus The King * Antigone * Electra
Euripides	Tragedy	* Medea * Hippolytus * The Cyclops
Aristophanes	Comedy	* The Clouds * The Birds
Menander	New Comedy	* The Grouch * The Arbitration * The Shorn Girl

Charts assist visual learners in seeing relationships and differences.

OUTLINES

Steps to Successful Speaking   p. 114

I. Select the Topic
  1. What are your talents
  2. Can you find sufficient materials
  3. Is the topic appropriate for the audience
II. Audience Analysis
  1. Conduct demographic study
  2. Use Maslow's Hierarchy of Basic Needs
III. Write a Purpose Statement
  1. What do you want your audience to understand
  2. What is the main idea of your speech
IV. Research Your Speech
  1. The Internet
  2. Personal interviews
  3. Electronic or print indexes
  4. Books
  5. Periodicals
V. Organize Your Speech
  1. Spatial organization
  2. Cause-effect
  3. Chronological
  4. Problem solving

Outlines organize information into clusters or under separate headings.

It's Not Over Until It's Over

Finally, if you are reading material that is completely new to you—difficult to understand yet important to remember—you may have to disregard paragraphs and paraphrase sections of a paragraph. This can be done with simple "tick marks" in your reading.

FIGURE 5.5 *Breaking Down the Meaning*

What Does It Mean to Be Healthy?

Most people consider themselves healthy. They believe that if they are not sick, they are healthy. However, the absence of illness does not mean that you are healthy; it simply means that you are currently without illness.

The World Health Organization defines health as "not merely the absence of disease or infirmity, but a state of complete physical, mental, and social well-being." Realistically, health is a continuum: on one end you have death, and on the other you have excellent health. Most students are somewhere in the middle of the continuum, experiencing neither excellent health nor debilitating diseases. Often students slip slowly into a state of unhealthiness, which if ignored, could lead to serious health problems. Most of us take our health for granted. We place undue stress on ourselves and assume that our bodies will continue to take this abuse. This chapter will afford you the opportunity to review your own health status and to explore some issues that might help you to lead a healthier lifestyle.

1. *Infirmity = the lack of power, a disability*

2. *Continuum = a whole where all parts work together.*

3. *Debilitating = to make weak.*

Just because you are not sick, this does not mean you are healthy

—Wellness = a state of complete physical, mental, and social health.

—Health is a whole part of life—one end is excellent health, the other end is death.

When you get to a point where you have "read enough," put a tick mark at that point. Continue reading until you get to the end of the paragraph, putting tick marks in the places where you feel you have read a complete thought.

When you get to the end of the paragraph, reread the first section that you marked off. Out to the side, paraphrase that section. Then go to the next section. Consider Figure 5.6.

Few techniques will assist your comprehension and retention more than this one because it requires you to be actively involved in the reading process. You are reading, paraphrasing, clarifying, and looking up words you do not know. This process is essential to you if your reading comprehension is not at the college level.

Recite

Recitation is simple, but crucial. Skipping this step may result in less than full mastery of the chapter. Once you have read a section using one or more of the techniques from above, ask yourself this simple question: "What was that all about?" Find a classmate, sit down together, and ask questions of each other. Discuss with each other the main points of the chapter. Try to explain the information to each other without looking at your notes. If you are at home, sit back in your chair, recite the information, and determine what it means. If you have trouble explaining the information to your friend or reciting it to yourself, you probably did not understand the section and you should go back and reread it. If you can tell your classmate and yourself exactly what you just read and what it means, you are ready to move on to the next section of the chapter.

Another way to practice reciting is to use the materials you produced as you read the chapter. Hopefully, you took notes,

YES YOU CAN !

IDEAS FOR Success

Consider the following strategies for making the most of your reading time:

▶ Reduce the distractions around you. Try to find an atmosphere that is comfortable and effective for you.

▶ Discover what time of day is best for you to read and concentrate on your material.

▶ Read with a healthy snack.

▶ Read in sections. Don't try to read an entire chapter in one sitting. Break it down and take breaks.

▶ Form questions about the material from headings as you are reading.

▶ Never just skip over words or phrases that you don't understand. Look them up in a dictionary.

▶ Allow yourself enough time to read the material effectively. Time management and reading comprehension go hand-in-hand.

FIGURE 5.6   *Reading Piece by Piece*

Negotiating Salary

If the company is interested in you, the interviewer might discuss salary and benefits with you on the second visit. Normally, you are advised not to bring up salary on the first interview. If, however, you detect that the company is not going to offer a salary that you can accept or if you have doubts that you are interested in working for that company, you might want to discuss this on the first interview.

→ Usually no salary discussions on 1st interview.

→ If there are doubts, you can discuss.

If you have several options and you are not quite sure about this company, you might say: "I know it's not considered good interviewing technique to discuss salary on the first interview, but I'm interested in knowing what the range is for this position. I want to be fair to you and not accept another interview and have you go to that expense if we're too far apart."

→ Talk to potential employer honestly about possibilities.

At the end of the second interview, if the interviewer hasn't mentioned salary, you should bring it up. You want the company to make the first move on salary. If the interviewer asks you, "If we are to make you an offer, what kind of salary are you looking for?" you can counter with this statement: "What is the range for this position?" This will give you something to go on.

→ If second interview comes and they do not discuss salary—you can bring it up by asking about the range.

If the interviewer then says, "The range is $27,000 to $32,000," you know if you are interested and you also know you want to go on the high side of this range. If   ›   ·   `tional grades and experience and you feel confi‐ dar·   try for a sal›·

Source: Capstone: Succeeding Beyond College, Sherfield, Montgomery, Moody (2001).

highlighted passages, underlined phrases, and paraphrased sections. From these, you can create flash cards, outlines, mind maps, timelines, and key word note cards. Using these materials is another way to "recite" the material.

Review

After you have read the chapter, immediately go back and read it again. "What? I just read it!" Yes, you did. And the best way to determine whether you have mastered the information is once again to survey the chapter; review marginal notes, highlighted areas, and vocabulary words; and determine whether you can answer the questions you posed during the question step of SQ3R. This step will help you store and retain this information in long-term memory.

Think About It
Chapter Reflection

SQ3R can be a lifesaver when it comes to understanding material that is overwhelming. It is an efficient, comprehensive, and *doable* practice that can dramatically assist you in your reading efforts. It may take more time than your old method, but you will begin to see the results almost immediately. Seriously considering and practicing the strategies outlined in this chapter will help increase your comprehension level and it will also help your ability to recall the information when you need it later on.

It has been suggested that if you can effectively read, write, and speak the English language, there is nothing that you can't accomplish. The power of knowledge is

monumental in your quest to become a productive and active citizen. Effective reading skills will help you acquire that knowledge.

As you continue to work to become an active, engaged learner, consider the following tips for reading comprehension and retention:

▶ Approach the text, chapter, or article with an *open mind.*

▶ *Free your mind* to focus on your reading.

▶ Always read with your "*six pack*" at your side.

▶ Underline and look up words you do not *understand.*

▶ Write down your *vocabulary words* and review them often.

▶ Use *SQ3R* and *Bloom's Taxonomy* to increase and test your comprehension.

▶ If you're having trouble, *get a tutor* to help you.

▶ Understand that *the more you read,* the better you'll become at it.

The knowledge of words is the gateway to learning.

—W. Wilson

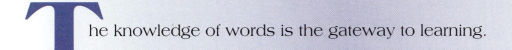

Knowledge in Bloom

Utilizes levels 1–6 of the taxonomy

Each chapter-end assessment is based on *Bloom's Taxonomy of Learning*. See the inside front cover for a quick review.

Increasing Your Reading Comprehension and Retention

Explanation: In Chapter 1's Knowledge in Bloom, the activity required you to use each of the six steps in Bloom's Taxonomy: Knowledge, Comprehension, Application, Analysis, Synthesis, and Evaluation. This chapter-end activity will ask you to do the same with a reading about a historical event.

Process: Read the following story carefully, looking up words that you do not understand, highlighting phrases that you think are important, and paraphrasing in the spaces provided. When you have read the story employing the SQ3R method, you will need to answer six questions (one for each level of learning).

The Life and Death of Harvey Milk

READ THIS SECTION, IDENTIFY UNFAMILIAR WORDS, HIGHLIGHT IMPORTANT WORDS AND PHRASES	LOOK UP YOUR IDENTIFIED WORDS THAT NEED TO BE DEFINED	PARAPHRASE THE MAIN IDEA IN YOUR OWN WORDS
More perplexing things have happened, but a Twinkie caused the death of Harvey Milk. That's right. In 1978, defense lawyers using the "Twinkie Defense" explained an inexplicable murder away. This was the first mainstream trial to use an "I am not responsible for my actions" defense.	Unfamiliar words and definitions	The main idea of this paragraph is

	Unfamiliar words and definitions	The main idea of this paragraph is
Harvey Milk was the first openly gay man elected to a significant office in America. In 1977, Milk was elected as a member of the San Francisco Board of Supervisors. This was quite arduous at this point in American history when most people, including many psychologists and religious leaders, still classified homosexuality as deviant and a mental illness.		
Harvey Milk is to the gay rights movement what Martin Luther King, Jr., is to the civil rights movement. Before King, little was happening with the CRM, and before Milk, little was happening with the GRM. He changed the face of California politics and paved the way for countless other gays and lesbians to enter the world of politics.	Unfamiliar words and definitions	The main idea of this paragraph is
Dan White, a staunch antigay advocate, served on the board with Milk. They were constantly at odds with each other and often engaged in verbal confrontations.	Unfamiliar words and definitions	The main idea of this paragraph is
White had been a policeman and a fireman in San Francisco before running for office. While running for office, he vowed to restore "family values" to the city government. He vowed to "rid San Francisco of radicals, social deviants, and incorrigibles."	Unfamiliar words and definitions	The main idea of this paragraph is
Dan White was one of the most conservative members of the board, and many proposals brought to the board by Milk and the mayor of San Francisco, George Moscone, were defeated because of the heavily conservative vote led by White.	Unfamiliar words and definitions	The main idea of this paragraph is
At that time, the Board of Supervisors was made up of eleven members; six of them, including Dan White, were conservative and had the power to defeat most, if not all of the liberal measures brought before the board. This did not fare well for Harvey Milk and the other liberal members of the board.	Unfamiliar words and definitions	The main idea of this paragraph is
Because the job offered diminutive wages, Dan White soon realized that he could not support his family on $9,800 per year, and he submitted his resignation to Mayor Moscone. This did not sit well with the people who elected him. They urged him to reconsider and when he tried to rescind his resignation, Mayor Moscone refused. This decision was made, in part, because Harvey Milk convinced Moscone to deny his reinstatement.	Unfamiliar words and definitions	The main idea of this paragraph is

In a fit of wrath over the decision, Dan White entered the San Francisco City Hall on the morning of November 27, 1978, through a basement window. He went to Mayor Moscone's office and shot him in the chest, and as he lay dying, shot him again in the head.	Unfamiliar words and definitions	The main idea of this paragraph is
He then walked calmly down the hall and asked to see Harvey Milk. Once inside the office, he slew Milk with two bullets to the brain. He then left City Hall, called his wife, spoke with her in person at St. Mary's Cathedral, and then turned himself in.	Unfamiliar words and definitions	The main idea of this paragraph is
It is reported that policemen representing the city of San Francisco shouted, cheered, and applauded when news of the murders reached the police department.	Unfamiliar words and definitions	The main idea of this paragraph is
Dan White's defense lawyers used a "diminished capacity" defense suggesting that he was led to his actions by too much sugar from junk food. The lawyers convinced a jury that he was not himself and his senses were off kilter. This became known as the "Twinkie Defense."	Unfamiliar words and definitions	The main idea of this paragraph is
Dan White was convicted of second-degree manslaughter and was sentenced to only seven years for two premeditated murders. After serving only five years, he was released. The "Twinkie Defense" had worked.	Unfamiliar words and definitions	The main idea of this paragraph is
In 1985, after being released from Soledad Prison, Dan White walked into his garage, took a rubber hose, connected it to his car's exhaust, and killed himself with carbon monoxide poisoning. He was 39 years old. His tomb reads, *"Daniel J. White (1946–October 21, 1985), Sgt. U.S. Army, Vietnam. Cause of death: Suicide."*	Unfamiliar words and definitions	The main idea of this paragraph is

Sources: "He Got Away with Murder" at www.findagrave.com; "Dan White" at www.backdoor.com/castro/milk; "The Pioneer Harvey Milk" at www.time.com; "Remembering Harvey Milk" at www.lambda.net.

Now answer the following questions on a separate sheet based on Bloom's Levels of Learning:

Question 1 **Knowledge**	Identify two members of the Board of Supervisors and the mayor of San Francisco.
Question 2 **Comprehension**	Based on the story given, explain why Dan White killed Harvey Milk and George Moscone.
Question 3 **Application**	Demonstrate how homophobia plays a similar role in American society today as it did in the 1970s.
Question 4 **Analysis**	How can defense lawyers justify using the "I am not responsible for my own actions defense" in a premeditated murder case?
Question 5 **Synthesis**	Design a plan by which you would have *prosecuted* or *defended* Dan White without using the "Twinkie Defense."
Question 6 **Evaluation**	Does Dan White deserve any sympathy? Justify your answer in detail.

Preparing for Success

Refer back to pages 94–95 of this chapter and answer the questions you developed from scanning this chapter's headings. You should also be able to answer the following questions if they were not on your list:

1. What are the five starter questions (words) you can use to construct test questions from headings?

   _____

2. What is reading comprehension? _____

   _____

3. Why is it important to know your reading speed? _____

   _____

4. What does frequency have to do with reading speed and comprehension? _____

   _____

6

Learn

We are
led to truth
by our
weaknesses
as well as our
strengths.

Parker Palmer

the big **WHY**

Why read and work through a chapter on learning and personality? *Why* will a chapter on discovering my learning style and personality type help me in college, at work, with my family, and beyond? *Why* is this information such a big deal to my college studies?

Everyone can do something that makes a difference.

—Todd Wagner

Learning *how to learn* and *how you learn* are two of the most important things you will ever do for yourself . . . especially as a college student. Learning *how to* learn means that you know where to find information, how to store that information in your brain so that it is easily retrievable, and how to make connections between one thing and another. *How you* learn means that you know your own learning style, your primary intelligence, and your personality type. *This chapter can help you:*

► Identify and use your learning style to increase active learning

► Identify and use your primary intelligence to increase active learning

► Identify and use your personality type to increase active learning

► Discuss the difference between learning styles and multiple intelligences

► Use your personality type to improve studying

Identifying and understanding if you are a visual, musical, and extroverted person *or* a verbal, naturalistic, and introverted person can help you as you study, communicate, and develop lasting relationships.

Scan &

Take a few moments and **scan this chapter.** As you scan, **list five questions** you can expect to learn the answers to while reading and studying Chapter 6.

Example:
► What is an introvert? (from page 133)
► What is the definition of tactile and how do you use it? (from page 129)

My Questions:

1. _____
   _____ from page _____

2. _____
   _____ from page _____

3. _____
   _____ from page _____

Name: La Dondo Faye Johnson
Institution: Houston Community College, Houston, TX
Major: Early Childhood Education
Age: 56

I am a very outgoing, open, interpersonal person. I love being around people and helping people in any way possible. I never thought this would have anything to do with my academic work or my chosen profession. Boy, was I wrong.

When I began my college studies, I took a class that helped me understand my personality type and learning style. It was not until then that I learned why some classes were easier than others and some situations were more comfortable than others. I had never really thought about my personality type and had heard very little about a learning style.

I found that I am a visual and auditory learner and a very extroverted person. By learning these two simple things about myself, I was able to take classes with professors that more closely taught to the way I learn. I also found that there were going to be times when I had to adjust my learning style to the way some professors taught. Both helped me greatly.

the big WHY
. . . from another perspective

I found that making note cards and repeating information out loud helped me learn better than anything ever had in the past. By focusing on my love of people and my desire to be involved (my extroverted personality), I was able to participate more in class and get involved in more things at Houston Community College.

By learning more about me and who I am and how I learn, my academic life has been greatly enriched. This chapter on learning styles, multiple intelligences, and personality type will help you identify what type of learner you are and what type of personality you have. The best thing to remember as you take the assessments is the advice my professor gave me: "An assessment will never measure who you are as a person." Good luck.

4. _____

_____

from page _____

5. _____

_____

from page _____

Question

Reminder: At the end of the chapter, come back to this page and answer these questions in your notebook, text margins, or online chapter notes.

There are many ways to learn a new activity. The learning technique that works best for you depends on many different factors, which may differ from situation to situation.

© Corbis

Understanding Your Strengths

Discovering and Polishing Your Talents

Lecture. Group discussion. Role playing. Case studies. Guided field trips. *Which way do you learn best?* Some students learn best by touching and doing, while others learn best by listening and reflecting. Some students prefer working with a group of people sitting outside under the trees, while others would rather be alone in the library. There are many factors that may influence the way we learn and process information.

You may be asking yourself, "Is there one 'best' way of learning?" The answer is no. The way you learn new information depends on many variables. Your learning style, your personal intelligence, your personality type, your past experiences, and your attitude all play a part in the way you process new information.

On the next few pages, you will have the opportunity to complete three inventories: one to assess your *learning style,* one to assess your *personality type,* and one to help you identify your *dominant intelligence.* We must say up front that these assessments are in no way intended to label you. They are not a measure of how smart you are. They do not measure your worth or your capacities as a student or citizen. The three assessments are included so that you might gain a better understanding of your multiple intelligences and identify your learning styles and your personality type.

There are no right or wrong answers and there is no one best way to learn. We hope that by the end of this chapter, you will have experienced a "Wow" or an "Ah-ha!" as you explore and discover new and exciting components of your education. We also hope that by the end of this chapter, you will have the skills needed to more effectively use your dominant traits and improve your less dominant traits.

Some educators and researchers do not even believe in the theory of learning styles or multiple intelligences. Anita Woolfolk (2001) states that "there has been considerable controversy over the meaning of intelligence. At a symposium on intelligence, 24 psychologists offered 24 different views about the nature of intelligence."

However, we include information on learning theory because many students have met with great success by identifying and molding their study environments and habits to reflect their learning style and personality type. If you have ever been in a class where you felt lost, inadequate, or simply out of place, it may have been because your professor was not teaching to your learning style. Conversely, if you are doing very well in a class, it may be because the information, professor, or class format matches the way you process information best. The following assessment will help you determine how you process information.

> **N**inety percent of the world's misery comes from people not knowing themselves, their abilities, their frailties, and even their real virtues. Most of us go almost all the way through life complete strangers to ourselves.
>
> —Sydney J. Harris

Where Are You . . .
AT THIS MOMENT

Before reading any further, take a moment and assess where you are at this moment with your knowledge and application of learning styles, multiple intelligences, and personality typing. Read each statement carefully and then respond accordingly.

1. I know my learning style. YES NO

2. I know my personality type. YES NO

3. I know my dominant intelligence. YES NO

4. When I study, I use a variety of methods to learn the material. YES NO

5. When learning something new, I try to incorporate what I see with what I hear and to "do something" with the information. YES NO

6. I know my weaknesses as a learner. YES NO

7. I know my strengths as a learner. YES NO

If you answered "Yes" to most of the questions (five or more), you know your learning style, dominant intelligence, and personality type and know how to apply each to create a positive learning experience. *If you answered "No"* to most of the questions, you need to pay very close attention to the material in this chapter so that you can identify how you learn best and how to apply the techniques to create a positive learning experience.

Take the MIS

The Multiple Intelligences Survey

Directions: Read each statement carefully and thoroughly. After reading the statement, rate your response using the following scale. There are no right or wrong answers. This is not a timed survey. The MIS is based, in part, on *Frames of Mind* by Howard Gardner (1983).

3 = Often applies
2 = Sometimes applies
1 = Never or almost never applies

_____ 1. When someone gives me directions, I have to visualize them in my mind in order to understand them.

_____ 2. I enjoy crossword puzzles and word games like Scrabble.

_____ 3. I enjoy dancing and can keep up with the beat of music.

_____ 4. I have little or no trouble conceptualizing information or facts.

_____ 5. I like to repair things that are broken such as toasters, small engines, bicycles, and cars.

_____ 6. I enjoy leadership activities on campus and in the community.

_____ 7. I have the ability to get others to listen to me.

Take the MIS
(continued)

_____ 8. I enjoy working with nature, animals, and plants.

_____ 9. I know where everything is in my home such as supplies, gloves, flashlights, camera, and compact discs.

_____ 10. I am a good speller.

_____ 11. I often sing or hum to myself in the shower or car, or while walking or just sitting.

_____ 12. I am a very logical, orderly thinker.

_____ 13. I use a lot of gestures when I talk to people.

_____ 14. I can recognize and empathize with people's attitudes and emotions.

_____ 15. I prefer to study alone.

_____ 16. I can name many different things in the environment such as cloud, rock, and plant types.

_____ 17. I like to draw pictures, graphs, or charts to better understand information.

_____ 18. I have a good memory for names and dates.

_____ 19. When I hear music, I "get into it" by moving, humming, tapping, or even singing.

_____ 20. I learn better by asking a lot of questions.

_____ 21. I enjoy playing competitive sports.

_____ 22. I communicate very well with other people.

_____ 23. I know what I want and I set goals to accomplish it.

_____ 24. I have some interest in herbal remedies and natural medicine.

_____ 25. I enjoy working puzzles or mazes.

_____ 26. I am a good storyteller.

_____ 27. I can easily remember the words and melodies of songs.

_____ 28. I enjoy solving problems in math and chemistry and working with computer programming problems.

_____ 29. I usually touch people or pat them on the back when I talk to them.

_____ 30. I understand my family and friends better than most other people do.

_____ 31. I don't always talk about my accomplishments with others.

_____ 32. I would rather work outside around nature than inside around people and equipment.

_____ 33. I enjoy and learn more when seeing movies, slides, or videos in class.

_____ 34. I am a very good listener and I enjoy listening to others' stories.

_____ 35. I need to study with music.

_____ 36. I enjoy games like Clue, Battleship, chess, and Rubik's cube.

_____ 37. I enjoy physical activities such as bicycling, jogging, dancing, snowboarding, skateboarding, or swimming.

_____ 38. I am good at solving people's problems and conflicts.

_____ 39. I have to have time alone to think about new information in order to remember it.

_____ 40. I enjoy sorting and organizing information, objects, and collectibles.

Take the MIS   *(continued)*

Refer to your score on each individual question. Place that score beside the appropriate question number. Then, tally each line at the side.

SCORE					TOTAL ACROSS	CODE
1 ___	9 ___	17 ___	25 ___	33 ___	_____	Visual/Spatial
2 ___	10 ___	18 ___	26 ___	34 ___	_____	Verbal/Linguistic
3 ___	11 ___	19 ___	27 ___	35 ___	_____	Musical/Rhythm
4 ___	12 ___	20 ___	28 ___	36 ___	_____	Logic/Math
5 ___	13 ___	21 ___	29 ___	37 ___	_____	Body/Kinesthetic
6 ___	14 ___	22 ___	30 ___	38 ___	_____	Interpersonal
7 ___	15 ___	23 ___	31 ___	39 ___	_____	Intrapersonal
8 ___	16 ___	24 ___	32 ___	40 ___	_____	Naturalistic

© Robert M. Sherfield, Ph.D., 1999, 2002, 2005, 2008

MIS TALLY

Multiple Intelligences

Look at the scores on the MIS. What are your top three scores? Write them in the spaces here.

Top score _____   Code _____
Second score _____   Code _____
Third score_____   Code _____

This tally can help you understand where some of your strengths may be. Again, this is not a measure of your worth or capacities, nor is it an indicator of your future successes. Read the following section to better understand multiple intelligences.

A NEW WAY OF LOOKING AT YOURSELF

Understanding Multiple Intelligences

In 1983, Howard Gardner, a Harvard University professor, developed a theory called multiple intelligences. In his book *Frames of Mind,* he outlines seven intelligences that he feels are possessed by everyone: visual/spatial, verbal/linguistic, musical/ rhythm, logic/math, body/kinesthetic, interpersonal, and intrapersonal. In 1996, he added an eighth intelligence: naturalistic. In short, when you have done things that came easily for you, you probably drew on one of your intelligences that is well developed. On the other hand, when you have tried to do things that are very difficult to master or understand, you may have been dealing with material that calls on one of your less developed intelligences. If playing the piano by ear comes easily to you, your musical/rhythm intelligence may be very strong. If you have trouble writing or understanding poetry, your verbal/linguistic intelligence may not be as well developed. This does not mean that you will never be able to write poetry; it simply means that this is not your dominant intelligence.

The Eight Intelligences

The "Smart" descriptors were adapted from Thomas Armstrong (1994).

Visual/Spatial (Picture Smart). Thinks in pictures; knows where things are in the house; loves to create images and work with graphs, charts, pictures, and maps.

Verbal/Linguistic (Word Smart). Communicates well through language, likes to write, is good at spelling, great at telling stories, loves to read books.

Musical/Rhythm (Music Smart). Loves to sing, hum, and whistle; comprehends music; responds to music immediately; performs music.

Logic/Math (Number Smart). Can easily conceptualize and reason, uses logic, has good problem-solving skills, enjoys math and science.

Body/Kinesthetic (Body Smart). Learns through body sensation, moves around a lot, enjoys work involving the hands, is graced with some athletic ability.

Interpersonal (People Smart). Loves to communicate with other people, possesses great leadership skills, has lots of friends, is involved in extracurricular activities.

Intrapersonal (Self-Smart). Has a deep awareness of own feelings, is very reflective, requires time to be alone, does not get involved with group activities.

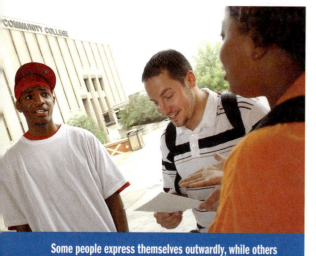

Some people express themselves outwardly, while others are more reflective. How would you describe yourself? Are there certain situations that cause you to be more or less extroverted than you are normally?

Patrick White/Merrill

Naturalistic (Environment Smart). Has interest in the environment and in nature; can easily recognize plants, animals, rocks, and cloud formations; may like hiking, camping, and fishing.

MAKING IT WORK FOR YOU

Using Multiple Intelligences to Enhance Studying and Learning

Following are some helpful tips to assist you in creating a study environment and study habits using your multiple intelligences. Read each category because you may need to use your less dominant intelligence in some of the classes you take. These lists can help you strengthen your less dominant areas.

Visual/Spatial

▶ Use visuals in your notes such as timelines, charts, graphs, and geometric shapes.

▶ Work to create a mental or visual picture of the information at hand.

▶ Use colored markers to make associations or to group items together.

▶ Use mapping or webbing so that your main points are easily recognized.

LEO G. BORGES
Co-founder and Former CEO, Borges and Mahoney, Inc.
San Francisco, CA

Tulare, California is still a farming community today, but in 1928 when I was born, it was totally agricultural and an exceptionally rural, detached part of the world. My parents had immigrated to California from the Azore Islands years earlier in search of a better life—*the American dream*. My father died when I was three years old and when I was 11, my mother passed away. Even though I lived with and was raised by my sisters, the feelings of aloneness and isolation were the two primary feelings I had growing up. We were orphans. We were poor. We were farm kids. We were Portuguese—not Americans. Every day, someone reminded us of these realities. One positive thing remained, however. My mother always told us that we could *be anything* or *have anything* if we believed in it and worked hard for it.

I left home at 17 to attend a program in advertising in San Francisco. Later that year, I moved to Los Angeles and began working for a major advertising firm. From there I enlisted in the Coast Guard, and when my duty was over, I worked for an oil company and then a major leasing firm. In each position, I worked my way up the ladder, strove to do my very best, and proved that I was capable of doing anything regardless of my background.

When I was in my early forties, my best friend, Cliff, and I decided to start our own business. We were tired of working in "middle management" and knew that we could be successful if we worked hard. After much research and consulting with companies across the country, we determined that we would start a company in the water treatment business.

You may be asking yourself, "What experience did an advertising agency, an oil company, and a leasing firm give me to start a business in water treatment?" The answer is *none*. However, Cliff was an excellent accountant and I was an excellent salesman. We found a third partner who was one of the leading water treatment experts in the world and we were off. It was not easy and we had to eat beans for many meals, but Borges and Mahoney, Inc. was born.

Our first office was a small storefront in San Francisco. Through the development of our superior products, expert advice to clients, and outstanding customer service, we grew and grew, finally moving to our largest location in San Rafael, California. By the time we sold our business some 20 years later, we had 15 full-time employees and annual revenues in the millions of dollars.

To this day, I attribute my success to the fact that I was determined to show everyone—my sisters, cousins, aunts and uncles, former co-workers, friends and foes—that I would never let my past, my heritage, my economic background, or my history hold me back. I knew that I could be a success. Through hard work, determination, and surrounding myself with supportive, brilliant people, I proved that the American dream my parents sought years earlier is truly possible for anyone who works hard, believes in him- or herself, and doesn't give up. It is possible for you, too.

▸ When taking notes, draw pictures in the margins to illustrate the main points.
▸ Visualize the information in your mind.

Verbal/Linguistic

▸ Establish study groups so that you will have the opportunity to talk about the information.
▸ Using the information you studied, create a story or a skit.
▸ Read as much information about related areas as possible.
▸ As you read chapters, outline them in your own words.
▸ Summarize and recite your notes aloud.

Musical/Rhythm

▸ Listen to music while studying (if it does not distract you).
▸ Write a song or rap about the chapter or information.
▸ Take short breaks from studying to listen to music.
▸ Commit the information being studied to the music from your favorite song.

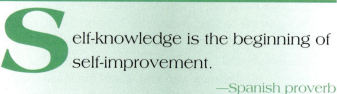

*S*elf-knowledge is the beginning of self-improvement.

—Spanish proverb

Logic/Math

▸ Strive to make connections between subjects.
▸ Don't just memorize the facts; apply them to real-life situations.
▸ As you study the information, think of problems in society and how this information could solve those problems.
▸ Create analyzing charts. Draw a line down the center of the page, put the information at hand in the left column and analyze, discuss, relate, and synthesize it in the right column.
▸ Allow yourself some time to reflect after studying.

Body/Kinesthetic

▸ Don't confine your study area to a desk or chair; move around, explore, go outside.
▸ Act out the information.
▸ Study in a group of people and change groups often.
▸ Use charts, posters, flash cards, and chalkboards to study.
▸ When appropriate or possible, build models using the information studied.
▸ Verbalize the information to others.
▸ Use games such as chess, Monopoly, Twister, or Clue when studying.
▸ Trace words as you study them.
▸ Use repetition to learn facts; write them many times.
▸ Make study sheets.

Interpersonal

▸ Study in groups.
▸ Share the information with other people.
▸ Teach the information to others.

▶ Interview outside sources to learn more about the material at hand.

▶ Have a debate with others about the information.

Intrapersonal

▶ Study in a quiet area.

▶ Study by yourself.

▶ Allow time for reflection and meditation about the subject matter.

▶ Study in short time blocks and then spend some time absorbing the information.

▶ Work at your own pace.

Naturalistic

▶ Study outside whenever possible.

▶ Relate the information to its effect on the environment whenever possible.

▶ When given the opportunity to choose your own topics or research projects, choose something related to nature.

▶ Collect your own study data and resources.

▶ Organize and label your information.

▶ Keep separate notebooks on individual topics so that you can add new information to each topic as it becomes available to you.

UNDERSTANDING LEARNING STYLES THEORY

Rita Dunn (2000) defines learning styles as "the way in which each learner begins to concentrate on, process, and retain new and difficult information." We must note that there is a difference between a *learning style* and a *learning strategy*. A learning strategy is how you might choose to learn or study, such as by using note cards, flip charts, color slides, or cooperative learning groups. Flip charts and slides are strategies. Learning styles are more sensory. They involve seeing, hearing, and touching.

Take the LEAD

The Learning Evaluation and Assessment Directory

Directions: Read each statement carefully and thoroughly. After reading the statement, rate your response using the following scale. There are no right or wrong answers. This is not a timed survey. The LEAD is based, in part, on research conducted by Rita Dunn.

3 = Often applies
2 = Sometimes applies
1 = Never or almost never applies

_____ 1. I remember information better if I write it down or draw a picture of it.

_____ 2. I remember things better when I hear them instead of just reading or seeing them.

Take the LEAD

(continued)

_____ 3. When I get something that has to be assembled, I just start doing it. I don't read the directions.

_____ 4. If I am taking a test, I can "see" the page of the text or lecture notes where the answer is located.

_____ 5. I would rather the professor explain a graph, chart, or diagram than just show it to me.

_____ 6. When learning new things, I want to do them rather than hear about them.

_____ 7. I would rather the instructor write the information on the board or overhead instead of just lecturing.

_____ 8. I would rather listen to a book on tape than read it.

_____ 9. I enjoy making things, putting things together, and working with my hands.

_____ 10. I am able to quickly conceptualize and visualize information.

_____ 11. I learn best by hearing words.

_____ 12. I have been called hyperactive by my parents, spouse, partner, or professor.

_____ 13. I have no trouble reading maps, charts, or diagrams.

_____ 14. I can usually pick up on small sounds like bells, crickets, or frogs, or distant sounds like train whistles.

_____ 15. I use my hands and gesture a lot when I speak to others.

Refer to your score on each individual question. Place that score beside the appropriate question number. Then, tally each line at the side.

SCORE					TOTAL ACROSS	CODE
1 _____	4 _____	7 _____	10 _____	13 _____	_____	Visual
2 _____	5 _____	8 _____	11 _____	14 _____	_____	Auditory
3 _____	6 _____	9 _____	12 _____	15 _____	_____	Tactile

©Robert M. Sherfield, Ph.D., 1999, 2002, 2005, 2008

LEAD SCORES

Learning Styles

Look at the scores on the LEAD. What is your top score?

Top Score _____   Code _____

If you learn best by _seeing_ information, you have a more dominant _visual_ learning style. If you learn best by _hearing_ information, you have a more dominant _auditory_ learning style. If you learn best by _touching or doing,_ you have a more dominant _tactile_ learning style. You may also hear the tactile learning style referred to as _kinesthetic_ or _hands-on._

Some of the most successful students have learned to use all three styles. If you were learning how to skateboard, you might learn best by hearing someone talk about the different styles or techniques. Others might learn best by watching a video of someone demonstrating the techniques. Still others would learn best by actually getting on the board and trying it. However, the student who involved all of his or her senses might gain the most. She might listen to the instructor tell about skateboarding, watch the video, and then go do it. Therefore, she would have involved all of her learning styles: visual, auditory, and tactile. Here are brief descriptions of the three styles.

Visual (Eye Smart). Thinks in pictures. Enjoys visual instructions, demonstrations, and descriptions; would rather read a text than listen to a lecture; avid note-taker; needs visual references; enjoys using charts, graphs, and pictures.

Auditory (Ear Smart). Prefers verbal instructions; would rather listen than read; often tapes lectures and listens to them in the car or at home; recites information out loud; enjoys talking, discussing issues, and verbal stimuli; talks out problems.

Tactile (Action Smart). Prefers hands-on approaches to learning; likes to take notes and uses a great deal of scratch paper; learns best by doing something, by touching it, or manipulating it; learns best while moving or while in action; often does not concentrate well when sitting and reading.

George Stroud/Getty Images Inc.–Hulton Archive Photos

Pablo Picasso, world-renowned trend-setting artist, was born in Spain. He had a hard time in school and is said to have had a very difficult time with reading. He was diagnosed with a learning disability and his formal education never really benefited him. He left his college-level courses at the Academy of Arts in Madrid after less than a year of study. However, because of his immense artistic talent, he changed the way the world looks at art through his cubist interpretation of the universe. He is listed in the Guinness Book of World Records as the most prolific painter in history—having completed nearly 14,000 paintings.

THE SIMILARITIES AND DIFFERENCES BETWEEN MULTIPLE INTELLIGENCES THEORY AND LEARNING STYLES THEORY

As you read over the components of MI theory and LS theory, you begin to see several common elements. Both theories deal with the visual, auditory, and tactile (or kinesthetic). Below the surface, there are also similarities.

Simply stated, you can be a visual learner (this is a learning style) and yet not have visual/spatial (this is one of the multiple intelligences) as your dominant intelligence. How can this be possible? It may be that you learn best by watching someone paint a picture—watching their brush strokes, their method of mixing paints, and their spatial layout—but it may be that you will not be as engaged or as talented at painting as the person you watched. Your painting may lack feeling, depth, and expression. This is an example of how your visual learning style can be strong but your visual/spatial intelligence may not be your dominant intelligence.

On the other hand, your learning style may be visual and your dominant intelligence may be verbal/linguistic. If that is the case, you would learn how to paint by watching someone go through the process. Then, using your verbal/linguistic intelligence, you would be masterful at describing how to paint and talking about the process you observed.

Bloom Level 2 question

In your own words, compare and contrast learning styles with multiple intelligences. _____

_____

_____

_____

_____

_____

_____

_____

WHAT CAN YOU LEARN ABOUT PERSONALITY?

Take the PAP

The Personality Assessment Profile

Directions: Read each statement carefully and thoroughly. After reading the statement, rate your response using the following scale. There are no right or wrong answers. This is not a timed survey. The PAP is based, in part, on the Myers-Briggs Type Indicator® (MBTI) by Katharine Briggs and Isabel Briggs-Myers.

3 = Often applies
2 = Sometimes applies
1 = Never or almost never applies

_____ 1a. I am a very talkative person.

_____ 1b. I am a more reflective person than a verbal person.

_____ 2a. I am a very factual and literal person.

_____ 2b. I look to the future and I can see possibilities.

_____ 3a. I value truth and justice over tact and emotion.

_____ 3b. I find it easy to empathize with other people.

_____ 4a. I am very orderly and efficient.

_____ 4b. I enjoy having freedom from control.

_____ 5a. I am a very friendly and social person.

_____ 5b. I enjoy listening to others more than talking.

_____ 6a. I enjoy being around and working with people who have a great deal of common sense.

_____ 6b. I enjoy being around and working with people who are dreamers and have a great deal of imagination.

_____ 7a. One of my motivating forces is to do a job very well.

_____ 7b. I like to be recognized for, and I am motivated by, my accomplishments and awards.

_____ 8a. I like to plan out my day before I go to bed.

_____ 8b. When I get up on a nonschool or nonwork day, I just like to let the day "plan itself."

Take the PAP

_____ 9a. I like to express my feelings and thoughts.

_____ 9b. I enjoy a great deal of tranquility and quiet time to myself.

_____10a. I am a very pragmatic and realistic person.

_____10b. I like to create new ideas, methods, or ways of doing things.

_____11a. I make decisions with my brain.

_____11b. I make decisions with my heart.

_____12a. I am a very disciplined and orderly person.

_____12b. I don't make a lot of plans.

_____13a. I like to work with a group of people.

_____13b. I would rather work independently.

_____14a. I learn best if I can see it, touch it, smell it, taste it, or hear it.

_____14b. I learn best by relying on my gut feelings or intuition.

_____15a. I am quick to criticize others.

_____15b. I compliment others very easily and quickly.

_____16a. My life is systematic and organized.

_____16b. I don't really pay attention to deadlines.

_____17a. I can be myself when I am around others.

_____17b. I can be myself when I am alone.

_____18a. I live in the here and now, in the present.

_____18b. I live in the future, planning and dreaming.

_____19a. I think that if someone breaks the rules, the person should be punished.

_____19b. I think that if someone breaks the rules, we should look at the person who broke the rules, examine the rules, and look at the situation at hand before a decision is made.

_____20a. I do my work, then I play.

_____20b. I play, then do my work.

Refer to your score on each individual question. Place that score beside the appropriate question number. Then, tally each line at the side.

SCORE

					TOTAL ACROSS	CODE
1a ____	5a ____	9a ____	13a ____	17a ____	_____	E Extrovert
1b ____	5b ____	9b ____	13b ____	17b ____	_____	I Introvert
2a ____	6a ____	10a ____	14a ____	18a ____	_____	S Sensing
2b ____	6b ____	10b ____	14b ____	18b ____	_____	N iNtuition
3a ____	7a ____	11a ____	15a ____	19a ____	_____	T Thinking
3b ____	7b ____	11b ____	15b ____	19b ____	_____	F Feeling
4a ____	8a ____	12a ____	16a ____	20a ____	_____	J Judging
4b ____	8b ____	12b ____	16b ____	20b ____	_____	P Perceiving

PAP Scores

Personality Indicator

Look at the scores on your PAP. Is your score higher in the E or I line? Is your score higher in the S or N line? Is your score higher in the T or F line? Is your score higher in the J or P line? Write the code to the side of each section.

Is your higher score E or I?   Code _____

Is your higher score S or N?   Code _____

Is your higher score T or F?   Code _____

Is your higher score J or P?   Code _____

Understanding Personality Typing (Typology)

The questions on the PAP helped you discover whether you are extroverted or introverted (E or I), sensing or intuitive (S or N), thinking or feeling (T or F), and judging or perceiving (J or P). These questions were based, in part, on work done by Carl Jung, Katharine Briggs, and Isabel Briggs-Myers.

In 1921, Swiss psychologist Carl Jung (1875–1961) published his work *Psychological Types*. In this book, Jung suggested that human behavior is not random. He felt that behavior follows patterns, and these patterns are caused by differences in the way people use their minds. In 1942, Isabel Briggs-Myers and her mother, Katharine Briggs, began to put Jung's theory into practice. They developed the Myers-Briggs Type Indicator®, which after more than 50 years of research and refinement has become the most widely used instrument for identifying and studying personality.

As indicated throughout this chapter, we must stress the fact that no part of this assessment measures your worth, your success potential, how smart you are, or your value as a human being. The questions on the PAP assisted you in identifying your type, but neither the PAP nor your authors want you to assume that one personality type is better or worse, more valuable or less valuable, or more likely to be successful. What personality typing can do is to "help us discover what best motivates and energizes each of us as individuals" (Tieger and Barron-Tieger, 2001).

Why Personality Matters

Functions of Typology

When all of the combinations of E/I, S/N, T/F, and J/P are combined, there are 16 personality types. Everyone will fit into one of the following categories:

ISTJ	ISFJ	INFJ	INTJ
ISTP	ISFP	INFP	INTP
ESTP	ESFP	ENFP	ENTP
ESTJ	ESFJ	ENFJ	ENTJ

Let's take a look at the four major categories of typing. Notice that the higher your score in one area, the stronger your personality type is for that area. For instance, if you scored 15 on the E (extroversion) questions, this means that you are a strong ex-

trovert. If you scored 15 on the I (introversion) questions, this means that you are a strong introvert. However, if you scored 7 on the E questions and 8 on the I questions, your score indicates that you possess almost the same amount of extroverted and introverted qualities. The same is true for every category on the PAP.

E versus I (Extroversion/Introversion)

This category deals with the way we *interact with others and the world around us.*

Extroverts prefer to live in the outside world, drawing their strength from other people. They are outgoing and love interaction. They usually make decisions with others in mind. They enjoy being the center of attention. There are usually few secrets about extroverts.

Introverts draw their strength from the inner world. They need to spend time alone to think and ponder. They are usually quiet and reflective. They usually make decisions by themselves. They do not like being the center of attention. They are private.

S versus N (Sensing/Intuition)

This category deals with the way we *learn and deal with information.*

Sensing types gather information through their five senses. They have a hard time believing something if it cannot be seen, touched, smelled, tasted, or heard. They like concrete facts and details. They do not rely on intuition or gut feelings. They usually have a great deal of common sense.

Intuitive types are not very detail-oriented. They can see possibilities, and they rely on their gut feelings. Usually, they are very innovative people. They tend to live in the future and often get bored once they have mastered a task.

T versus F (Thinking/Feeling)

This category deals with the way we *make decisions.*

Thinkers are very logical people. They do not make decisions based on feelings or emotion. They are analytical and sometimes do not take others' values into consideration when making decisions. They can easily identify the flaws of others. They can be seen as insensitive and lacking compassion.

Feelers make decisions based on what they feel is right and just. They like to have harmony, and they value others' opinions and feelings. They are usually very tactful people who like to please others. They are very warm people.

J versus P (Judging/Perceiving)

This category deals with the way we *live.*

Judgers are very orderly people. They must have a great deal of structure in their lives. They are good at setting goals and sticking to their goals. They are the type of people who would seldom, if ever, play before their work was completed.

Perceivers are just the opposite. They are less structured and more spontaneous. They do not like timelines. Unlike the judger, they will play before their work is done. They will take every chance to delay a decision or judgment. Sometimes, they can become involved in too many things at one time.

YES YOU CAN !

IDEAS FOR *Success*

Consider the following strategies for making the most of your learning style, personality type, and dominant intelligence:

► Understand that everyone has a strength and aptitude for some skill or task.

► Improve your weaker learning styles by incorporating at least one aspect of those learning styles into your daily study plans.

► If your personality type clashes with your professor's personality type, try to make adjustments that enable you to get through the class successfully.

► Strengthen your less dominant intelligences by involving yourself in activities that cause you to use them.

► Adjust your learning style to match your professor's teaching style if possible.

► Understand that your primary intelligence can help you decide your life's vocation.

After you have studied the following chart and other information in the chapter regarding your personality type, you can make some decisions about your study habits and even your career choices. For instance, if you scored very strong in the extroversion section, it may not serve you well to pursue a career where you would be forced to work alone. It would probably be unwise to try to spend all of your time studying alone. If you are a strong extrovert, you will want to work and study around people.

A Closer Look at Your Personality Type

ISTJ 7–10% OF AMERICA	**ISFJ** 7–10% OF AMERICA	**INFJ** 2–3% OF AMERICA	**INTJ** 2–3% OF AMERICA
Have great power of concentration; very serious; dependable; logical and realistic; take responsibility for their own actions; they are not easily distracted.	Hard workers; detail-oriented; considerate of others' feelings; friendly and warm to others; very conscientious; they are down-to-earth and like to be around the same.	Enjoy an atmosphere where all get along; they do what is needed of them; they have strong beliefs and principles; enjoy helping others achieve their goals.	They are very independent; enjoy challenges; inventors; can be skeptical; they are perfectionists; they believe in their own work, sometimes to a fault.
ISTP 4–7% OF AMERICA	**ISFP** 5–7% OF AMERICA	**INFP** 3–4% OF AMERICA	**INTP** 3–4% OF AMERICA
Very reserved; good at making things clear to others; interested in how and why things work; like to work with their hands; can sometimes be misunderstood as idle.	Very sensitive and modest; adapt easily to change; they are respectful of others' feelings and values; take criticism personally; don't enjoy leadership roles.	They work well alone; must know others well to interact; faithful to others and their jobs; excellent at communication; open-minded; dreamers; tend to do too much.	Extremely logical; very analytical; good at planning; love to learn; excellent problem solvers; they don't enjoy needless conversation; hard to understand at times.
ESTP 6–8% OF AMERICA	**ESFP** 8–10% OF AMERICA	**ENFP** 6–7% OF AMERICA	**ENTP** 4–6% OF AMERICA
They are usually very happy; they don't let trivial things upset them; they have very good memories; very good at working with things and taking them apart.	Very good at sports and active exercises; good common sense; easygoing; good at communication; can be impulsive; do not enjoy working alone; have fun and enjoy living and life.	Creative and industrious; can easily find success in activities and projects that interest them; good at motivating others; organized; do not like routine.	Great problem solvers; love to argue either side; can do almost anything; good at speaking/motivating; love challenges; very creative; do not like routine; overconfident.
ESTJ 12–15% OF AMERICA	**ESFJ** 11–14% OF AMERICA	**ENFJ** 3–5% OF AMERICA	**ENTJ** 3–5% OF AMERICA
They are "take charge" people; they like to get things done; focus on results; very good at organizing; good at seeing what will not work; responsible; realists.	Enjoy many friendly relationships; popular; love to help others; do not take criticism very well; need praise; need to work with people; organized; talkative; active.	Very concerned about others' feelings; respect others; good leaders; usually popular; good at public speaking; can make decisions too quickly; trust easily.	Excellent leaders; speak very well; hard-working; may be workaholics; may not give enough praise; like to learn; great planners; enjoy helping others reach their goals.

All percentages taken from Tieger and Barron-Tieger, *Do What You Are,* 3rd ed. (2001).

Think About It
Chapter Reflection

The most important thing to remember about learning styles, multiple intelligences, and personality typology is that, unlike an IQ test, they do not pretend to determine if you are "smart" or not. They simply allow you to look more closely at how you learn, what strengths you have in your innate personality, and what your dominant intelligence may be.

Discovering your learning style can greatly enhance your classroom performance. For example, finally understanding that your learning style is visual and that your professor's teaching style is totally verbal (oral) can answer many questions about why you may have performed poorly in the past. Now you have the knowledge and the tools to make your learning style work for you, not against you. As you continue to use your learning style, dominant intelligence, and personality type to enhance learning, consider the following suggestions:

- ► Get involved in a *variety* of learning and social situations.
- ► Use your less dominant areas more often to *strengthen* them.
- ► *Read more* about personality typing and learning styles.
- ► Remember that inventories *do not* measure your worth.
- ► Work to *improve* your less dominant areas.
- ► *Surround yourself* with people who are very different from you.
- ► Try *different ways* of learning and studying.

By understanding how you learn, learning can become an entirely new and exciting venture for you. Good luck to you on this new journey.

 Education is learning what you did not know you did not know.

—Daniel Boorstin

Knowledge in Bloom

Each chapter-end assessment is based on *Bloom's Taxonomy of Learning*. See the inside front cover for a quick review.

Utilizes levels 4 and 5 of the taxonomy

Creating Your Personal Life Profile

In this chapter, you have discovered three things about the way you learn best: your multiple intelligence, your learning style, and your personality type. Write them down in the space here:

My *dominant intelligence* is _____

My *learning style* is _____

My *personality type* is _____

Now that you see them all together, think of them as a puzzle and "connect the dots." In other words, put them all together and what do they look like? What do they mean? How do they affect your studies, your relationships, your communication skills, and your career choices?

Example: If Mike's dominant intelligence is *interpersonal*, his learning style is *verbal,* and his personality type is *ENFJ,* connecting the dots may suggest that he is the type of person who loves to be around other people; he is an extrovert who learns best by listening to other people or explaining how something is done. He is a person who would probably speak out in class, be more of a leader than a follower, and start a study group if one did not exist because he is outgoing, organized, and very much a goal setter. Mike is the type of person who values relationships and listens to what others are saying. He is a person who shares and does not mind taking the time to explain things to others. He could easily become a good friend.

Some of the challenges Mike could encounter might involve taking a class where discussions are rare, having to sit and never share ideas or views, or having a professor who is not very organized and skips around. He would not deal very well with peers who were disrespectful or did not pull their own weight in the study group. He might also have a hard time with group members or classmates who are very quiet and prefer to observe rather than become involved. He would have trouble being around people who have no goals or direction in life. He might also run into some trouble because he is a very social person and loves to be around others in social settings. He may overcommit himself to groups and clubs and on occasion, he may socialize more than study.

As you can see, by connecting the dots, Mike's Personal Life Profile tells us a great deal about his strengths and challenges. It also gives him an understanding of how to approach many different situations.

Now it is your turn. Take your time and refer to your chapter for any information you may need. Examine your assessments and create your own profile in the four areas listed here. Discuss your strengths and challenges for each area.

The Personal Life Profile of _____

Academic Strengths: I found that I . . .

_____

_____

_____

_____

Academic Challenges: I found that I . . .

_____

_____

_____

_____

Communication Strengths: I found that I . . .

_____

_____

_____

_____

Communication Challenges: I found that I . . .

_____

_____

_____

_____

Relationship Strengths: I found that I . . .

_____

_____

_____

_____

Relationship Challenges: I found that I . . .

_____

_____

_____

_____

Career Strengths: I found that I . . .

_____

_____

_____

Career Challenges: I found that I . . .

_____

_____

_____

_____

Preparing for Success

Refer back to pages 118–119 of this chapter and answer the questions you developed from scanning this chapter's headings. You should also be able to answer the following questions if they were not on your list:

1. Explain the difference between a learning style and a dominant intelligence. _____

_____

_____

2. How can your personality type affect your study time? _____

_____

3. What is the difference between a visual learning style and a visual intelligence? _____

_____

_____

4. Briefly discuss each of the three learning styles. _____

_____

_____

_____

_____

7

Record

To **achieve** the **impossible,** it is **precisely** the **unthinkable** that must be **thought.**

Tom Robbins

Why do I need to become a better listener? Why will a chapter on listening and note taking help me in college, at work, with my family, and beyond? Why do college professors make such a big deal about note taking?

Listening is a magnetic and strange thing, a creative force. When we are listened to, it creates us, makes us unfold and expand. Ideas actually begin to grow within us and come to life. When we listen to people there is an alternating current, and this recharges us so that we never get tired of each other.

—Brenda Ueland

Listening is considered by many communication experts to be the most essential skill for building healthy relationships, solving problems, learning new information, and getting along in life. Listening is certainly essential to your success as a college student. It will help you in terms of retaining information and becoming actively involved in the learning process. The ability to listen in a variety of situations will also help you become a more efficient note taker. Notes create a history of your time in class, what you have read in your text and various articles, and what you have studied with a group. *This chapter can help you*:

► Understand the difference between listening and hearing

► Understand and apply the Chinese definition of listening to everyday situations
► Overcome the obstacles to listening
► Identify key words in a lecture that indicate important information
► Learn and use the L-STAR note-taking system
► Identify and choose the best note-taking system for you
► Determine what to do if you get lost during a lecture

Some students have incredible memory and don't need to take many notes, but most of us are not so lucky. We need to write information down so that we can refer to it later. This chapter will help you become a better listener and note taker.

Take a few moments and **scan this chapter.** As you scan, **list five questions** you can expect to learn the answers to while reading and studying Chapter 7.

Example:
► What are the four components of the Chinese verb "to listen"? (from page 146)
► Why is it important to identify key words during a lecture? (from page 148)

My Questions:

1. _____

_____ from page _____

2. _____

_____ from page _____

Name: Damion Saunders
Institution: Western Career College
Major: Veterinary Technology
Age: 31

When I returned to school 10 years after graduating from high school, it was a major adjustment being in class five or six hours a day and then having to find time to study every night, work part-time, and care for my family. I also found that the old ways that I took notes and studied in high school were not working so well for me at WCC.

The wake-up call that I got was on a critical care exam. This should have been easy for me since I was already working in a vet's office. I thought I knew the material and did not need to review my notes or study much at all. I failed the test, and most of my classmates did, too. I realized this was serious business and I was spending serious money and I needed to learn how to read the text, take notes from the text, take better notes in class, and study properly. I finally realized that the only way to master the material was to get involved with it, read it, take notes on it, study it, and basically live it.

the big WHY

. . . from another perspective

This chapter on note taking will help you become more involved in learning. It will show you different note-taking styles that can help you develop notes that actually do you some good when it comes time for the test. Using the information from this chapter helped me greatly. I learned that I needed to read a chapter more than once. I began making note cards, highlighting main points when I read, and keeping a separate notebook for text notes. I made flash cards and bookmarks to help me. We formed a study group and compared notes and helped each other.

Today, as I finish my classes and begin my 200-hour externship, I'm glad that I finally learned how to get actively involved in learning. I would not be at this point in my life if I had not.

3. _____

_____

from page _____

4. _____

_____

from page _____

5. _____

_____

from page _____

Question

PS **Reminder:** At the end of the chapter, come back to this page and answer these questions in your notebook, text margins, or online chapter notes.

College classes demand active critical listening skills.

© EyeWire, Inc.

© BananaStock Ltd.

> **Y**ou can not truly listen to anyone and do anything else at the same time.
>
> —M. Scott Peck

THE IMPORTANCE OF LISTENING

Listening's Value in Classes, Relationships, and Avoiding Misunderstandings

Listening is a survival skill. Period! It is that simple. "I know listening is important," you might say, but few ever think of the paramount significance listening has in our everyday lives. It is essential for life's necessities:

- ▶ Establishing and improving relationships
- ▶ Personal growth
- ▶ Showing respect to others
- ▶ Professional rapport
- ▶ Showing empathy and compassion
- ▶ Learning new information
- ▶ Understanding others' opinions and views
- ▶ Basic survival
- ▶ Entertainment
- ▶ Health

How much time do you think you spend listening every day? Research suggests that we spend almost 70% of our waking time communicating, and *53% of that time is spent in listening situations* (Adler, Rosenfeld, and Towne, 2001). Effective listening skills can mean the difference between success or failure, As or Fs, relationships or loneliness, and in some cases and careers, life or death.

For students, good listening skills are critical. Over the next two to four years, you will be given a lot of information through lectures. Cultivating and improving your active listening skills will help you to understand the material, take accurate notes, participate in class discussions, communicate with your peers more effectively, and become more actively engaged in your learning process.

The Difference Between Listening and Hearing

No doubt you've been in a communication situation where a misunderstanding took place. Either you hear something incorrectly or someone hears you incorrectly, or it could be that someone hears your message but misinterprets it. These communication blunders arise because we tend to view listening (and communication in general) as an automatic response when in fact it is not.

Listening is a learned, voluntary activity. You must choose to do it. It is a skill just like driving a car, painting a picture, or playing the piano. Becoming an active listener requires practice, time, mistakes, guidance, and active participation.

Hearing, however, is not learned; it is automatic and involuntary. If you are within range of a sound you will probably hear it although you may not be listening to it. Hearing a sound does not guarantee that you know what it is or what made it. Listening actively, though, means making a conscious effort to focus on the sound and to determine what it is.

Where Are You . . .   AT THIS MOMENT

Before reading any further, take a moment and assess where you are at this moment with your knowledge and application of listening and note-taking skills. Read each statement carefully and then respond accordingly.

1. When I am listening to someone, I give him or her my full, undivided attention.   YES NO

2. I know how to listen for key words and phrases during a lecture.   YES NO

3. When I am listening, I try to relate the new information to something I already know.   YES NO

4. I know the difference between listening and hearing.   YES NO

5. I know how to avoid the obstacles of prejudging, talking too much, and being too emotional when listening in conversation or a lecture.   YES NO

6. I know how to listen in class to take the most effective notes possible.   YES NO

7. I know how to use several different note-taking styles.   YES NO

8. I know how to use my own individualized style of shorthand when taking notes.   YES NO

9. I know what to do with my notes when I get lost in class.   YES NO

If you answered "Yes" to most of the questions (seven or more), you have a firm grasp on the listening process, and you know how to listen effectively in class and in other situations. You have developed a strong note-taking system and use your own note-taking style. *If you answered "No"* to most of the questions, you may be experiencing difficulty listening in the classroom and beyond. You may have trouble with your note-taking skills because of your listening challenges. You have not developed your own note-taking style, and you are not sure how to listen for clues in the classroom. You may need to practice your listening and note-taking skills outside the classroom.

Listening Defined

According to Ronald Adler (Adler et al., 2001), the drawing of the Chinese verb "to listen" (Figure 7.1) provides a comprehensive and practical definition of listening.

To the Chinese, listening involves the ears, the eyes, undivided attention, and the heart. Do you make it a habit to listen with more than your ears? The Chinese view listening as a whole-body experience. People from Western cultures seem to have lost the ability to involve their whole body in the listening process. We tend to use only our ears, and sometimes we don't even use them very well.

At its core, listening is "the ability to hear, understand, analyze, respect, and appropriately respond to the meaning of another person's spoken and nonverbal messages" (Daly and Engleberg, 2002). Although this definition involves the word "hear," listening goes far beyond just the physical ability to catch sound waves.

The first step in listening *is* hearing, but true listening involves one's full attention and the ability to filter out distractions, emotional barriers, cultural differences, and religious biases. Listening means that you are making a conscious decision to understand and show respect for the other person's communication efforts.

Listening needs to be personalized and internalized. To understand listening as a whole-body experience, we can define it on three levels:

1. Listening with a *purpose*
2. Listening *objectively*
3. Listening *constructively*

FIGURE 7.1 *The Chinese Pictograph for "Listen"*

Ear

Eyes

Undivided attention

Heart

Listening with a purpose suggests a need to recognize different types of listening situations—for example, class, worship, entertainment, and relationships. People do not listen the same way in every situation.

Listening objectively means listening with an open mind. You will give yourself few greater gifts than the gift of knowing how to listen without bias and prejudice. This is perhaps the most difficult aspect of listening. If you have been cut off in mid-conversation or mid-sentence by someone who disagreed with you, or if someone has left the room while you were giving your opinion of a situation, you have had the experience of talking to people who do not know how to listen objectively.

Listening constructively means listening with the attitude: "How can this be helpful to my life, my education, my career, or my finances?" This type of listening involves evaluating the information you are hearing and determining whether it has meaning to your life. Sound easy? It is more difficult than it sounds because, again, we all tend to shut out information that we do not view as immediately helpful or useful. To listen constructively, you need to know how to listen and store information for later.

WHAT DID YOU SAY?

Obstacles to Listening

Several major obstacles stand in the way of becoming an effective listener. To begin building active listening skills, you first have to remove some barriers.

Obstacle One: Prejudging

Prejudging means that you automatically shut out what is being said; it is one of the biggest obstacles to active listening. You may prejudge because you don't like or

Listening to people from different cultures, backgrounds, and religions can open many doors.

agree with the information or the person communicating. You may also have pre-judging problems because of your environment, culture, social status, or attitude.

Do You Prejudge Information or Its Source?

Answer yes or no to the following questions:

1. I tune out when something is boring.	YES	NO
2. I tune out when I do not agree with the information.	YES	NO
3. I argue mentally with the speaker about information.	YES	NO
4. I do not listen to people I do not like.	YES	NO
5. I make decisions about information before I understand all of its implications or consequences.	YES	NO

If you answered yes to two or more of these questions, you tend to prejudge in a listening situation.

Tips for Overcoming Prejudging

▶ Listen for information that may be valuable to you as a student. Some material may not be pleasant to hear but may be useful to you later on.

▶ Listen to the message, not the messenger. If you do not like the speaker, try to go beyond personality and listen to what is being said, without regard to the person saying it. Conversely, you may like the speaker so much that you automatically accept the message without listening objectively to what is being said.

▶ Try to remove cultural, racial, gender, social, and environmental barriers. Just because a person is different from you or holds a different point of view does not make that person wrong; and just because a person is like you and holds a similar point of view does not make that person right. Sometimes, you have to cross cultural and environmental barriers to learn new material and see with clearer eyes.

Obstacle Two: Talking

Not even the best listener in the world can listen while he or she is talking. The next time you are in a conversation with a friend, try speaking while your friend is speaking—then see if you know what your friend said. To become an effective listener, you need to learn the power of silence. Silence gives you the opportunity to think about what is being said before you respond.

Are You a Talker Rather Than a Listener?

Answer yes or no to the following questions:

1. I often interrupt the speaker so that I can say what I want.	YES	NO
2. I am thinking of my next statement while others are talking.	YES	NO
3. My mind wanders when others talk.	YES	NO
4. I answer my own questions.	YES	NO
5. I answer questions that are asked of other people.	YES	NO

If you answered yes to two or more questions, you tend to talk too much in a listening situation.

Tips for Overcoming the Urge to Talk Too Much

▶ Avoid interrupting the speaker. Force yourself to be silent at parties, family gatherings, and friendly get-togethers. We're not saying you should be unsociable, but force yourself to be silent for 10 minutes. You'll be surprised at what you hear. You may also be surprised how hard it is to do this. Test yourself.

▶ Ask someone a question and then allow that person to answer the question.

▶ Too often we ask questions and answer them ourselves. Force yourself to wait until the person has formulated a response. If you ask questions and wait for answers, you will force yourself to listen.

▶ Concentrate on what is being said at the moment, not what you want to say next.

Obstacle Three: Becoming Too Emotional

Emotions can form a strong barrier to active listening. Worries, problems, fears, and anger can keep you from listening to the best of your ability. Have you ever sat in a lecture, and before you knew it, your mind was a million miles away because you were angry or worried about something? If you have, you know what it's like to bring your emotions to the table.

Do You Bring Your Emotions to the Listening Situation?

Answer yes or no to the following questions:

1. I get angry before I hear the whole story.	YES	NO
2. I look for underlying or hidden messages in information.	YES	NO
3. Sometimes I begin listening on a negative note.	YES	NO
4. I base my opinions of information on what others are saying or doing.	YES	NO
5. I readily accept information as correct from people I like or respect.	YES	NO

If you answered yes to two or more of these questions, you tend to bring your emotions to a listening situation.

Tips for Overcoming Emotions

▶ Know how you feel before you begin the listening experience. Take stock of your emotions and feelings ahead of time.

▶ Focus on the message; determine how to use the information.

▶ Create a positive image about the message you are hearing.

▶ Avoid overreacting or jumping to conclusions.

"FOR EXAMPLE, YOU SHOULD BE ABLE TO . . ."

Listening for Key Words, Phrases, and Hints

Learning how to listen for key words, phrases, and hints can help you become an active listener and an effective note taker. For example, if your English professor begins a lecture saying, "There are 10 basic elements to writing poetry," jot down the number 10 under the heading "Poetry" or number your notebook page 1 through 10, leaving space for notes. If at the end of class you listed six elements to writing poetry, you know that you missed a part of the lecture. At this point, you need to ask the professor some questions or partner with your study group.

Here are some key phrases and words to listen for:

▶ in addition	▶ another way	▶ above all
▶ most important	▶ such as	▶ specifically
▶ you'll see this again	▶ therefore	▶ finally
▶ for example	▶ to illustrate	▶ as stated earlier
▶ in contrast	▶ in comparison	▶ nevertheless
▶ the characteristics of	▶ the main issue is	▶ moreover
▶ on the other hand	▶ as a result of	▶ because

Picking up on *transition words* will help you filter out less-important information and thus listen more carefully to what is most important. There are other indicators of key information, too. Listen carefully when the professor does these things:

Writes something on the board

Uses an overhead

Uses computer-aided graphics

Speaks in a louder tone or changes vocal patterns

Uses gestures more than usual

Draws on a flip chart

LISTENING WHEN ENGLISH IS YOUR SECOND LANGUAGE

Suggestions for ESL Students

For students whose first language is not English, the college classroom can present some uniquely challenging situations. One of the most pressing and important challenges is the ability to listen, translate, understand, and capture the message on paper in a quick and continuous manner. According to Lynn Forkos, professor and coordinator of the Conversation Center for International Students at the Community College of Southern Nevada, the following tips can be beneficial:

▶ Don't be afraid to stop the professor to ask for clarification. Asking questions allows you to take an active part in the listening process. If the professor doesn't answer your questions sufficiently, be certain to make an appointment to speak with him or her during his or her office hours.

▶ If you are in a situation where the professor can't stop or you're watching a movie or video in class, listen for words that you do understand and try to figure out unfamiliar words in the context of the sentence.

▶ Enhance your vocabulary by watching and listening to TV programs such as *Dateline, 20/20, Primetime, 60 Minutes,* and the evening news. You might also try listening to radio stations such as National Public Radio as you walk or drive.

© Hulton-Deutsch Collection/Corbis

Thomas Edison invented the light bulb, the phonograph, the battery, the forerunner to the movie camera, and 1089 other creations. He was also kicked out of school at age 12. His teachers thought he was too stupid to remain in class because of his constant questioning. He was deaf in one ear and 80% deaf in the other. He also had what would today be called ADHD. At one point during his career, he had to borrow money from a friend to avoid starvation.

Edison read constantly, had an incredible memory, and sometimes worked 20 hours a day.

He was one of the most important scientists in history whose inventions led the world into modern society.

DID YOU KNOW?

▶ Be certain that you write down everything that the professor puts on the board, overhead, or PowerPoint. You may not need every piece of this information, but this technique gives you (and hopefully your study group) the ability to sift through the information outside of class. It gives you a visual history of what the professor said.

▶ Finally, if there is a conversation group or club that meets on campus, take the opportunity to join. By practicing language, you become more attuned to common words and phrases. If a conversation group is not available, consider starting one of your own.

WHY TAKE NOTES?

Is It Just a Big, Crazy Chore?

Go to class, listen, and write it down. Read a text, take notes. Watch a film, take notes. Is it really that important? Actually, knowing how to take useful, accurate notes can dramatically improve your life as a student. If you are an effective listener and note taker, you have two of the most valuable skills any student could ever use. There are several reasons why it is important to take notes:

▶ You become an active part of the listening process.

▶ You create a history of your course content when you take notes.

▶ You have written criteria to follow when studying.

▶ You create a visual aid for your material.

▶ Studying becomes much easier.

WRITING IT RIGHT

Tips for Effective Note Taking

You have already learned several skills you will need to take notes such as cultivating your active listening skills, overcoming obstacles to effective listening, and familiarizing yourself with key phrases used by professors. Next, prepare yourself mentally and physically to take effective notes that are going to be helpful to you. Consider the following ideas as you think about expanding your note-taking abilities.

▶ *Attend class.* This may sound obvious, but it is surprising how many college students feel they do not need to go to class.

▶ *Come to class prepared.* Scan, read, and use your textbook to establish a basic understanding of the material before coming to class. It is always easier to take notes when you have a preliminary understanding of what is being said. Coming to class prepared also means bringing the proper materials for taking notes: lab manuals, pens, a notebook, and a highlighter.

▶ *Bring your textbook to class.* Although many students think they do not need to bring their textbook to class if they have read the homework, you will find that many professors repeatedly refer to the text while lecturing. The professor may ask you to highlight, underline, or refer to the text in class, and following along in the text as the professor lectures may also help you organize your notes.

Good note-taking skills help you do more than simply record what you learn in class or read in a book so that you can recall it. These skills can also help to reinforce that information so that you actually know it.

© BananaStock Ltd.

▶ *Ask questions and participate in class.* Two of the most critical actions you can perform in class are to ask questions and to participate in the class discussion. If you do not understand a concept or theory, ask questions. Don't leave class without understanding what has happened and assume you'll pick it up on your own.

YOU'LL BE SEEING STARS

The L-STAR System

One of the most effective ways to take notes begins with the L-STAR system. This system involves the following skills:

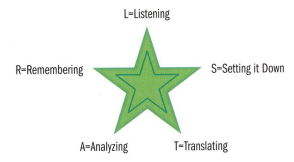

This five-step program will enable you to compile complete, accurate, and visual notes for future reference. Along with improving your note-taking skills, using this system will enhance your ability to participate in class, help other students, study more effectively, and perform well on exams and quizzes.

L—Listening

One of the best ways to become an effective note taker is to become an active listener. A concrete step you can take toward becoming an active listener in class is to sit near the front of the room where you can hear the professor and see the board and overheads. Choose a spot that allows you to see the professor's mouth and facial expressions. If you see that the professor's face has become animated or expressive, you can bet that you are hearing important information. Write it down. If you sit in the back of the room, you may miss out on these important clues.

S—Setting It Down

The actual writing of notes can be a difficult task. Some professors are organized in their delivery of information; others are not. Your listening skills, once again, are going to play an important role in determining what needs to be written down. In most cases, you will not have time to take notes verbatim. You will have to be selective about the information you choose to set down. One of the best ways to keep up with the information being presented is to develop a shorthand system of your own. Many of the symbols you use will be universal, but you may use

some symbols, pictures, and markings that are uniquely your own. These are some
of the more common symbols:

w/	with	w/o	without
=	equals	≠	does not equal
<	less than	>	greater than
%	percentage	#	number
&	and	∧	increase
+	plus or addition	−	minus
*	important	etc	and so on
eg	for example	vs	against
esp	especially	"	quote
?	question	. . .	and so on

These symbols can save you valuable time when taking notes. Because you will use
them frequently, it is a good idea to memorize them.

T—Translating

Translating can save you hours of work as you begin to study for exams. Many students feel that this step is not important, or too time-consuming, and leave it out.
Don't. Often, students take notes so quickly that they make mistakes or use abbreviations that they may not be able to decipher later.

After each class, go to the library or some other quiet place and review your notes.
You don't have to do this immediately after class, but before the end of the day, you
will need to rewrite and translate your classroom notes. This process gives you the
opportunity to put the notes in your own words and to incorporate your text notes
into your classroom notes.

Translating your notes helps you make connections among previous material
discussed, your own personal experiences and readings, and new material presented. Translating aids in recalling and applying new information. Few things are
more difficult than trying to reconstruct your notes the night before a test, especially
when they were made several weeks earlier.

A—Analyzing

This step takes place while you translate your notes from class. When you analyze
your notes, you are asking two basic questions: (1) What does this mean? and (2) Why
is it important? If you can answer these two questions about your material, you have
almost mastered the information. Though some instructors will want you to spit
back the exact same information you were given, others will ask you for a more detailed understanding and a synthesis of the material. When you are translating your
notes, begin to answer these two questions using your notes, textbook, supplemental materials, and information gathered from outside research. Once again, this
process is not simple or quick, but testing your understanding of the material is important. Remember that many lectures are built on past lectures. If you do not understand what happened in class on September 17, you may not be able to
understand what happens on September 19. Analyzing your notes while translating
them will give you a more complete understanding of the material.

R—Remembering

Once you have listened to the lecture, set your notes on paper, and translated and analyzed the material, it is time to study, or remember, the information. Some effec-

tive ways to remember information include creating a visual picture, speaking the notes out loud, using mnemonic devices, and finding a study partner. Chapter 9 will help you with these techniques and other study aids.

NOT EVERYONE WORKS AND LEARNS THE SAME WAY

Three Common Note-Taking Systems

There are three common note-taking systems: (1) the outline technique; (2) the Cornell, or split-page, technique (also called the T system); and (3) the mapping technique.

It's as Simple as A, B, C—1, 2, 3: The Outline Technique

The outline system uses a series of major headings and multiple subheadings formatted in hierarchical order (see Figure 7.2). The outline technique is one of the most commonly used note-taking systems, yet it is also one of the most misused systems. It can be difficult to outline notes in class, especially if your professor does not follow an outline while lecturing.

FIGURE 7.2   *The Outline Technique*

Study Skills 101   Oct. 17
                                                     Wednesday

Topic: Listening

I. The Process of Listening (ROAR)
    A. R = Receiving
        1. W/in range of sound
        2. Hearing the information
    B. O = Organizing & focusing
        1. Choose to listen actively
        2. Observe the origin, direction & intent
    C. A = Assignment
        1. You assign a meaning
        2. May have to hear it more than once
    D. R = Reacting
        1. Our response to what we heard
        2. Reaction can be anything
II. Definitions of Listening (POC)
    A. P = Listening w/ a purpose
    B. O = Listening w/ objectivity
    C. C = Listening constructively

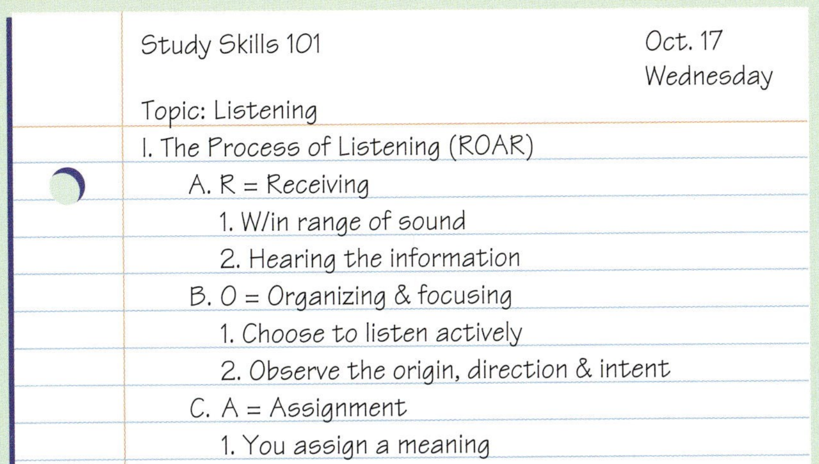

Chances are that sometime in your college career you'll find yourself in a large lecture hall class where it can be difficult to ask questions or seek clarification.

© Image 100 Ltd.

When using the outline system, it is best to get all the information from the lecture and afterward combine your lecture notes and text notes to create an outline. Most professors would advise against using the outline system of note taking in class, although you may be able to use a modified version. The most important thing to remember is not to get bogged down in a system during class; what is critical is getting the ideas down on paper. You can always go back after class and rearrange your notes as needed.

If you are going to use a modified or informal outline while taking notes in class, you may want to consider grouping information together under a heading as a means of outlining. It is easier to remember information that is logically grouped than to remember information that is scattered across several pages. If your study skills lecture is on listening, you might outline your notes using the headings "The Process of Listening" and "Definitions of Listening."

After you have rewritten your notes using class lecture information and material from your textbook, your notes may look like those in Figure 7.2.

It's a Split Decision: The Cornell (Modified Cornell, Split Page, or T) System

The basic principle of the Cornell system, developed by Dr. Walter Pauk of Cornell University, is to split the page into two sections, each to be used for different information (see Figure 7.3). Section A is used for questions that summarize information

FIGURE 7.3 *A Blank Cornell Frame*

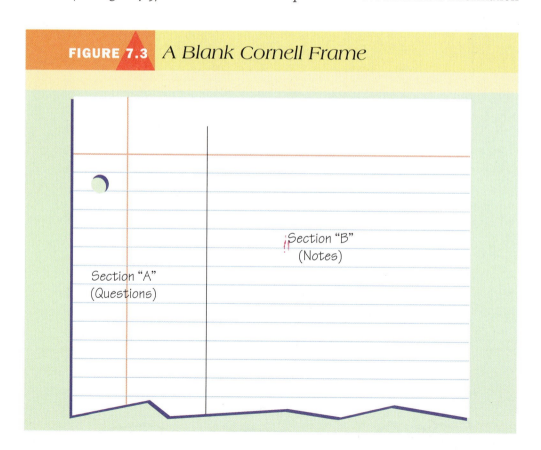

Section "A"
(Questions)

Section "B"
(Notes)

FIGURE 7.4 *Outline Using a Cornell Frame*

| Study Skills 101 | | Oct. 19 |
| Topic: Listening | | Friday |

What is the listening process? (ROAR)	*The Listening Process (ROAR)
	A= Receiving
	1. Within range of sound
	2. Hearing the information
	B = Organizing
	1. Choose to listen actively
	2. Observe origin
Definition of Listening (POC)	*Listening Defined
	A. Listening w/ a purpose
	B. Listening objectively
	C. Listening constructively
Obstacles (PET)	*What interferes w/ listening
	A. Prejudging
	B. Emotions
	C. Talking

The listening process involves Receiving, Organizing, Assigning & Reacting - Talking, Prejudging & Emotions are obstacles.

found in Section B; Section B is used for the actual notes from class. The blank note-taking page should be divided as shown.

The Cornell system is shown in Figures 7.4 and 7.5. Sometimes the basic Cornell layout is modified to include a third section at the bottom of the page for additional or summary comments. In such cases the layout is referred to as a T system for its resemblance to an upside-down T. To implement the Cornell system, you will want to choose the technique that is most comfortable and beneficial for you; you might use mapping (discussed below) or outlining on a Cornell page. An example of notes outlined using the Cornell system appears in Figure 7.4.

Going Around in Circles: The Mapping System

If you are a visual learner, this system may be especially useful for you. The mapping system of note taking generates a picture of information (see Figure 7.5 and 7.6). The mapping system creates a map, or web, of information that allows you to see the relationships among facts or ideas. A mapping system might look something like the notes in Figure 7.6.

The most important thing to remember about each note-taking system is that *it must work for you.* Do not use a system because your friends use it or because you feel

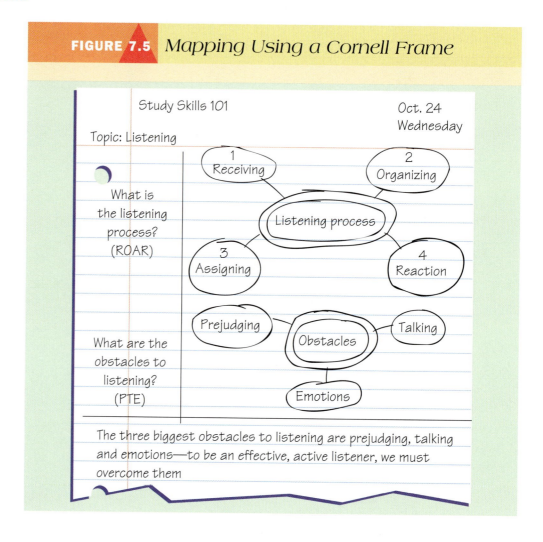

FIGURE 7.5   *Mapping Using a Cornell Frame*

Study Skills 101   Oct. 24
                                                           Wednesday
Topic: Listening

What is the listening process? (ROAR)

1 Receiving   2 Organizing
Listening process
3 Assigning   4 Reaction

What are the obstacles to listening? (PTE)

Prejudging   Obstacles   Talking
                Emotions

The three biggest obstacles to listening are prejudging, talking and emotions—to be an effective, active listener, we must overcome them

that you should use it. Experiment with each system or combination to determine which is best for you.

Always remember to keep your notes organized, dated, and neat. Notes that cannot be read are no good to you or to anyone else.

WHAT TO DO IF YOU GET LOST DURING THE LECTURE

Have you ever been in a classroom trying to take notes and the professor is speaking so rapidly that you cannot possibly get all of the information? Just when you think you're caught up, you realize that he or she has made an important statement and you missed it. What do you do? How can you handle, or avoid, this difficult note-taking situation? Here are several hints:

▶ Raise your hand and ask the professor to repeat the information.

▶ Ask your professor to slow down.

▶ If he or she will do neither, leave a blank space with a question mark at the side margin (see Figure 7.7). You can get this information after class. This can be a difficult task to master. The key is to focus on the information at hand. Focus on what is being said at the exact moment.

FIGURE 7.6   *The Mapping System*

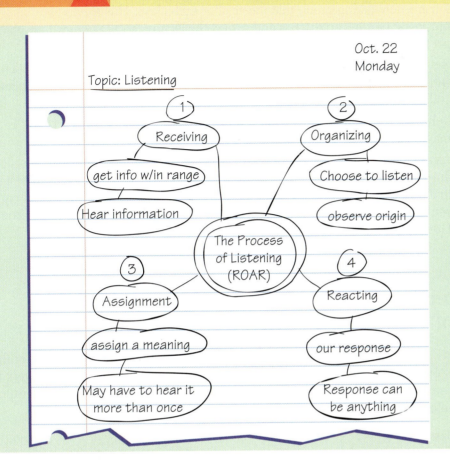

Oct. 22
Monday

Topic: Listening

1 Receiving
- get info w/in range
- Hear information

2 Organizing
- Choose to listen
- observe origin

The Process of Listening (ROAR)

3 Assignment
- assign a meaning
- May have to hear it more than once

4 Reacting
- our response
- Response can be anything

FIGURE 7.7   *What to Do When You Get Lost*

Public Speaking   Oct. 7
Lecture: Types of Research for Speeches

*Periodicals	- Magazines, trade & professional
*Newspapers	Local, state & national (some international as well)
*Reference materials	Specialized . . . (?) } If you missed it, leave it blank
*Government documents	- Maps, reports, federal proceedings

> ► Meet with your professor immediately after class or at the earliest time convenient for both of you.

> ► Form a note-taking group that meets after each class. This serves two purposes: (1) you can discuss and review the lecture, and (2) you will be able to get the notes from one of your note-taking buddies.

> ► Never lean over and ask questions of another student during the lecture. This will cause them to lose the information too. It will probably annoy your peers and the professor as well.

> ► Rehearse your note-taking skills at home by taking notes from TV news magazines or channels like the History Channel.

> ► As a last resort, you can ask the professor's permission to use a tape recorder during the lecture. Do not record a lecture without permission. We suggest that you try to use other avenues, such as the ones listed here, instead of taping your notes. It is a time-consuming task to listen to the lecture a second time. However, if this system works for you, use it.

Using Your Laptop Computer for Note Taking

In this age of high technology, some students prefer to take notes or transfer their notes onto their computers. Some students bring laptops to class while others immediately type and reorganize their notes after class. If you choose to use a computer for note taking, use the following tips:

In Class

> ► Come to class early to set up your computer. Don't disturb others by arriving late.

> ► Try to sit where you can see the professor and projection screen, but also be respectful of other students. Tapping on the keyboard can disturb others' concentration.

> ► Don't worry too much about spelling or grammar. You can run the spelling and grammar checker after class while cleaning up your notes.

> ► Set your tabs before you begin. You can set them to use an outline format or the Cornell format.

Out of Class

> ► If you are going to type your notes into the computer, do so as quickly after class as possible. The information obtained in class needs to be fresh in your mind. Try to reorganize your notes within 24 hours.

> ► Combine your textbook notes and lecture notes. This will help you access the big picture of the information.

General Hints

> ► Save your notes on both a disk and your hard drive.

> ► Always print your notes after each entry. It can be catastrophic if all of your notes are on one disk or one hard drive and the computer crashes or the disk is lost.

> ► After you have printed your notes, use a three-hole punch and place your notes in a three-ring binder. Arrange computer notes with related handouts.

A last note about copying your notes by hand or into a computer: This technique, while valuable to some students, does not constitute studying. Dr. Walter Pauk (2005), creator of the Cornell note-taking system, suggests that "contrary to what most people think, almost no learning takes place during the keyboarding of scribbled notes." Finally, don't be threatened by those who decide to use the computer in class or those who come to class with typewritten, printed notes. *Cornerstone* in general, and this chapter specifically, is about choices. You have to find and use a system that is convenient, easy, and useful to you.

If you remember the concepts of the L-STAR system (listening, setting it down, translating, analyzing, and remembering) and use this system as a study pattern, and if you find a note-taking system that is comfortable and useful for you, then you will begin to see significant improvement in your ability as a note taker and in your performance as a student.

Think About It
Chapter Reflection

Yes, listening is a learned skill, but it is more than that. It is a gift that you give to yourself. It is a gift that promotes knowledge, understanding, stronger relationships, and open-mindedness. Good listening skills can help you manage conflict, avoid misunderstandings, and establish trusting relationships. Perhaps most importantly at this point in your life, listening can help you become a more successful student. Once you learn how to listen with your whole body and mind, you will begin to see how your notes, your grades, your attitude, your relationships, and your learning process change. As you work toward improving your listening skills and developing your note-taking system, remember the following:

▶ When listening, evaluate the content before you judge the messenger.
▶ Keep your emotions and preconceived notions in check while listening.
▶ Sit where you can see and hear the professor.
▶ Listen for "how" something is said.
▶ Listen to the entire story before making a judgment call.
▶ Listen for major ideas and key words.
▶ Use a separate notebook for every class.
▶ Use abbreviations whenever possible.
▶ Write down what the professor puts on the board or PowerPoint.

Becoming adept at listening and developing your own note-taking system are two essential skills that can help you become a more active learner.

Listening is an attitude of the heart, a genuine desire to be with another person.

—J. Isham

Knowledge in Bloom

Each chapter-end assessment is based on *Bloom's Taxonomy of Learning*. See the inside front cover for a quick review.

Utilizes levels 4 and 6 of the taxonomy

Listening with an Open Mind

Explanation: Seldom (if ever) would you pop in a CD, click your iPod, or tune your radio to a station that you strongly disliked. It just does not seem like a good use of time and it is not something that you would probably enjoy on a daily basis. However, for this exercise, we are going to ask that you do precisely what we've described above.

Process: Over the course of the next few days, find a song from your *least favorite* genre. If you are a huge fan of R&B, then choose something from a genre of which you are not particularly fond. You might choose an old country song or a song from rap or bluegrass. If you enjoy listening to "Easy Love Songs," try something different such as metal or swing. The only stipulation is that *the song must have lyrics*.

You will have to listen to the song several times to answer the following questions. However, it is important to read the questions *before* you listen to the song—particularly question 2. The key to this exercise is to practice listening with an open mind, listening for content, and listening to words when barriers are in the way (the barrier would be the actual music itself).

1. What is the song's title and who is the artist? _____

_____

2. What emotional and mental response to the music did you have the first time you listened to it? Why do you think you had this response? _____

_____

_____

_____

_____

3. While listening to the song, what happened to your appreciation level? Did it increase or decrease? _____

_____

_____

_____

_____

4. In your opinion, what is the message of the song? _____

_____

_____

_____

_____

5. What surprised you most about the song? The lyrics? The actual music? Your like or dislike of the song? The artist's voice? _____

_____

_____

_____

_____

6. If you *had* to say that you gained or learned one positive thing from this song, wha ould it be? _____

_____

_____

_____

7. From memory, list at least five statements, comments, or quotes from the ng. _____

_____

_____

_____

_____

Preparing for Success

Refer to pages 142–143 of this chapter and answer the questions you developed from scanning this chapter's headings. You should also be able to answer the following questions if they were not on your list:

1. What is objective listening? _____

_____

2. Discuss the five steps in the L-STAR note-taking system. _____

_____

3. List and discuss the four aspects of the Chinese verb "to listen." _____

_____

4. When would be the best time to use the mapping system of note taking? Justify your answer. _____

_____

8

Remember

Anyone who stops **learning** is **old,** whether at **20** or **80.** **Anyone** who keeps learning **stays young.** **The** greatest thing in **life** is to **keep** your mind young.

Henry Ford

the big **WHY**

Why do I need to remember any more than I remember right now? *Why* will a chapter on studying and remembering information help me at work, with my family, and beyond? *Why* is it so important to sharpen my memory about what goes on in class?

You live and you learn or you don't live long.

—Robert Heinlein

You've just learned that Whoopi Goldberg has dyslexia, or that turtles can have upper respiratory tract disease diagnosed by dehydration and nasal discharge, or that the first copying machine was invented in 1778, or that Germany was the first foreign country to have a McDonald's. *Wow!* How did you learn this? Through reading, listening, attending class, conversing with peers, and studying new material.

While these facts may not stun the world or cure cancer, studying for the sake of learning and understanding new material can be as exciting (or as dull) as you want it to be. It does not have to be the dreaded routine that you may be used to. With a plan, you can learn *almost anything that is known to mankind. Anything!* This chapter is about learning how to study so that you can learn what you need and want. *This chapter can help you:*

- ▶ Understand how your memory works and how to help it work better
- ▶ Identify the differences between short-term and long-term memory
- ▶ Learn to commit information to long-term memory
- ▶ Identify and avoid the issues that hinder memory
- ▶ Understand the role of sleep in memory and learning
- ▶ Know the difference between memorizing and knowing information
- ▶ Use mnemonics to help you remember information
- ▶ Develop strategies for studying math and science

Learning how to study smart instead of studying hard will save you countless hours and more stress than you can imagine.

Scan &

Take a few moments and **scan this chapter**. As you scan, **list five questions** you can expect to learn the answers to while reading and studying Chapter 8.

Example:
- ▶ What are three strategies for studying math? (from page 180)
- ▶ Why are mnemonics important? (from page 177)

My Questions:

1. _____
   _____ from page _____

2. _____
   _____ from page _____

3. _____
   _____ from page _____

Name: **Joey Luna**
Institution: **El Paso Community College, El Paso, TX and California State University—Los Angeles, CA**
Major: **Physician's assistant**
Age: **22**

... from another perspective

It's even hard for *me* to believe, but I have been accepted at California State University—Los Angeles. I will be transferring in the fall to complete my studies as a physician's assistant. The reason that this is hard for me to believe is that just three years ago when I began my first year at El Paso Community College, I immediately dropped my first nine credit hours of classes. I kept a math class because it was the only class that did not require a great deal of reading.

My second semester, I registered for 12 hours and dropped them all in the course of a few weeks because of the reading load and my inability to study. I never took notes while trying to read chapters, I never planned any time for studying, and soon, I was too far behind and very frustrated.

In the *Cornerstone* textbook, you will have the opportunity to read and discuss Chapter 8. This chapter deals with memory development and learning how to

become a better student through proper study habits. Because of the information and tips in this chapter, I learned how to take notes when studying, how to verbally repeat information at the end of a chapter, and how to reduce the amount of anxiety I suffered while studying for tests. Most importantly, I learned that as a college student, I *had* to plan time to study. Making time to study was the important lesson I learned for passing classes.

As I look back on my first year, completing only three credits, I am so excited that my dream of working in the health profession is well on its way to becoming a reality. This is now possible for me because I learned how to be a better student through mastering my study habits. I know that you can do the same thing, too.

4. _____

_____

from page _____

5. _____

_____

from page _____

Question

PS **Reminder:** At the end of the chapter, come back to this page and answer these questions in your notebook, text margins, or online chapter notes.

You may choose a nontraditional study environment, but be sure that you are able to study effectively in it.

© Corbis

WHY STUDY?

I Can Fake It

Studying for college classes can be quite different from studying for high school classes. The types of questions asked may be different, and the required depth of your response will almost certainly be different. In high school, you may have studied at the lower levels of Bloom's Taxonomy and learned simple facts, dates, places, and names. You'll need to know information at these levels in college, but you'll also be asked to analyze and evaluate information, too. You'll need to be able to defend your diagnosis of an upper respiratory tract disease in that turtle. And you'll have to know how to compile a treatment plan to save his life. These are examples of the higher-level learning skills required in college.

You may be saying to yourself, "I didn't have to study very hard in high school; why should I do it now?" Some students believe that they can glance at their notes for a moment and fake it. Quite truthfully, some students are able to do this because their learning style, professors, type of test given, and memory lend themselves to this type of studying technique. More than you may imagine, however, this is not the case. College professors are notorious for giving thorough exams, lengthy essay questions, tricky true-false statements, and multiple choices that would confuse Einstein. If you want to succeed in your classes in college, you will need to make studying at a higher level a way of life.

Effective studying requires a great deal of commitment, but learning how to get organized, taking effective notes, reading a textbook, listening in class, developing personalized study skills, and building memory techniques will serve you well in becoming a successful graduate. Faking it is now a thing of the past.

THE IMPORTANCE OF YOUR STUDY ENVIRONMENT

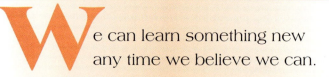

We can learn something new any time we believe we can.

—Virginia Satir

You may wonder why your study place is important. The study environment can determine how well your study time passes. If the location is too hot, too noisy, too dark, or too crowded, your study time may not be productive. In a room that is too hot and dimly lit, you may have a tendency to fall asleep. In a room that is too cold, you may spend time trying to warm yourself. Choose a location that is comfortable for you.

Different students need different study environments. You may need to have a degree of noise in the background, or you may need complete quiet. You have to make this decision. If you always have music in the background while you are studying, try studying in a quiet place one time to see if there is a difference. If you always try to study where it is quiet, try putting soft music in the background to see if it helps you. You may have to try several environments before you find the one that is right for you.

I FORGOT TO REMEMBER!

Understanding How Your Memory Functions

"My brain is full." *Myth*

"I can't remember another thing." *Myth*

Where Are You. . .   AT THIS MOMENT

Before reading any further, take a moment and assess where you are at this moment with your knowledge and application of memory and studying. Read each statement carefully and then respond accordingly.

1. I am comfortable studying for math and science classes.   YES   NO

2. I know which environments are best for me when I am studying.   YES   NO

3. When I study, I try to think of examples to illustrate and reinforce the material.   YES   NO

4. I know how to use mnemonic devices to aid my memory.   YES   NO

5. I am comfortable studying in groups.   YES   NO

6. I study new material over time and in moderation rather than cramming all at one time.   YES   NO

7. I would rather know the information than simply memorize it.   YES   NO

8. I try to use pictures to visualize what I am studying.   YES   NO

9. I know how to transfer information into my long-term memory.   YES   NO

If you answered "Yes" to most of the questions (seven or more), you understand the importance of your study environment. You know how to visualize the information you are studying, and you know that studying over time is a better technique than cramming. *If you answered "No"* to most of the questions, you will need to examine how you process new information. You will need to look carefully at the section on mnemonics to increase your memory power. You will also need to examine other new ways of transferring information into your long-term memory. You may benefit from a study group or a study buddy.

Several studies suggest that it is impossible to fill our brains full. One study in the 1970s concluded that if our brains were fed 10 new items of information every second for the rest of our lives, we would never fill even half of our memory's capacity (Texas A&M University).

At times, you may feel that if you study or read or learn any more, you'll forget everything. Some researchers suggest that we never forget anything—that the material is simply "covered up" by other material, but it is still in our brain. The reason we can't recall the information is that it was not important enough, not stored properly, or not used enough to keep it from being covered up.

So, why is it so hard to remember the dates of the Civil War or who flew with Amelia Earhart or how to calculate the liquidation value of stocks or the six factors in the communication process? The primary problem is that we never properly filed or stored this information.

What would happen if you typed your English research paper into the computer and did not give it a file name? When you needed to retrieve that paper, you would not know how to find it. You would have to search through every file until you came across the

Choosing the best study environment can be challenging. The best study place may depend on the different accommodations available to you and may vary with the kinds of studying required. What kind of study environment has worked best for you?

information you needed. Memory works in much the same way. We have to store it properly if we are to retrieve it easily at a later time.

This section will detail how memory works and why it is important to your studying efforts. Here are some basic facts about memory.

- ▸ Everyone remembers some information and forgets other information.
- ▸ Your senses help you take in information.
- ▸ With very little effort, you can remember some information.
- ▸ With rehearsal (study), you can remember a great deal of information.
- ▸ Without rehearsal or use, information is forgotten.
- ▸ Incoming information needs to be filed in the brain if you are to retain it.
- ▸ Information stored, or filed, in the brain must have a retrieval method.
- ▸ Mnemonic devices, repetition, association, and rehearsal can help you store and retrieve information.

Psychologists have determined that there are three types of memory: *sensory* memory; *short-term, or working* memory; and *long-term* memory.

Sensory memory stores information gathered from the five senses: taste, touch, smell, hearing, and sight. Sensory memory is usually temporary, lasting about one to three seconds, unless you decide that the information is of particular importance to you and make an effort to transfer it to long-term memory.

Short-term, or working memory holds information for a short amount of time. Your working memory bank can hold a limited amount of information, usually about five to nine separate new facts or pieces of information at once (Woolfolk, 2001). Although it is sometimes frustrating to forget information, it is also useful and necessary to do so. If you never forgot anything, you would not be able to function. As a student, you would never be able to remember all that your professor said during a 50-minute lecture. You have to take steps to help remember information. Taking notes, making associations, drawing pictures, and visualizing information are all techniques that can help you move information from your short-term memory to your long-term memory bank.

SHORT-TERM MEMORY ASSESSMENT

Theo, Gene, and Suzanne were on their way home from class. As they drove down Highway 415 toward the Greengate subdivision, they saw a 2001 Honda Civic pull out in front of a 1998 Nissan Maxima. There was a crash as the two cars collided. Theo stopped the car. Gene and Suzanne jumped from the car to see if they could help. Suzanne yelled for someone to call 911; Robertina, a bystander, ran to the pay phone at the corner of Mason and Long streets. Within 10 minutes, an ambulance arrived and took Margaret, the driver of the Maxima, to St. Mary's Hospital. Tim, the driver of the Honda, was not badly injured.

Cover this scenario with a piece of paper and answer the following questions.
1. Who was driving the Honda? _____
2. What highway were they driving on? _____
3. Who called 911? _____
4. What hospital was used? _____
5. What year was the Maxima? _____

How many questions did you answer correctly? If you answered four or five questions correctly, your working memory is strong. If you answered only one or two questions correctly, you will need to discover ways to commit more information to your short-term, or working, memory. Some techniques for doing this are discussed later in this chapter.

Long-term memory stores a lot of information. It is almost like a computer disk. You have to make an effort to put something in your long-term memory, but with effort and memory techniques, such as rehearsal and practice, you can store anything you want to remember there. Long-term memory consists of information that you have heard often, information that you use often, information that you might see often, and information that you have determined is necessary. Just as you name a file on a computer disk, you name the files in your long-term memory. Sometimes, you have to wait a moment for the information to come to you. While you are waiting, your brain disk is spinning; if the information you seek is in long-term memory, your brain will eventually find it. You may have to assist your brain in locating the information by using mnemonics and other memory devices.

LONG-TERM MEMORY ASSESSMENT

Without using any reference materials, quickly answer the following questions using your long-term memory.
 1. What is your mother's maiden name? _____
 2. Who was the first U.S. president? _____
 3. What is the capital of California? _____
 4. Who write *A Christmas Carol*? _____
 5. What shape is a stop sign? _____
 6. What is your Social Security number? _____
 7. Name one of the tallest buildings in America. _____
 8. What is the title of Dr. Martin Luther King's famous speech?

 _____
 9. What does the "A" stand for in the L-STAR note-taking method?

 _____
 10. What does the acronym "IBM" stand for? _____

Did the answers come to you quickly? If you review your answers, you will probably find that you responded quickly to those questions whose content you deal with fairly frequently, such as your Social Security number. Although you were probably able to answer all the questions, in some instances your brain had to search longer and harder to find the answer. This is how long-term memory works.

THIS ISN'T YOUR DADDY'S VCR

Using *VCR3* to Increase Memory Power

Countless pieces of information are stored in your long-term memory. Some of it is triggered by necessity, some may be triggered by the five senses, and some may be triggered by experiences. The best way to commit information to long-term memory and retrieve it when needed can be expressed by VCR3:

V Visualizing

C Concentrating

R Relating

R Repeating

R Reviewing

Consider the following story.

As Katherine walked back to the dorm room after her evening class, she heard someone behind her. She turned to see two students holding hands walking about 20 feet behind her. She was relieved. This was the first night that she had walked back to the residence hall alone.

Katherine pulled her book bag closer to her as she increased her pace along the dimly lit sidewalk between the Salk Biology Building and the Horn Center for the Arts. "I can't believe that Shana didn't call me," she thought to herself. "She knows I hate to leave class alone."

As Katherine turned the corner onto Suddith Street, she heard someone else behind her. She turned but did not see anyone. As she continued to walk toward the residence hall, she heard the sound again. Turning to see if anyone was there, she saw a shadow disappear into the grove of hedges along the sidewalk.

Startled and frightened, Katherine crossed the street to walk beneath the streetlights and sped up to get closer to a group of students about 30 feet in front of her. She turned once more to see if anyone was behind her. Thankfully, she did not see anyone.

By this time, she was only one block from her residence hall. The lighting was better and other students were around. She felt better, but vowed never again to leave class alone at night.

To *visualize* information, try to create word pictures in your mind as you hear the information. If you are being told about the Revolutionary War battle of Camden, SC, try to see the soldiers and the battlefield, or try to paint a mind picture that will help you to remember the information. You may also want to create visual aids as you read or study information.

As you read Katherine's story, were you able to visualize her journey? Could you see her walking along the sidewalk? Did you see the two buildings? What did they look like? Could you see the darkness of her path? Could you see that shadow disappearing into the bushes? Could you see her increasing her pace to catch up to the other students? What was she wearing?

> If a man is given a fish, he eats for a day. If a man learns to fish, he eats forever.
>
> —Chinese Proverb

If you did this, then you are using your visual skills—your mind's eye. This is one of the most effective ways to commit information to long-term memory. See it, live it, feel it, and touch it as you read it and study it, and it will become yours. Consider the following tips:

Concentrating on the information given will help you commit it to long-term memory. Don't let your mind wander. Stay focused. If you find yourself having trouble concentrating, take a small break (two to five minutes).

Relating the information to something that you already know or understand will assist you in filing or storing the information for easy retrieval. Relating the appearance of the African zebra to the American horse can help you remember what the zebra looks like. You may not know what the building in Katherine's story looked like, but try to see her in front of a building on *your campus*. All of these relationships increase retention.

Repeating the information out loud to yourself or to a study partner facilitates its transfer to long-term memory. Some people have to hear information many times before they can commit it to long-term memory. Memory experts agree that repetition is one of the *strongest* tools to increase the retention of material.

Reviewing the information is another means of repetition. The more you see and use the information, the easier it will be to remember it when the time comes. As you review, try to remember the main points of the information.

Walter Pauk, educator and inventor of the Cornell note-taking method, found in a study that people reading a textbook chapter forgot 81% of what they had read after 28 days (Pauk, 2001). With this in mind, you might want to review the material in your texts on a regular basis. Reviewing is a method of repetition and of keeping information fresh.

Remembering Katherine

Without looking back, answer the following questions about Katherine. Use your visualization and concentration skills to recall the information.

1. What was the name of the biology building? _____

2. Did she see the shadow before or after she saw the two people behind her? _____

3. What were the two people behind her doing? _____

4. What was the name of the arts building? _____

5. Why did she cross the street? _____

6. How far ahead of her was the group of students? _____

7. When she saw the group of students in front of her, how far was she from her residence? _____

8. What was Katherine's friend's name? _____

WHAT HELPS? WHAT HURTS?

Attending to Your Memory

For any part of the body, there are things that help you and hurt you. Your memory is no different. Just as your body will begin to fail you without proper attention, exercise, and nutrition, if neglected or mistreated, your memory will do the same. Consider the following things that can help or hinder your memory.

Memory Helpers
- Proper sleep
- Proper nutrition/diet
- Exercise
- Mental exercises such as crossword puzzles, brain teasers, name games
- A positive mind-set
- The proper environment
- Scheduled study breaks
- Repetition and visualization

Memory Hindrances
- Internal and external distractions
- Alcohol
- Drugs
- Stress
- Closed-mindedness (tuning out things you don't like)
- Inability to distinguish important facts from unimportant facts

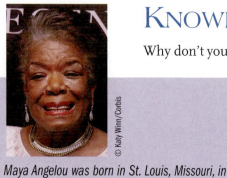

© Katy Winn/Corbis

DID YOU KNOW?

Maya Angelou was born in St. Louis, Missouri, in 1928. As a young girl, she was raped by her mother's boyfriend and did not speak again for four years. By the time she was in her twenties she had been a cook, streetcar conductor, cocktail waitress, dancer, madam, high school dropout, and an unwed mother.

Today, Dr. Angelou is a world-renowned poet, civil rights activist, historian, screenwriter, and director. She is only the second poet in history to write and deliver an original poem at a presidential inauguration (Clinton).

She has won three Grammy awards in the spoken word category and has been nominated twice for Broadway's prestigious Tony award.

KNOWING VERSUS MEMORIZING

Why don't you forget your name? Why don't you forget your address? The answer is that you *know* that information. You *own* it. It belongs to you. You've used it often enough and repeated it often enough that it is highly unlikely that you will ever forget it. Conversely, why can't you remember the details of Erickson's stages of development or Maslow's hierarchy of basic needs or Darwin's theory of evolution? Most likely because you memorized it and never "owned" it.

If you think back to what you can and can't remember, memorization plays a great role. Rote memory is when you literally memorize something and days later it is gone. You memorized it because you needed it for something like a test or a discussion, but it was not important enough to you to know it for life.

Knowing something means that you have made a personal commitment to make this information a part of your life. For example, if you needed to remember the name Stephen and his phone number of 925-6813, the likelihood of your remembering this depends on *attitude*. Do you need to recall this information because he is in your study group and you might need to call him, or because he is the caregiver for your infant daughter while you are in class? How badly you need that name and number will determine the commitment level that you make to just *memorizing* it (and maybe forgetting it) or *knowing* it (and making it a part of your life).

Think about your study habits for a moment. When you are reading your chapter, listening in class, or studying at home, what is your commitment level? How much energy, brainpower, zeal, and fervor do you put into it? Again, it will depend on how you perceive the value of that information.

To *own* knowledge, you have to work from many angles, and Bloom's Taxonomy can help you do that. After you have read a chapter, visualized the information, related it to something you already know, and reviewed it for accuracy, ask yourself a few questions. These questions can help you *know* the information, thus helping you transfer it to long-term memory and *lifelong ownership*.

Questions such as these can help you move from simple memorization to ownership of the material:

▶ Can I relate x to y?

▶ Can I illustrate how x does y?

▶ Can I compare and contrast x to y?

▶ Can I apply x to y in the real world?

▶ Can I distinguish x from y?

▶ Can I define, identify, name, and describe x?

▶ Can I solve the problem of x?

▶ Can I modify or rearrange x to make it work with y?

▶ Can I support the theory of x and y?

▶ Can I defend my knowledge of x or y?

By asking questions from Bloom's Taxonomy, you can begin to own that information.

Consider the following picture. Study it carefully and completely. Look at everything in the picture from top to bottom, left to right.

© Sonya Etchison—FOTOLIA

Now, look at the picture again, paying close attention to the areas marked by the arrows.

Notice the number of people on the trampoline

Notice the storage building

Notice the color of the protective padding

Notice the green foliage

Notice the utility meter

Now, *cover the pictures* and answer the following questions:

1. How many people are on the trampoline? _____

2. What color is the protective padding? _____

3. What is the season of the year based on the foliage color? _____

4. What colors are used on the storage building? _____

5. Is there one utility meter or two? _____

6. How many children are in the air? _____

7. Are the children all male, all female, or mixed? _____

8. How many people are wearing striped shirts? _____

9. What type of fence surrounds the house? _____

10. What colors are used on the house? _____

11. Is the house made of one material or more? _____

12. What colors are the flowers on the bush? _____

Could you answer all the questions without looking? The purpose of this exercise is to help you understand the real difference between casually looking at something and *really* looking at something. To truly know something, you have to go beyond what is given. You have to look at and examine more than you are told or more than what is pointed out for you. In order to own information, you have to be totally committed to examining every detail, every inch, and every angle of it. You will need to practice and master the technique of "going beyond."

READY, SET, GO!

Memory and Studying

All it takes is a positive attitude and an open mind. Next, you'll learn about three methods of studying that you can use to put yourself in charge of the material. The following box provides a brief summary of these methods and they are discussed in more detail below.

Three Studying Strategies

SQ3R METHOD	MNEMONICS	COOPERATIVE LEARNING
Best used for scanning and reading textbooks	Can be used when studying lecture or text notes	Can be used when studying in groups for tests, projects, note sharing, and analysis
Scan	Jingles/rhymes	Questioning
Question	Sentences	Comparing
Read	Words	Drilling
Recite	Story lines	Brainstorming
Review	Acronyms	Sharing
	Pegs	Mapping

The SQ3R Method

You were introduced to this method in Chapter 5. This method can help you commit material to memory. As a quick review, here's how to use SQ3R:

▶ Scan the chapter: headings, photos, quotes, indentions, boldfaced words, and so on.

▶ Write questions from headings: use *who, what, when, where, why, how.*

▶ Read the chapter: look up unfamiliar words, highlight important sections, take notes while reading, paraphrase the information.

▶ Recite the information: close the text and determine if you can "tell the story" of the chapter.

▶ Review the chapter: return to the chapter often and look over the information.

Using SQ3R as a study method can help you increase your understanding of the material and commit the information to long-term memory.

Mnemonic Devices

Mnemonic, pronounced (ni-mōn-ik), devices are memory tricks or techniques that assist you in putting information into your long-term memory and pulling it out when you need it. I recently gave a test on the basic principles of public speaking. A student asked if she had to know the parts of the communication process in order. When I replied that she should be able to recall them in

> The illiterate of the 21st century will not be those who cannot read and write, but those who cannot learn, unlearn, and relearn.
>
> —Alvin Toffler

order, she became nervous and said that she had not learned them in order. Another student overheard the conversation and said, "Some men can read backward fast." The first student asked, "What do you mean by that?" I laughed and said that the mnemonic was great! The student had created a sentence to remember **s**ource, **m**essage, **c**hannel, **r**eceiver, **b**arriers, and **f**eedback. The relationship worked like this:

Some	=	Source
Men	=	Message
Can	=	Channel
Read	=	Receiver
Backward	=	Barriers
Fast	=	Feedback

This is a perfect example of how using memory tricks can help you retrieve information easily.

The following types of mnemonic devices may help you with your long-term memory.

Jingles/Rhymes. You can make up rhymes, songs, poems, or sayings to assist in remembering information; for example, "Columbus sailed the ocean blue in fourteen hundred and ninety-two."

As a child, you learned many things through jingles and rhymes. You probably learned your ABCs through a song pattern, as well as your numbers. If you think about it, you can still sing your ABCs, and maybe your numbers through the "Ten Little Indians" song. You could probably sing every word to the opening of *The Brady Bunch* or *Gilligan's Island* because of the continual reruns on TV. Jingles and rhymes have a strong and lasting impact on our memory—especially when repetition is involved.

Sentences. You can make up sentences such as "Some men can read backward fast" to help remember information. Another example is "Please excuse my dear Aunt Sally," which corresponds to the order of mathematical operations: parentheses, exponents, multiplication, division, addition, and subtraction.

Here are sentences for other academic areas:

1. *My Very Elderly Mother Just Sat Up Nights.* This is a sentence mnemonic for the eight planets in order from the sun: Mercury, Venus, Earth, Mars, Jupiter, Saturn, Uranus, Neptune.

2. *Every Good Bird Does Fly* is a sentence mnemonic for the line notes in the treble clef in music.

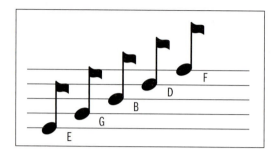

3. *Some Men Help Each Other* is a sentence mnemonic for the Great Lakes from west to east: Superior, Michigan, Huron, Erie, Ontario.

Words. You can create words. For example, the name *Roy G. Biv* may help you to remember the colors of the rainbow: *r*ed, *o*range, *y*ellow, *g*reen, *b*lue, *i*ndigo, and *v*iolet. Here are two other word mnemonics:

1. *HOMES* is a word for the Great Lakes in no particular order: *H*uron, *O*ntario, *M*ichigan, *E*rie, *S*uperior.

2. *FACE* is a word mnemonic for the space notes in the treble clef.

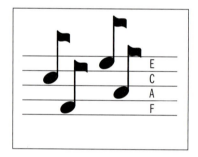

Story Lines. If you find it easier to remember stories than raw information, you may want to process the information into a story that you can tell. Weave the data and facts into a creative story that can be easily retrieved from your long-term memory. This technique is especially beneficial if your professor gives essay exams, because the "story" that you remember can be what was actually told in class.

Acronyms. An acronym is a word that is formed from the first letters of other words. You may see reruns for the famed TV show *M*A*S*H*. This is an acronym for Mobile Army Surgical Hospital. If you scuba dive, you know that *SCUBA* is an acronym for Self-Contained Underwater Breathing Apparatus. Other common acronyms include the following:

NASA (National Aeronautics and Space Administration)

NASCAR (National Association for Stock Car Auto Racing)

NASDAQ (National Association of Securities Dealers Automated Quotation)

NATO (North Atlantic Treaty Organization)

BART (Bay Area Rapid Transit)

Pegging. The peg system uses association, visualization, and attachment for remembering. With this system, you "attach" what you want to remember to something that is already familiar to you. This is a visual means of remembering lists, sequences, and even categories of information.

Most peg systems use numbers and rhyming words to correspond:

1	= sun	6 =	sticks
2	= shoe	7 =	heaven
3	= bee	8 =	gate
4	= shore	9 =	fine
5	= alive	10 =	pen

To attach information to the number, you visually attach a word (such as sun, shoe, bee, shore) to the word you want to remember. For example, if you wanted to remember a shopping list that included ice cream, rice, Ajax, milk, water, and cookies, this might be your plan:

You see ice cream melting in the *sun*.

You see rice filling a *shoe*.

You see Ajax sprinkled on a *bee*.

You see milk rushing to the *shore*.

You see water keeping you *alive* on a deserted island.

You see cookies being offered to you on a *stick* (like a s'more).

Cooperative Learning

There is strength in numbers. Many times, groups of people can accomplish what a single individual cannot. This is the idea behind cooperative learning. Cooperative learning can benefit you because you have pulled together a group of people who have your same interests and goals: to pass the course.

Here are some tips for forming an effective cooperative study group:

▶ Limit the group size to five to seven people.

▶ Search for students who participate in class.

▶ Include people who take notes in class.

▶ Include people who ask questions in class.

▶ Include people who will work diligently.

▶ Include people who do their share for the group.

▶ Invite people who are doing well in a specific area; they may not attend every meeting, but they may be of assistance periodically.

Have you ever studied with a group of people? What were some of the benefits that you experienced? What are some advantages over studying alone?

© BananaStock Ltd.

Once the group is formed, you can engage in several different activities to learn, share, and reinforce information.

▶ **Questioning.** With this technique, group members bring several questions to the session. These may be predicted exam questions, questions about methods or formulas, or questions that the member was not able to answer individually.

> **W**hen you stop learning, stop listening, stop looking and asking questions, always new questions, then it is time to die.
>
> —Lillian Smith

- **Comparing.** The study group is a good place to compare notes taken in class or from the text.

- **Drilling.** This technique assists you with long-term memory development. Repetition is an important step in transferring information to long-term memory.

- **Brainstorming.** During each session, members can use this technique (discussed in detail in the chapter on critical thinking) to predict exam questions, review information, and develop topic ideas for research, projects, future study sessions, and papers.

- **Sharing.** The study group is a time when you can give and receive. At the beginning or end of each session, students in the group can share the most important aspect of the lecture or readings.

- **Mapping.** This technique can be used in a variety of ways. It is similar to the mapping system discussed in the note-taking chapter. On a board or large sheet of paper, one member writes a word, idea, or concept in the center. The next student adds information, thus creating a map or diagram of information and related facts. This can help the group make connections and associations and assist members in identifying where gaps in knowledge exist.

A Quick Reference Guide for Studying Math and Science
© *Robert M. Sherfield, 2005*

Before Class

- *Never* take a math or science course (or any course for that matter) for which you are not prepared. If you test into, or think you need, a basic, remedial, or transitional class, *take it!* Look at it as a chance to start over with new hope and knowledge.

- *Understand* that most math and science classes build on previous knowledge. If you begin the class with a weak background, you must work very hard to learn missed information.

- *Avoid* taking math or science classes during "short" terms if possible. The more time you spend with the material, the better.

- *Know* your own learning style. If you're visual, use colors, charts, and photos. If you're auditory, practice your listening skills. If you're tactile, work to create situations where you can "act out" or touch the material.

- *Prepare* yourself *before class* by reading the chapter, *even* if you don't understand all of it. Read through the material and write down questions about material you did not understand.

- *Scan* all of the introductory and summation materials provided in the text or study guides.

- *Join* a study group, and if there is no group, start one. Cooperative learning teams can be life savers.

- *Seek* tutorial assistance on campus from the first day. Don't wait until you get behind.

During Class

- *Come to every* class, study group, or lab.

- *Control* your own anger and frustration. The past is the past and you can't change any part of it—but you can change *your* future. Learn to make your negative self-talker "be quiet"!

CHEF ODETTE SMITH-RANSOME
Hospitality Instructor, The Art Institute of Pittsburgh
Pittsburgh, PA

At the age of 15, I found myself constantly in conflict with my mother until one day I stood before her as she held a gun to my head. It was at that moment I knew I had to leave my parents' home not just for my emotional well-being, but for my actual life and survival. My father was a good man, but he did not understand the entire situation with my mother's alcohol and diet pill addiction and he could do little to smooth out the situation with my mother and me. To complicate matters even more, my brother had just returned home from fighting in Vietnam and everyone was trying to adjust. It was a horrible time in the house where my ancestors had lived for over 100 years. So I packed my clothes, dropped out of the tenth grade, and ran away over 1,000 miles to Charleston, South Carolina.

My first job was as a waitress. I worked in that job for over three years realizing more every day that I was not using my talents and that without an education, I was doomed to work for minimum wage for the rest of my life. During this time, I had met a friend in Charleston who was in the Navy. When he was released, he offered to take me back to Pittsburgh. I agreed and upon my return, I went to work in the kitchen of a family-owned restaurant. They began to take an interest in me and made me feel proud of my work. I decided to get my GED and determine what road to take that would allow me to use my culinary talents and help others at the same time.

I began my associate's degree, which required that students complete an apprenticeship. We worked 40 hours per week, Monday through Thursday, under the direction of a master chef and we were in class eight hours a day on Friday. My apprenticeship was at the Hyatt Regency in Pittsburgh. In order to obtain your degree, you had to pass the apprenticeship, all of the classes, and a bank of tests that proved your proficiency in a variety of areas. If you failed one part of the tests, you could not get your degree. Proudly, I passed every test, every class, and my apprenticeship.

My first professional job came to me upon the recommendation of a friend. I interviewed and was hired to become the private chef for the chancellor of the University of Pittsburgh. I loved the job and it afforded me the opportunity to get my bachelor's degree. I juggled a full-time job, a two-year-old child, and a full load of classes. As I neared the end of my degree, I was offered a fellowship at the University of Pittsburgh that trained people how to teach students with special needs. I graduated cum laude and began teaching and working at Connelley Academy with people who had cerebral palsy. I loved the work and that position solidified my desire to work with adults.

From there I taught at the Good Will Training Center and later at the Pittsburgh Job Corps where my culinary team won a major national competition. Today, I am an instructor at The Art Institute® of Pittsburgh helping others reach their dreams of working in the hospitality industry. In 2005, I was named Culinary Educator of the Year by the American Culinary Federation®. I try to let my life and my struggles serve as a light for students who have faced adversity and may have felt that their past was going to determine their future. My advice to my students—and to you—is this: *Never* let anyone tell you that you can't do it, that you're not able to do it, that you don't have the means to do it, or that you'll never succeed. *You* set your own course in life and *you* determine the direction of your future.

- *Ask* questions. *Ask* questions. *Ask* questions. *Ask* questions . . . and be specific in your questioning. Don't just say, "I don't understand that." Say, "I don't understand why $f(x + h)$ doesn't equal $f(x) + f(h)$." Or, "I don't understand the difference between 'algia' and 'dynia.' Why are two different words used for pain?"

- *Slow down* and read the material carefully.

- *Find* the formulas and write them down on note cards.

- *Write* down the explanatory remarks made by the instructor:

  How you get from one step to the next

  How this problem differs from other problems

  Why you need to use formula x instead of formula y

  Why any steps were combined, or why not

- *Try* to learn from a *general to specific* end. That is, try to get a feeling of the overall goal of the material before you hone in on smaller problems.

- *Write down* any theorem, formula, or technique that the instructor puts on the board, overhead, or PowerPoint.

- *Leave* a space in your notes for any material you missed or did not understand. This will help you keep your notes organized when you go back after class and add the explanation.

- *Bring* Post-it® Notes, strips of paper, or bookmarks to class with you so that you can "tag" pages with important information and concepts.

After Class

- *Visit* your instructor's office (make an appointment to visit during office hours).

- *Fill in* the information missing in your notes by reviewing the text, going to your study group, or getting clarification from your instructor.

- *Practice* the problems in your text or study guide and then practice them again, and again, and again until they become second nature. Much of math and science is learned by *doing* . . . so *do* . . . and then *do* again.

- *Apply* what you learned in class or lab. Find a way to make it "speak" to your life in a practical way.

- *Continually* review all of the theorems, formulas, concepts, and terms from each chapter.

- When doing practice tests, *pretend* that you are in an actual test and adhere to the timelines, rules, and policies of your instructor. This helps replicate the actual testing situation.

Before the Test

- *Ask* questions that will reduce your anxiety:

  What is the point value of each question?

  How many questions will be on the test?

  Will the questions be multiple choice (and so forth)?

  What materials do I need to bring to class?

  Will I be allowed to use a calculator or any other technology?

  Is there a time limit on the test?

  What is the overall grade value of the test?

- *Make* every effort to attend any study or review sessions offered by the instructor or your peers.

During Tests

▶ *Read* the directions carefully.

▶ *Quickly* glance over the test to determine the number of questions and the degree of difficulty in relation to the time you have to complete the test.

▶ *Work* by the clock. If you have 60 minutes to take the test and 120 questions, this means you have about 30 seconds per question.

▶ *Begin* by working the problems that are easiest or most familiar to you.

▶ *Read* the questions on the test carefully and *more* than once.

▶ *Determine* which formulas you will need to use.

▶ *Decide* how you want to solve the problem.

▶ *Check* your work by using multiple solving techniques. (For example, if the problem is division, can it be checked with multiplication? This is called opposite operations.)

▶ *Draw* pictures if you encounter word problems. Visualization is very important.

▶ *Show* all of your work, even if it is not required. This will help the instructor (and you) see what you did correctly or incorrectly.

▶ *Recheck* every answer if you have time.

▶ *Work* backwards if at all possible. This may help answer the question and catch mistakes.

▶ After you've completed the answer, *reread* the question to determine if you did everything the question asked you to do to.

▶ *Never* erase your margin work or mistakes. This wastes time and you may erase something that you need (or worse, something that was correct).

After Tests

▶ *Immediately* after the test, try to determine if the majority of test questions came from classroom notes, your textbook, your study guide, or from your homework. This will help you prepare for the next test.

▶ *Think* about the way you studied for this test and how you could improve your techniques for the next time. Consider the amount of time spent studying for this test.

▶ Once the test is graded, *determine* what caused you to lose the most points: Simple errors? Applying incorrect formulas or theorems? Misunderstanding the questions? Intensified test anxiety? Poor study habits in general?

HAKUNA MATATA

Studying with Small Children in the House

For many college students, finding a place or time to study is the hardest part of studying. Some students live at home with younger siblings; some students have children of their own. If you have young children in the home, you may find the following hints helpful when it comes time to study.

YES YOU CAN !

IDEAS FOR Success

Consider the following strategies when selecting a professor for math or science classes:

▶ Talk to peers who have taken math and science classes and get their advice regarding the most effective professors. Don't think in terms of "easiest professor," but in terms of teaching excellence, fairness, accessibility, and patience.

▶ Ask your advisor to help you find a math/science professor whose teaching style matches your learning style.

▶ Choose a professor who appreciates students' questions during class.

▶ Choose a professor who keeps regular office hours on campus.

▶ Choose a professor who is known for his or her patience.

▶ Choose a professor who holds frequent review and study sessions beyond the classroom.

▶ Choose a professor who works closely with the tutorial center or math labs

▶ Choose a professor who also teaches the lab component of the class.

If you view your studying responsibilities positively, your children will too. Try to separate the time you spend with your family from the time you need to spend on your school work.

© Corbis

Study at school. Your schedule may have you running from work to school, then directly home. Try to squeeze in even as little as half an hour at school for studying, perhaps immediately before or after class. A half hour of pure study time can prove more valuable than five hours at home with constant interruptions.

Create crafts and hobbies. Your children need to be occupied while you study. It may help if you have crafts and hobbies available that they can do while you are involved with studying. Choose projects your children can do by themselves, without your help. Depending on their ages, children can make masks from paper plates, color, create pipe cleaner art or papier-mâché, use modeling clay or dough, or build a block city. Explain to your children that you are studying and that they can use this time to be creative; when everyone is finished, you'll share what you've done with each other.

Study with your children. One of the best ways to instill the value of education in your children is to let them see you participating in your own education. Set aside one or two hours per night when you and your children study. You may be able to study in one place, or you may have separate study areas. If your children know that you are studying and you have explained to them how you value your education, you are killing two birds with one stone: you are able to study, and you are providing a positive role model as your children study with you and watch you.

Rent movies or let your children watch TV. Research has shown that viewing a limited amount of educational television, such as *Sesame Street, Reading Rainbow,* or *Barney and Friends,* can be beneficial for children. If you do not like what is on television, you might consider renting or purchasing age-appropriate educational videos for your children. This can keep them busy while you study, and it can help them learn as well.

Don't just learn something from every experience learn something positive.

—Al Neuharth

Invite your children's friends over. What? That's right. A child who has a friend to play or study with may create less of a distraction for you. Chances are your children would rather be occupied with someone their own age, and you will gain valuable study time.

Hire a sitter or exchange sitting services with another student. Arrange to have a sitter come to your house a couple of times a week. If you have a classmate who also has children at home, you might take turns watching the children for each other. You could each take the children for one day a week, or devise any schedule that suits you both best. Or you could study together and let your children play together while you study, alternating homes.

Ask if your college has an on-site daycare center such as the Boys and Girls Club. Some colleges provide daycare facilities at a reduced cost, and some provide daycare at no charge. It is certainly worth checking out.

Talk to the financial aid office on your campus. In some instances, there will be grants or aid to assist you in finding affordable daycare for your child.

Studying at any time is hard work. It is even harder when you have to attend to a partner, children, family responsibilities, work, and a social life as well. You will have to be creative in order to complete your degree. You are going to have to do things and make sacrifices that you never thought possible. But if you explore the options, plan ahead, and ask questions of other students with children and with responsibilities outside the classroom, you can and will succeed.

WHAT DO YOU MEAN THE TEST IS TOMORROW?

Studying in a Crunch

No study skills textbook will ever advise you to cram. It is simply a dangerous and often futile exercise in desperation. You'll never read the words, "Don't waste your party time studying, *cram* the night before." Cramming is just the opposite of what this whole chapter is about—knowing versus memorizing. Cramming will never help you know; it can only help you memorize a few things for storage in short-term memory. You may spend several hours cramming, and shortly after the test, the information is gone, evaporated, vanished!

But let's be straight about something else. We know that you may have obligations that take numerous hours from your week. This is simply a matter of fact in the 21st century. So, there may be times when time runs out and the only option is to cram. If you find yourself in this spot, consider the following tips and suggestions for cramming. These probably won't get you an A, but they may help you with a few questions.

Depressurize. Just tell yourself up front what you are doing. Don't pretend that cramming is going to save you. Let yourself realize that you are memorizing material for short-term gain and that you won't be able to keep it all. With this admission, your stress will diminish.

Ditch the blame game. You know you're at fault, so accept that and move on. Sitting around bemoaning your fate will not help. Just tell yourself, "I messed up this time; I won't let it happen again."

Know what. When cramming, it is important to know what you're cramming for. If you're cramming for a multiple-choice test, you'll need different types of information than for an essay test. Know the type of test for which you are studying.

Read it quickly. Think about H2 FLIB. This is a mnemonic for read the Headings, Highlight the important words, read the First sentence of every paragraph, read the Last sentence of every paragraph, and read the Indented and Boxed material. This can help you get through the chapter when pinched for time.

Make connections. As you are reading, quickly determine if any of the information has a connection with something else you know. Is there a comparison or contrast? Is there a relationship of any kind? Is there a cause and effect in motion? Can you pinpoint an example to clarify the information? These questions can help you with retention.

Use your syllabus or study guide. If your professor lists questions that you should know (mastery questions) in the syllabus, or if he or she gave you a study sheet, this is the place to start. Answer those questions. If you don't have either, look to see if the text gives study questions at the end of the chapter. Try to answer the questions using the text *and* your lecture notes.

See it. Visualizing the information through mapping, diagrams, photos, drawings, and outlines can help you commit this information to short-term memory.

Repeat! Repeat! Repeat! Repetition is the key to committing information to memory. After you read information from the text or lecture notes, repeat it time and time again. When you think you've got it, write it down, then repeat it again.

Choose wisely. If you're cramming, you can't do it all. Make wise choices about which material you plan to study. This can be driven by your study sheet, your lecture notes, or questions in your syllabus (if they are listed).

One of the most important things to remember about cramming is that this information is going to leave you. Don't rely on it for the next test or the final. You will need to go back, relearn, and truly understand this information to commit it to long-term memory. Good luck!

Think About It
Chapter Reflection

Just as reading is a learned skill, so is memory development. You can improve your memory, but it will take practice, patience, and persistence. By making the decision that "this information is important to me and my life," you've won the battle; for when you make that decision, your studying becomes easier.

Making a commitment to *truly understand* and own the material instead of just memorizing it can help you establish a knowledge base that you never imagined. It can help you retain information that otherwise would have been lost. It can help you amass a powerful vocabulary, and it can help you apply information from one class to another for papers, speeches, reports, and discussions.

- Study your hardest material first.
- Review your classroom and textbook notes frequently.
- Use mnemonics to help remember lists.
- Take small breaks every half hour.
- Study in a brightly lit, cool environment.
- Have a healthy snack.
- Learn the material from many different directions.

Your memory needs constant care and attention. If you provide the proper rest, nutrition, and exercise, it will carry you through your degree (and beyond) with flying colors.

Research shows that you begin learning in the womb and go right on learning until the moment you pass on. Your brain has a capacity for learning that is virtually limitless, which makes every human a potential genius.

—Michael Gelb

Knowledge in Bloom

Utilizes level 4 of the taxonomy

Creating Your Own Learning Mnemonics

Explanation: There are going to be times when you must memorize information first in order to transfer it to long-term memory and eventually "own" it. Following are lists of the cranial nerves (from anatomy/physiology) and factors of production (from business). Using the mnemonic strategies listed, devise "memory tricks" to remember each list. One example is given.

Biology 101
The Cranial Nerves in the Brain

Olfactory	Facial
Optic	Auditory
Oculomotor	Glossopharyngeal
Trochlear	Varus
Trigeminal	Spinal
Abducens	Hypoglossal

Example: Mnemonic: Sentence
"*O*n *O*ld *O*lympus, *T*ommy *T*une *A*nd *F*armer *A*nnie *G*ot *V*ery *S*pecial *H*elp"

Now, you try it.

Mnemonic: Sentence

_____

_____

_____

Mnemonic: Acronym

_____

_____

_____

_____

_____

Mnemonic: Pegging

_____

_____

_____

_____

_____

_____

_____

Small Business Management 101
Factors of Production

Labor

Capital

Entrepreneurs

Physical resources

Information resources

Mnemonic: Sentence

_____

_____

Mnemonic: Acronym

_____

_____

_____

_____

Mnemonic: Pegging

_____

_____

_____

_____

_____

_____

_____

_____

Preparing for Success

Refer to pages 166–167 of this chapter and answer the questions you developed from scanning this chapter's headings. You should also be able to answer the following questions if they were not on your list:

1. What is the difference between short-term and long-term memory? _____

   _____

2. Discuss the five steps in VCR3. _____

   _____

3. How does repetition help? _____

   _____

4. What is H2 FLIB and how can it help you? _____

   _____

9

Assess

A
little knowledge
that performs
is
worth infinitely
more
than a lot of
knowledge
that is idle.

Kahlil Gibran

the big
WHY

Why read and work through this chapter when I already know how to take tests? *Why* will a chapter on test taking help me at work, with my family, and beyond? *Why* is it so important for me to learn how to take a test when college is the only place I'll ever have to take them?

Learning is not attained by chance; it must be attained by diligence.

—Abigail Adams

Yes, tests can be a manipulative tool, but they can also give you a chance to show how much you know. They can seem like cruel treatment by professors, but they can also provide external motivation for learning. Testing is necessary and even useful. You have to be tested to drive a car; to continue in school; to join the armed services; to become a teacher, a lawyer, a doctor, or a nurse; and often to be promoted at work.

In the past, you may have dreaded tests for a variety of reasons, but by preparing for a test and reducing test anxiety, you can become a more confident test taker and put those fears behind you. *This chapter can help you*:

▶ Identify the causes of your test anxiety
▶ Learn to reduce your test anxiety
▶ Learn how to predict test questions for upcoming assessments

▶ Navigate the three types of testing responses
▶ Develop successful strategies for taking essay tests
▶ Develop successful strategies for taking true-false tests
▶ Develop successful strategies for taking matching tests
▶ Develop successful strategies for taking short-answer tests
▶ Develop successful strategies for taking multiple-choice tests
▶ Understand the internal and external ramifications of integrity

Optimism and test taking can exist in harmony. By applying the techniques learned in earlier chapters and utilizing the information in this chapter, test taking can become much less stressful and much more rewarding.

Scan &

Take a few moments and **scan this chapter**. As you scan, **list five questions** you can expect to learn the answers to while reading and studying Chapter 9.

Example:
▶ What is academic integrity? (from page 204)
▶ What are five types of academic dishonesty? (from page 205)

My Questions:

1._____

_____ from page _____

2._____

_____ from page _____

3._____

_____ from page _____

Name: Oscar Bowser, Jr.
Institution: Midlands Technical College, Columbia, SC
Major: Nursing
Age: 55

I am a former Marine, an ex–New York state public safety officer, an ex-correctional officer, and a certified rescue scuba diver. Over the course of my life, there have been very few things that I have feared and not conquered. It may sound strange, but after all of my experiences and life lessons from 55 years, I was afraid of math.

I knew that I wanted to become a professional registered nurse, but I also knew that math was an "enemy" standing in my way. For a few semesters, I would avoid registering for math classes or register and quickly withdraw due to my anxiety over math tests.

One day it dawned on me: I've been tested my whole life—everyone has. I was tested in high school, I was tested to get my driver's license, I was tested for positions in the military, and I was tested at work for promotions. Tests had been a part of my life and I had never really thought of it that way before. Finally, I realized that my fear was not math tests at all. I realized that all of my fear about math tests

the big WHY

. . . from another perspective

and tests in general was this: the lack of knowing. If you study hard and *know the material*, then a test is nothing more than a way to prove what you know. And if you know something, there is no need to fear it.

This chapter on learning how to be a better test taker and reduce test anxiety is going to be very beneficial to you because the earlier you learn to take tests, the more confident you'll become, the more comfortable you'll become, and the better you'll do on all tests in your life. And believe me, you'll have tests the rest of your life.

If there is no way around it, you have to find a way through it. The information in this chapter regarding beating test anxiety, getting proper sleep, and the tips for taking certain types of tests will help you "get through it" with flying colors.

---

4. _____

_____

from page _____

5. _____

_____

from page _____

Question

PS Reminder: At the end of the chapter, come back to this page and answer these questions in your notebook, text margins, or online chapter notes.

THINKING ABOUT TESTING

Your Attitude Makes All the Difference

A student jokes with her professor, "I have five thousand dollars in my savings account and it is yours if you don't make us take the test!" Well, this may be a bit extreme, but many students would do almost anything to get out of taking exams. Some students proudly walk into the classroom on test day relaxed, poised, and optimistic. Others have physical reactions to testing, including nausea, headaches, and blackouts. Those negative reactions may be a result of being underprepared or not knowing how to take an exam.

If you asked the relaxed and poised student why he or she feels so optimistic, the response may be something like the following:

▶ I studied over the past week and feel great about the material.

▶ I'm ready and I know I'm going to do a great job.

▶ I used some helpful study techniques to remember information.

▶ I tested myself at home using the techniques of Bloom's Taxonomy.

▶ I've learned so much in this class.

Conversely, if you asked the student who is pale and about to throw up, the response may be along these lines:

▶ I didn't know what to study.

▶ I just know I'm going to fail this miserable test.

▶ I crammed all night and I can't remember half of what I studied.

▶ I hate this class and the professor. I should have dropped it weeks ago.

▶ When am I ever going to have to use this stuff?

> Optimism is the faith that leads to achievement. Nothing can be done without hope and confidence.
>
> —Helen Keller

A positive or negative attitude can truly mean the difference between success and failure. With an attitude adjustment from negative to positive and some basic preparation, you can overcome a good deal of your anxiety about tests and do well. You can reduce anxiety when you are in control of the situation, and you can gain control by convincing yourself that you can and will be successful. If you think positively and can honestly say that you have done everything possible to prepare for a test, then the results will most likely be positive.

No test is an indication of who you are as a person or a measure of your worth as a human being. No one can be good at all things. You will have areas of strength and weakness. You will spare yourself a great deal of anxiety and frustration if you understand from the start that you may not score 100 on every test. If you expect absolute perfection on everything, you are setting yourself up for great disappointment. Think positively, prepare well, and do your best. No one can ask for more.

To gain a basic understanding of your test anxiety level, complete the following checklist.

If you check off more than five items on this list, you experience test anxiety. If you check off 10 or more, you have severe test anxiety. This chapter will discuss how to reduce test anxiety and look at tests with a more positive attitude.

TEST ANXIETY SCALE

Check the items that apply to you when preparing for a test.

- ☐ I do not sleep well the night before a test.
- ☐ I get sick if I eat anything before a test.
- ☐ I am irritable and hard to be around before a test.
- ☐ I see the test as a measure of my worth as a student.
- ☐ I blank out during the test and am unable to recall information.
- ☐ I worry when other students are still testing and I am finished.
- ☐ I worry when others finish and I am still testing.
- ☐ I am always afraid that I will run out of time.
- ☐ I get frustrated during the test.
- ☐ I have a negative attitude about testing.
- ☐ I think about skipping the test.
- ☐ I always average my grades before a test.
- ☐ My body reacts negatively to testing (sweats, nervousness, butterflies).

Where Are You . . .   AT THIS MOMENT

Before reading any further, take a moment and assess where you are at this moment with your knowledge and application of test-taking strategies and reducing test anxiety. Read each statement carefully and then respond accordingly.

1. I know how to control my nerves and anxiety during a test.   YES | NO

2. I approach most tests with an open mind and optimism.   YES | NO

3. I remember information I've studied even after I've taken the test.   YES | NO

4. I know how to physically prepare myself for a test.   YES | NO

5. I know and use strategies for different kinds of test questions (such as essay, matching, etc.).   YES | NO

6. I ask my professors questions about the test before the actual test day.   YES | NO

7. I read the directions on a test and know how to look for key words and verbs.   YES | NO

8. I look forward to coming to class the day of a test so I can prove what I know.   YES | NO

9. I answer the easiest questions first and come back to the harder ones.   YES | NO

If you answered "Yes" to most of the questions (seven or more), you have a firm grasp on how to be optimistic about a test. You employ different types of strategies to ready yourself for the test; you know how to control test anxiety. *If you answered "No"* to most of the questions, you probably experience a great deal of test anxiety. You probably approach most assessments with a pessimistic attitude. It will be helpful for you to study the techniques in this chapter and to visit your college's testing center for advice on testing.

I Know I Can, I Know I Can, I Know I Can . . .

Reducing Test Anxiety

As you learned in Chapter 4, some stress is a good thing. It is the bad stress (distress) that can cause problems at physical, emotional, and mental levels. Test anxiety can be described as distress. A little bit of nervousness and good stress (eustress) can help you focus, increase your energy level, and keep you sharp. The most powerful stress-reduction strategy that you can use is to *silence your negative self-talk* about the exam or change your self-talk to a positive tone. Consider the following tips for reducing test anxiety during your next test. You will not be able to employ them all, but if you learn and use a few new ones each time, before you know it, you'll be a testing pro!

HELPFUL REMINDERS FOR REDUCING TEST ANXIETY

- ☑ Approach the test with an "I can" attitude.
- ☑ Prepare yourself emotionally for the test, control your self-talk, and be positive.
- ☑ Remind yourself that you studied and that you know the material.
- ☑ Overlearn the material—you can't study too much.
- ☑ Chew gum or eat hard candy during the test if allowed; it may help you relax.
- ☑ Go to bed early. Do not pull an all-nighter before the test.
- ☑ Eat a healthy meal before the test.
- ☑ Arrive early for the test (at least 15 minutes early).
- ☑ Sit back, relax, breathe, and clear your mind if you become nervous.
- ☑ Come to the test with everything you need: pencils, calculator, and other supplies.
- ☑ Read over the entire test first; read all the directions; highlight the directions.
- ☑ Listen to the professor before the test begins.
- ☑ Keep an eye on the clock.
- ☑ Answer what you know first: the questions that are easiest for you.
- ☑ Check your answers, but remember, your first response is usually correct.
- ☑ Find out about the test before it is given; ask the professor what types of questions will be on the test.
- ☑ Find out exactly what the test will cover ahead of time.
- ☑ Ask the professor for a study sheet; you may not get one, but it does not hurt to ask!
- ☑ Know the rules of the test and of the professor.
- ☑ Attend the review session if one is offered.
- ☑ Know what grade value the test holds.
- ☑ Ask about extra credit or bonus questions on the test.
- ☑ When you get the test, jot down any mnemonic you might have developed on the back or at the top of a page.
- ☑ Never look at another student's test or let anyone see your test.

"Now, Calculate the Following Equation Using . . ."

Quizzing Your Professor and Predicting Exam Questions

Several classes before the test is scheduled, *quiz your professor* about the logistics of the test. This information can help you study more effectively and eliminate the anxiety

Strategies for True-False Questions

True-false tests ask if a statement is true or not. True-false questions can be some of the trickiest questions ever developed. Some students like them; some hate them. There is a 50/50 chance of answering correctly, but you can use the following strategies to increase your odds on true-false tests:

► Read each statement carefully.

► Watch for key words in each statement; for example, negatives.

► Read each statement for double negatives, such as "not untruthful."

► Pay attention to words that may indicate that a statement is true, such as "some," "few," "many," and "often."

► Pay attention to words that may indicate that a statement is false, such as "never," "all," "every," and "only."

► Remember that if any part of a statement is false, the entire statement is false.

► Answer every question unless there is a penalty for guessing.

Sample Test #2

Place "T" for true or "F" for false beside each statement.

NOTE-TAKING SKILLS

1. _____ Note taking creates a history of your course content.
2. _____ "Most importantly" is not a key phrase.
3. _____ You should always write down everything the professor says.
4. _____ You should never ask questions in class.
5. _____ The L-STAR system is a way of studying.
6. _____ W/O is not a piece of shorthand.
7. _____ You should use 4-by-6-inch paper to take classroom notes.
8. _____ The outline technique is best used with lecture notes.
9. _____ The Cornell method should never be used with textbook notes.
10. _____ The mapping system is done with a series of circles.

Strategies for Multiple-Choice Questions

Many college professors give multiple-choice tests because they are easy to grade and provide quick, precise responses. A multiple-choice question asks you to choose from among two to five answers to complete a sentence. Some strategies for increasing your success in answering multiple-choice questions are the following:

► Read the question and try to answer it before you read the answers provided.

► Look for similar answers; one of them is usually the correct response.

► Recognize that answers containing extreme modifiers, such as *always, every,* and *never,* are usually wrong.

► Cross off answers that you know are incorrect.

► Read all the options before selecting your answer. Even if you believe that A is the correct response, read them all.

► Recognize that when the answers are all numbers, the highest and lowest numbers are usually incorrect.

▶ Recognize that a joke is usually wrong.

▶ Understand that the most inclusive answer is often correct.

▶ Understand that the longest answer is often correct.

▶ If you cannot answer a question, move on to the next one and continue through the test; another question may trigger the answer you missed.

▶ Make an educated guess if you must.

▶ Answer every question unless there is a penalty for guessing.

Sample Test #3

Directions: Read each statement and select the best response from the answers given below.

STUDY SKILLS

1. Which statement is true according to the 2000 Census?
   a. Men earn more than women.
   b. Women earn more than men.
   c. People with a bachelor's degree earn the most money of any education level.
   d. Males and females earn just about the same amount of money.
2. To calculate a GPA, you would:
   a. divide quality points by the number of semester hours.
   b. multiply total points by quality points.
   c. divide total points by the number of semester hours.
   d. multiply the quality points by the total points.
3. To be an effective priority manager, you have to:
   a. be very structured and organized.
   b. be very unstructured and disorganized.
   c. be mildly structured and organized.
   d. know what type of person you are and work from that point.
4. Objective listening is:
   a. judging the speaker and not the message.
   b. listening with an open mind.
   c. mentally arguing with the speaker so you can formulate questions.
   d. listening using the elements of the Korean verb "to listen."

Travel the path of integrity without looking back; for there is never a wrong time to do the right thing.

—Anonymous

Strategies for Short-Answer Questions

Short-answer questions, also called fill-in-the-blanks, ask you to supply the answer yourself instead of selecting it from a list. Although "short answer" sounds easy, these questions are often very difficult. Short-answer questions require you to draw from your long-term memory. The following hints can help you answer this type of question successfully:

▶ Read each question and be sure that you know what is being asked.

▶ Be brief in your response.

▶ Give the same number of answers as there are blanks; for example, _____ and _____ would require two answers.

▶ Never assume that the length of the blank has anything to do with the length of the answer.

▶ Remember that your initial response is usually correct.

▶ Pay close attention to the word immediately preceding the blank; if the word is "an," give a response that begins with a vowel (a, e, i, o, u).

▶ Look for key words in the sentence that may trigger a response.

Sample Test #4

Directions: Fill in the blanks with the correct response. Write clearly.

LISTENING SKILLS

1. Listening is a _____ act. We choose to do it.
2. The three elements of listening involve listening objectively, _____ and _____.
3. _____ is the same as listening with an open mind.
4. Prejudging is an _____ to listening.
5. Leaning forward, giving eye contact, being patient, and leaving your emotions at home are characteristics of _____ listeners.

Strategies for Essay Questions

Most students look at essay questions with dismay because they take more time. Yet essay tests can be some of the easiest tests to take because they give you a chance to show what you really know. An essay question requires you to supply the information. If you have studied, you will find that once you begin to answer an essay question, your answer will flow easily. Some tips for answering essay questions are the following:

▶ More is not always better; sometimes more is just more. Try to be as concise and informative as possible. A professor would rather see one page of excellent material than five pages of fluff.

▶ Pay close attention to the action word used in the question and respond with the appropriate type of answer. Key words used in questions include the following:

discuss	illustrate	enumerate	describe
compare	define	relate	list
contrast	summarize	analyze	explain
trace	evaluate	critique	interpret
diagram	argue	justify	prove

▶ Write a thesis statement for each answer.

▶ Outline your thoughts before you begin to write.

▶ Watch your spelling, grammar, and punctuation.

▶ Use details, such as times, dates, places, and proper names where appropriate.

▶ Be sure to answer all parts of the question; some discussion questions have more than one part.

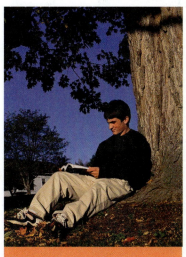

Using proper study techniques and remembering testing tips can increase your chances of success on most tests.

© Corbis

▶ Summarize your main ideas near the end of your answer.

▶ Write neatly.

▶ Proofread your answer.

Sample Test #5

Directions: Answer each question completely. Use a separate paper if you wish.

STUDY SKILLS

1. Identify and discuss two examples of mnemonics.
2. Justify why it is important to use the SQ3R method when reading.
3. Draw and illustrate each level of Bloom's Taxonomy, giving a brief definition of each level.
4. Compare an effective study environment with an ineffective study environment.

Learning how to take a test and learning how to reduce your anxiety are two of the most important gifts you can give yourself as a student. Although tips and hints may help you, don't forget that there is no substitute for studying and knowing the material.

ACADEMIC AND PERSONAL INTEGRITY

Making the Right Decisions

As a college student, you will be faced with temptations that require you to make hard choices. You have probably already been forced to make decisions based on ethics. Do I cheat and make a higher grade so I can compete with top students? Will cheating help me earn higher grades so I get a better job? Do I copy this paper from the Internet? Who will know? No one said specifically that copying from the Internet is wrong. Why shouldn't I do this if everybody else is copying? Why shouldn't I buy one of the term papers that is floating around my fraternity? What if I lose my scholarship? What if I just copy someone's homework and not cheat on a test? What if I lie to the instructor and say I was sick so I can get more time for a test for which I am not prepared? What if I let someone look on my paper during a test; I'm not cheating, am I? These are all ethical questions that require you to use your personal integrity to make the right decision.

Integrity is purely and simply doing what you think is right. It's about understanding who you are as a person and making decisions about what is right and wrong according to your personal code of ethics. What will you do when nobody knows but you? It is also making decisions about what is right and wrong according to your institution's standards. As a college student, you will see many people do things that you think are not right. You have to decide what is right for you and follow your values no matter what others may be doing. Just because "everyone is doing it" doesn't make it right, and certainly it doesn't make it right for you.

Your college years should refine your character and hopefully help you assess and evaluate your value system. You will no doubt find some of your views and values changing over the next few years. One of your challenges is to ensure that you are improving your character rather than compromising who you are and hope to become. You are building yourself today for the long haul—not for a few short years!

Listen to Your Conscience

What does your conscience tell you? If it nags at you about an action you are about to take, don't do it! Making ethical decisions can be as simple as listening to your conscience. If you have a nagging, recurring feeling that what you are doing is not right, it probably isn't. If you can't sleep at night because you have done something that you cannot respect, chances are you need to reflect on your decisions. Real integrity is doing the right thing when nobody knows but you, or refraining when you could probably get away with copying a test question or committing an infraction of the rules. Your personal code of ethics is based on your value system, the standards and ideals that you use to make tough decisions.

Even if you cheat and don't get caught, you lose. You lose respect for yourself, your self-esteem is likely to decline, and you cheat yourself of the knowledge for which you are paying. You also lose because you damage your character and the person you hope to become. Cheating can cause you to feel guilty and stressed because you are afraid that someone might find out.

Eventually, cheating will become a crutch that you lean on in order to pass and make good grades, and it will become easy to decide to cheat instead of working and earning your grades. The habit of cheating is likely to carry over into the workplace if you have embraced it as a way of life in college. Gradually, day by day, you are building the person you want to become. Ultimately, the person who is harmed the most by cheating is the one who does it. In some shape or fashion, cheating will always come back to haunt you. You, personally, will pay the price.

Academic integrity says a lot about who you are and what you believe in. Following a code of ethics is important for another reason as well. If you are honest, work hard, and do your own work, you will most likely get a good education. Your future depends on what you are learning today!

YES YOU CAN !

IDEAS FOR *Success*

Ask yourself the following "Top 10" questions about your personal ethics and integrity:

1. If your family knew about your decision, would they be proud of you?
2. If this action were to appear in the headlines of the newspaper tomorrow morning, would you feel proud?
3. Is it the right thing to do?
4. Have you made a carefully thought out, responsible, mature decision regardless of what everyone else is doing?
5. Does your decision make you proud of who you are as a person?
6. Is your decision fair to all people concerned?
7. How would you feel about being expelled from school for this action?
8. Is it worth failing the course if the professor learns you cheated?
9. Is the action you are taking worth the risk and the stress?
10. If other people found out about your actions, could you defend what you did?

What Do You Need to Know about Academic Misconduct?

It is important to know what constitutes dishonesty in an academic setting. Following is a list of offenses that most colleges consider academic misconduct.

▶ Looking on another person's test paper for answers.

▶ Giving another student answers on tests, homework, or lab projects.

▶ Using any kind of "cheat sheets" on a test or project.

▶ Using a computer, calculator, dictionary, or notes when not approved.

▶ Discussing exam questions with students who are taking the same class at another time.

- ▶ Plagiarism or using the words or works of others without giving proper credit. This includes the Internet!
- ▶ Stealing another student's class notes.
- ▶ Using an annotated instructor's edition of a text.
- ▶ Having tutors do your homework for you.
- ▶ Submitting the same paper for more than one class during any semester.
- ▶ Copying files from a lab computer or borrowing someone else's disk with the work on it.
- ▶ Bribing a student for answers or academic work such as papers or projects.
- ▶ Buying or acquiring papers from individuals or the Internet.
- ▶ Assisting others with dishonest acts.
- ▶ Lying about reasons you missed a test or a class.

Think About It
Chapter Reflection

Learning to deal with test anxiety and get your fears under control early in your college years can lead to greater success as you move through your college career. With the right kinds of practice, you can become much more adept at test taking and can greatly reduce your stress.

Another important part of this chapter deals with academic and personal integrity. You can't control anyone's behavior but your own. Your challenge is to focus on developing excellent test-taking abilities and study habits while earning the best grades you can. When you have done this, you can look in the mirror and be proud of the person you see without having to be ashamed of your character or having to worry about being caught cheating. When taking your next test, remember these points:

- ▶ *Ask* questions of the professor before the test.
- ▶ Maintain your personal *integrity*.
- ▶ *Never* use drugs or alcohol to get through a test.
- ▶ Glance at the entire test *before* beginning.
- ▶ *Check* punctuation, spelling, and grammar on essay answers.
- ▶ Write your *name* on every test page.
- ▶ *Ignore* the pace of your classmates.
- ▶ Answer *all* questions if there is no penalty for guessing.
- ▶ Watch *time* limits.
- ▶ Think *positively*.
- ▶ Write *clearly*.

As you study and learn to enter your chosen profession, remember this: You are building your character for the long haul—not just a few short years.

Change occurs, progress is made, and difficulties resolved if people merely do the right thing—and rarely do people *not know* what the right thing is.

—Father Hessburg

Knowledge in Bloom

Utilizes level 5 of the taxnomy

Each chapter-end assessment is based on *Bloom's Taxonomy of Learning.* See the inside front cover for a quick review.

Creating Your Plan for Test Anxiety Reduction

Explanation: Now that you have read and studied this chapter, and no doubt taken a few tests this semester, you have a better understanding of what happens to you physically and mentally during an exam.

The following table lists six of the common physical or mental symptoms of anxiety reported by students while testing.

Process: Beside each symptom, *create a list* of at least three concrete, doable, realistic strategies to overcome this physical or emotional anxiety symptom before or during a testing situation.

SYMPTOM	HOW TO REDUCE IT
Fatigue	1.
	2.
	3.
Frustration	1.
	2.
	3.
Fear	1.
	2.
	3.
Anger	1.
	2.
	3.
Nervousness/Nausea	1.
	2.
	3.
Uncertainty/Doubt	1.
	2.
	3.

Preparing for Success

Refer to pages 192–193 of this chapter and answer the questions you developed from scanning this chapter's headings. You should also be able to answer the following questions if they were not on your list:

1. Why is integrity important to you as a college student? _____

   _____

2. Discuss five ways to reduce text anxiety. _____

   _____

3. Identify and discuss five ways to get a better night's sleep. _____

   _____

4. What are the three types of testing responses? _____

   _____

10

Think

Many people **think** they are thinking when they are merely rearranging their **prejudices.**

William James

the big **WHY**

Why do I need to read a chapter on critical thinking when I'm thinking all the time? *Why* will a chapter on problem solving and thinking logically help me in college, at work, with my family, and beyond? *Why* is information on thinking logically such a big deal?

What we need is not the will to believe but the will to find out.

—Bertrand Russell

You use critical and creative thinking on a daily basis: when you go to the grocery store, when you purchase gasoline, when you choose your TV program at night, when you select classes for your degree, and when you talk with your friends. Critical and creative thinking are major parts of our daily lives. They help us make decisions that will aid our quality of life and make things easier for us. Can you think of a time when you did not use your critical (or creative) thinking skills and life did not turn out as you had hoped? Perhaps it was when you decided to cut class and a major quiz was given that day, or when you engaged in a heated discussion with another person over a topic of great interest to you and you let your emotions overwhelm you. Your ability to think on a critical and creative level will help you greatly as a college student. *This chapter can help you:*

▶ Understand the vast importance of critical thinking
▶ Use emotional restraint to aid in thinking more logically
▶ Analyze information
▶ Ask questions that get at the heart of the matter
▶ Solve problems and conflicts more effectively
▶ Learn the difference between fact and opinion
▶ Think more creatively
▶ Use critical and creative thinking more effectively on a daily basis

Critical thinking can help you defend your positions on difficult issues, research and write better papers and speeches, plan your time more effectively, and do things that others never would have considered.

Scan &

Take a few moments and **scan this chapter**. As you scan, **list five questions** you can expect to learn the answers to while reading and studying Chapter 10.

Example:
▶ Why is emotional restraint important? (from page 217)
▶ What is the difference between fact and opinion? (from page 225)

My Questions:

1. _____
   _____ from page _____

2. _____
   _____ from page _____

3. _____
   _____ from page _____

Name: E. J. Grant
Institution: East Central College, Union, MO
Major: Nuclear engineering
Age: 20

the big WHY

. . . from another perspective

I like seeing "the big picture." Sure, I love the small pieces that make up the big picture, but I enjoy understanding every aspect of how something works, every facet of how something comes together, and every detail of how one thing is related to another thing. To me, this is what critical thinking is all about.

Learning to look at the fine details of a project has helped me in many of my classes, especially math and science. By looking at all of the pieces and then trying to figure out how each one fits into the grand scheme of things, I am better able to understand how things work. This process even helps me when I write papers for English or history or psychology.

By learning to think critically and look at every angle of an issue, I am able to expand my views by looking at things from others' perspectives. I am able to make my papers flow better because I have more information from a variety of sources. I am able to incorporate credible Internet research into papers and speeches, and I am able to know what questions to ask to get at the real problem or the heart of the matter.

Outside the classroom, I have found that my critical thinking skills help me analyze things better and mange my time more effectively. But one of the best things I love about being able to think more openly is that I get to see how my small job plays a role in the bigger picture of the entire company.

This chapter can open so many doors for you as a student and also as a person in the working world. If I had to say what the most important thing has been to me about critical thinking, I would say that it has allowed me to go beyond memorizing information and really begin to understand it. The contents of this chapter can help you do the same.

Question

4. _____

_____

from page _____

5. _____

_____

from page _____

PS **Reminder:** At the end of the chapter, come back to this page and answer these questions in your notebook, text margins, or online chapter notes.

213

THINKING ABOUT THINKING

Same-sex couples should be able to marry and adopt children. Think about that statement for a moment. As a matter of fact, you probably don't even have to think about it. You may already have an opinion about the issue. Do you think that your emotions cloud your thoughts on the issue? Is there a right or wrong side to this debate? What are you thinking right now? More importantly, why are you thinking the way you are right now? What is causing you to believe, feel, or think one way or the other on this issue? What are the facts and/or opinions that have led you to your conclusion?

At this moment, are you basing your thoughts about this issue on emotions or facts, fallacies or truths, data or opinions, interviews or hearsay, reason or misjudgment, fear or empathy? Are your opinions rooted in religion and your home environment or elsewhere?

We purposefully chose a "hot topic" issue to open this chapter because understanding why and how we formulate thoughts and ideas is the main objective of this chapter. This chapter is about believing and disbelieving, seeking, uncovering, debunking myths, and proving the impossible possible. It is about proof, logic, evidence, and developing ideas and opinions based on hard-core facts or credible research. This chapter is about seeking truth and expanding your mind to unimaginable limits. This chapter is about the fundamental aspect of becoming an educated citizen; it is about human thought and reasoning.

Almost any profession you choose to go into will require the ability to think through problems, make decisions, and apply other critical thinking skills.

© Image Source Limited

WHAT IS IT, ANYWAY?

A Working Definition of Critical Thinking

All right, it is your turn. Suppose your best friend asked you why you favored (or did not favor) same-sex marriage. What would your answer be? If you are *for* the issue, would you say that it is justified, necessary, and constitutional? If you are *against* the issue, would you say that it goes against biblical teachings, social norms, and the fabric of our environment?

For those of you who are *for* same-sex marriage, let's say that you believe it to be *constitutional*. For those of you who are *against* same-sex marriage, let's say that you hold the issue to be *blasphemous*.

> Not everything that is faced can be solved, and nothing can be solved until it is faced.
>
> —James Baldwin

Before you go any further, explain to your friend just what constitutional (or blasphemous) really means. Make him or her understand it. Make him or her understand your reason for using that word. Can you do it? You know what you mean, but can you make your friend understand your position? Can you explain in great detail what the word is and how it applies to same-sex marriage? Can you define the word? Can you explain what it implies? Can you give examples of the word as related to the issue at hand? If you had to, could you expand on the issue? Could you support your views with facts instead of opinions? Could you discuss some of the social, cultural, economic, artistic, or political complexities of the issue?

The technique detailed above and developed by Peter Facione (1998) is the best way to define critical thinking. Critical thinking is what you are doing with that word (constitutional or blasphemous) *right this instant.* Critical thinking is searching, plotting, making associations, explaining, analyzing, probing for multiple angles, justifying, scrutinizing, making decisions, solving problems, and investigating. *It is literally thinking about something from many angles.*

Another way to define critical thinking is to consider people who use critical thinking in their daily lives:

- ▶ The doctor who searched deeply enough, ordered the correct tests, and found the cancer that was missed by three other physicians
- ▶ The computer repair technician who found the one tiny circuit problem in your computer
- ▶ The auto repair person who found the faulty wiring in your car
- ▶ The nurse who sensed something was wrong and noticed the error in the medication chart
- ▶ The teacher who finally found a way to teach Johnny to read with pictures
- ▶ The marketing expert who developed the winning campaign for Mountain Dew
- ▶ The student who discovered that reading the material before class made listening easier

These people and their discoveries define critical thinking better than any definition we could provide here.

Critical thinking is about making informed, enlightened, educated, open-minded decisions in college, in relationships, in finances, and in life in general.

Where Are You . . .   AT THIS MOMENT

Before reading any further, take a moment and assess where you are at this moment with your knowledge and application of critical thinking and problem solving. Read each statement carefully and then respond accordingly.

1. I am usually very skeptical about information I get from the TV, radio, or newspaper.   YES   NO

2. I question and scrutinize the facts I get from others.   YES   NO

3. I understand the value of critical thinking beyond the classroom.   YES   NO

4. I know how to tell if a statement is fact or opinion.   YES   NO

5. I know how to control my emotions when I am listening to a controversial issue.   YES   NO

6. I know how to look at an issue from many different angles.   YES   NO

7. I always research both sides of an issue before I make up my mind.   YES   NO

If you answered "Yes" to most of the questions (five or more), you have a clear understanding of how to critically evaluate and scrutinize an issue. You look at multiple sources and you do not take statements at face value. *If you answered "No"* to most of the questions, you tend to believe the mass media and reject researching issues on your own. You may be prone to formulate your opinions and judgments based on one source or opinion only. You may benefit from a course in critical thinking or logic.

WHEN WILL I EVER USE IT?

The Importance of Critical Thinking

Have you ever made a decision that turned out to be a mistake? Have you ever said to yourself, "If only I could go back . . . "? Have you ever regretted actions you took toward a person or situation? Have you ever planned an event or function that went off flawlessly? Have you ever had to make a hard, painful decision that turned out to be the best decision of your life? If the answer to any of these questions is yes, you might be able to trace the consequences back to your thought process at the time of the decision. Let's face it, sometimes good and bad things happen out of luck. More often than not, however, the events in our lives are driven by the thought processes involved when we make the initial decision.

Critical thinking can serve us in many areas as students and citizens in society. As a student, critical thinking can help you focus on issues; gather relevant, accurate information; remember facts; organize thoughts logically; analyze questions and problems; and manage your priorities. It can assist in your problem-solving skills and help you control your emotions so that you can make rational judgments. It can help you produce new knowledge through research and analysis and help you determine the accuracy of printed and spoken words. It can help you detect bias and determine the relevance of arguments and persuasion.

How Critical Thinking Can Help You Beyond the Classroom

THE SITUATION	CRITICAL THINKING CAN HELP YOU DECIDE . . .
Relationships	▶ Whom to date ▶ Whom to trust ▶ In whom you can confide ▶ How seriously involved you should get
Goal Setting	▶ If the goal is realistic ▶ How to develop a plan of action ▶ What resources you need and how to get them
Finances	▶ How to develop a realistic budget ▶ If you should charge or lay away ▶ How much to save to pay tuition and fees ▶ How to search for scholarships
Decision Making	▶ How to approach a difficult decision ▶ How to analyze your options ▶ How the decision will affect your life ▶ If the decision is a solid one
Problem Solving	▶ How to identify the real problem ▶ How to solicit assistance ▶ How serious the problem really is ▶ When to implement the solution
Environmental Issues	▶ Whether to buy an SUV or "green" car ▶ How recycling helps the earth ▶ How you contribute to the warming effect
Civic Duties	▶ For whom to cast your vote ▶ How to get involved in your community ▶ For which organization to volunteer ▶ To which organization to donate money

A PLAN FOR CRITICAL THINKING

Making It Work for You

As you begin to build and expand your critical-thinking skills, consider the steps involved. Critical-thinking skill development involves several aspects.

- ▶ Restraining emotions
- ▶ Looking at things differently
- ▶ Analyzing information
- ▶ Asking questions
- ▶ Solving problems
- ▶ Distinguishing fact from opinion
- ▶ Seeking truth in argument and persuasion

The remainder of this chapter will detail, through explanation, exploration, and exercises, how to build a critical-thinking plan for your academic and personal success.

Step One: Restraining Emotions

Did James Earl Ray really kill Martin Luther King, Jr.? Is there life on other planets? Should gangsta rap be banned from music stores and performance arenas? Should the drinking age be lowered to 18? Should 16-year-olds be allowed to drive a car? Should hate crime laws be abolished? Should evolution be taught in schools? What emotions are you feeling right now? Did you immediately formulate answers to these questions in your mind? Are your emotions driving your thinking process?

Emotions play a vital role in our lives. They help us feel compassion, help others, reach out in times of need, and relate to others. On the other hand, emotions can cause some problems in your critical-thinking process. You do not have to eliminate emotions from your thoughts, but it is crucial that you know when your emotions are clouding an issue.

Consider the following topics:

- ▶ Should drugs and prostitution be legalized?
- ▶ Can the theories of evolution and creationism coexist?
- ▶ Is affirmative action reverse discrimination?
- ▶ Should illegal aliens be given amnesty and made U.S. citizens?
- ▶ Should terminally ill patients have the right to state-assisted and/or privately assisted suicide?

As you read these topics, did you immediately form an opinion? Did old arguments surface? Did you feel your emotions coming into play as you thought about the questions? If you had an immediate answer, it is likely that you allowed some past judgments, opinions, and emotions to enter the decision-making process, unless you have just done a comprehensive, unbiased study of one of these issues. As you discuss these topics in class or with your friends, how do you feel? Do you get angry? Do you find yourself groping for words? Do you find it hard to explain why you hold the opinion that you voice? If so, these are warning signs that you are allowing your emotions to drive your decisions. If we allow our emotions to run rampant (not using restraint) and fail to use research, logic, and evidence (expansive thinking), we will not be able to examine the issues critically or have a logical discussion regarding the statements.

If you feel that your emotions cause you to be less than objective, you might consider the following tips when you are faced with an emotional decision:

► Listen to all sides of the argument or statement before you make a decision or form an opinion.

► Make a conscious effort to identify which emotions are causing you to lose objectivity.

► Do not let your emotions make you withdraw or turn you away from the situation.

► Don't let yourself become engaged in "I'm right, you're wrong" situations.

► Work to understand why others feel their side is valid.

► Physiological reactions, such as increased heart rate and blood pressure and an increase in adrenaline flow, should be recognized as an emotional red flag. If you begin to experience these reactions, relax, take a deep breath, and concentrate on being open-minded.

► Control your negative self-talk or inner voice toward the other person(s) or situation.

► Determine whether your emotions are irrational.

Candid discussions and sometimes brutal honesty are useful and necessary when you are addressing complex or difficult issues. However, be careful not to let emotions take over your objectivity.

© Image 100 Ltd.

In the space provided, develop a step-by-step plan to evaluate one of the controversial topics listed previously. You do not have to answer the question; your task is to *create a plan to look at (research) the topic critically* without emotional interference.

For example: Do violent TV programs and movies cause violent crime? Before you answer yes or no, your first step might be to define violent TV/movies. A second step might be to define violent crime. A third step might be to research the connection between the two. A fourth step might be to evaluate the research objectively, asking the following questions: (1) Where does the research originate: the TV or movie industry, a parental guidance group, or a completely independent agency? (2) How old is the research? (3) For how long a period was the research conducted? This type of questioning does not allow your emotions to rule the outcome.

Select one of the topics from those listed on page 217, or develop your own statement, and devise a plan for critical analysis.

Statement _____

Step 1. _____

Step 2. _____

Step 3. _____

Step 4. _____

Step 5. _____

Bloom Level 2 question

Step Two: Looking at Things Differently

Critical thinking involves looking at an issue from many different angles. It encourages you to dig deeper than you have before; get below the surface; struggle, experiment, and expand. It asks you to look at something from an entirely different angle so that you might develop new insights and understand more about the problem, situation, or question. Thinking on a higher level involves looking at something that you may never have seen before, or something that you may have seen many times, and trying to think about it more critically than before.

As you begin to look "with different eyes," take a moment to complete the following activities. They are provided to encourage you to look at simple, common situations in a new light. Remember, these exercises do not measure intelligence.

Review the following examples of brain teasers and solve the remaining teasers. You will need to break down a few barriers in thought and look at them from a new angle to get them all.

BRAIN TEASERS

Examples: *4 W on a C*   4 Wheels on a Car
                   13 O C   13 Original Colonies

1. *SW and the 7 D* _____
2. *I H a D by MLK* _____
3. *2 P's in a P* _____
4. *HDD (TMRUTC)* _____
5. *3 S to a T* _____
6. *100 P in a D* _____
7. *T no PLH* _____
8. *4 Q in a G* _____
9. *I a SWAA* _____
10. *50 S in TU* _____

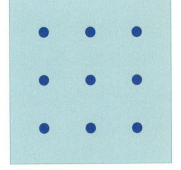

How did you do? Was it hard to look at the situation backward? Most of us are not used to that. As you continue to build your critical-thinking skills, look at the design of nine dots at right. Your mission is to connect all nine dots with four straight lines without removing your pencil or pen from the paper. Do not retrace your lines. Can you do it?

Finally, as you begin to think beyond the obvious, examine the penny shown here. You will see the front and back sides of the penny. Pretend that the world has ended and all traces of civilization are gone. Someone from another planet, who speaks our language, has come to earth and the only thing left from our civilization is one penny. Below, list the things that could be assumed or inferred about our civilization from this one small penny. You should find at least 10.

1. _____   6. _____
2. _____   7. _____
3. _____   8. _____
4. _____   9. _____
5. _____   10. _____

While these activities may seem somewhat trivial, they are provided to help you begin to think about and consider information from a different angle. This is a major step in becoming a critical thinker: looking beyond the obvious, thinking outside the box, examining details, and exploring possibilities.

Step Three: Analyzing Information

Critical thinking goes further than thinking on a different or higher level or using emotional restraint; it also involves analyzing information. To analyze, you break a topic, statement, or problem into parts to understand it more clearly. This is a simple, yet crucial step in critical thinking. An easy way to analyze is to create a chart of the information using right- and left-hand columns. Consider the following example that examines the death penalty topic.

Example

Why should the death penalty be abolished?

It is barbaric.	The United States is the last industrialized nation in the world to use capital punishment. We are in the company of the Congo, Iran, and China.
It is racist.	More African Americans and Hispanics are put to death than Caucasians. The proportion of African American and Hispanic inmates on death row is greater than their proportion of the general population.
It is expensive.	It costs over $3 million to put a person to death, while it costs slightly more than $500,000 to imprison him or her for 40 years.

As you can see, a question properly analyzed prevents you from simply answering with a bland and poor answer such as, "It's good," or "It's bad." It can also prevent you from becoming too emotional because you must rely on facts to support your answer. An analysis forces you to ask *why* it is good or bad, right or wrong, proper or improper.

Now it's your turn. Analyze the following question: *How can an undeclared student take steps to decide on a career?* Hint: The answer can be found in Chapter 15 of *Cornerstone.*

Column A (Answer)   **Column B (Explanation)**

_____   _____

_____   _____

_____   _____

_____   _____

_____   _____

_____   _____

_____   _____

_____   _____

This method can also be used to formulate new information on a subject. If you read a chapter or an article, hear a conversation, or are faced with a problem, you can analyze it by creating questions that need to be answered in Column A and providing the answer in Column B. You may have to use more than one source of information to answer the questions you posed in Column A.

Step Four: Asking Questions

You've asked questions all your life. As a child, you asked your parents, "What's that?" a million times. You probably asked them, "Why do I have to do this?" In later years, you've asked questions of your friends, teachers, strangers, store clerks, and significant others. Questioning is not new to you, but it may be a new technique for exploring, developing, and acquiring new knowledge. Curiosity may have killed the cat, but it was a smart cat when it died! Your curiosity is one of the most important traits you possess. It helps you grow and learn, and it may sometimes cause you to be uncomfortable. That's OK. This section is provided to assist you in learning how to ask questions to promote knowledge, solve problems, foster strong relationships, and critically analyze difficult situations.

Let's start with a simple questioning exercise. If you could meet anyone on earth and ask five questions, who would you meet, why would you meet that person, and what questions would you ask?

I'd like to meet _____

because _____

_____

_____

_____

_____

_____

_____

I'd ask the person:
1. _____
2. _____
3. _____
4. _____
5. _____

Sometimes you want to ask questions of experts or those whose opinions you value to aid your own thinking. Are there questions you have for any of these people?

Asking questions can be fun in many situations. They help us gain insight where we may have limited knowledge. They can also challenge us to look at issues from many different angles. Answering properly posed questions can help us expand our knowledge base.

If you were assigned to write a paper or give a speech on the topic of creationism vs. evolution, what five questions would you definitely want that paper or speech to answer when you were finished? Take some time to think about the issue. Write down at least five questions.

My five questions are:
1. _____
2. _____
3. _____
4. _____
5. _____

Questioning also involves going beyond the obvious. Examine the advertisement shown here. The car dealership has provided some information, but it is not enough to make an educated decision. What other questions would you ask to make sure that you are getting a good deal?

1. _____
2. _____
3. _____
4. _____
5. _____

Step Five: Solving Problems

You face problems every day; some are larger and more difficult than others. You may have transportation problems. You may have child-care problems. You may have academic problems or interpersonal problems. Many people don't know how to solve problems at school, home, or work. They simply let the problem go unaddressed until it is too late to reach a satisfactory solution. There are many ways to address and solve problems. In this section, we will discuss how to identify and narrow the problem, research and develop alternatives, evaluate the alternatives, and solve the problem.

It is important to remember that every problem does have a solution, but the solution may not be what we wanted. It is also imperative to remember the words of Mary Hatwood Futrell, president of the NEA. She states that "finding the right answer is important, of course. But more important is developing the ability to see that problems have multiple solutions, that getting from X to Y demands basic skills and mental agility, imagination, persistence, patience."

> **W**hen I'm getting ready to reason with a man, I spend one-third of my time thinking about myself and what I am going to say—and two-thirds thinking about him and what he is going to say.
>
> —Abraham Lincoln

Identify and narrow the problem. Put your problem in writing. When doing this, be sure to jot down all aspects of the problem, such as why it is a problem, whom it affects, and what type of problem it is. Examine the following situation: You have just failed two tests this week and you are dreadfully behind on an English paper. Now, that's a problem . . . or is it? If you examine and reflect on the problem, you begin to realize that because of your nighttime job, you always get to class late, you are tired and irritable when you get there, and you never have time to study. So the real problem is not that you can't do the work; the problem is that your job is interfering with your study time. Now that you have identified and narrowed the problem, you can begin to work toward a solution.

Research and develop alternatives. A valuable method of gathering ideas, formulating questions, and solving problems is brainstorming. To brainstorm, gather a group of people and ask them to let ideas flow. A brainstorming session allows all thoughts to be heard without any fear of ridicule. You can brainstorm any matter, almost anywhere. You may want to set some guidelines for your sessions, like those on page 224, to make them more productive.

CATHERINE SCHLEIGH
Retail Consultant, Kinkos-FedEx, Inc.
Philadelphia, PA

I don't like to speculate, but I would say that few college students in America have to take a bus two and a half hours each way to attend classes each day. I did. I would also speculate that few college students became the primary caregiver for their mother at the age of seven. I did. I might also speculate that few people feel as lucky, proud, and honored as I do to simply hold their head high and say, "I made it." My name is Catherine Schleigh and despite my past family history and personal struggles, I am a first-generation college graduate and hold a professional position with a major corporation in one of America's most wonderful cities.

Growing up, I had no real family to speak of. My dad left my mom and me when I was young and from the age of seven, I was left to care for my mother who is a diagnosed paranoid schizophrenic. Growing up, I received no help, no support, and no encouragement from her or any member of my family. Often, she would not take her medications (or the medications had been improperly prescribed) and she would be physically, emotionally, and verbally abusive to me. It was hard to watch her talk to herself or invisible people. We lived in a very poor, drug-infested, gang-populated area of Philly and many times, I could not see how I would ever survive.

I managed to complete high school and I began attending Job Corps studying business. From there, I began my college studies majoring in business administration. I had to work very hard and the adjustment from high school to college was massive. I had to learn how to motivate myself, but the most important thing I learned was that there are people in this world who will help you if you let them. My

professors and mentors at Katharine Gibbs School, such as Brian Kester, became monumental in helping me adapt, build my self-esteem, and learn how to put myself first.

Some of my professors did not understand my situation at first. I cried a lot in class, did not have my projects completed from time to time, and basically lived the life of an introvert. Once everyone learned that I was caring for my mother, traveling five hours a day to class, and struggling just to eat, they became my family. They taught me that I had to put my education first. They taught me that without an education, I would most likely have to work in dead-end jobs for the rest of my life. I began to really look at all of the people in my neighborhood and I made a committed decision that I was not going to fall prey to the temptations of alcohol, sex, unemployment, and drugs.

As I began to succeed in classes, my self-esteem became healthier. I began to understand how to support myself, take pride in my successes, and help others in any way possible. I still struggle with my mother as she seeks therapy and better medical care, but I also know that I must take care of my own life and keep working toward my own goals. My life is my first priority.

Today, I am a college graduate. I completed my bachelor of arts in business administration with a GPA of 3.5. At the graduation ceremony, I was presented an award by the faculty and staff for my dedication, hard work, and for overcoming all odds to obtain my degree. I hope in some small way that my story can help you "hold on" and reach your dreams. Happiness and success are possible for you.

- ▶ Identify the topic, problem, or statement to be discussed.
- ▶ Set a time limit for the entire brainstorming session.
- ▶ Write all ideas on a board or flip chart.
- ▶ Let everyone speak.
- ▶ Don't criticize people for their remarks.
- ▶ Concentrate on the issue; let all of your ideas flow.
- ▶ Suspend judgment until all ideas are produced or the time is up.
- ▶ If you're using the session to generate questions rather than solutions, each participant should pose questions rather than make statements.

Using the problem just identified (my nighttime job is causing me to not have enough time for sleep or study), jot down the first few alternatives that come to mind. Don't worry about content, clarity, or quality. Just let your ideas flow. Verbalize these ideas when the class brainstorms this problem.

Ideas: _____

_____

_____

_____

_____

When solving a problem, it is helpful to look at all possible alternatives and decide on the best one. Sometimes there is one right answer, but often you'll have to settle for the best answer.

© Image Source Limited

Evaluate the alternatives. Some of your ideas or your classmates' ideas may not be logical in solving the problem. After careful study and deliberation, without emotional interference, analyze the ideas and determine if they are appropriate or inappropriate for the solution. To analyze, create Columns A and B. Write the idea in Column A and a comment in Column B.

Example:

A (Idea)	B (Comments)
Quit the job.	Very hard to do. I need the money for tuition and car.
Cut my hours at work.	Will ask my boss.
Find a new job.	Hard to do because of the job market—but will look into it.
Get a student loan.	Visit financial aid office tomorrow.
Quit school.	No—it is my only chance for a promotion.

With your comments in Column B, you can now begin to eliminate some of the alternatives that are inappropriate at this time.

Solve the problem. Now that you have a few strong alternatives, you have some work to do. You will need to talk to your boss, go to the financial aid office, and possibly begin to search for a new job with flexible hours. After you have researched each alternative, you will be able to make a decision based on solid information and facts.

Your Turn

Pretend that your best friend, Nathan, has just come to you with an unusual problem. He tells you that his parents are really coming down hard on him for going to college. It is a strange problem. They believe that Nathan should be working full time and that he is just wasting his time and money, since he did not do well in high school. They have threatened to take away his car and kick him out of the house if he does not find a full-time job. Nathan is doing well and does not want to leave college. In the space provided, formulate a plan with multiple alternatives to help Nathan solve this problem.

A (Idea)   **B (Comments)**

Step Six: Distinguishing Fact from Opinion

One of the most important aspects of critical thinking is the ability to distinguish fact from opinion. In most situations—real life, TV, radio, friendly conversations, and the professional arena—opinions surface more often than facts. *Reread the previous sentence.* This is an example of an opinion cloaked as a fact. There is no research supporting this opinion. It sounds as if it could be true, but without evidence and proof, it is just an opinion.

A fact is something that can be proven, something that can be objectively verified. An opinion is a statement that is held to be true, but one that has no objective proof. *Statements that cannot be proved should always be treated as opinion.* Statements that offer valid proof and verification from credible, reliable sources can be treated as factual.

When trying to distinguish between fact and opinion, you should take the following guidelines into consideration:

► If you are in doubt, ask questions and listen for solid proof and documentation to support the statement.

► Listen for what is not said in a statement.

► Don't be led astray by those you assume are trustworthy and loyal.

▶ Don't be turned off by those you fear or consider untruthful.

▶ Do your own homework on the issue. Read, research, and question.

▶ If you are unsure about the credibility of the source or information, treat the statement as opinion.

Examine the following statements. Before you glance at the answer, try to determine if you think the statement is a fact or an opinion. Circle one.

Gone With the Wind is a movie.	Fact	Opinion
Gone With the Wind is a movie made in 1939.	Fact	Opinion
Gone With the Wind is the best movie ever made.	Fact	Opinion
Tom Hanks is an actor.	Fact	Opinion
There is a "heaven" and a "hell."	Fact	Opinion
Some people believe in a "heaven" and a "hell."	Fact	Opinion
Lincoln was the best president ever to head the U.S.	Fact	Opinion

STATEMENT	ANSWER	EVIDENCE
Gone With the Wind is a movie.	Fact	This can be proven by watching the movie and by reading movie reviews.
Gone With the Wind is a movie made in 1939.	Fact	This can be verified by many movie sources and by the Motion Picture Association of America.
Gone With the Wind is the best movie ever made.	Opinion	This is only the opinion of some critics and could never be proven.
Tom Hanks is an actor.	Fact	This can be proven by viewing his movies and verifying his two Academy Awards® for acting.
There is a "heaven" and a "hell."	Opinion	As controversial as this answer is, the exsistence of heaven and hell has never been scientifically proven. Both are opinions of various religions.
Some people believe in a "heaven" and a "hell."	Fact	This can be verified by many books and articles and by simply taking a poll of people you know.
Lincoln was the best president ever to head the United States.	Opinion	This is only an opinion that can be disputed by many people. This cannot be proven.

There is nothing so powerful as truth, and often, nothing so strange.

—Daniel Webster

Step Seven: Seeking Truth in Arguments and Persuasion

Whether or not you realize it, arguments and persuasive efforts are around you daily—hourly, for that matter. They are in newspaper and TV ads, editorials, news commentaries, talk shows, TV magazine shows, political statements, and religious services. It seems at times that almost everyone is trying to persuade us through argument or advice. This section is included to assist you in recognizing faulty arguments and implausible or deceptive persuasion.

First, let's start with a list of terms used to describe faulty arguments and deceptive persuasion. As you read through the list, try to identify situations in which you have heard arguments that fit these descriptions.

Terminology for Fallacious Arguments

Ad baculum	Ad baculum is an argument that tries to persuade based on force. Threats of alienation, disapproval, or even violence may accompany this type of argument.
Ad hominem	Ad hominem is when someone initiates a personal attack on a person rather than listening to and rationally debating his or her ideas. This is also referred to as slander.
Ad populum	An ad populum argument is based on the opinions of the majority of people. It assumes that because the majority says X is right, then Y is not. It uses little logic.
Ad verecundiam	This argument uses quotes and phrases from people in authority or popular people to support its own views.
Bandwagon	The bandwagon approach tries to convince you to do something just because everyone else is doing it. It is also referred to as peer pressure.
Scare tactic	A scare tactic is used as a desperate measure to put fear in your life: If you don't do X, then Y is going to happen to you.
Straw argument	The straw argument attacks the opponent's argument to make one's own argument stronger. It does not necessarily make argument A stronger; it simply discounts argument B.
Appeal to tradition	This argument looks only at the past and suggests that we have always done it "this way" and we should continue to do it "this way."
Plain folks	This type of persuasion is used to make you feel that the people making the argument are just like you. Usually, they are not; they are only using this appeal to connect with your sense of space and time.
Patriotism	This form of persuasion asks you to ignore reason and logic and support what is right for state A or city B or nation C.
Glittering generalities	This type of persuasion or argumentation is an appeal to generalities (Bosak, 1976). It suggests that a person or candidate or professional is for all the "right" things: justice, low taxes, no inflation, rebates, full employment, low crime, free tuition, progress, privacy, and truth.

IDENTIFYING FALLACIOUS ARGUMENTS

Here are some statements intended to persuade you or argue for a cause. Beside each statement, identify which type of faulty persuasion is used.

AB	Ad baculum	SA	Straw argument
AH	Ad hominem	AT	Appeal to tradition
AP	Ad populum	PF	Plain folks
AV	Ad verecundiam	PM	Patriotism
BW	Bandwagon	GG	Glittering generalities
ST	Scare tactic		

_____ **1.** This country has never faltered in the face of adversity. Our strong, united military has seen us through many troubled times, and it will see us through our current situation. This is your country; support your military.

_____ **2.** If I am elected to office, I will personally lobby for lower taxes, a new comprehensive crime bill, a $2,500 tax cut on every new home, and better education, and I will personally work to lower the unemployment rate.

_____ **3.** This is the best college in the region. All of your friends will be attending this fall. You don't want to be left out; you should join us, too.

_____ **4.** If you really listen to Governor Wise's proposal on health care, you will see there is no way that we can have a national system. You will not be able to select your doctor, you will not be able to go to the hospital of your choice, and you will not be able to get immediate attention. His proposal is not as comprehensive as our proposal.

_____ **5.** My father went to Honors College, I went to Honors College, and you will go to Honors College. It is the way things have been for the people in this family. There is no need to break with tradition now.

_____ **6.** The witness's testimony is useless. He is an alcoholic; he is dishonest and corrupt. To make matters worse, he was a member of the Leftist party.

_____ **7.** The gentleman on the witness stand is your neighbor, he is your friend, he is just like you. Sure, he may have more money and drive a Mercedes, but his heart never left Elm Community.

_____ **8.** John F. Kennedy once said, "Ask not what your country can do for you; ask what you can do for your country." This is the time to act, my fellow citizens. You can give $200 to our cause and you will be fulfilling the wish of President Kennedy.

_____ **9.** Out of the 7,000 people polled, 72% believed that there is life beyond our planet. Therefore, there must be life beyond Earth.

_____ **10.** Without this new medication, you will die.

_____ **11.** I don't care what anyone says. If you don't come around to our way of thinking, you'd better start watching your back.

As you develop your critical-thinking skills, you will begin to recognize the illogical nature of thoughts, the falsehoods of statements, the deception in some advertisements, and the irrational fears used to persuade. You will also begin to understand the depths to which you should delve to achieve objectivity, the thought and care that should be given to your own decisions and statements, and the methods by which you can build logical, truthful arguments.

CREATIVE THINKING

From Ridiculous to Possible

Creative thinking is much like critical thinking in that you are producing something that is uniquely yours. You are introducing something to the world that is new, innovative, and useful. Creative thinking does not mean that you have to be an artist, a musician, or a writer. Creative thinking means that you have examined a situation and developed a new way of explaining information, delivering a product, or using an item. It can be as simple as discovering that you can use a small rolling suitcase to carry your books around campus instead of the traditional backpack. Creative thinking means that you have opened your mind to possibilities!

Creative thinking and critical thinking both require that you "loosen up" your brain and be more flexible in your approaches and tactics. In her book _The Artist's Way: A Spiritual Path to_

YES YOU CAN !

IDEAS FOR Success

Consider the following strategies for creative thinking:

▶ Understand that the creative process is not an organized process. It can be chaotic and disorderly—downright crazy at times.

▶ Never be afraid to ask any question, even those you think may be silly.

▶ Jot your weirdest and funkiest ideas down; you may need them later.

▶ Take risks! Greatness has never been achieved by playing it safe. Dream, and dream big.

▶ Hone your sense of adventure and exploration by playing and thinking like a child.

▶ Force yourself to develop at least five creative solutions to any problem you face.

▶ Force yourself to do something old in a new way.

Higher Creativity (1992), Julia Cameron suggests that there are basic principles of creativity:

► Creativity is the natural order of life.
► There is an underlying, indwelling creative force infusing all of life.
► We are, ourselves, creations. And we, in turn, are meant to create ourselves.
► The refusal to be creative is counter to our true nature.

So how do we become more creative in our thought process? It may be easier than you think. Your individual creativity can be revealed if you make a daily effort to hone and use your creative skills. Consider the tips in the box on page 228.

As you explore your own creativity, you may find yourself struggling and even at odds with your own opinions. That is perfectly OK. Remember, if everything is easy and smooth, it only means that you are not challenging and stretching yourself. Thinking creatively and critically is *not* easy for everyone, but can benefit you greatly.

To begin the creative process, consider the items in the following chart. These are some of the characteristics that creative thinkers have in common.

Creative Thinking Involves . . .

Compassion	Creative thinkers have a zest for life and genuinely care for the spirit of others.	**Example:** More than 40 years ago, community members who wanted to feed the elderly created Meals on Wheels, now a national organization feeding the elderly.
Courage	Creative thinkers are unafraid to try new things, to implement new thoughts and actions.	**Example:** An NBC executive moves the *Today Show* out of a closed studio onto the streets of New York, creating the number-one morning news show in America.
Truth	Creative thinkers search for the true meaning of things.	**Example:** The astronomer and scientist Copernicus sought to prove that Earth was *not* the center of the universe—an unpopular view at the time.
Dreams	Creative thinkers allow themselves time to dream and ponder the unknown. They can see what is possible, not just what is actual.	**Example:** John F. Kennedy dreamed that space exploration was possible. His dream became reality.
Risk taking	Creative thinkers take positive risks every day. They are not afraid to go against popular opinion.	**Example:** WWF wrestler Jesse "The Body" Ventura took a risk and ran for mayor in a small Minnesota town, never having had any experience in politics. Later, he became governor of the state.
Innovation	Creative thinkers find new ways to do old things.	**Example:** Instead of continuing to fill the earth with waste such as aluminum, plastic, metal, and old cars, means were developed to recycle these materials for future productive use.
Competition	Creative thinkers strive to be better, to think bolder thoughts, to do what is good, and to be the best at any task.	**Example:** Andre Agassi had a several-year slump in tennis. Most people thought he was a "has-been." He came back to win tournament after tournament because he knew that he could.
Individuality	Creative thinkers are not carbon copies of other people. They strive to be true to themselves.	**Example:** A young man decides to take tap dancing instead of playing baseball. He excels and wins a fine arts dancing scholarship to college.
Thinking	Creative thinkers are always thinking about the world, people, and new ideas.	**Example:** A scientist is not afraid to take time to sit alone with his or her data to study and ponder the results, make connections, and develop ways to use the information.
Curiosity	Creative thinkers are interested in all things; they want to know much about many things.	**Example:** A 65-year-old retired college professor goes back to college to learn more about music appreciation and computer programming to expand her possibilities.
Perseverance	Creative thinkers do not give up. They stick to a project to its logical and reasonable end.	**Example:** Dr. Martin Luther King, Jr., did not give up on his dream in the face of adversity, danger, and death threats.

Why should we use our creative power? Because there is nothing that makes people so generous, joyful, lively, bold, and compassionate.

—Brenda Ueland

Using your imagination and innovative ideas, think about how you would *creatively* solve the following problem. Write down at least five possibilities. Come on, make it count!

The Problem

Jennifer is a first-year student who does not have enough money to pay her tuition, buy her books, and purchase a few new outfits and shoes to wear to class and her work-study job on campus.

What should she do? Should she pay her tuition and purchase her books, or pay her tuition and buy new clothes and shoes to wear to class and work? What creative ideas (solutions) can you give Jennifer?

My Creative Solutions:

1. _____
2. _____
3. _____
4. _____
5. _____

Think About It
Chapter Reflection

Both critical and creative thinking require a great deal of commitment on your part. Critical and creative thinking are not easy for everyone, but with practice, dedication, and an understanding of the need, everyone can achieve both.

Critical and creative thinking can affect the way you live your life, from relationships to purchasing a new car, from solving family problems to investing money, from taking the appropriate classes for graduation to getting a promotion at work.

As you continue on in the semester and work toward personal and professional motivation, consider the following ideas:

- ► Use only *credible* and *reliable* sources.
- ► Distinguish *fact* from *opinion*.
- ► Be *flexible* in your thinking.
- ► Use emotional *restraint*.
- ► *Avoid* generalizations.
- ► Avoid *stereotyping* and prejudging.
- ► Strive for *objectivity* in all your thinking.
- ► *Reserve* judgment until you have looked at every side.
- ► Do *not* assume—do the research.
- ► *Ask* questions—and strive to ask the proper questions.
- ► Seek *truth*.

Creative and critical thinking are truly the hallmarks of an educated person. They are hallmarks of character and integrity, and they are hallmarks of successful students. Let them be yours.

The significant problems we face cannot be solved at the same level of thinking we were at when we created them.

—Albert Einstein

Knowledge in Bloom

Utilizes level 3 of the taxonomy

Each chapter-end assessment is based on *Bloom's Taxonomy of Learning*. See the inside front cover for a quick review.

Developing a Rational, Logical Argument

Explanation: Thousands of articles are written every day for magazines, newspapers, online journals, and other print media. Depending on the article or where it is published, it can have a slant. You may have heard this called bias (as in liberal or conservative bias). One of journalism's objectives should be to present the *facts* of an incident or the *facts* of what is being discussed. Bias should not enter the argument unless it is an editorial.

Process: For this activity, you are to find an article (not an editorial) in a mainstream newspaper or magazine (*USA Today, Newsweek, Time, New York Times, Washington Post*, etc.), read the article, and determine if the article has bias, unsubstantiated opinions, or research that is weak.

To assist you in this project, use this list of questions to evaluate and assess your article.

Name of the article: _____

Writer of the article: _____

His/her affiliation: _____

Publication in which the article was found: _____

Date of publication: _____

After reading the article, what do you think is the author's main reason for writing it? _____

_____

_____

_____

What is the most important fact(s) or information in the article? _____

_____

_____

_____

By writing this article, what is the author implying? _____

_____

_____

_____

By writing this article, what is the author proving? _____

_____

_____

_____

In writing this article, what assumptions were made? _____

_____

_____

_____

What sources or research does the writer cite to prove his or her point? _____

_____

_____

_____

Is the article fairly presented? In other words, does the author examine both sides of the issue or just one side?

_____

_____

_____

_____

Do you believe and trust the article? Why or why not? Justify your answer. _____

_____

_____

_____

_____

_____

If this article is accurate (or inaccurate, depending on your judgment), what are the implications for society?

_____

_____

_____

_____

(This project is adapted, in part, from the work of Richard Paul and Linda Elder.)

Preparing for Success

Refer to pages 212–213 of this chapter and answer the questions you developed from scanning this chapter's headings. You should also be able to answer the following questions if they were not on your list:

1. Why is asking questions so important in critical thinking? _____

   _____

2. Define fact and opinion and give an example of each. _____

   _____

3. Define ad hominem and find an example of this in a recent newspaper or magazine. _____

   _____

4. Why is creative thinking important? _____

   _____

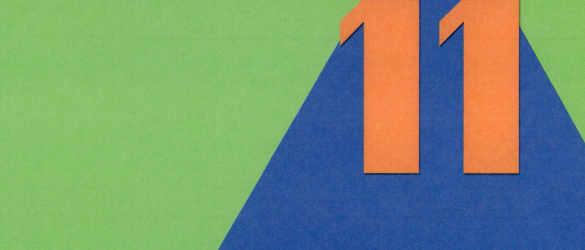

11

Prosper

© Getty Images

Money can't buy everything— for example, poverty.

Nelson Algren

the big **WHY**

Why is learning to manage money so important at this stage of my life? *Why* is it such a big deal to learn to invest for the future? *Why* do I need to pay attention to all this information about credit cards, loans, and debt?

Money will come when you are doing the right thing the right way with the right people.

—Mike Phillips

The things you learn in this chapter will impact your life forever. This chapter is designed to help you make wise decisions today about student loans, credit cards, and impulse buying. Just as important, the chapter is designed to prompt you to start thinking about your future and investments you need to make for your security. While every chapter in this book is valuable and will have long-lasting impact on your life, this information can be the difference in whether you are financially secure or debt-ridden, whether you have a high credit score or one so bad that you can't finance a car or a house, whether you make wise decisions about borrowing money to finance college expenses or spend with no thought for tomorrow.

Learning to manage your money is one of the most important skills you can develop because so many other things in your life depend on it. *This chapter will help you:*

▶ Learn to evaluate different types of loans and grants.
▶ Make wise decisions about borrowing money.
▶ Construct and use a budget.
▶ Protect your credit cards and other vital information from identity theft.
▶ Understand your credit score.
▶ Practice fiscal fitness.

Make wise decisions today that will have long-lasting implications for a prosperous future. The skills you learn here can help you to implement sound financial practices and become a wise manager of money.

Scan &

Take a few minutes and **scan this chapter**. As you scan, **list five questions** you can expect to learn the answers to while reading and studying Chapter 11.

Example:
▶ What is a Pell grant? (from page 240)
▶ How does a grant differ from a loan? (from page 239)

My Questions:

1. _____
   _____ From page _____

2. _____
   _____ From page _____

3. _____
   _____ From page _____

Name: Martin Zavala
Institution: Texas State University, San Marcos, TX
Major: Geography and Urban/Regional Planning
Age: 31

You know those credit card invitations that you see hanging all over campus? *"Preapproved." "Automatic Acceptance!" "Apply Today!"* Well, all I can say to you is this: *Run!* This chapter is about learning how to "run" from bad money decisions. I only wish I had known the information discussed here much earlier in my college career.

By the time I finished my first semester in college, I had seven or eight credit cards all maxed to the limit. Cards just kept coming, one right after the other, and I thought it was fine to use them. I had every intention of paying them off each month, but as I look back, I wonder how I thought that I could because I was only working part-time.

I began getting collection calls at my parents' home and things began to spiral out of control from that point. Before I knew it, my credit was ruined and I was in debt over my head for things I could not even remember buying—new clothes, food, entertainment, and the like.

the big **WHY**

. . . from another perspective

This whole terrible ordeal taught me two important lessons: (1) You must be responsible with your credit and spending habits. (2) There is a huge difference between *need* and *want.* I thought I needed all those things that I charged, but in retrospect, I only wanted them. I found that I *need* a place to live, water, food, electricity, and transportation. Everything else was a *want* at that point in my life.

As I got older, the lessons of that ordeal kept coming. I could not get a car in my name because the interest rate was going to be 17%. One company even wanted to charge me 23% interest. I had trouble finding an apartment because my credit was trashed. Bad credit follows you for a very long time, and it can ruin many aspects of your life.

This chapter will help you avoid the mistakes I made when it comes to money and debt management. Read it carefully and use the information wisely.

4. _____

_____

From page _____

5. _____

_____

From page _____

Question

PS Reminder: At the end of the chapter, come back to this page and answer these questions in your notebook, text margins, or online chapter notes.

Practicing Fiscal Fitness

Are You Managing Your Money or Is It Managing You?

Can you imagine getting information in your hands that is so important that you will use it for the rest of your life? What if you knew that information in this chapter could be the difference between graduating with lower debts or with huge financial burdens? How serious would you be about this content if you knew that learning to invest properly at an early age is the difference between retiring with $10,000 or $1,000,000? The principles and exercises discussed in this chapter on money management are so important that they will have lasting implications for the rest of your life. Learning to budget, avoid credit card debt, stay away from impulse buying, invest well, and capitalize on scholarships can be lessons that will serve you well now—and years later. This chapter is crucial to you as you begin your journey as a college student because money management has such long-lasting implications for you, your spouse or partner, and your children.

Many students arrive on college campuses never having had to manage their own money. In some cases, their parents have just handed them money to cover their expenses without assigning responsibility for managing finances. Quite a few students worked in high school, but they were free to spend their money as they pleased while their parents put a roof over their heads, fed, and clothed them. When you were living at home and not paying high tuition costs, this was easier for your parents to manage, but college education costs change things drastically for most families, especially if they have not prepared well for it. Even if your family has saved money for college, expenses are rising so rapidly that it is a rare student who will not need to manage money very carefully and strategically.

Many, if not most, students who attend college today will be required to learn to manage money much better than they have in the past. Often first-year students have a very difficult time making ends meet unless their parents continue to hand over money with no consequences attached. Unfortunately, for most students this scenario is not going to happen. You will most likely have to stay on a budget. In many cases, students will be totally on their own and will be supporting themselves with rent and car payments, insurance, food expenses, and entertainment, as well as paying for tuition and books. Some college freshmen already have families and in addition to all the expenses mentioned above, they also must support children with all the accompanying expenses of family care.

Although managing your money is challenging, it is an opportunity to grow, to learn to resist impulse buying, to invest wisely, to become more disciplined, and to prepare for future success.

Pennies from Heaven

The Secret World of Financial Aid

You may feel that it is crazy to talk about financial aid at this point. After all, you had to have found the money to enroll in college or you would not be in this orientation class. Still, financial aid comes in many forms, and there may be some sources you have not yet thought about that can help you through the rest of your college years.

The most well-known sources of assistance are from federal and state governments. Federal and state financial aid programs have been in place for many years, are a staple of assistance for many college students, and include the following:

Where Are You . . .

Before reading any further, take a moment and assess where you are at this moment with your knowledge and application of managing your money and your debts. Read each statement carefully and then respond accordingly.

1. I have had instruction on money management in high school and believe I understand how it works. ☐ YES ☐ NO

2. I know how to construct and follow a budget. ☐ YES ☐ NO

3. I understand the dangers of impulse buying. ☐ YES ☐ NO

4. I have a habit of saving and putting aside money for emergencies. ☐ YES ☐ NO

5. I avoid using my credit card for things I don't really need. ☐ YES ☐ NO

6. I understand how to avoid identity theft. ☐ YES ☐ NO

7. I realize the dangers of high-interest credit cards. ☐ YES ☐ NO

8. I have read and understand the regulations relative to repaying student loans. ☐ YES ☐ NO

9. I have developed and managed my own budget very successfully. ☐ YES ☐ NO

If you answered "Yes" to most of the questions (seven or more), you have a better than average knowledge of money management. You usually make good decisions relative to spending and borrowing money. *If you answered "No"* to most of the questions, you will need to study this chapter carefully and consider enrolling in a personal finance course. You will need to be especially careful about accumulating large debts while you are in college.

- ▶ Federal and state loans
- ▶ Federal and state grants
- ▶ Scholarships (local, regional, and national)
- ▶ Work-study programs

Not every school participates in every federal assistance program. To determine which type of aid is available at your school, you need to contact the financial aid office.

Some students may be confused about the differences between loans, grants, and work-study programs. The following definitions are supplied by *The Student Guide,* published by the U.S. Department of Education:

- ▶ Grants—Monies that you don't have to repay
- ▶ Work study—Money earned for work that you do at the college that does not have to be repaid
- ▶ Loans—Borrowed money that you must repay with interest

An undergraduate may receive any of these types of assistance, whereas graduate students cannot receive Pell grants or Federal Supplemental Educational Opportunity grants (FSEOGs).

One of the biggest mistakes students make when thinking about financial aid is forgetting about scholarships from private industry and social or civic organizations. Each year, millions of dollars are unclaimed because students do not know about these scholarships or where to find the necessary information. Following is a list of resources that can help you research and apply for all types of financial aid.

Types of Federal Financial Aid

Pell grant. This is a need-based grant awarded to qualified undergraduate students who have not been awarded a previous degree. Amounts vary based on need and costs.

Federal Supplemental Educational Opportunity grant (FSEOG). This is a need-based grant awarded to institutions to allocate to students through their financial aid offices.

Stafford loan (formerly known as the Guaranteed Student Loan). The Stafford Direct Loan program is a low-interest, subsidized loan. You must show need to qualify. The government pays the interest while you are in school, but you must be registered for at least half-time status. You begin repayments six months after you leave school.

Unsubsidized Stafford loan. This Stafford loan is a low interest, non-subsidized loan. You *do not* have to show need to qualify. You are responsible for the interest on the loan while you are enrolled. Even though the government does not pay the interest, you can defer the interest and the payment until six months after you have left school.

PLUS loan. This is a federally funded, but state administered, low-interest loan to qualified parents of students in college. The student must be enrolled at least half-time. Parents must pass a credit check and payments begin 60 days after the last loan payment.

Work study. Work study is a federally funded, need-based program that pays students an hourly wage for working on (and sometimes off) campus. Students earn at least minimum wage.

Hope Scholarship tax credit. This tax credit is for students in their first two years of college and who are enrolled at least half-time in a degree or certificate program. For each student, taxpayers may receive a 100% tax credit for each year for the first $1,000 of qualified out-of-pocket expenses. They also may claim a 50% credit on the second $1,000 used for qualified expenses (U.S. Bank, 2002).

Perkins loan. This is a need-based loan. The amount of money you can borrow is determined by the government and the availability of funds. The interest rate is 5% and repayment begins nine months after you leave school or drop below half-time status. You can take up to 10 years to repay the loan. (Note: The federal government may have eliminated this program by the time this book is published.)

Drugs and Money

What do drugs and money have in common? More than you might think! Did you know that when applying for federal financial aid, you must complete a drug conviction worksheet? This worksheet will be used to determine if you can receive *any* type of federal aid. Be warned!

The questions on the worksheet include the following:

▶ Have you ever been convicted of selling or possessing drugs?
▶ Have you completed an acceptable drug rehab program since your last conviction?
▶ Do you have more than two convictions for possessing drugs?
▶ Do you have more than one conviction for selling drugs?

FIGURE 11.1 *Financial Aid Glossary*

Borrower—The person who borrows the funds and agrees to repay them.

COA—Cost of attendance. This is the total amount it will cost you to go to college.

Cosigner—A person who signs a promissory note and agrees to repay the debt should the borrower default.

Default—The term used when you do not repay your student loan. This will prevent you from receiving any further funding. Your wages can be garnished until full restitution is made. Your tax refunds will also be held until full payment is made. This default will also be reported to credit agencies and your credit will be scarred for seven to 10 years.

Deferment—A period of time when you do not have to make loan payments. This period usually applies to education loans and usually lasts only six to nine months.

EFC—Expected Family Contribution. The amount of money your family contributes to your educational costs.

FAFSA—Free Application for Federal Student Aid. The application that you (or your parents) fill out to determine your financial needs. This is the first step in any financial aid process.

FAT—Financial Aid Transcript. A record of your financial assistance from all institutions.

Gross income—Your income before taxes and deductions.

Interest—The fee (or amount of money) charged to you to borrow money.

Late fee—A fee charged to you if you do not make your payment on time.

Need analysis—A formula established by Congress to determine your financial need. This is based on your FAFSA form.

Net income—Your income after taxes and deductions.

Payoff—The total amount owed on a loan if you were to pay it off in one lump sum.

Principal—The exact dollar amount that you borrowed and the amount on which interest is charged.

Promissory note—A legal document that obligates the borrower to repay funds.

Selective Service Registration—If you are required by law to register with Selective Service, you must do so before you can qualify for federal student aid.

FIGURE 11.2 *Student Eligibility for Federal Financial Aid**

To receive aid from the major federal student aid programs, you must:
- ☑ Have financial need, except for some loan programs.
- ☑ Hold a high school diploma or GED, pass an independently administered test approved by the U.S. Department of Education, or meet the standards established by your state.
- ☑ Be enrolled as a regular student working toward a degree or certificate in an eligible program. You may not receive aid for correspondence or telecommunications courses unless they are a part of an associate, bachelor, or graduate degree program.
- ☑ Be a U.S. citizen.
- ☑ Have a valid Social Security number.
- ☑ Make satisfactory academic progress.
- ☑ Sign a statement of educational purpose.
- ☑ Sign a statement of updated information.
- ☑ Register with the Selective Service, if required.

*Some federal financial aid may be dependent on your not having a previous drug conviction.

Source: Adapted from *The Student Guide: Financial Aid from the U.S. Department of Education.* U.S. Dept. of Education, Washington, DC, 2005–2006.

Scholarships

Each year, millions and millions of scholarship dollars go unclaimed simply because no one applied for them. Scholarships are given to students based on academic excellence, talent, need, affiliation, sporting abilities, social interests, community involvement, and a variety of other attributes.

When looking for scholarships, use the Internet as a tool for tracking down appropriate sources. Your local bookstore will also carry many books that offer sources and even applications.

Tips for Applying for Financial Aid

▶ *Do not miss a deadline.* There are *no* exceptions for making up deadlines for federal financial aid!

▶ *Read all instructions* before beginning the process.

▶ Always fill out the application completely and have someone proof your work.

▶ If documentation is required, submit it according to the instructions. Do not fail to do all that the application asks you to do.

▶ Never lie about your financial status.

▶ Begin the application process as soon as possible. Do not wait until the last moment. Some aid is given on a first-come, first-served basis. Income tax preparation time is usually financial aid application time.

▶ Talk to the financial aid officer at the institution you will attend. Person-to-person contact is always best. Never assume anything until you get it in writing.

▶ Take copies of fliers and brochures that are available from the financial aid office. Private companies and civic groups will often notify the financial aid office if they have funds available.

▶ Always apply for admission as well as financial aid. Many awards are given by the college to students who are already accepted.

▶ If you are running late with an application, find out if there are electronic means of filing.

▶ Always keep a copy of your tax returns for each year!

▶ To receive almost any money, including some scholarships, you must fill out the Free Application for Federal Student Aid form.

▶ Apply for everything possible. You will get nothing if you do not apply.

Student Loans

A Day of Reckoning Will Come

The high cost of college makes tuition out of reach for many families. For many students, the only way they can attend college is via student loans. If this is the only way you can go to college, borrow the money—but borrow no more than you absolutely must. Try not to borrow anything but tuition and perhaps room and board. Get a job, budget, cut out extras, work in the summers, take fewer credits even though it delays graduation—do everything possible not to borrow more money than you must.

If you have to borrow a great deal of money, ask yourself a few very important questions: "Am I majoring in a field that is going to pay me enough money to repay

these loans and live a desirable lifestyle? Will I ever be able to afford a house? Can I afford to get married and have a family?" You should have a good idea of how much money you can make when you get out of college. Be realistic. Can you pay this money back with the major you are in right now? If you owe a lot of money, should you rethink your future career choice? Perhaps a current major might become a minor. While it is very important to work at something you love, it is equally important to be able to pay your bills. According to Watson (2002), the median student loan debt is at record levels due to rising tuition costs—$17,000 versus $2000 when baby boomers were in their twenties. You will have to repay this money that you have borrowed. Even bankruptcy will not relieve you of this debt; so again, don't borrow any money you can do without.

Good financial habits in college will serve you well after graduation.

©Stockdisc

PRIORITIZING YOUR FINANCES

Getting a Handle on Debt Before it Gets Out of Control

College students, as a whole, typically don't have a great deal of extra money to manage, but it is never too early to learn the basic principles of managing money and accumulating wealth. One of the most important things you want to do while in college is to avoid borrowing more money than you absolutely have to. In recent years, tuition has skyrocketed causing many students to borrow large sums of money to finance their educations, buy books and materials, and pay their day-to-day living expenses. According to *Young Money* (2005), a money publication for younger adults, "the biggest problem facing college students is rising tuition and other costs." For many students, indeed most, borrowing money has become a necessity since tuition has risen faster than family income. All the more reason to manage money carefully and strategically.

Credit card debt—the worse kind of debt—is rising rapidly among college students as they struggle to pay tuition, buy books, and cover day-to-day living expenses. According to a Nellie Mae study (2004), 76% of all undergraduate college students have at least one credit card and carry an average balance of $2,169. One of the results of

No man's credit is as good as his money.

—Edgar Watson Howe

high credit card debt is lower GPAs and a higher dropout rate (Cooper-Arnold, 2006).

It is one thing to talk about credit card debt and something else to live without charging books, food, tuition, and so forth if you have no other means to pay these bills. While many students have the luxury of having their parents pay for college expenses, many others are totally responsible for these expenses and most students have to resort to some kind of financial assistance. If you are one of these students, learn everything you can learn about grants and scholarships. Find a job that pays as much as possible, ideally one that prepares you for a career of your choice. Use your credit card only if you absolutely have to, preferably for expenses that can be paid off each month.

Work in the summers, live at home, and save everything you can save. Consider a cooperative program in which you work for a semester or a year and go to college for a semester or a year, alternating this practice. This is a better plan than leaving college owing excessive amounts of money, even if it takes you longer to graduate. The average college student now takes at least five years to graduate, and many take six or more. In most cases, this is due to rising tuition costs.

UNDERSTANDING YOUR CREDIT SCORE

Long-Lasting Implications

College students rarely know—or even think about—their credit score, yet this score is the single most important factor in determining your approval for a mortgage, car loan, credit card, insurance, and so on. Furthermore, even if you get approved this credit score will determine the rate of interest you have to pay (Broderick, 2003). You can order a free credit score online by accessing the Web site for Equifax, Experian, or Transunion (www.annualcreditreport.com/cra/index.jsp).

To fully maximize your financial resources, you need to establish a budget and learn to live within your means. According to Konowalow (2003), watching and calculating how much money is coming in each month and how much you spend is important in taking control of your finances and protecting your credit score. Although not having control of your income and expenditures may not be a problem this week or next, it is sure to become one soon if the money you are spending each month exceeds the money coming in. This can quickly turn your good credit into a credit nightmare.

> Your credit past is your credit future.
>
> —Steve Konowalow

B IS FOR BUDGETING

Knowing Where Your Money Goes

Most people have no idea where their money goes. Many just spend and spend and then borrow on credit cards to pay for additional expenses for which they have not budgeted. Knowing how much money you have and exactly how you spend it is a very important step toward financial security.

One of the main reasons to budget is to determine the exact amount of money you need to borrow to finance your college education. Poor planning while in college can easily result in a lower standard of life after you graduate and have to begin paying back enormous loans. Deciding how much to borrow will impact your life long after you have completed your degree. You should also remember that you will be required to repay your student loans even if you do not graduate.

When budgeting, you must first determine how much income you earn monthly. Complete the following chart.

SOURCE OF INCOME	ESTIMATED AMOUNT
Work	$_____
Spouse's income	$_____
Parental contributions	$_____
Scholarships	$_____
Loans	$_____
Savings	$_____
Investments	$_____
Other	$_____
Total Income	$_____

Next, you must determine how much money you spend in a month. Complete the following chart.

Tuition	$_____
Books and supplies	$_____
Housing	$_____
Utilities	$_____
Phone	$_____
Car payment	$_____
Insurance	$_____
Gas	$_____
Clothing	$_____
Food	$_____
Household items	$_____
Personal hygiene items	$_____
Health care and/or health insurance	$_____
Entertainment/fun	$_____
Other	$_____
Total Expenditures	$_____

If the amount of your total expenditures is smaller than your monthly income, you are on your way to controlling your finances. If your total expenditures figure is larger than your monthly income (as is the case for many students), you are heading for a financial crisis. Furthermore, you are establishing bad habits of money management that will carry over into your professional life.

LIVING ON BORROWED MONEY

Credit Cards—The Worst Kind of Debt

Credit card companies have been waiting for you to arrive at college. They have your name and address on file, and they will start sending you credit card applications right away. They want you to begin the dangerous habit of living off borrowed money. Don't let them get their tentacles wrapped around you and your money! Getting yourself too deeply in debt by abusing credit cards can bring you many sleepless nights and years of debt with high interest rates.

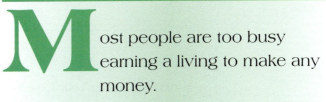

Most people are too busy earning a living to make any money.

—Anonymous

Approximately 20% of all credit card holders have credit card debt in the $6,000 to $15,000 range, and 6% have credit card debt that exceeds $15,000 (DebtSteps.com, 2006). College students should try to keep their debt below 65% of the total limit on the credit card to avoid a bad reflection on credit scores (College Credit Cards, 2006).

Most credit card companies charge a very high rate of interest—18% to 21% or higher. For every $1,000 you charge, you will pay from $180 to $210 each year, states Konowalow (2003). Don't be fooled by the ploy of "1.5% interest." This means 1.5% each month, which equates to 18% per year. If you make only the minimum required payment, you will begin paying interest on interest before the debt is paid off. If you have an extra $180, invest it. Years from now, it most likely will have doubled and even tripled. On the other hand, if you owe $1,000 and make only minimum payments, you will probably still owe $1,000 at the end of a year of making minimum payments even if you don't continue to charge. Credit cards are a bad trap for people who use them unwisely. The best practice is to charge no more than you can pay off each month while avoiding high interest rates.

According to statistics, the average college student is a better risk than the general adult population, with 67% of students sticking with one credit card. The bad news is that 33% have difficulty handling credit, according to Konowalow (2003). They fall into the instant gratification trap rather than saving until they can pay for something. Charging for extravagant items in the beginning, many people then begin charging for essentials because it seems like easy money. Nothing could be further from the truth!

Instead of using credit cards to pay for the expenditures that cause you to go over your budget, modify your expenditures. Almost every line on the expenditure chart can be modified. For example, adding a roommate or moving can lower your housing expense. You can change your car to a less expensive one or consider using public transportation or carpooling with colleagues. Gasoline is a very high-priced budget item today and this is unlikely to change.

List five ways you can modify your expenditures to avoid overwhelming credit card debt:

1. _____

_____

2. _____

_____

3. _____

_____

4. _____

_____

5. _____

_____

Hints for Cutting Your Expenses

▶ Control impulse buying. (Don't buy anything that costs more than $15 until you have waited 72 hours. It is amazing how often you decide you don't need the item that you thought you had to have.)

▶ Carpool, take public transportation, or walk to classes.

▶ Don't eat out as often. Make your own meals. On weekends, make enough meals for several days to save time.

▶ Use coupons and buy during sales.

▶ Live more simply by getting rid of unnecessary items like cell phones, beepers, and cable television.

> I must say I hate money, but it's the lack of it that I hate most.
>
> —Katherine Mansfield

FACTS YOU NEED TO KNOW ABOUT CREDIT CARDS

What You Don't Know Can Wreck Your Credit Rating and Ruin Your Life

Here are some of the most important things you can learn about managing money:

▶ Understand that credit cards are nothing more than high-interest loans—in some cases, very high!

▶ Carry only one or two credit cards so you can manage your debt and not get in over your head. Do not accept or sign up for cards that you don't need.

▶ When you accept a card, sign it right away and keep records of your credit card numbers and the phone number to contact in case they are lost or stolen. If you lose your card, report it immediately to avoid charges. Usually, you will not have to pay more than $50.

▶ Avoid credit cards that charge an annual fee. Most likely, you don't need a gold or platinum card. Does your card allow for a grace period before interest is charged?

▶ Avoid the temptation to charge. You should use credit cards only when you absolutely must and only when you can pay the full amount before interest is added. "Buy now, pay later" is a dangerous game.

▶ Determine if you can get cash advances from your card if you really need to in an emergency situation.

▶ When you pay off a card, celebrate and don't use that as a reason to charge again.

▶ If you have credit card debt, always pay more than the minimum.

▶ Pay your credit card payment early enough to avoid late charges, which now average $29.84. Send the payment at least five days in advance. Late fees now represent the third-largest revenue stream for banks. If you are assessed a late fee, call and complain. If you normally pay on time and don't max out your limit, you will probably get it removed. If you get more than two late fees in a year, you could be assessed a higher interest rate on your balance.

▶ Call the credit card company and negotiate a better rate. If they won't give you a better rate, tell them you are going to transfer the debt.

▶ If you have several credit card debts, consolidate all the amounts on the card where you have the lowest balance. Ask for a lower rate when you do. Destroy all the other cards so you don't accumulate debts again.

▶ If you pay off the full amount every month, some credit card companies allow you only 20 days from a purchase before they charge interest. If you carry a debt with them, however, they will allow you to have 25 days before your payment is due.

▶ Having a large number of credit cards with balances can seriously impact your credit rating. What you do today may inhibit your ability to buy a car, purchase a house, and even get some jobs!

▶ You only need one or two credit cards. Destroy all applications that come to you in the mail.

▶ Handle your credit cards carefully. Write down the card account numbers and the phone numbers of the issuing companies in case your cards are lost or stolen. Contact the company immediately if you cannot find your cards.

▶ Do not leave any personal information (credit cards, Social Security number, checking accounts) in places where roommates or other students have access to them. Purchase a metal file box with a lock and keep it in a secure place. Your roommates and friends may be very trustworthy, but others are not!

▶ Use your credit card only for plane tickets, hotel rooms, and other travel necessities that you can pay for within 20 days.

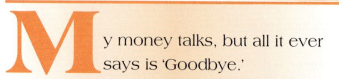

y money talks, but all it ever says is 'Goodbye.'

—American proverb

▶ If you have already gotten into credit card trouble, get counseling. One of the best agencies is the National Foundation for Credit Counseling (NFCC). An ethical professional can help you reduce your interest rates, get control of your debt, and get relief from your creditors while you pay off the debt.

▶ Be very careful not to get involved with high-pressure credit card counseling agencies who may cause you even more problems. Not all credit counselors are ethical.

▶ Be aware that using a credit card carelessly is similar to a drug addiction.

▶ Ask yourself these questions: "If I can't pay this credit card in full this month, what is going to change next month? Will I have extra income or will I reduce my spending enough to pay for this purchase?" If the answers are "No," you don't need to make the purchase.

▶ This may help you stop unnecessary spending: "How much do I have saved for fun, exciting plans for which I have a deadline?"

▶ Realize that you are building your future credit rating even though you are a student.

Bloom Level 4 & 5 question

Research and read two articles about credit card debt. Analyze your own credit card situation relative to the information you read in the articles. Predict where you will be in two years if you stay on the same course that you are on now.

_____

_____

_____

_____

_____

_____

THE PITFALLS OF PAYDAY LOANS, CAR TITLE LOANS, AND RENT-TO-OWN CONTRACTS

There's Someone on Every Corner to Take Your Money

Many unsuspecting consumers have been duped into signing car title loans, payday loans, or rent-to-own contracts that resulted in very high monthly payments and penalties. Some were told by their title loan broker before they signed the contract that they could make a partial payment if they needed to and this would be OK. Unfortunately, the unsuspecting victims find out too late that their car is going to be re-

possessed due to one late or partial payment. Others realize too late that on a loan of $400, they must pay back over $500 that month. According to recent reports from consumer affairs groups, some institutions have been charging as much as 250% interest on an annualized basis (Cojonet, 2003). In some instances interest rates as high as 900% have been charged due to poor government regulatory policies.

By using rent-to-own companies, you are paying double and sometimes triple the actual cost of the item. Try never to walk into the door of a rent-to-own company.

The main point that you need to remember is that you should only borrow money from a reputable bank or credit union. *Never* get involved in a payday loan or car title loan. Not only could you lose your car, you can ruin your credit. There are indeed people on every corner who will take your money if you don't manage your affairs very carefully.

> **I**f you can make a million by starting to invest after 45, how much more could you accumulate if you started at 25?
>
> —Price Pritchett

FIGURE 11.3 *Glossary of Financial Terms*

Annual fee—Amount charged by a lender to keep a credit card.
Annual percentage rate—The cost of credit at an annual rate.
Bankruptcy—Chapter 7 bankruptcy allows one's unprotected assets to be sold and disbursed to creditors. Chapter 13 allows the debtor time to pay debts.
Budget—A plan that takes into consideration one's income, expenses, and savings.
Car title loans—Loans made against one's car, usually at a very high rate of interest.
Collateral—Assets that may be used to secure a loan.
Credit—A promise to buy now and pay later.
Credit history—A record of one's loans and credit card debts and how one has repaid the debts.
Credit line—The amount of credit issued by a lender.
Credit report—Your credit history, compiled by several companies and made available to banks and other financial services companies.
Debit card—Card allows purchases to be charged directly to one's personal bank account.
Default—Failure to repay a debt.
Delinquency—Past due payment on a loan.
Discretionary income—Amount of money one has left after all expenses have been paid.
Disposable income—Money left over after taxes have been deducted.
Fixed expenses—Expenses that remain the same every month.
Flexible expenses—Expenses that vary from month to month.
Grace period—Period one has to pay a debt before being charged finance charges.
Identity fraud—Crime that occurs when someone assumes another person's identity.
Income taxes—A percentage of one's income that is assessed by the federal and some state governments and deducted from one's paycheck.
Installment loan—A debt in which the amount and number of payments are predetermined.
Interest—Cost of borrowing or lending money.
Interest rate—Percentage charged by the lender.
Investment—Buying stock, real estate, art, bonds, and so on with the idea that the investment will appreciate in value.
Late fee—Charges made to a delinquent account.
Payday loans—Loans made against one's next paycheck, usually at a very high rate of interest.
Principal—The outstanding balance of a loan exclusive of interest.
Repossession—Creditor legally takes back something purchased and not paid for.

Donald Trump is internationally known today as a billionaire real estate developer, TV star, and author. He has many luxurious buildings with the Trump name emblazoned on them. He can be seen flying in his personal helicopter and living in a penthouse.

In 1994, however, Donald Trump faced business and personal bankruptcy. One columnist wrote, "If we had debtors' prison, Donald Trump would be in the dungeon."

He restructured his $3.5 billion business debt and his worth today is estimated at $2.7 billion.

THE LATTE FACTOR®

In his book *The Finish Rich Notebook* (2003), Bach states, "How much you earn has no bearing on whether or not you will build wealth." As a rule, the more we make, the more we spend. Many people spend far more than they make and subject themselves to stress, exorbitant debt, fear, and an ultimate future of poverty.

Bach uses the Latte Factor® to call our attention to how much money we carelessly throw away when we should be saving and investing for the future. He uses the story of a young woman who said she could not invest because she had no money. Yet almost every day she bought a large latte for $3.50 and a muffin for $1.50. If you add a candy bar here, a drink there, a shake at the gym, you could easily be spending $10 a day that could be invested.

If you take that $10 per day and invest it faithfully at 10%, in 34 years you will have $1 million. This is the power of compound interest! If you are a relatively young person, you will probably work that many years and more, so you could retire with an extra $1 million in addition to any other savings you might have accumulated.

The point is that most of us have the ability to become rich, but we either lack the knowledge or the discipline to do so. Remember the Latte Factor® as you begin your college career and practice it, along with other sound financial strategies, if you want to become a millionaire.

Calculate Your Own Latte Factor®

For example, if you buy one McDonald's large Diet Coke each morning at $1.81, then your Latte Factor® is $685.84 per year. ($1.81 × 7 days/week × 52 weeks/year).

My daily "have to have it" is _____

My Latte Factor® is $ _____

PROTECT YOURSELF FROM IDENTITY THEFT

Living Large on Your Good Name

Every year thousands of people are victims of identity theft. In other words, someone uses their name and personal information and makes charges on their credit cards. Identity theft may also include filing fraudulent tax returns, accessing bank accounts, and other crimes. *Never* put any personal information in the garbage that has not been shredded. Buy an inexpensive shredder and use it! Many identity theft victims have spent over 175 hours and over $10,000 per incident to resolve their problems.

People who may steal your identity are roommates, relatives, friends, estranged spouses, restaurant servers, and household workers who have ready access to your papers. They may steal your wallet, go through your trash, or take your mail. They can even legally photocopy your vital information at the courthouse if, for example, you have been divorced. The Internet provides thieves many other opportunities to use official-looking e-mail messages designed to obtain your personal information.

It is very difficult, if not impossible, to catch identity thieves. While you may not be liable, you still have to spend your time filing expensive legal affidavits, writing letters, and making telephone calls to clear your good name.

Victims of identity theft can suffer staggering consequences:

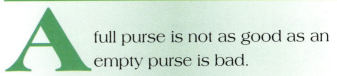

A full purse is not as good as an empty purse is bad.

—Yiddish proverb

- ▸ They must resolve unauthorized debts and delinquent accounts.
- ▸ Some have lost their jobs.
- ▸ Some have faced criminal investigation, arrest, or conviction.
- ▸ Victims may not even know their identity has been stolen until, after several months, a negative situation arises and they realize they have a problem.

Order a credit report once a year to be sure you have no major problems!

How to Minimize Identity Theft Risk

Criminals are very clever, and many are adept at using electronic means to steal your information. Here are ways to avoid having this kind of problem:

- ▸ Carry only the ID and cards you need at any given time.
- ▸ Sign all new credit cards immediately with permanent ink and write across the back of them *"Check ID"* in bold red letters.
- ▸ Do not make Internet purchases from sites that are unsecured (check for a padlock icon to ensure safety).
- ▸ Do not write your PIN number, Social Security number, or passcode on any information that can be stolen or that you are discarding.
- ▸ Try to memorize your passwords instead of recording them on paper or in the computer.
- ▸ Get someone you trust to check your mail in your absence.
- ▸ Destroy all carbons.
- ▸ Be aware of "shoulder surfers." Shield your numbers when using an ATM.
- ▸ Avoid providing your Social Security number to any organization until you have verified its legitimacy.
- ▸ Check your credit file periodically by requesting a copy of your report.

(Adapted from *Identity Theft and Fraud*, 2005).

If Your Credit Cards Are Stolen

- ▸ Contact your local police immediately.
- ▸ Notify your creditors immediately and request that your accounts be closed.
- ▸ Ask the card company to furnish copies of documents that show any fraudulent transactions.
- ▸ Refuse to pay any bill or portion of any bill that is a result of identity theft.
- ▸ Report the theft or fraud to credit reporting agencies.

If You Lose Your Driver's License

- ▸ Notify the state office of the Department of Motor Vehicles and place a fraud alert on your license number.
- ▸ Request a new driver's license.

Think About It
Chapter Reflection

Although many young people fail in the management of their personal finances, there is no reason that you cannot manage your financial affairs well. You should think about personal finance and the management of money and investments as basic survival skills that are very important to you now and for the rest of your life.

Only 10% of high school students graduate from high school with any kind of instruction in personal finance. Learning to budget, make wise investments, and avoid credit card debt is a priority need of all college students. As you move toward establishing yourself in a career, it is important to remember that to get what you want out of life, a significant part of your success will depend on your ability to make sound money decisions. En route to becoming a good money manager, the following tips will assist you:

- ▶ Don't get caught in the credit card trap.
- ▶ Know exactly how you are spending your money.
- ▶ Protect your credit rating by using wise money management strategies.
- ▶ Learn all you can about scholarships and grants.
- ▶ Understand the regulations about repaying student loans.
- ▶ Don't borrow any more money than you absolutely have to.
- ▶ Ask for your credit score at least once a year and be sure you have a good one.
- ▶ Use only one or two credit cards.
- ▶ Try to pay off your credit card each month before any interest is charged.
- ▶ Write down your credit card numbers and keep them in a safe place in case your cards are lost or stolen.
- ▶ If you get into credit card trouble, get counseling.

Learning to manage your money and protect your credit rating will be as important to you as getting your degree. It is never too early to learn about money management. If you can do it when you have just a little money, it is easier when you have more.

ever work just for money or for power. They won't save your soul or help you sleep at night.

—Marian Wright Edelman

Knowledge in Bloom

Each chapter-end assessment is based on *Bloom's Taxonomy of Learning*. See the inside front cover for a quick review.

Utilizes levels 4, 5, and 6 of the taxonomy

Improving Your Money Management Skills

Process: As a beginning college student, it is not too early to map out your financial future. In this exercise, you will be asked to analyze your current financial management profile, design a plan for improvement, and critique your plan after practicing it for a week.

Using the information you have studied in this chapter, analyze your current financial management practices. Discuss your income, your expenses, student loans, credit card debt, impulse buying habits, and overall financial situation at the moment. Be sure to list financial concerns.

_____

_____

_____

_____

_____

_____

_____

Now that you have been honest with yourself and have identified your current financial practices and concerns, design a plan for improvement by listing steps that you will employ to practice better financial management.

_____

_____

_____

_____

_____

_____

_____

_____

Follow your plan for a week. Write down everything you spend, the things you resist that before you might have bought, and strategies you have employed to improve. After a week, evaluate your plan and your discipline to stick with this plan at this point.

_____

_____

_____

_____

_____

_____

_____

_____

_____

_____

_____

Preparing for Success

Refer to pages 236–237 of this chapter and answer the questions you developed from scanning this chapter's headings. You should also be able to answer the following questions if they were not on your list:

1. What have you learned that might help you make better decisions about student loans? _____

   _____

2. What are some of the dangers of credit card debt? _____

   _____

3. Why is budgeting so important? _____

   _____

4. What practices will you employ to avoid identity theft? _____

   _____

12

Communicate

© Getty Images

What
you find
in
your mind
is
what you
put there.

Mary Ford

Why will I ever be asked to use this stuff? *Why* will a chapter on communication help me in college, at work, with my family, and beyond? *Why* is this information on speaking and writing such a big deal?

T he language of the heart, which comes from the heart, is always simple, graceful, and full of power.

—Bovee

The things you learn in this chapter will be useful to you now while you are in college and later when you start a career. This chapter is designed to help you express yourself in your classes in both speaking and writing, but you will also find that this information will help you with all kinds of situations where you need to express yourself well. Good communication skills will help you improve your relationships at school, work, and home. This chapter will build research skills that you will use in almost every course you take.

Learning to communicate well is a necessary skill that will help you be successful in so many endeavors while at school and beyond. *This chapter can help you:*

▶ Develop research skills that help in writing and presenting papers
▶ Select topics and themes for written and oral presentations
▶ Understand and appreciate the power of words
▶ Hone skills that employers value greatly
▶ Learn to analyze a variety of types of audiences
▶ Organize and deliver quality speeches

This chapter will help you improve your writing, speaking, and research skills as you work toward becoming an accomplished speaker and writer. The skills you learn in this chapter will be useful to you in all your classes and will go with you when you move into your career.

Scan &

Take a few moments and **scan this chapter**. As you scan, **list five questions** you can expect to learn the answers to while reading and studying Chapter 12.

Example:
▶ What is a thesis statement? (from page 264)
▶ How do you evaluate Internet resources? (from page 265)

My Questions:

1. _____
   _____ from page _____

2. _____
   _____ from page _____

3. _____
   _____ from page _____

Name: Jackie Montgomery
Institution: University of Nevada—Las Vegas, Las Vegas, NV
Major: Business Administration
Age: 21

Having a chapter on written and oral communication is going to be very interesting and informative for you. I quickly found out that college papers and presentations were not like high school papers and presentations. In high school, the teachers gave you more directions and sometimes even gave you the subject. However, in college I have found this is not the case. I had to quickly learn how to identify my own topic, develop my own ideas, and use many sources of credible research to support those ideas. This chapter will help you do all of those things, too.

This chapter also discusses the importance of oral communication and how to put together a presentation for any class. So many of my classmates and I were very afraid of "public speaking," but once we learned the techniques of speaking, rehearsal, and delivery, it became easier. I'm thankful that it did because there have been so few classes in my college life thus far that have not required a personal or group oral presentation.

the big WHY

. . . from another perspective

Recently, I went on a series of interviews for a part-time job. I found myself using many of the communication skills I learned in class, and from this book, in those interviews. Everything from eye contact to hand shakes to a strong verbal tone all played a role in my interviews.

I have also found that communication is so very important to every type of relationship in our lives. It does not matter if you're trying to talk to your parents, friends, spouse, or partner, good communication skills can mean the difference between keeping that relationship solid or watching it go down the drain. By focusing on the information in this chapter, you'll begin to see how quickly you start using it in and out of the classroom.

4. _____

_____

from page _____

5. _____

_____

from page _____

Question

PS **Reminder:** At the end of the chapter, come back to this page and answer these questions in your notebook, text margins, or online chapter notes.

YOUR CHANCE TO SHINE

Writing! Research! Public Speaking!

"If I wanted to write papers or speak in front of people, I would have taken a writing class or a public speaking course," you might be saying at this moment. Relax. You are not alone in your anxiety about writing papers or speaking publicly. In fact, according to *The Book of Lists,* 3,000 Americans surveyed listed public speaking as their number one fear. Public speaking came in ahead of sickness, insects, financial troubles, deep water, and even death! So why do we include a chapter on writing and public speaking in a first-year orientation text? You probably won't like the answer, but the simple truth is that you are going to be asked to write and speak in many of your classes; from history to chemistry, from engineering to computer programming, writing and speaking are a way of life for today's college students. The more you know about writing papers and speeches and delivering speeches, the more confident you are going to feel in every class.

THE POWER OF WORDS

The benefits and value of written and oral communication cannot be measured. The power of words has changed nations, built civilizations, preserved traditions, freed masses, and prevented destruction. Think of the words written or spoken by Dr. Martin Luther King, Jr., Lorraine Hansbury, Maya Angelou, Booker T. Washington, Franklin Roosevelt, Frederick Douglass, Spike Lee, Ann Richards, Steven Spielberg, and Princess Diana. Good or bad, right or wrong, appropriate or inappropriate, their words have changed many lives.

The ability to write and speak with confidence and credibility is empowering. According to Beebe and Beebe (2002), learning to speak well will give you an edge that people with lesser skills lack. Even if someone else has superior knowledge, skills, and experience, if you can speak better, you may come across better. The ability to speak and write positions you to move to the next level. A survey of top executives who earned more than $ 250,000 per year was conducted by a large executive search firm. The survey found that these executives believe their communication skills were the number one factor that carried them to the top (Advanced Public Speaking Institute, 2003).

Numerous studies have reported that clear communication is imperative for one's success. In the marketplace of ideas, the person who communicates clearly is also the person who is seen as thinking clearly. Oral and written communications are not only job-securing, but job-holding skills. The ability to speak and write tops the list of skills that are sought after by corporations. Survey after survey reveals that the most important thing a college graduate can learn to do is speak and write well.

I f all my talents and powers were to be taken from me, and I had the choice of keeping but one, I would unhesitatingly ask to be allowed to keep the power of speaking, for through it, I would quickly recover the rest.

—Daniel Webster

Ten Steps to Communication Success

OVERVIEW OF SIMILARITIES AND DIFFERENCES BETWEEN WRITING AND SPEAKING

STEPS	WRITER	SPEAKING
Topic	Most likely assigned by the professor	May be assigned by the professor, most likely chosen by the student
	Can be very broad to appeal to a mass audience	Usually narrowed for a specific audience or class
	Can be narrative, informative, biographical, technical, analytical, etc.	Will usually be informative, demonstrative, or persuasive for classroom purposes
Audience Analysis	Usually written for the professor	Usually written and delivered for the class
Purpose Statement	Referred to as a thesis statement, it is usually at the beginning of the paragraph and introduces the topic	Referred to as a purpose or transition statement, it is usually at the end of the introduction and serves as a bridge to the body of the speech
Research Process	Research based on your topic and thesis statement	Research based on your topic and thesis statement
Organizational Process	May be assigned by the professor May use a formal outline	Usually determined by the type of speech Will probably use a less formal outline
Writing Process	Writer can create a draft and revise until polished	Speaker can create a draft and rehearse until polished
	May be allowed a rewrite after a grade is assigned	Seldom allowed a second chance for another grade
Documentation	Written at the end of the paper as a bibliography or reference page, depending on documentation style	Research and sources usually documented verbally during speech and may be written at the end of the speech as required by the professor
Outlining Delivery Notes	Not required for a written paper	Speaker can use a variety of notes such as key word outlines, note cards, or overheads if allowed by the professor
Audiovisual	Not required for a written paper	Adds strength to the presentation Increases audience attention and retention Speaker must rehearse with the aids used
Rehearsal and Delivery	Not required for a written paper	Speaker must spend a great deal of time in rehearsal to deliver a polished presentation

STEP 1: TOPIC SELECTION

Almost every writing and speaking expert will tell you to select a topic on which you are an expert, or a topic on which you have a keen interest and enough preparation time to become an expert. This does not mean that you cannot write or speak on topics that are new or unfamiliar to you, but if you choose such a topic, your preparation time will need to be extended. If you have a choice for your paper or speech, keep the following tips in mind.

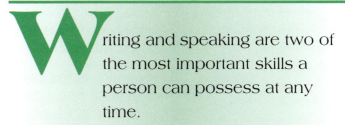

Writing and speaking are two of the most important skills a person can possess at any time.

—Dr. P. G. Moody

Tips for Topic Selection

▶ Know what type of paper or speech you will be writing and/or delivering.

▶ What are your talents, interests, and experiences?

Where Are You . . .

Before reading any further, take a moment and assess where you are at this moment with your knowledge and application of communications skills. Read each statement carefully and then respond accordingly.

1. I feel confident about speaking in front of a group of people. YES NO

2. I have no difficulty clearly explaining my thoughts to others. YES NO

3. I know how to select a topic for a paper or presentation in class. YES NO

4. I know how to access necessary research materials at the library. YES NO

5. When organizing materials for a paper or presentation, I always use an outline. YES NO

6. I always document the source of the facts I use for papers and projects. YES NO

7. I know how to use visual aids to complement a presentation. YES NO

8. I know how to analyze an audience and prepare a presentation that relates to them. YES NO

9. I know how to control my speaking anxiety. YES NO

If you answered "Yes" to most of the questions (seven or more), you most likely feel comfortable in researching and writing a paper. You feel somewhat comfortable in your ability to analyze an audience and prepare appropriate visual aids. *If you answered "No"* to most of the questions, you will need to examine why you feel inadequate when preparing and presenting a speech or writing a paper. If you feel less than comfortable, this will be an important chapter for you. You will need to push yourself in the beginning to step out of your comfort zone while learning to be comfortable speaking in front of a group.

▶ Can you find sufficient material and information for your paper or speech?

▶ Is your topic appropriate to you and your audience?

▶ Can you adequately discuss the topic within the given time frame or page length?

▶ Can the topic be narrowed down and still be beneficial?

▶ When researching your topic, narrow your search. If your subject is *rape,* for example, it may be too broad. You may have to narrow that search to *date rape,* or you could use the words college-date-rape if you wanted to see data pertaining only to rape on college campuses. By narrowing your topic at this stage, you save yourself hours of work later on.

As you work your way through this chapter, you will be asked to build a paper or speech. Following your instructor's guidelines, begin to develop your paper or speech by identifying a topic or using the topic given to you in class.

My topic is (be sure to narrow it down):

_____

_____

_____

Why have you chosen this topic?

_____

_____

_____

_____

As a writer or speaker, knowing your audience can create a positive rapport.

© Image 100 Ltd.

STEP 2: AUDIENCE ANALYSIS

Have you ever read a paper that was boring or listened to someone speak about a topic that was so technical that you understood very little of it? It could be because the paper or the speech was poorly written, but it may be that the boring paper or technical speech was inaccessible to you because it was written for a different audience. If you don't understand your audience, it is unlikely that you will be able to maintain their attention, inform or persuade them, or expect them to act on your advice. Although your immediate paper or speech will be written for your professor or class, there will be instances in the future when it will be advantageous to complete an analysis of your audience. This analysis will assist you in learning more about the diversity or homogeneity of your audience. Figure 12.1 will guide you in developing a comprehensive audience analysis.

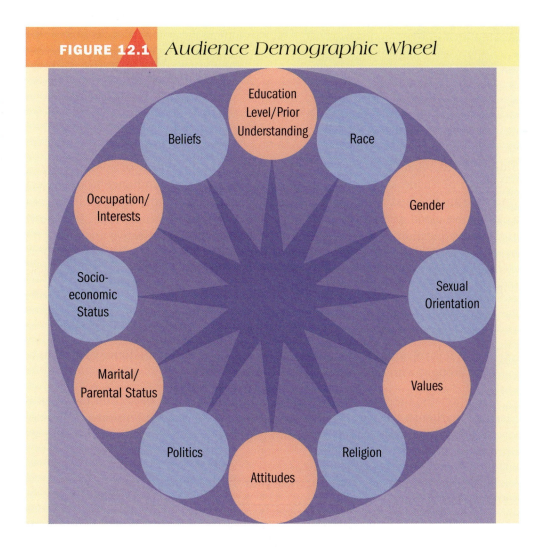

FIGURE 12.1 _Audience Demographic Wheel_

Education Level/Prior Understanding

Beliefs

Race

Occupation/Interests

Gender

Socio-economic Status

Sexual Orientation

Marital/Parental Status

Values

Politics

Religion

Attitudes

> nyone who wishes to fulfill a mission in the world must have an overmastering purpose that guides and controls them.
>
> —Unknown

An audience analysis might also consist of customized questions about your topic. If you were writing a paper or delivering a speech on genetic engineering, you might poll your audience to find out how many people believe that we should clone human beings.

Using your classroom setting as your audience, write a brief analysis of this audience. You may have to make some educated guesses based on observation and keen listening skills, but you may also have to interview them or issue a questionnaire. As a basis for your understanding, you will want to seek answers to the 12 factors in the demographic wheel. You may also need to answer questions such as, "What do I know about them?" "What do I need to find out?" "What do they expect?" and "What does my analysis mean to my paper or speech?"

Brief analysis of your classroom audience:

_____

_____

_____

_____

_____

_____

STEP 3: WRITING A THESIS STATEMENT

Simply stated, what do you want to accomplish? Are you writing or speaking to entertain, to persuade, or to inform? What do you want your audience to do or feel when you are finished? Do you want them to change their minds, sign a petition, join a cause, give blood, practice safer sex, or enjoy a trip down memory lane? If you can answer this question, you are well on your way to writing an effective and engaging paper or speech.

Your thesis statement is one sentence that tells your audience *exactly* what you hope to accomplish. Examples of some thesis statements are the following:

- ▶ You will understand the effects of domestic abuse, know how to look for warning signs, and know where to turn for assistance.
- ▶ Today, it is my intent to persuade you to complete the organ donor cards that I have brought with me.

Traditionally, the thesis will come at the end of the first or second paragraph. Placing it earlier in the paper or speech does not serve as an attention-gaining device. More will be discussed about gaining attention in the section on writing an introduction.

Using the topic you selected earlier, write your thesis statement here.

_____

_____

_____

_____

STEP 4: RESEARCHING YOUR SPEECH OR PAPER

Now that you have selected and narrowed your topic, analyzed your audience, and developed your purpose statement, you are ready to begin accumulating information to support your paper or speech. As you begin to consider resources, you will want to investigate and explore a variety of sources, including the following:

- ▶ Personal interviews with experts on your topic
- ▶ Electronic and print indexes, such as the *Reader's Guide* and *Humanities Index*
- ▶ Books
- ▶ Electronic card catalogs and computerized databases
- ▶ The Internet (start with Yahoo!, Infoseek, Dogpile, or Google, for example)
- ▶ Periodicals such as *Newsweek, Vital Speeches*, and *American Psychologist*
- ▶ Newspapers such as *The New York Times, Chicago Sun-Times*, and *Atlanta Constitution*
- ▶ Reference materials such as encyclopedias, dictionaries, directories, atlases, almanacs and yearbooks, books of quotations, and bibliographical directories
- ▶ Government documents

As you begin to collect your data, you may want to consider the following tips to keep your information orderly:

- ▶ Collect and keep copies of articles, pages of books, or chapters. You may want to copy them if the copyright laws permit.
- ▶ Always keep hard copies of your Internet research. Be sure to write the URL and the date you accessed it on each article.
- ▶ When taking notes from articles, chapters, pages, or the Internet, try to take them in an organized manner to save time later in the writing process.

Validity of Sources and Authors

As a researcher, you should know the validity of the sources and research that you plan to use to write your papers and speeches. The credibility of your sources can mean the difference between having a valid argument or thesis and having unsubstantiated opinions. With the Internet becoming an increasingly popular source for information, it is of ultimate importance that you know the validity of your Internet resources.

To evaluate Internet resources, you need to identify the audience that the article was intended for while bearing in mind that many things on the Internet are not valid. Therefore, you should check the author's validity and reputation, perhaps through checking refereed journal articles.

You should always feel free to ask the librarian for assistance and advice regarding Internet resources. Also, to critically analyze any information sources, whether Internet or print, use the following guidelines by Ormondroyd, Engle, and Cosgrave (2001) from Cornell University Libraries:

Internet research can be helpful, quick, and timely. But you must watch for false or misleading information.

© BananaStock Ltd.

- Who is the author and what are his or her credentials, educational background, past writings, and experience? Has your instructor mentioned the author? Is he or she cited in other works? Is the author associated with any organizations or institutes?

- When was the source published? If it is a Web page, the date is usually found on the last page or the home page. Is the source current or out of date for your topic?

- What edition is the source? Second and third editions suggest that the source has been updated to reflect changes and new knowledge.

- Who is the publisher? If the source is published by a university press, it is likely to be a scholarly publication.

- What is the title of the source? This will help you determine if the source is popular, sensational, or scholarly and indicates the level of complexity.

- Popular journals are resources such as *Time, Newsweek, Vogue, Ebony*, and *Reader's Digest*. They seldom cite their sources.

- Sensational resources are often inflammatory and written on an elementary level. They usually have flashy headlines, and they cater to popular superstitions. Examples are *The Globe, The National Enquirer*, and *The Star*.

- Scholarly resources are defined as having a solid base. They are substantial. They always cite their sources and are usually written by scholars in their fields. Usually, they report on original research.

- What is the intended audience of your source? Is the information too simple, too advanced, or too technical for your needs?

- Is the source factually objective, is it opinionated, or is it propaganda? Objective sources look at all angles and report on each one honestly. Sources of opinion give unfounded information. Propaganda is information that spreads the same message over and over until it is believed by the masses.

- Does the information appear to be valid and well researched or does it just gloss over the material? Is it supported by evidence? Usually, the more in-depth the source, the more substantial it is going to be to your research.

- When using the Internet for resources, use extreme caution. Anyone can create a Web page or present information on the Internet. This can be good, but it can also create a situation where you have little control over the validity of your resources. Laura Cohen (1996a) of the University of Albany Libraries suggests, "Internet sites change over time according to the commitment and inclination of the creator. Some sites demonstrate an expert's knowledge, while others are amateur efforts. Some may be updated daily, while others may be outdated."

To evaluate Web pages (UC Berkeley, 2005), you should train your mind to think critically, even suspiciously, by asking a series of questions that will help you decide how much a Web page is to be trusted:

- Is it someone's personal page? Personal pages are not necessarily bad, but they may need to be investigated very carefully.

- What kind of domain does it come from? Look for appropriateness. What do you think is the most reliable source for your topic?

- Look for the date when the article was last updated.

- Who wrote the paper? Look for the name of the author or organization, agency, or institution that is responsible for the page.

- Is the page dated? Is it current enough for your research or is it "stale" or "dusty"?

- ▶ What are the author's credentials? Anyone can put anything on the Web. Your task is to distinguish between the reliable and the questionable.
- ▶ Are sources documented with footnotes or links? In scholarly works, the credibility of most writings is proven through the footnote documentation.
- ▶ Ask yourself, "Why was this page put on the Web?"
- ▶ Could the article be parody, humor, or satire?
- ▶ Is this as good a resource as you could find if you used the library?

Access the magazine *Biography* at www.biography.com and *The National Enquirer* at www.nationalenquirer.com or a similar tabloid and conduct a brief review of the background of the entertainer Beyoncé. Compare and contrast the reliability of the information you find on both sites. If you were writing a formal paper, which site offers you the most credible research? Why?

_____

_____

_____

_____

_____

_____

_____

_____

_____

_____

_____

_____

Bloom Level 4 question

STEP 5: ORGANIZING YOUR PAPER OR SPEECH

Now that you have gathered enough information from a variety of resources, what are the most effective ways to present your findings and ideas? As you know, every good paper and speech will have an introduction, body, and conclusion. A complete discussion of introductions and conclusions will follow in the next section on writing.

Organizing the body of your paper or speech can be done using one of several proven methods.

Spatial organization is when you arrange information or items according to their direction or location.

Example: If you were describing the mall in Washington, DC, you could begin with the Lincoln Memorial and then move on to the reflecting pond, the Washington Monument, and the Smithsonian.

Cause-effect organization is when you arrange your information in the cause-and-effect order. You would discuss the causes of a problem and then explore its effects.

Example: If you were speaking about high blood pressure, you would first examine the causes of high blood pressure such as diet, hereditary factors, and weight, and then move on to the effects such as heart attack and stroke.

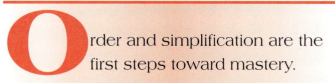

rder and simplification are the first steps toward mastery.

—Thomas Mann

Chronological organization is presenting information in the order in which it happened. Speeches that deal with historical facts and how-to speeches often use chronological organization.

Example: If you were giving a speech or writing a paper on the history of automobiles in America since 1950, you would begin with the '50s and move to the '60s, '70s, '80s, and '90s. If you were giving a how-to speech on refinishing a table, you would begin with the first process of stripping the old paint or varnish and move forward to the last step of applying a new coat of paint or varnish.

Problem-solving organization is often used in persuasive papers and speeches. Usually, you are trying to get your reader or audience to accept your proposal. You first begin by pointing out the major problem(s) and then move on to revealing the solutions and the advantages of the solutions.

Example: If you were writing or speaking about crime on college campuses, you would begin by informing the reader or listener about the problems, the crime statistics, and the personal toll on students. You would then propose solutions and tell how the solutions would help all students.

Topical/categorical organization is when you group information into subdivisions or cluster information into categories. Some information naturally falls into specific categories, such as the different types of palm trees or the types of rollerblades available.

Example: If you were writing a speech or paper on taxes in the United States, you might categorize your information into local taxes, state taxes, federal taxes, luxury taxes, "sin" taxes, and special taxes.

Compare/contrast organization is when you present your information in a fashion that shows its similarities to and differences from other information.

Example: You may be writing a paper or speech that compares the health care system in the United States to that of England or Canada.

Importance/priority organization allows you to arrange information from the most important issue to the least or the least important to the most important. You can also arrange your information from the top priority to the lowest priority or vice versa.

Example: If you were writing a paper or delivering a speech to inform readers and listeners about buying diamonds, you might arrange your information so that you speak first about the most important aspects of diamond buying and later about less important factors.

Using the topic that you selected at the beginning of the chapter, and referring to the up-to-date, valid research that you have gathered, how do you plan to organize your paper or speech? Why is this the best way?

_____

_____

_____

CHUCK DELPH (Posthumously, 2006)
Chief Tool Engineer (Retired), The DaimlerChrysler Corporation
Kokomo, IN

I never took a shower until I was in high school. I loved to play sports, but I never owned a pair of tennis shoes until I was in junior high school. I was born and raised in the small town of Tipton, Indiana as one of eight children. To say we were "poor" would be as much of an understatement as saying that the sun's surface gets a little warm. We lived in a two-bedroom house where all eight children slept in one bedroom—four to a bed. My father was an alcoholic who worked in a poor-paying job for the railroad company. My siblings and I got along, but we had a harsh relationship with our father. My mother stayed home and cared for my siblings and me as best she could. Many meals consisted of rice or cereal or pig brains—things that went a long way for a small amount of money.

My father built our small house from materials he was able to salvage from the railroad company. He used railroad ties as the beams for the floors and old wood from inside boxcars for the walls. The windows were bought from salvage yards and we had no bathroom. We had to wash our clothes and dishes in the same sink, and each Saturday, we pulled a metal tub into the middle of the kitchen so we could have our weekly bath. My years in elementary school were very difficult as I tried to cover the shame of our poverty, the embarrassment over our house, and the humiliation of wearing hand-made, hand-me-down clothes. I had to begin working when I was seven years old. I found a job as a golf caddy. From hoeing corn to working on the railroad, there was never a time in my life, from that point forward, that I did not hold a job.

I was always good at sports but often I was not allowed to play because I was too poor to afford the equipment or uniform. I liked math in high school and worked hard to be successful in my classes. I looked around and saw that the guys who had the cars, got the girls, and went on to college were not just

successful in sports, but in academics as well. I began to understand that a college education was the only way to escape my past. It was my road map out of Tipton.

I passed the entrance exam for college and began pursuing my love of bridge engineering. There was no such thing as work-study and my grades were not good enough to earn a scholarship. Eventually, I had to leave college because I simply could not pay for it. My father was able to get me a job at the railroad company as a car man's helper, rebuilding old boxcars. Eventually, I was promoted to car man and this led to my hearing about, applying for, and being accepted into a two-year apprentice program for the Chrysler Corporation. Finally, my abilities in math and my experience at the railroad began to pay off.

My first job at Chrysler was helping to build the new plant in Kokomo, Indiana. I worked hard and studied under skilled and talented tradesmen until I finally became a tool and die maker. It took over 8,000 hours and four years, but I made it. During this time, I married, had three children and began working on my associate's degree. I knew I had to know more to move up the ladder. I advanced to maintenance engineer supervisor and then went on to become a chief tool engineer. By the time I received my degree, I was an engineering manager at Chrysler's Kokomo Transmission Plant supervising over 1,500 people.

I left Chrysler years later and served in several management positions, including vice president for U.S. manufacturing for Bendix Corporation in Detroit. The proudest moments of my life, however, were watching all three of my children graduate from college. One is a geophysicist, one is a lawyer, and one is a college professor and writer. Nothing will ever match the joy of knowing that my children and their children had the opportunity and means to transcend the poverty that I knew as a child.

Step 6: Writing Your Paper or Speech

At some point in time, we have all made written or verbal blunders that caused us embarrassment or even hurt someone. The power of words is phenomenal. They make us laugh and cry, feel pain and joy, understand and react. When writing your papers and speeches, it is important to remember that you have the power of words at your side. They can be used for good or bad, strengthening or weakening, building or tearing down, love or hatred. The choice is always up to you.

Ethical Considerations

As a writer and speaker, you have a personal responsibility to consider the ethics and consequences of your statements.

Gamble and Gamble, in their book *Public Speaking in the Age of Diversity* (1998), suggest that you follow these guidelines when considering the ethical dimensions of writing and speaking:

▶ Share only what you know to be true.

▶ Be fully prepared and informed.

▶ Consider the best interest of your receivers.

▶ Make it easy for your receivers to understand your message.

▶ Refrain from using words as weapons.

▶ Don't wrap information in a positive spin just to succeed.

▶ Respect the cultural diversity of your receivers.

▶ Remember you are accountable for what you say.

Using Language

As you begin to write your paper or speech, several factors will assist you in building colorful, meaningful, and memorable work. When writing, consider the following:

▶ Use colorful, vivid language to evoke images and word pictures.

   Example: Instead of telling the reader or listener about a dog, tell about the six-week-old, black, playful Labrador retriever. This helps your reader or listener "see" rather than imagine.

▶ Use unbiased, nonsexist, nonracist, nonageist language.

   Example: Instead of writing or saying, "Everyone should bring his lab kit to class tomorrow," the proper language would be, "Everyone should bring his or her lab kit to class tomorrow."

▶ Use simple, nontechnical, familiar, layperson terminology (the language should suit the audience).

   Example: Instead of writing or speaking about the absence of monocholorodifloromethane, simply say that the air conditioner was out of Freon. Your audience will appreciate it; so will your spellchecker.

▶ Use concrete language.

   Example: Instead of saying, "She drove a very expensive car," say, "She drove a Lexus." Instead of saying, "The building was crummy," say, "The building's foundation was crumbling, the walls were dirty, and the roof was in need of repair."

▶ Use parallelism for balance.

Example: If you open by telling a story about the abuses suffered by a mother and her child, you can mention them in the body and end the story in the conclusion. Martin Luther King, Jr., used parallelism in his "I Have a Dream" speech by repeating throughout the speech, "I have a dream . . . ".

Selecting the Main Ideas and Issues

At this point, you have carefully selected and narrowed your topic. You have taken a careful look at your audience; you have decided on the basic needs you plan to address; you have written a comprehensive thesis; and you have collected your research. Upon reviewing your research, you have decided on an organizational pattern, and finally, you have examined some interesting and creative ways to add variety and color to your paper or speech. Now, based on your research, you are ready to decide on the main issues and major details that you plan to share with your readers or audience. The main issues are going to be derived from your research and your thesis statement. Main issues are the major divisions of your paper or speech. David Zarefsky, in his book *Public Speaking: Strategies for Success* (2001), suggests that you can identify main ideas and issues by asking the following questions:

▶ What does it mean?
▶ What are the facts?
▶ What are the reasons?
▶ How often does it occur?
▶ What is my view?
▶ What are the parts?
▶ What is the reasoning?

▶ What is the cause?
▶ How will it happen?
▶ Who is involved?
▶ What are some examples?
▶ What are some objections?
▶ What is the effect?
▶ What is preventing it?

© Flip Schulke/Corbis

Martin Luther King, Jr. was only in his thirties and pastor of a small Baptist church in Montgomery, Alabama, when he was thrust into the national spotlight as a leader of protests against segregation.

The movements and marches he led brought significant changes in the fabric of American life through his courage and selfless devotion. He was arrested over 20 times, traveled 6,000,000 miles and spoke over 2,500 times wherever there was injustice or protest.

Martin Luther King and Coretta Scott King had four children, all of whom are involved in different aspects of civil rights.

He was awarded the Nobel Peace Prize at the age of 35, the youngest man ever to receive the award. Dr. King was assassinated in 1968 in Memphis, Tennessee.

Organizing the Body

One of the most effective ways to begin composing your paper or speech is to create a rough outline of the points you would like to cover. As you begin to outline, remember that your organizational pattern should guide you through this phase. The following is an example of a generic outline:

Types of Evidence
    I. Point 1 or Major Issue 1
        a. Who, what, when, where, and why?
        b. Statistics, polls, results
        c. Personal testimonials, case studies
        d. Causes
        e. Problems and solutions
    II. Point 2 or Major Issue 2
        a. Who, what, when, where, and why?
        b. Statistics, polls, results

c. Personal testimonials, case studies

d. Causes

e. Problems and solutions

III. Point 3 or Major Issue 3

a. Who, what, when, where, and why?

b. Statistics, polls, results

c. Personal testimonials, case studies

d. Causes

e. Problems and solutions

Once you have developed your outline, you can begin to write your paper or speech. Using the topic you selected earlier, organize the body of your paper or speech by completing an outline of your resources. Use a separate sheet of paper for this exercise

YES YOU CAN!

IDEAS FOR Success

Consider the following strategies for improving your presentations:

▶ Select topics that interest you and your audience.

▶ Analyze your audience and how you might relate to them.

▶ Carefully research your papers and presentations.

▶ Document your sources carefully.

▶ Pay extra attention to Internet resources.

▶ Polish your presentation by practicing aloud many times.

▶ Face your fears about speaking by presenting in public as often as you can.

▶ Keep in mind the slogan, "This is your moment in the sun." Use it wisely.

Introductions

Throughout the day, you are bombarded with ideas, messages, and ads begging for your attention. How do you decide on the messages to which you will direct your attention? Is it the low-key, dull message or idea that grabs you? Is it the idea or message that you have heard countless times? No, it is the message that is vibrant, new, creative, and alive that catches your attention and holds you long enough to hear the information. You are now at the point where you will need to consider the introduction and conclusion to your paper or speech.

The introduction to your work will, in a very large part, determine how the reader or audience perceives you and your work, and it will determine if you are going to obtain and maintain their interest. While the introduction is a very small part of your overall piece, it should never be taken lightly. It is the first few lines that will lure your audience to your message or turn them to thoughts of last night's supper. Attention spans are short, so you must use attention-getting devices.

As you study the techniques of introducing that are detailed here, think about the topic you chose earlier. Determine which technique would best suit your individual writing and/or delivery style, which would most greatly appeal to your audience, and which technique you feel would best gain their attention. Introductions are not necessarily written first. Many writers and speakers write their introduction last. Keep this in mind as you begin to compose. Here are a variety of techniques used to create effective introductions:

▶ Telling a story or creating a vivid, visual illustration

▶ Using startling facts or statistics

▶ Referring to an accident with which the audience or reader is familiar

▶ Asking rhetorical, yet pertinent questions

▶ Using novel ideas or striking statements

▶ Using quotations

▶ Using humor or humorous stories

▶ Showing a visual

The following is an example of an introduction using the technique of telling a story. Note the thesis statement at the end of the introduction:

It was a normal Friday, just like every other Friday for the past 10 years. Jane had gone to the grocery store, driven home, pulled into her driveway, and started unloading the groceries from the car. Just as she opened the trunk, she heard a loud scream from inside the house. She threw the groceries back into the trunk and ran toward the house. The front door was slightly ajar. As she entered the front door, her greatest horror was realized. Her 6-year-old son Jeff was sitting in the middle of the floor with blood on the front of his shirt. He was holding his left arm, crying and screaming. Immediately, Jane thought, "Did he fall out of that treehouse again? Did he have another accident on his bicycle?" The answer came when she saw her husband coming down the hall with a Ping Pong paddle in his hand and blood on his shirt—drinking again.

What Jane began to realize at this moment was that two years ago when Jeff had a broken arm, he had fallen out of the treehouse, and last month, when he suffered two cracked ribs, he had not fallen off his bicycle. What she began to realize was that Jeff was suffering from the same thing that she had suffered from for nine years—domestic abuse.

(Thesis or Purpose Statement) This paper will inform you about (or, Today, I am going to speak to you about) the causes, effects, and signs of domestic abuse. I will also provide information that will help you gain assistance if you are involved in an abusive relationship or know someone who is.

In the space provided, choose one technique or a combination of the techniques we've discussed to construct an introduction to your topic.

Technique(s) used

_____

_____

Introduction

_____

_____

_____

_____

_____

_____

Conclusions

Without exception, the conclusion should be one of the most carefully crafted components of your paper or speech. Long after your reader has finished reading or your audience has finished listening, the last part of your work is more than likely going to be the part they remember the most. Some writers and speakers suggest that you write your conclusion *first,* so that your paper or speech is directed toward a specific end result. That decision, of course, is up to you. However, a great piece of advice from writing experts tells us that captivating writers always know how their stories will end long before they begin writing them.

The following are some techniques for concluding a paper or speech:

▶ Summarize and reemphasize the main points.

▶ Make a final appeal for action or challenge.

▶ Refer to the introduction (story, quote, or joke); this is parallelism.

▶ Complete the opening story.

▶ Reemphasize the impact of your topic.

▶ Use a vivid analogy or simile.

▶ End powerfully.

The following is an example of a conclusion using the technique of referring to the introduction (parallelism) and making an appeal for action.

> Jane had denied the abusive situation for so long that she could not see how it was affecting her son. Just as the individual men and women profiled in this speech (paper) feared retaliation and more violence if they left the relationship, so do larger groups in our society. However, we saw that there are a variety of resources available for assistance such as the Women's Program for Abuse, Sister Care, Americans for an Abuse Free Nation, and local police departments. I call on you today, if you are in an abusive relationship or know someone who is, to act deliberately and immediately. Tomorrow may be one day too late.

In the space provided and using your topic from the beginning of the chapter, write a memorable, creative conclusion.

Technique(s) used _____
Conclusion _____
_____
_____
_____
_____

STEP 7: DOCUMENTING YOUR PAPER OR SPEECH

When writing your paper or speech, and certainly once it has been written, you should take careful precautions to document all research and information that is not your own. If you have written a paper, you will need to document and cite all statistics, quotes, and excerpts from works that you referenced. The most common means of doing this is by quoting within the paper and then compiling a reference list or bibliography at the end. If you have written a speech, you can verbally document researched facts, statistics, quotes, and excerpts. The following is an example of verbal documentation:

> Jane and her son Jeff are not alone in their abusive situation. According to Ronald Cohen in his book, *Psychology and Adjustment,* over 1.5 million cases of abuse occur in the United States every year.

This allows the listeners to focus on the research and lets them know where the facts, statistics, or excerpts came from.

If you have questions about what to document, consider the following list by Kirszner and Mandell (1995):

▶ Direct quotations

▶ Opinions, judgments, and insights of others that you summarize or paraphrase

▶ Information that is not widely known

▶ Information that is open to dispute

▶ Information that is not commonly accepted

▶ Tables, charts, graphs, and statistics taken from a source

There are several popular documentation styles used today. They include, but are not limited to, *The Modern Language Association* (MLA), *The American Psychological Association* (APA), and *The Chicago Manual of Style* (CMS).

Using your topic, choose two of your research sources, choose a documentation style, and properly document them here.

Style chosen:

_____

_____

Source #1

_____

_____

_____

Source #2

_____

_____

_____

STEP 8: OUTLINING YOUR NOTES FOR DELIVERY

The techniques for outlining a speech are exclusive to delivery only. If you have used this chapter as a guideline for writing papers, this section and the last two sections on audiovisual aids and rehearsal will not be relevant to you at this time.

If you have ever watched and heard a disorganized speaker, or had to endure a speaker _reading_ an entire presentation, then you know the value of well-designed speaking notes.

After your speech has been formally written, it is time to outline your speaking notes. It is the mark of an unprofessional, unprepared speaker to read verbatim from pages and pages of typed notes. Instead, with rehearsal and a comprehensive key-word outline, you can use surprisingly few notes as you gain experience.

An outline should be used to keep you organized and to assist you should you get lost or blank out during your presentation. It should not be used for reading your speech to the audience. Some speakers prefer to use note cards (3 × 5 or 5 × 7), while others prefer to use several sheets of paper in outline form. The choice is yours unless specified otherwise by your professor. Examples of a note card and a note outline are provided in Figure 12.2.

In the space provided here, outline the introduction that you wrote earlier in the chapter. Remember, use only key words. Do not write it out verbatim.

_____

_____

_____

_____

_____

_____

_____

_____

_____

_____

_____

_____

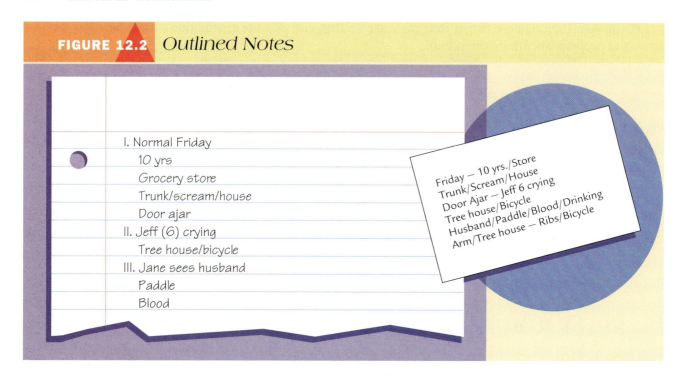

FIGURE 12.2   *Outlined Notes*

I. Normal Friday
   10 yrs
   Grocery store
   Trunk/scream/house
   Door ajar
II. Jeff (6) crying
   Tree house/bicycle
III. Jane sees husband
   Paddle
   Blood

Friday — 10 yrs./Store
Trunk/Scream/House
Door Ajar — Jeff 6 crying
Tree house/Bicycle
Husband/Paddle/Blood/Drinking
Arm/Tree house — Ribs/Bicycle

STEP 9: USING AUDIOVISUAL AIDS

You have heard it said, "A picture is worth a thousand words." Nowhere is that more true than in public speaking. Visual aids can assist your audience in retaining the information longer. If you simply tell an audience a fact, three days later, they will remember only 10% of what you said. If you tell them and show them, three days later, they will remember 65% of what you said (Gamble and Gamble, 1998).

Several important factors should be considered when developing your visual aids. First, an audiovisual aid is a supplement to, not a substitute for, a presentation. Simply stated, even the most wonderfully creative visual aid will not support a poorly written and delivered speech. When choosing your aid, consider your audience, the location, and your time limits. You should also consider your comfort level with the aid that you have chosen. There are many types of aids available to you:

> *S*peeches cannot be made long enough for the speakers, nor short enough for the hearers.
>
> —Perry

- ▶ Physical objects
- ▶ Models
- ▶ Drawings
- ▶ Maps
- ▶ Videotapes
- ▶ Audio recordings
- ▶ Real people

- ▶ Overhead transparencies
- ▶ Graphs, tables, and charts
- ▶ Photographs and slides
- ▶ Slick boards and chalkboards
- ▶ Yourself (probably the most important)
- ▶ Posters and flip charts
- ▶ Computer-generated presentations (such as PowerPoint slides) and CD-ROMs

For a smooth, clean, polished presentation, consider the following guidelines when using your visual aids:

- ▶ *Always* rehearse with your audiovisual (AV) aids.
- ▶ Make sure your AV is visible to all audience members.

- ▸ Make sure all equipment works before you begin your speech.
- ▸ Bring any item that you might need to make your AV work (such as extension cords, tape, push pins, and magic markers).
- ▸ Reveal each AV when you are ready to use it, not all at once.
- ▸ Explain each AV as it is revealed.
- ▸ Do not pass any AV around the room.
- ▸ Remove the AV when you have finished using it.
- ▸ Use any living AV with caution.
- ▸ Don't speak to the AV; speak to your audience.
- ▸ Use handouts with extreme caution. They should be issued only at the very end of your speech.

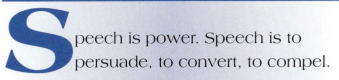

Speech is power. Speech is to persuade, to convert, to compel.

—Ralph Waldo Emerson

Consider the information and research that you plan to share. What type of audiovisual aid would best suit you, your presentation, and your audience?

Type of AV_____

Why? _____

_____

STEP 10: REHEARSAL AND DELIVERY

The time has come! All of your hard work, creativity, and energy will culminate in this one moment in the sun. You have taken all of the necessary steps for a successful presentation. Now, you only need to consider a few more details before taking the lectern.

Public speaking is an unfair beast. If you study for an exam and do well or fail to study and do poorly, the results are known only to you and the professor. However, the results of your public speaking performance are known to all present. You are evaluated immediately. That is just an accepted fact in the art of speaking. In order to do your very best, consider the following anxiety-reducing and delivery tips.

Reducing Anxiety

As we mentioned earlier in the chapter, the fear of public speaking is rated as the number one fear among Americans. According to Gamble and Gamble (1998), there are several reasons why we fear public speaking:

- ▸ Fear of failure
- ▸ Fear of the unknown
- ▸ Fear of evaluation
- ▸ Fear of being the center of attention
- ▸ Fear of difference
- ▸ Fear imposed by culture

Most of our obstacles would melt away if instead of cowering before them, we should make up our minds to walk boldly through them.

—Orison Swett Marden

These fears are real, but they are also manageable. When faced with anxiety over public speaking, keep the following tips in mind:

► A certain degree of anxiety is good for you. Use it to create energy.

► Choose a topic about which you know a great deal and one about which you care deeply.

► Prepare for your speech thoroughly!

► When rehearsing, try to recreate the speaking environment, or if possible, rehearse in the room where the speech will be delivered.

► Approach the speech with an "I can" attitude. The more confident you act, the more confident you will eventually become.

► After your first speech, jot down what happened to you physically; that is, did your heart beat faster, did you sweat, did your breathing become erratic? Keep a running list of these reactions so that you can recognize them and begin to control them.

► Realize that your small mistakes will not be seen and will rarely be heard by the audience; they are magnified in your own mind.

► Remember that listeners want you to succeed; most audiences are supportive.

► Instead of looking at the entire audience as a "room full of people," choose one person and look at him or her for a brief moment. Then, move on to the next person, and so on. This creates the feeling of speaking to only one person at a time.

► Don't try to be something that you are not. Just be yourself; use your own voice, your own gestures, and your own style.

► Don't concentrate on the evaluation. If you are prepared and do your best, you will be evaluated fairly.

► Visualize your success; the power of positive thinking is vastly underrated.

Rehearsal and Delivery

The moment is close at hand. Your topic is sterling, you have all of the information that you need to succeed, and you have prepared and rehearsed. To achieve a polished and professional touch, keep these final tips in mind:

► Always practice aloud so that you can practice your volume, tone, pace, and articulation.

► Rehearse from beginning to end without stopping.

► Rehearse at least once in front of a mirror so you can see your gestures, facial expressions, and body language.

► Rehearse using minimal notes.

► Rehearse using a tape recorder so that you may evaluate your own performance.

► When rehearsing, use a timer so that you can adjust your speech accordingly.

► Never, ever, under any circumstances, apologize for your speech or presentation.

- ▶ Watch your nonverbal communication (body language, facial expressions, and gestures).
- ▶ Remove temptations to fidget with things such as keys, change in your pocket, pens, and clips.
- ▶ Always maintain eye contact with your audience.
- ▶ The occasion should dictate your dress, so dress for the occasion.
- ▶ Don't stand in front of an audience and read; know your topic and simply talk to them.

The steps outlined in this chapter will assist you in writing and delivering a paper and public speech. However, without a positive "I can" attitude, much of your preparation will be fruitless. Public speaking is an exciting, rewarding experience that will assist you in almost every endeavor of your collegiate and professional life. The more you practice, the better you'll become!

Think About It
Chapter Reflection

As you learn to speak and write well, you will be following a tradition that has been practiced by scholars for thousands of years. Effective speechmaking principles can be traced to Plato, Socrates, Cicero, and Quintilian. By learning to construct and deliver your own presentations and write your own papers, you are becoming accomplished in skills that will serve you well all your life.

Learning to write well and to make effective presentations will help you succeed in every class you take. More than likely, the skills learned in this chapter will assist you in improving your relationships with friends and family. While you further hone your communications abilities, you will want to practice the following points:

- ▶ Use a comprehensive thesis statement.
- ▶ Use credible, documented research.
- ▶ Be sure to investigate carefully sources found on the Internet.
- ▶ Always rehearse aloud. Rehearse often.
- ▶ Take every opportunity to speak in public.
- ▶ Use a logical organization pattern.
- ▶ Employ a variety of research sources.
- ▶ Develop an "I can" attitude.
- ▶ Speak on subjects that you know.
- ▶ Use a key word outline.
- ▶ Analyze the audience and relate to them.
- ▶ Use vivid, colorful language.
- ▶ Learn to use technology to complement your presentations.

Do more than exist, LIVE.
Do more than touch, FEEL.
Do more than look, OBSERVE.
Do more than read, ABSORB.
Do more than hear, LISTEN.
Do more than listen, UNDERSTAND.
Do more than think, PONDER.
Do more than talk, SAY SOMETHING.

—John H. Rhoades

Remember, *This is your moment in the sun! Shine!*

Knowledge in Bloom

Each chapter-end assessment is based on *Bloom's Taxonomy of Learning.* See the inside front cover for a quick review.

Utilizes levels 1–6 of the taxonomy

Improving Your Research Skills and Applications

Explanation: In Chapter 1's Knowledge in Bloom, the activity required you to use each of the six steps in Bloom's Taxonomy: Knowledge, Comprehension, Application, Analysis, Synthesis, and Evaluation. This chapter-end activity will ask you to do the same.

Process: The exercises will ask you to use your research skills to find out all that you can about the singer and movie star, Queen Latifah, as if you were going to write a paper or deliver a speech on her life. The questions below will guide you in making a proper search and narrowing your topic. You can use the Internet or any valid print media to answer the questions.

Locate Queen Latifah's real name:

_____

Using research, briefly discuss in 200 words or less Queen Latifah's background.

_____

_____

_____

_____

_____

What was her first CD? What was her first movie? What else has she done in her life on the stage or screen that you would want your audience to know?

_____

_____

_____

_____

_____

Based on what you have learned about Queen Latifah, deduce from the information you found through your research the main things in her background that have driven her to be successful.

_____

_____

_____

_____

_____

Based on your research of Queen Latifah and what you have discovered about her virtues, compile a list of positive attributes that she has that you would like to share with your audience.

_____

_____

_____

_____

Based on your research, what adversities or setbacks has Queen Latifah had in her past that you feel your audience needs to know?

_____

_____

_____

_____

_____

Evaluate two of the Web sites you used to find this information. Are they useful, valid, reliable?

Web Site #1

_____

_____

_____

_____

_____

Web Site #2

_____

_____

_____

_____

_____

Preparing for Success

Refer to pages 258–259 of this chapter and answer the questions you developed from scanning this chapter's headings. You should also be able to answer the following questions if they were not on your list:

1. How do people like Steven Spielberg, Maya Angelou, or Beyoncé use communications and the power of words in their careers?_____
   _____

2. Why is it important to analyze an audience before you prepare a presentation to deliver to them? ___
   _____

3. Why is it important to know something about a topic before you make a presentation?_____
   _____

4. What role does a strong thesis sentence play in making an overall good presentation or writing a comprehensive paper? _____
   _____

13

Relate

© Getty Images

Success is empty if you arrive at the finish line alone. The best reward is to get there surrounded by winners. The more winners you bring with you—the more gratifying the victory.

Howard Schultz

the big
WHY

Why is it important to study about relationships? *Why* can't everyone just get along? *Why* will a chapter on relationships help me be able to get along with other people at college, work, or in the neighborhood?

N o road is long with good company.

—Turkish proverb

Life is about relationships. You would literally have to be shipwrecked on an island to be free of relationships with other humans, but you would still have relationships with nature and animals. People do not live in a vacuum. We are the sum total of all of our relationships.

For many of you, this has been a rather homogenized sum. If you grew up in a big city, you have been exposed to a wider variety of cultures. For those from smaller communities, there might not have been much opportunity to explore other cultures. Higher education is designed to give you the opportunity to meet, study with, befriend, and come to understand people who walk a different path—be it a different age, gender, race, religion, culture, sexual orientation, or physical challenge. *This chapter can help you:*

▶ Understand why relationships are important
▶ Develop a community during your college experience
▶ Learn about cultures that differ from your own
▶ Learn how to appreciate other cultures
▶ Manage conflict
▶ Understand the components of culture

Addressing every aspect of relationships is important to understanding any of them. This chapter looks at relationships with our friends, family, peers, and professors, and examines the components of culture and how understanding diversity can help us all.

Scan &

Take a few moments and **scan this chapter**. As you scan, **list five questions** you can expect to learn the answers to while reading and studying Chapter 13.

Example:
▶ Why are relationships important? (from page 288)
▶ What does it mean to be a culture of one? (from page 293)

My Questions:

1. _____
   _____ from page _____

2. _____
   _____ from page _____

3. _____
   _____ from page _____

Name: Sheena Moses
Institution: Florence Darlington Technical College, Florence, SC
Major: Paralegal studies
Age: 23

I am employed by my college in the work-study program and I work for the department chair of math, science, and humanities. Every day, so many people from so many backgrounds, interests, and walks of life come through the office. I'm lucky that I enjoy meeting new people and learning from everyone.

All of the work-study participants had to attend a development workshop last semester. We were assigned a partner and it turned out that my partner was quite different from me. The first thing I noticed was how she carried herself; how she acted and how she dressed. The most interesting thing about her was that she wore a garment that covered her face. I was not sure if it was cultural or religious—and I did not ask.

What I did find out in the course of our conversation was that she and I shared the same religion. In our spare time, that was the topic of conversation. What I loved was

the big WHY

. . . from another perspective

discovering that even though we are quite different, we had a very common path together—our religion. So, getting beyond the outward appearance and obvious cultural difference, we had a great deal in common. I enjoyed her company and conversation.

That is what this whole chapter is about. The information in Chapter 13 offers advice on how to interact and learn from people who may not be like you. I think that one of the best lessons of my life has been this: Talk to others and have an open mind. By doing both, we learn from others, grow from their knowledge of the world, and understand that just because someone is different from us, this does not make him or her wrong or bad.

4. _____

_____

from page _____

5. _____

_____

from page _____

PS **Reminder:** At the end of the chapter, come back to this page and answer these questions in your notebook, text margins, or online chapter notes.

Question

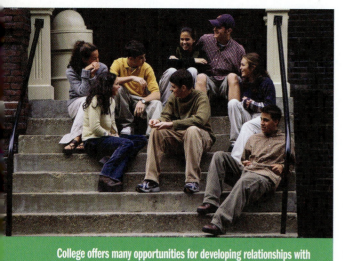

College offers many opportunities for developing relationships with people from backgrounds that may be different from your own.

© Corbis

WHY ARE RELATIONSHIPS IMPORTANT?

To function in a happy and healthy manner, human beings need one another. Everything we learn in this life comes through and from our relationships with others. We need each other to help us laugh, help us cry, help us learn, help us work, help us provide for the survival of the species, and help us die when the time comes.

Throughout our lives, we experience a myriad of relationships. We are someone's son or daughter, we may be someone's brother or sister, and we probably will be someone's friend and someone's lover, as well as someone's helpmate through life. Each of these relationships has its own individual dynamics, but all successful relationships have some similarities.

Communities

Most, if not all, of our relationships take place within a community. Shaffer and Amundsen, in their book *Creating Community Anywhere* (1994), define a community as a dynamic whole that emerges when a group of people do the following:

▶ Participate in common practices

▶ Depend on one another

▶ Make decisions together

▶ Identify themselves as part of something larger than the sum of their individual relationships

▶ Commit themselves for the long term to their own, to one another's, and to the group's well-being

I am part of all that I have met.

—Alfred Tennyson

You may find yourself involved in several separate communities: a home community, a school community, a work community. Communities may involve a group of diverse individuals. This can be rewarding. You may also find that your communities overlap at times, adding more balance to your life.

What is your current community like? Your community has most likely changed recently because of your entry into higher education. In the past, your community may have been dictated by your physical surroundings, your parents and extended family, or the school you attended. Now you have many more choices in how your community looks and feels, and you also have more say about who will be a part of your community.

RELATIONSHIP WITH FAMILY

Almost everyone has a family in one form or another, be it a biological family, an adoptive family, or one pulled together from friends and loved ones. There is nothing that promises that any one of these families will be any more functional than the others. They can either help you succeed or help you fail. The power you give them

Where Are You . . .

Before reading any further, take a moment and assess where you are at this moment with your knowledge and application of relationships and cultural diversity. Read each statement carefully and then respond accordingly.

1. I am aware of my prejudices and attitudes toward other people.   YES   NO

2. I make an effort to learn about a person without judging them.   YES   NO

3. Defensiveness and/or anger do not get the best of me during conflicts.   YES   NO

4. I am good at managing all the different relationships (friends, family, romantic, community) in my life.   YES   NO

5. I see how my relationship with myself impacts my other social relationships.   YES   NO

6. I know where to turn for help if I feel I am a victim of prejudice or discrimination.   YES   NO

7. I am patient with or tolerant of people who come from other cultures.   YES   NO

If you answered "Yes" to most of the questions (five or more), you know how important relationships are to your success in college and your life beyond. You have probably had good luck in your past with friendships and family ties. *If you answered "No"* to most of the questions, you will need to examine why you are struggling with relationships and cultures that are different from your own. You may need to speak with your advisor or counselor to find assistance on campus or in the community to help you focus on improving your relationship skills.

to control your life is up to you. Regardless of what your choices might be, a family can be either your biggest fan or number one critic.

When dealing with your family (regardless of its makeup), here are a few pointers:

▶ Honesty is the best policy—all of us, at one time or another, have tried lying to our parents, friends, or loved ones and paid the price for it. Just remember the old saying, "Honesty without love is brutality."

▶ Talk things out; remember, you have two ears and one mouth. Use them in that proportion.

▶ Family is forever, whether it's the one you were born into or the one you have chosen. Your connections are powerful and should not be taken lightly or abused because of a whim or a passing bad mood.

▶ The words spoken cannot be unspoken. This is not to say you won't be forgiven, but forgiving is different from forgetting. The wounds your words cause may last a lifetime, so choose them carefully.

RELATIONSHIP WITH FRIENDS

It has been said that a very lucky person has three to four good friends at any given time in his or her life. True friends are hard to find, and even harder to keep! Many of us approach friendship as if it just happens, and, in some cases, it does. Think about your best friend. How did you meet? Probably by chance. Perhaps fate brought you together. Sometimes circumstances can cause you to drift apart.

Why is it important to build strong friendships? Friendships can bring you comfort, understanding from another person, and loyalty, and they give you someone to

*T*he worst solitude is to be destitute of sincere friendship.

—Francis Bacon

talk with about joys and sorrows. You can share your hopes and dreams and fears with good friends. Another reason for developing friendships is to have people with whom you share common interests and who allow you to have uninhibited fun. Really good friends bring joy into your life. Close and trusted friends are among the most important components of your personal community. When making new friends, consider adding these people to your life:

▶ They treat you well and equally.

▶ They have ambition and courage.

▶ They have healthy work habits and a strong work ethic.

▶ They have pride in their name.

▶ They enjoy college and learning new things.

▶ They are outgoing and adventurous.

▶ They have found their goals and mission in life.

LOVE RELATIONSHIPS

There are many types and degrees of love relationships. The love between two old friends differs tremendously from the passion of two lovers. Love can be as relaxing and comfortable as an easy chair or as tumultuous and exhilarating as any roller-coaster ride. The way love is manifested in a relationship does not necessarily attest to the degree or intensity of the love.

Loving someone means caring about that person's happiness, trying to understand and to be understood by that person, and giving as well as receiving emotional support. Most love relationships involve intimacy to some degree. Intimacy is not synonymous with sex; it may or may not involve sexual relations. Intimacy refers to the emotional openness that usually develops over time between two people who love each other. Intimacy allows people to share hopes and dreams as well as pain and sorrows.

Some of you will meet and fall in love with your lifelong partner in college, and the ritual you will most likely use to become acquainted is dating. Keep the following tips in mind when you begin dating a person:

▶ Don't go out alone with a stranger; go out in a group until you are better acquainted with your date.

▶ Make sure someone else knows with whom you are going out, where you are going, and the approximate time you'll return; call that person if your plans change.

▶ Have your own transportation so that you can leave if you are uncomfortable.

▶ Don't go to someone's home unless you know that person very well.

▶ Establish a friendship before you try a relationship.

WHEN RELATIONSHIPS GO SOUR

Every relationship, whether it is a friendship or love relationship, has its period of exhilaration when nothing the other person does is wrong. Everything in the world is brighter because this person is in your life. You also know that these feelings may taper off. After the newness of a relationship wears off, you discover whether or not it will continue to be part of your life. This is the ordinary cycle of a relationship. If a person is meant to be a part of your life, you begin to settle into a rhythm that works for both of you; if not, hopefully you part ways in a friendly manner that hurts no one.

> **T**here is no greater hatred than the hatred between two people who once loved.
>
> —Sophocles

Unfortunately, there are times when this is not possible, when one or both parties hang on because they are not emotionally prepared to go it alone. Often, this leads to a very toxic situation. What does a toxic situation look like? You may have seen one or even participated in one. Here are some things to look for:

- One person's inability to function apart from the other.
- Blaming each other (or perhaps just one of you) for everything that is going wrong in your lives (life).
- Using abusive language and/or trying to control through intimidation.
- Using intimate knowledge of your weaknesses to hurt you or someone else.
- Using intimate knowledge to manipulate you or someone else.
- The use of physical violence or any controlling technique.
- Sexual harassment may be involved.

Sexual Harassment

Those of us in higher education would like to believe that we are immune to problems of sexual harassment, that we foster an atmosphere in which such behavior is not tolerated. But the cold, hard facts prove otherwise. On many campuses, sexual harassment takes place among students, between students and faculty, among faculty, and between faculty and administration.

Male and female professors have been accused and convicted of sexual harassment involving students. Most colleges have adopted strict policies on student-faculty relationships. No faculty member has a right to ask you to be personally involved. If you have been verbally harassed, threatened, or coerced into an unwanted sexual or personal situation, contact your department chair and/or the professor's department chair. He or she is required to act on this grievance. If the department chair does not act on your grievance, go to his or her dean.

The federal government defines sexual harassment as deliberate or repeated unsolicited verbal comments, gestures, or physical contact of a sexual nature that is considered to be unwelcome by the recipient, male *or* female. These are included:

- Verbal abuse or harassment (i.e., dirty jokes, unwanted letters, telephone calls, or written materials)
- Unwelcome sexual overtures or advances
- Pressure for dates or to engage in sexual activity
- Remarks about a person's body, clothing, or sexual activities
- Personal questions of a sexual nature
- Touching of any kind
- Referring to people as babes, hunks, dolls, honey, boy toy, and so forth

If you are faced with a situation that you believe is sexual harassment, you can take several steps to protect yourself.

1. Make a conscious effort to keep interactions between you and the person harassing you as impersonal as possible.

2. Avoid being alone with the person harassing you. If that person is your professor, bring a friend with you to meetings and arrange to meet in a classroom either right before or right after class.

3. Keep a record of the harassment in case you have to bring formal charges.

4. Tell the harasser that you believe he or she is harassing you and you want the behavior to stop. Be very specific, so that the person knows what you perceive as harassment.

5. Tell your academic advisor or a campus counselor about the events. Seek their counsel.

6. See a lawyer. Sexual harassment is against the law, and you may need to bring formal charges.

In some worst-case scenarios, sexual harassment has led to acts of violence, stalking, and even rape. The following section provides advice on how to decrease the chances of being raped by an acquaintance or a stranger.

Rape

Rape is a cause of fear and concern among college students, and date, or acquaintance, rape has become as much a concern as rape by strangers. You can take steps to reduce the possibility of rape.

To Decrease the Chances of Rape by a Stranger
1. Become familiar with campus security systems.

2. Set up signals with other students in your residence hall to alert one another in case of a problem.

3. Be aware of your surroundings and avoid unsafe places.

4. Vary your route and walk in groups whenever possible.

5. Use dead-bolt locks on your doors and keep windows locked.

6. Always check the identification of people such as utility workers, security officers, or salespeople who come to your door.

To Decrease the Chances of Acquaintance or Date Rape
1. Until you are very familiar with your date, avoid being alone together or going to secluded places.

2. Stay sober.

3. Be very clear about your sexual intentions.

4. Tell a friend whom you are out with, where you are going, and when you expect to return home.

5. Use your own transportation.

6. Learn the signs of date rape and "club" drugs.

College is an environment fraught with new experiences, new relationships, and new behaviors. It is our hope that this chapter will help you think about the situations you may find yourself in and prompt you to make responsible decisions.

RELATIONSHIPS WITH DIVERSE OTHERS

We have discussed the closest relationships you might form with family, friends, and lovers. The remainder of this chapter will focus on your relationships with people of different cultures, religions, ages, gender, or sexual orientation who may have beliefs and values different from your own. One of the biggest advantages of going to college is the fact that you live and study in an international community. If you approach diverse populations with an open mind and heart, you can benefit greatly from the exposure to people who are different from you.

The Power of an Open Mind

To experience other people and to receive the benefits of knowing someone, you need to enter all relationships with an open mind. If you have a derogatory mind-set toward a race, an ethnic group, a sexual orientation, or a religion, for example, you have internal barriers that can keep you from getting to know who a person really is.

Learning to interact with people from different cultures is a matter of keeping an open mind and looking at each person as an individual, not as a race, a class, or a religion. We cannot help but be influenced by what we have been taught and what we have experienced, but we can overcome prejudices and biases if we view people as individuals. If you intend to grow as an educated person and as a human being, you will need to expand your capacity to accept and understand people from different cultures within and outside your country.

> Y ou have to move to another level of thinking, which is true of me and everybody else. Everybody has to learn to think differently, think bigger, to be open to possibilities.
>
> —Oprah Winfrey

You Are a Culture of One

During our formative years, each of us develops a unique set of values, beliefs, and customs. We are virtually programmed, based on who raises us, our race, our nationality, where we live, where we go to school, our religion or lack of religion, our friends, our relatives, and our experiences and opportunities. Like fingerprints, no two people with their beliefs, customs, and experiences are exactly alike. This amazing phenomenon is what makes human beings interesting and makes the differences we see in people from cultures other than our own especially interesting as well as personally educational.

Culture is learned. People are born into a culture, but their culture is not a physical trait, such as eye color or hair texture. You probably developed, or absorbed, most of your personal culture from your family. The process is almost like osmosis in plants; it is as though culture seeps gradually through your skin. Many of the beliefs and values you embrace have been passed from one generation to another.

How can getting to know people from different backgrounds or cultures enhance your personal education?

© EyeWire, Inc.

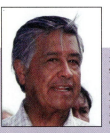

DID YOU KNOW?

César Chávez, who was raised during the Great Depression and in unspeakable poverty, spent his youth working as a migrant worker and only completed formal schooling up to the eigth grade. Chávez joined the Navy and then later founded the United Farm Workers, an organization responsible for increasing public awareness of the plight of migrant workers in America.

In college, you are likely to find your values, beliefs, and actions changing as you meet new people and become involved in new situations and as your horizons broaden. Quite simply, your college experience enhances your understanding, and your cultural beliefs change as a result. This change is known as cultural adjustment. You can, and should, expect to have your beliefs greatly tested—and perhaps adjusted—before you graduate.

Cultural adjustment doesn't mean that you must abandon your family, church, basic values, and friends. It may mean, however, that you need to reevaluate why you feel the way you do about certain situations and certain groups. You may have been taught that people belonging to a certain group are not acceptable. As you learn and grow, you may find that they are not bad at all, just different from you. You may discover that this different culture is one to be celebrated.

THE TIES THAT BIND

Components of Culture

Sometimes we can tell that people are from a different culture or ethnic group because of the way they look and dress or by the way they speak—dress and speech are two visible signs of culture. Other components of culture are not so visible. Sociologist David Popenoe (1993) identifies five components of culture:

- ▶ Symbols
- ▶ Language
- ▶ Values
- ▶ Norms
- ▶ Sanctions

Symbols are items that stand for something, such as the American flag. Most Americans respect the flag and know that it stands for honor, duty, patriotism, service, and freedom. People of other nationalities might not understand that the stars and stripes on the American flag are significant symbols in American culture. The key to relating to people from any culture is understanding. Some common symbols and what they stand for are the following:

Purple signifies royalty in some cultures.

A *pineapple* is a sign of welcome and hospitality in the southern United States.

Red is associated with anger in some cultures.

An *octagon sign* indicates "Stop!" in several countries.

Language is another important component of culture; the meaning of a word can vary across cultures. For example, if you were to ask for a biscuit in England, you would get a cookie. How many different words can you think of for that nonalcoholic, carbonated beverage many of us like to drink? Pop? Soda? Soft drink? Coke?

If you know someone with a disability, have you ever talked about or compared your experiences?

Scott Cunningham/Merrill

Values are typically based on family traditions and religious beliefs. What is unacceptable in one society may be acceptable in another. Most young people in the United States would be unwilling to allow their parents to choose their future spouse, yet in many countries this practice is still common. Some religious services are joyous celebrations; others are formal and solemn. The

> **I** am a citizen, not of Athens or Greece, but of the world.
>
> —Socrates

African American AME church is usually filled with soulful, joyous singing, while the Primitive Baptist Church may include songs not accompanied by musical instruments and may be more solemn. There is no one proper way to conduct a religious ceremony. Like so much else, what is correct depends on the culture.

Norms relate directly to the values of a culture or society. They are how we expect people to act based on those values. In an elegant restaurant, for example, you expect people to conduct themselves with more dignity than you might expect in a fast-food restaurant.

Sanctions are the ways in which a society enforces its norms. When a society adopts a set of norms that are upheld as valuable, it typically seeks a way to enforce these norms through formal laws. In every society, there are people who do not abide by the rules; people who break the law. A person in the United States who breaks the law may be sent to jail or may be required to perform community service. In some cultures, punishment is much more severe. For example, the punishment for stealing in some Middle Eastern cultures may be to sever the thief's hand. In the United States, this punishment would not be acceptable, but elsewhere it is.

CONFLICT IS INEVITABLE

How Do You Deal with It?

Many people intensely dislike conflict and will go to extreme measures to avoid it. On the other hand, some people seem to thrive on conflict and enjoy creating situations that put people at odds with each other. While in college, you certainly will not be sheltered from conflicts. In fact, on a college campus where a very diverse population lives and learns together, conflict is likely to arise on a regular basis. The simple truth is, conflict is pervasive in our culture, and you simply cannot avoid having some confrontations with other people. Therefore, you should not try to avoid conflict; rather, you can use it to create better relationships by exploring workable solutions.

You may experience conflict in a classroom when another student takes issue with your opinions and continues to harass you about your ideas after the class is over. You could be placed son a team where conflicts arise among the members. A major conflict could erupt in the parking lot if someone thoughtlessly pulls into a parking space that you have been waiting for. You could even experience conflict with a faculty member because you intensely disagree with the grade he or she assigned you on a project. Conflict can occur in any relationship, whether it is your parents, your girlfriend or boyfriend, your best friend, a roommate, a spouse or partner, your children, or a total stranger.

As you consider conflicts in your life and relationships, take a moment and complete the Conflict Management Assessment.

Conflict Management Assessment

Read the following questions carefully and respond according to the following key. Take your time and be honest with yourself.

1 = *Never* typical of the way I address conflict
2 = *Sometimes* typical of the way I address conflict
3 = *Often* typical of the way I address conflict
4 = *Almost always* typical of the way I address conflict

1. When someone verbally attacks me, I can let it go and move on.	1	2	3	4
2. I would rather resolve an issue than have to "be right" about it.	1	2	3	4
3. I try to avoid arguments and verbal confrontations at all costs.	1	2	3	4
4. Once I've had a conflict with someone, I can forget it and get along with that person just fine.	1	2	3	4
5. I look at conflicts in my relationships as positive growth opportunities.	1	2	3	4
6. When I'm in a conflict, I will try many ways to resolve it.	1	2	3	4
7. When I'm in a conflict, I try not to verbally attack or abuse the other person.	1	2	3	4
8. When I'm in a conflict, I try never to blame the other person; rather, I look at every side.	1	2	3	4
9. When I'm in a conflict, I try not to avoid the other person.	1	2	3	4
10. When I'm in a conflict, I try to talk through the issue with the other person.	1	2	3	4
11. When I'm in a conflict, I often feel empathy for the other person.	1	2	3	4
12. When I'm in a conflict, I do not try to manipulate the other person.	1	2	3	4
13. When I'm in a conflict, I try never to withhold my love or affection for that person.	1	2	3	4
14. When I'm in a conflict, I try never to attack the person; I concentrate on their actions.	1	2	3	4
15. When I'm in a conflict, I try never to insult the other person.	1	2	3	4
16. I believe in give and take when trying to resolve a conflict.	1	2	3	4
17. I understand *and use* the concept that kindness can solve more conflicts than cruelty.	1	2	3	4
18. I am able to control my defensive attitude when I'm in a conflict.	1	2	3	4
19. I keep my temper in check and do not yell and scream during conflicts.	1	2	3	4
20. I am able to accept "defeat" at the end of a conflict.	1	2	3	4

Total number of 1s _____   Total number of 3s _____
Total number of 2s _____   Total number of 4s _____

If you have more 1s, you do not handle conflict very well and have few tools for conflict management. You have a tendency to anger quickly and lose your temper during the conflict.

If you have more 2s, you have a tendency to want to work through conflict, but you lack the skills to carry this tendency through. You can hold your anger and temper for a while, but eventually, it gets the best of you.

If you have more 3s, you have some helpful skills in handling conflict. You tend to work very hard for a peaceful and mutually beneficial outcome for all parties.

If you have more 4s, you are very adept at handling conflict and do well with mediation, negotiation, and anger management. You are very approachable; people turn to you for advice about conflicts and their resolution.

The world is full of difficult people, but most of them can be dealt with if you keep a lid on your own hostility. The basic idea of resolving conflict is to get a handle on your own emotions. You need to remove threatening behaviors, words, and body language and be prepared to compromise so everyone leaves feeling as if they won something. Think of conflict resolution as a way to gain a new friend instead of adding a new enemy. Never allow yourself to become the person you're trying to avoid.

THE GOLDEN RULE FOR CELEBRATING DIVERSITY

At one time or another, most of us have been exposed to the Golden Rule: Do unto others as you would have them do unto you. As you work to improve and expand your knowledge of cultural diversity, it may help you to look at this rule from a different angle. In considering the following scenarios, first by yourself and then with a group, see if you can apply a new version of the Golden Rule: Do unto others as they would have you do unto them.

I Think I Would . . . An Exercise in Cultural Understanding

Respond to each scenario in the space provided. Discuss how the situation makes you feel, how you would feel if you were the person in the cultural minority depicted, and what you might do or say to improve this situation for everyone involved.

Your class may be asked by the instructor to discuss your responses to these scenarios in an open discussion. If so, be aware that these scenarios contain information sensitive to some of your classmates, perhaps to you. While the purpose of the discussion will be to help everyone understand how their classmates feel, each person in the class should be mindful of others' feelings. Think before you speak. Speak your mind openly, but carefully, to avoid damaging others' self-esteem. Remember, we all take in "messages" about ourselves from others. Be aware of your body language as well as your words.

You may find that some of your beliefs change slightly—or maybe even dramatically—as you work on these exercises. Growth that allows you to open up your mind, to move beyond biases and prejudices, and to seek to understand people who are different from you is positive growth.

Scenario 1

You and Jack, a friend from high school, are attending the same college. Jack has a physical disability that requires him to use a wheelchair. He was an outstanding basketball player and swimmer prior to a diving accident, which left him a paraplegic. Jack is an honor roll student. He is an avid basketball fan, attends all the games, and plays on a wheelchair team. He has a great sense of humor. He long ago dealt with his personal situation and now he even jokes about it. Jack is one of your favorite people.

Since you and Jack have been in class together, you have been noticing that people tend to treat him differently from others. Sometimes people talk loudly when talking to Jack, as if he can't hear. Because getting to and from classes is difficult, Jack has someone to help him maneuver around campus. One day you overhear a student talking to the person who is helping Jack as if Jack weren't there. "What happened to him? Can he use his arms?" Although Jack is handsome, friendly, and personable, he is usually left out of the many social activities in which other classmates participate. You know that your classmates would like and admire Jack if they got to know him.

How do you think Jack feels when people treat him as though he doesn't exist?

Why do you think some people have difficulty relating to people who have physical disabilities?

What could you say to classmates that might help them understand how to relate to Jack better and might make them and him feel more comfortable?

Scenario 2

Douglas met Andy on the first day of class. Douglas struck up a conversation with Andy because he saw a tennis racket in Andy's gym bag—a welcome sight. Douglas had not found anyone to play tennis with since his arrival on campus. The two decided to get together later in the afternoon to play a game. When the game was over, each knew that he had found a friend. They discovered that they lived in the same residence hall, had the same professor for English, only at different times, and both loved to play tennis. As the semester progressed, Douglas and Andy became very close friends; they studied history together, went to parties together, ate together when their schedules permitted, and double-dated once or twice.

Douglas and Andy enjoyed many of the same sports and movies and had similar tastes in music. Douglas felt that he had met a true soul mate, and Andy could not have been happier to have Douglas to talk to and hang around with. Andy knew, however, that things could soon change. He had made a serious decision; before the Christmas break, he would tell Douglas that he was gay.

Exams ended on Wednesday. Andy decided to break the news to Douglas on Tuesday night. They talked and laughed sitting on a bench outside the athletic center; then the conversation grew still, and Andy chose his words carefully. He told Douglas that he was gay and that he had been involved with someone at home for almost a year.

If you were Douglas, what would your reaction have been?

Should Andy have told Douglas about his sexual orientation? If so, should he have told him sooner? Why or why not?

Imagine that Douglas, a heterosexual, accepted Andy's orientation; but that Andy went on to say that he was interested in having a relationship with Douglas. How do you think Douglas would have reacted?

Does being gay carry a cultural or social stigma? Why or why not?

Scenario 3

Tonya was a first-year student at a major research university. She had an excellent academic background. She had always loved science and math and was seriously considering a major that would allow her to incorporate her love of these subjects into a career. In her second semester at the university, she enrolled in a calculus class taught by Dr. Ralph Bartlett. This class was especially important to Tonya for two reasons. First, Dr. Bartlett was the department chair for the program she was considering pursuing, and second, the course was her first college math course, so she wanted to start off strong.

On the first day of class, Dr. Bartlett made some disparaging jokes about women in the field of science. Although these comments made Tonya uncomfortable, she thought perhaps she was being oversensitive. As the semester progressed, so did Dr. Bartlett's derogatory asides about women. Nonetheless, Tonya loved the course; she was earning As and she felt that she had found her niche. She decided to major in this area. Tonya made an appointment to discuss possible career opportunities with Dr. Bartlett. Shortly into the appointment, Dr. Bartlett made it clear to Tonya that he didn't think she could cut it and suggested that she look for another program.

How would you feel if you were in Tonya's shoes?

Should you allow one person's assessment of your abilities to dictate your course in life?

How would you feel if you were a male in Tonya's class?

Why do you think women face discrimination in higher education? In the workforce?

Scenario 4

Rebecca is a nontraditional student who is 38 years old. She is a single parent and has two young children. Although she is not a college graduate, she has been promoted through the ranks to a responsible position at a major bank. Because she has now reached the highest level she can achieve without a college degree, she has returned to school. Rebecca has developed excellent computer skills from her on-the-job experience. Working full time, parenting two young children alone, and going back to school constitute a heavy load for Rebecca.

You notice that Rebecca comes into class at the last possible moment since she must rush to school from work and find a parking place. As soon as class is over, she makes a dash for her car so she can get back to work. Her classmates have very little time to get to know her and she tends to get left out of discussions.

You and Rebecca have been assigned to a team that has to work together to complete a group project. All of the team members except Rebecca are traditional students. At the first meeting, your group discusses times to meet, and most agree that 1:30 on Tuesday afternoons meets your schedules. When Rebecca tells the group that she can only meet at night because of her job and only on Wednesday nights when her mother can take care of her children, one of the team members makes the following hostile remark to Rebecca: "Well, perhaps you will have to find a way to meet when the rest of us want to since you are the only one causing a problem."

How can you use the conflict resolution techniques discussed earlier in this chapter to immediately ease the tension between team members?

If Rebecca is unable to attend meetings held during her work hours, how can you help her catch up on what she needs to do to be an effective member of your team?

What special skills and attributes can traditional students learn from a nontraditional student like Rebecca?

Scenario 5

Jermale, an 18-year-old student of African American and Asian heritage, often feels left out because he doesn't seem to belong to either race. African Americans seem to feel that he is white and Asian Americans believe he is African American. Although he has friends of different races, he is sometimes the brunt of ignorant remarks. Jermale often feels lonely and fears that he might be the victim of a hate crime.

While returning to his residence hall one evening after a fraternity meeting, Jermale is frightened when a pickup truck slows to match his pace as he walks along the sidewalk. One of the two young men in the truck leans out the window and yells racial slurs at him and spits in his direction before the truck speeds away.

Upon reaching his residence hall, Jermale notices the same truck, now empty, parked outside the building. As he nears the front door, Jermale again hears loud racial slurs being yelled at him from a third-story window directly above the entrance to the dorm. Clearly, the students are very drunk and obnoxious, and they are waiting for him to arrive. As Jermale enters the door, the slurs become mixed with threats to urinate on him. He enters the residence hall just as drops of liquid fall around him. Angry and frightened, Jermale rushes to his room and locks the door.

How would you feel if you were Jermale?

What action, if any, do you think Jermale should take?

Do you think racial discrimination is a problem on college campuses?

SLAMMING THE DOOR ON HATE

What Can You Do to Make a Difference?

Because we are a diverse population with people from all over the world making up our neighborhoods, our communities and individuals are often the victims of hate crimes. Hate crimes are vicious attacks on society in general and on communities and individuals specifically. The people who perpetrate hate crimes are usually misguided individuals who, nevertheless, cause great harm to many people. Hatemongers represent a very small minority of people on the fringes of society, yet they are serious stumbling blocks to racial harmony. Hate crimes can be directed at many diverse targets. They can be racially motivated or the result of religious intolerance. Sometimes, they are directed at people who have different sexual orientations. Intolerance of differences might be directed at gays and lesbians, Jews, African Americans, Native Americans, Hispanics, and others.

Regardless of the reason for the hate crime, the victims are left frightened, vulnerable, and feeling alone. According to the Southern Poverty Law Center (2000), "Somewhere in America, every hour someone commits a hate crime. Every day at least eight blacks, three whites, three gays, three Jews and one Latino become hate crime victims. Every week a cross is burned [in someone's yard]." Blacks are terrified of burning crosses because of the history of this evil act. A swastika is a symbol that brings back horrible images to Jews and tells them their lives are at risk. Hate crimes are aimed at entire groups of people, although they may directly impact only one person. Primarily the result of ignorance, lack of education, and inbred hatred passed from one generation to another, hate crimes hurt all of us. Because we are a diverse population, every American citizen needs to take a stand against all forms of hatred and intolerance.

Getting Involved and Making a Difference

Individuals and small groups of people can make a major difference in putting a stop to hate crimes. A list of things you can do to make a difference follows:

▶ Become knowledgeable about the kinds of hate crimes and how to combat each type.

▶ Take a stand for decency. If you see someone being mistreated because he or she is different, stand up for the person. Get other people to join you. Make a phone call; organize a group to paint over hate graffiti; march with people who are standing up against hatred.

▶ Let the victims know they are not alone. Encourage neighbors to welcome racially diverse families.

▶ When a hate group does something vicious, organize something to counteract their actions. Paint a house in a minority neighborhood or organize a rally of decent people who are appalled at hate crimes.

▶ Speak up in positive ways and get community business leaders and politicians involved in taking a stand against intolerance.

▶ Teach tolerance to young children. Your group might be an elementary class, or you might teach your younger siblings and cousins.

▶ Talk to friends who demonstrate intolerance through their actions, words, or jokes. Tolerance can be learned; attitudes can be changed. You can be the catalyst.

Truth, kindness, and love by good, decent, caring people always wins out over hatred, intolerance, and bigotry. If you take a stand for what is right, you will have other good people step up and stand with you.

This chapter has presented a great deal of information about relationships both good and bad. You have been given the opportunity to review the components of culture and to discuss five scenarios addressing real-life situations that many of you might face in the future.

Think About It
Chapter Reflection

As a college student, you can learn almost as much from the diverse population of students and peers as you can from the lessons you hear in the classroom. If you will open up your heart and mind to all of the possibilities, you will leave college a much more enlightened person than you were when you arrived.

College will provide you an opportunity to expand your horizons. Here you will have classes with people from all over the world. They will not only speak and dress differently; they will most likely have different religions, beliefs, customs, values, and experiences. Rather than close out people who are different from you, embrace new and different cultures. While you don't have to be just like these new people, you are certain to learn to appreciate and benefit from the relationships.

Remember, we are motivated by what we value. As you continue on in the semester and work toward personal and professional growth, consider the following ideas:

▶ Examine your personal values and beliefs to determine if cultural adjustments are needed.

▶ Listen to people and try to understand them.

▶ Stand up against intolerance of any kind.

▶ Help others understand the importance of organizing against hate crimes.

▶ Develop relationships with people from a variety of backgrounds.

▶ Learn to appreciate differences.

▶ Maintain close friendships.

The best relationship is the one in which your love for each other exceeds your need for each other.

—Unknown

Knowledge in Bloom

Each chapter-end assessment is based on *Bloom's Taxonomy of Learning*. See the inside front cover for a quick review.

Utilizes levels 4 and 6 of the taxonomy

Cultural Research and Understanding Project

Explanation: Select one culture, subculture, or religion that you are not a part of and research that culture, subculture, or religion. You may use interviews, books, journals, the Internet, or newspapers as your resources.

The culture, subculture, or religion that I have chosen is: _____

because: _____

_____

_____

_____

_____

_____

What is one value that this culture or religion holds? _____

_____

_____

_____

_____

_____

What is one norm that this culture or religion holds? _____

_____

_____

_____

_____

_____

_____

What is one unique example of language used by this culture? _____

_____

_____

_____

_____

_____

What is the most surprising or interesting thing that you learned about this culture or religion? Why?

_____

_____

_____

_____

Now that you have had a chance to learn about another culture other than your own culture, how has this knowledge impacted how you view your own culture? _____

_____

_____

_____

_____

_____

_____

_____

Preparing for Success

Refer to pages 286–287 of this chapter and answer the questions you developed from scanning this chapter's headings. You should also be able to answer the following questions if they were not on your list:

1. Explain why relationships are important. _____

   _____

2. What are the different components of culture? _____

   _____

3. What constitutes sexual harassment? _____

   _____

4. How are you a culture of one? _____

   _____

14

Live

The
purpose of **life**
is to **live it**,
to **taste** your
experiences
to the **utmost**,
to **reach out**
eagerly and
without **fear** for
newer and **richer**
experiences.
Eleanor Roosevelt

Why will I ever be asked to use information on my own health? *Why* will a chapter on developing a plan for wellness and personal responsibility help me in college, at work, with my family, and beyond? *Why* is this information such a big deal?

The mind is never right but when it is at peace within itself.

—Lucius Annaeus Seneca

This book has focused on both your personal and professional development. This chapter is about helping you maintain balance in your life during the educational process. It is designed to help alert you to the powerful role health plays in your educational process. This chapter introduces the body, mind, and soul connection to you so that you can begin to understand the importance of caring for all aspects of yourself throughout your college career and beyond.

Many of us take our health for granted. We place undue stress on ourselves and assume that our bodies will continue to take this abuse. This chapter will afford you the opportunity to review your own health status and to explore some issues that might help you lead a healthier lifestyle. *This chapter can help you:*

► Understand the relationship among the body, mind, and soul in your personal wellness
► Understand what a holistic approach to wellness is
► Learn how to develop a personal plan for wellness
► Learn the role you play in your own safety on campus
► Understand the different types of sexually transmitted diseases, protection from them, and treatment for them

In the pages to come we have given you information that will help you make informed choices about what you do with your body, because some of the choices you make may have consequences for the rest of your life.

Scan &

Take a few moments and **scan this chapter**. As you scan, **list five questions** you can expect to learn the answers to while reading and studying Chapter 14.

Example:
► What does it mean to have a holistic approach to health? (from page 310)
► What effect does the mind have on wellness? (from page 311)

My Questions:

1. _____

_____ from page _____

2. _____

_____ from page _____

Name: Sakinah Pendergrass
Institution: The Art Institute of Philadelphia, Philadelphia, PA
Major: Hospitality–Culinary Arts
Age: 25

There were times when I thought I might not make it. I struggled with some of my classes and had a few problems that almost sidetracked me, but I was determined to be a success and after my first year, I was determined to take better care of my entire body, mind, and soul. The information and tips in this chapter will help you live better, too.

I quickly found that taking care of my entire "self" was very important to every aspect of my life. When you're going to college, working, studying, and trying to have a life, your body begins to shut down and everything suffers if you don't take care of your "self." By learning to eat properly, getting the correct amount of rest, and taking time for my own personal spirituality, I began to see a change in my attitude, my performance, my grades, and my overall quality of life.

College students face many demands on their time such as studying, being in class, working, completing

the big WHY
. . . from another perspective

projects, and often, home life. I have found that for me, the easiest way to take care of my body and mind is to focus on my end goal and how that goal is going to help me and my family. By keeping the goal in mind, I am constantly reminded that my body, mind, and soul have to be in shape to reach that goal.

There are so many ways that we can abuse our bodies, minds, and souls. From alcohol or drug usage to unprotected sex, from not getting enough rest to being too busy, each one plays a major role in how we are able to function and learn. Chapter 14 will help you understand how to take better care of your machine, to nurture it, fuel it correctly, and provide it with the care it demands.

3. _____

_____

from page _____

4. _____

_____

from page _____

5. _____

_____

from page _____

Question

PS Reminder: At the end of the chapter, come back to this page and answer these questions in your notebook, text margins, or online chapter notes.

The Mind, Soul, and Body

A Holistic Approach to Wellness

Maintaining a healthy body, mind, and soul is one of the most exciting and challenging aspects of your college career. Think about a time when you felt absolutely wonderful! Your world was working perfectly—school was going great, your social life was incredible, and work was providing the income necessary to care for your family and friends. This is the perfect scenario—isn't it? It is, if you are healthy.

Approaching your health from a holistic standpoint means that you don't ignore any aspect—neither your body, nor your mind, nor your soul. In the Indian tradition, life is said to have four aims—wealth, pleasure, ethical conduct, or goodness, and enlightenment—and they are meant to be held in balance. How would your life be if you were to cultivate each of these areas?

> I am seeking, I am striving, I am in it with all my heart.
>
> —Vincent van Gogh

Think about your wellness in relationship to these three areas: your body, mind, and soul. Becoming aware of how your body, mind, and soul are functioning is paramount to your success in college and in life after college. Developing self-awareness is part of the personal responsibility that will be discussed in this chapter. How to continuously monitor and sustain balance in your body, mind, and soul is the key to maintaining a healthy lifestyle. This becomes far more difficult as exams, work, and other realities of life crowd into your schedule.

You cannot address your mental health without taking into account your physical well-being; you cannot talk about fitness without including nutrition in your dis-

Where Are You . . . AT THIS MOMENT

Before reading any further, take a moment and assess where you are at this moment with your knowledge and application of wellness and personal responsibility. Read each statement carefully and then respond accordingly.

1. My physical health is very important to me.   YES   NO

2. I am knowledgeable about the many types of STDs, including prevention and symptoms.   YES   NO

3. I know how to make myself feel better when I'm feeling depressed.   YES   NO

4. I frequently consume alcohol in large quantities (binge drinking).   YES   NO

5. I know where to get help if I need it to become more mentally healthy.   YES   NO

6. I am physically active, including involvement in a variety of activities.   YES   NO

7. I know how legal and illegal drugs affect my mental and physical health.   YES   NO

If you answered "Yes" to most of the questions (five or more), you know how important a holistic approach to wellness is to your success in college. You understand the interaction of the body, mind, and soul in wellness. *If you answered "No"* to most of the questions, you will need to reevaluate your wellness plan. You may need to speak with your advisor or counselor to find assistance on campus or in the community to help you focus on your wellness plan and develop a healthier attitude.

cussion. If your body, mind, and soul are to function in a healthy manner, then your approach to wellness should be balanced. You need to explore and develop a holistic approach to wellness.

THE MIND'S EFFECT ON WELLNESS

The mind is an incredibly complex organ. The health industry has not begun to tap the awesome power the mind has over a person's physical health. Very basic studies have shown that the mind is a vital link to physical health. Your emotions play a tremendous role in how you approach your overall wellness program. Your emotional well-being impacts all aspects of your general wellness and therefore is the platform for all health. Christopher Reeve once discussed the importance that his mental state played in his recovery from what people thought would be a life-ending fall in 1990. Instead Reeve, although remaining a quadriplegic until his death in 2005, was able to continue acting, directing, and producing and was a very influential activist in the field of stem cell research.

Ignoring your mental health can be dangerous. When was the last time you took a mental health break?

© BananaStock Ltd.

People who are mentally healthy possess these qualities:

▶ Have a positive sense of self-worth
▶ Are determined to make an effort to be healthy
▶ Can love and have meaningful relationships
▶ Understand reality and the limitations placed on them
▶ Have compassion for others
▶ Understand that the world does not revolve around them

DEPRESSION AND ANXIETY DISORDERS

Depression is a term used to describe feelings ranging from feeling blue to utter hopelessness. The use of "I'm depressed" to mean "I'm sad" or "I'm down" is a far cry from the illness of clinical depression. Depression is a sickness that can creep up on an individual and render that person helplessly lost if it is not detected and properly treated. Signs of depression include the following (Donatelle and Davis, 2002):

▶ Lingering sadness
▶ Inability to find joy in pleasure-giving activities
▶ Loss of interest in work or school
▶ Unexplainable fatigue
▶ Sleep disorders, including insomnia or early-morning awakenings
▶ Loss of sex drive
▶ Withdrawal from friends and family
▶ Feelings of hopelessness and worthlessness
▶ Desire to die

© Steve Azzara/Corbis

DID YOU KNOW?

Sheryl Crow, singer, song writer, and activist was diagnosed with breast cancer at age 44 just after the debut of her Grammy-nominated Wildflower CD was released. Those closest to Crow stated that it was her commitment to a holistic approach to living that kept her centered during her recovery from surgery.

According to the Anxiety Disorders Associations of America, anxiety disorders are the most common mental illness in America—with more than 13% of American adults suffering from some form of an anxiety disorder. Learning to cope with anxiety allows you to focus and maintain balance in your health and academic welfare. There are several ways to proactively approach dealing with anxiety: relaxation techniques such as yoga, music or dance therapy, and meditation; cognitive behavior therapy, other forms of therapy, and medication.

If you are feeling depressed or your anxiety has reached a level where you cannot control it, but your depression seems minor or situational, try some of these helpful hints for picking yourself up out of the blues:

▶ Get physical exercise because it causes the release of endorphins, which help to stimulate you and give you a personal high.

▶ Spend time talking with a good friend; share your thoughts and feelings.

▶ Control your self-talk. If you're playing a negative tune, change to a positive song.

▶ Do something special for yourself: Take a long walk in the park, watch a favorite movie, listen to a special CD, or eat a hot fudge sundae. It doesn't really matter what you do as long as it's something special.

▶ Nurture yourself by doing things you love and enjoy and that bring you peace.

▶ *Never* be afraid or ashamed to seek professional assistance.

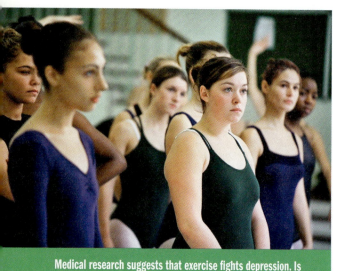

Medical research suggests that exercise fights depression. Is there a physical activity that you particularly enjoy? Do you have access or opportunity to do it?

© Image Source Ltd.

THE SOUL'S EFFECT ON WELLNESS

The human being is an insatiably inquisitive creature. Our quest for the greater meaning of life is equaled only by our quest for eternal life. For some, these two quests become one in the search for spiritual meaning. Some people find the true meaning of life in the teachings of Jesus Christ; others study the Koran or the teachings of Buddha or worship the wonder of Nature. Whether they follow a formal religion or not, people have their own beliefs about the universe, human nature, and the significance of life. How we approach our beliefs is related to our perception of our own spiritual nature, or the state of our soul. Spirituality guides many aspects of our daily lives. From character development to ethics to personal responsibility to managing conflict, your spiritual nature helps determine how you act and how you treat others.

Spirituality is also about caring for yourself and appreciating your talents and natural gifts. It can also help reduce stress by bringing you a degree of peace and understanding. "Spirituality is concerned with self-determination and being able to face problems without going to pieces. It is about learning to solve problems and learning to come to conclusions that are positive for yourself, others, and the earth" (Sherfield, 2004).

If you are interested in expanding your spiritual nature, consider the following suggestions:

▶ Read books about different religions, spiritual journeys, and inspirational persons.

▶ Join a group on campus or in the community that explores different spiritual themes.

▶ Keep an open mind and listen to a variety of perspectives.

▶ Join a meditation group.

▶ Begin journaling (possibly in your online journal) about your feelings, desires, aspirations, and contributions you want to make to the world.

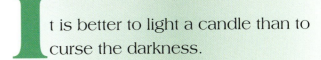

I t is better to light a candle than to curse the darkness.

—Chinese proverb

Your time in higher education provides an outstanding opportunity for you to explore the true meaning of life. Many campus organizations can help you in your quest for spirituality. Take this opportunity to explore your spirituality and to provide food for your soul. To ignore this aspect of yourself is to shut off a potentially rich and wonderful source of joy.

THE BODY'S EFFECT ON WELLNESS

Physical fitness is different for everyone. Why is physical fitness important? The list of reasons for maintaining an activity level that will keep you physically fit is lengthy. Among other benefits, physical fitness gives you these:

▶ Helps you have more energy

▶ Gives you increased confidence

▶ Helps you deal with stress

▶ Improves the health of your skin

▶ Prevents insomnia

▶ Reduces your risk of heart disease

▶ Helps control blood-serum cholesterol levels

▶ Helps control high blood pressure and diabetes

▶ Increases longevity of bone structure

▶ Helps maintain your quality of life

There is no universal fitness plan or program that fits everyone, but there are universal components of fitness. Cardiovascular fitness, flexibility, muscular strength, and muscular endurance are the four components of fitness.

Cardiovascular fitness is by far the most important component. Some aerobic activities are walking, jogging, biking, swimming, jumping rope, dancing, and cross-country skiing. The benefits of aerobic exercise include reducing the risk of heart disease, keeping blood pressure down, increasing the level of HDL (good cholesterol), and helping control weight. Flexibility is the ability of joints to move through the full range of their motion. Good flexibility is believed to prevent pulls, tears, and other damage to your muscles and is particularly important in preventing back pain. The key to flexibility is stretching correctly. You should stretch in a slow relaxed movement.

Muscular strength is the muscles' ability to exert force in one motion, such as a jump or lift. Muscular endurance is the muscles' ability to perform repeated muscular contractions. These two components

Finding an exercise buddy can increase your motivation to exercise regularly.

Patrick White/Merrill

DACIE JACKSON-PETERS
Student—Emergency Medical Paramedic
Delgado Community College and Southwest Tennessee Community College
New Orleans, LA and Memphis, TN

One minute your life is fine. You're in college studying in a field you love, your child is doing well in school, your husband is great, your home is secure, and life is good. The next moment, your home is gone, your school is underwater, your child is crying and terrified, and you're being airlifted from the roof of your home and taken to a state and city where you know no one. Yes, my family and I endured Hurricane Katrina. But we survived and even after all of this, I can say I am truly blessed.

I am a native of New Orleans. My family and I have lived in Louisiana all our lives until August of 2005 when the levees failed and washed our lives away. I was studying to work in the health care profession and was close to graduation when my life changed forever. After the rescue, my family and I were taken to a shelter in Arkansas and later moved to another in Memphis, TN. I never thought that anything like this could happen to me and my family, but at 32 years old, the word "normal" disappeared from my dictionary.

We spent much of September through December just trying to survive, finding a place to live, looking for new jobs, and caring for our child. I found myself mad at everything and everybody. I was scared, I had watched everything disappear that I had worked for since high school, my child had to begin counseling to help her cope with the massive changes, and my life seemed out of control. Then it dawned on me. I knew

that I had to "get up" and start over. I had to find my footing again and get my family back on track. The first thing I did was to find a college in Memphis, transfer my credits, and begin to complete my degree. In January of 2006, I enrolled in classes and am now working toward the completion of my degree as an emergency medical paramedic.

I learned that when you are down, you have to look up. I learned that there are people who will help you and guide you. One of my past professors from Delgado Community College, Melanie Deffendall, will forever be a role model and guardian angel to me. She lost everything in Katrina, too. As I write this, she is living in a FEMA trailer. But through e-mail and later phone calls, she encouraged me, guided me, and is helping me complete my degree. She never put herself first and I can only imagine the number of other students she helped during this time.

I plan to return to my home of New Orleans in the coming months, purchase a home, rebuild my life there, and help others in any way possible. I want to be the type of person and role model to my child that Ms. Deffendall and others were to me. I have learned that this is what life is all about—helping others rise up.

As you can tell by my story, my family and I have been through quite an ordeal, but as I wrote earlier, I am able to stand up today and say, *I am truly, truly blessed.*

are interrelated in that most muscular contractions use some degree of muscular strength. You can increase both strength and endurance by doing exercises that involve resistance, usually weights. You gain strength by conditioning your body to resist more and more weight; you improve endurance by increasing repetitions at the same weight.

Although an active lifestyle should include all four fitness components to some degree, the extent to which each is included is determined by your goals and the level of activity you wish to achieve in your life. If you would like to have a high level of activity so that you can work out or play a sport, here are some suggestions for getting started. Start your program slowly.

▶ If it hurts, stop!

▶ Wear the proper gear.

▶ Learn the proper form and technique.

▶ Always warm up and cool down.

"I don't have time to join the gym," you might say. The following suggestions can help you be more active in your daily life.

> **I**nside of a ring or out, ain't nothing wrong with going down. It's staying down that's wrong.
>
> —Muhammad Ali

▶ Walk to class rather than drive or ride the bus.

▶ Walk up stairs instead of taking the elevator.

▶ Develop a hobby that involves physical activity, such as gardening or bowling.

▶ Do volunteer work that involves physical activity.

▶ Make a commitment to include some form of physical activity in your daily routine.

Almost everyone has at one time or another made a New Year's resolution or some other form of pledge to become more physically fit. Most people don't have trouble starting exercise programs; they only have trouble sticking with them.

ARE YOU WHAT YOU EAT?

The Body and Food

Eating has become Americans' favorite hobby. Rather than eating to live, many of us live to eat. We socialize around food—dinner and a movie, pizza and a beer with friends, and so on. Virtually every holiday or celebration we observe has a food focus.

As you enter into this new stage of your life, balancing schedules, studying, and caring for others, you need to understand that your body will be undergoing tremendous biological stress. The hormonal changes that tend to coincide with the traditional college age, 18 to 22, may cause you to experience an alteration in your basal metabolic rate; you will no longer be able to eat like a horse and not gain a pound. At the same time, your lifestyle in college is likely to be more sedentary than was your lifestyle prior to college. As a result, you may well end up gaining the additional weight commonly

When you're on the run it is easy to ignore your eating habits. How many times per day do you sit down to a balanced meal? Per week? Per month?

Patrick White/Merrill

referred to as the "freshman 15." Take advantage of the many guides available to help you make the correct choices of foods and develop a healthy eating plan.

What You Do Matters

Personal Responsibility and Wellness

College and life are about choices. You will find few places in this book where we say, "you must," or "you have to," or "you should." It is not our intention to tell you how to live your life or how to make life choices. Whether you are 18 or 58, we consider you an intelligent, rational adult and we have tried to address you accordingly. The following section will not break tradition. We do not plan to tell you how you should live, whom you should see, what you should or should not drink or use, or with whom you should have intimate relations. These are your choices, and for us to tell you which ones to make would counter all the decision-making skills we have tried to provide you throughout this book.

The following section will simply provide you with information that you can study and from there, make intelligent decisions about drinking, drug usage, smoking, and sexual behavior. The only thing we ask is that you consider carefully this fact: Everything you put into your body and do with and to your body has a direct effect, either positively or negatively, on your overall wellness.

Drugs and Alcohol

First, let us state that alcohol *is* a drug. It is legal for people over 21, but it is a drug just as cocaine and Ecstasy are drugs. Drugs can basically be divided into two categories—legal and illegal. It may sound strange, but drugs run the gamut from caffeine to crystal methamphetamine. The decision to use a drug, legal or illegal, is yours and it is personal. However, every drug—from tobacco to roofies—has ramifications and health consequences. The charts on pages 317 to 318 are provided to give you a better understanding of many legal and illegal drugs.

Prescription Drugs and the College Student

More Americans today are addicted to prescription drugs than to illegal drugs, and college campuses are only a microcosm of the country. Nonmedical use of prescription drugs for either recreational purposes or for purposes other than their prescribed intent has reached epidemic proportions. The three classes of prescription drugs most commonly abused are pain medications, antianxiety and sleep medications, and stimulants. All of these medications have had a history of being overprescribed, and if students don't come to campus with pills or prescriptions from their homes, they acquire them through the Internet or other means. These drugs, because of their familiarity to the user, can be more dangerous and therefore more addictive. Casual use may unwittingly escalate into an addiction.

It is also common practice among young adults to share prescriptions with their friends. Some areas have even coined a phrase for "prescription parties" that feature

Commonly Used and Abused Legal Drugs

NAME	USE	SOURCES	NEGATIVE EFFECTS
Caffeine	Alertness, pleasure, energy, reduce fatigue	Coffee, tea, chocolate, some soft drinks, medications	A stimulant, increased anxiety, highly addictive, increased urination, irregular heartbeat, indigestion
Alcohol	Relaxation, mood enhancer, overcome depression, overcome shyness, social acceptance, relieve tension, celebrate, bonding	Beer, wine, liquor, medications, some foods	Liver disease, memory loss, blackouts, false euphoria, depression, hangovers, birth defects, loss of balance, mental impairment, increased suicide rate, death
Tobacco	Stimulant, relaxation, social acceptance, curb appetite, increase alertness	Cigarettes, cigars, pipes, snuff, chewing tobacco	Highly addictive, increased heart and respiratory rate, increased blood pressure, decreased taste sensations, increased risk of cancer, decreased hunger, lung disease, gum disease, birth defects, strokes, cardiovascular disease
Over-the-counter drugs	Weight loss, alertness, sleeping, body building, depression, pain relief	Laxatives, diet medications, sleep enhancers, stimulants, herbal medications, nasal sprays, cough medications, pain relievers	Addiction, organ damage, nausea, vomiting, reduced absorption of vitamins and minerals, liver damage
Prescription drugs	Weight loss, alertness, sleeping, depression, pain relief, mood enhancers, muscle relaxers	Found in many forms, prescribed by medical professionals from every area of medical science	Addiction, impaired judgment, loss of memory, weight loss/gain, blackouts, death

sharing what is in one another's medicine cabinet. This is *never* a good practice. If you believe you or someone you know have developed an addiction to prescription medications, this addiction should be treated as seriously as any other drug addiction.

Several drugs need to be discussed separately. These drugs are more commonly called "cocktail drugs" or "club drugs." They are called that because they are most commonly found in dance clubs, raves, and other places where people are interacting and inhibitions are low.

It is important to note that they are extremely dangerous, even to the most casual user. The effects of club drugs (and many others) can range from elevated body temperatures to dehydration to increased blood pressure to adverse effects of serotonin in the brain. Club drugs include the following:

▶ Ecstasy
▶ Roofies
▶ Sextasy
▶ Destiny

Sextasy is a mixture of Ecstasy and Viagra. *Ecstasy* alters one's senses, but can hinder sexual functioning. To increase sexual functioning, many people have begun taking Viagra, whose real purpose is to treat impotence and assist prostate cancer

Commonly Used Illegal Drugs

SUBSTANCE	STREET NAME	ADMINISTRATION	HOW IT MAKES YOU FEEL (EFFECTS)
MDMA	Ecstasy, E	Oral	Distortion of time and perception and enhanced enjoyment from tactile experiences
MDMA and Viagra	Sextasy	Oral	Heightens sexual experience, rapid heart rate, increased blood pressure
Synthetic Heroin	Destiny, D	Oral	Drowsy, floating, without pain
Rohypnol	Roofies, date rape drug	Oral and in drinks	Sedation, muscle relaxation, reduction in anxiety with partial amnesia
Gamma Hydroxybutyrate	GHB	Oral and in drinks	Induces relaxation before sleep and eventual coma and/or death
Cocaine	Coke, crack, flake, rocks, snow	Injected, smoked, sniffed	Central nervous system stimulant, restlessness, irritability and anxiety
Amphetamines	Black beauties, crosses, hearts	Injected, oral, smoked, sniffed	Central nervous system stimulant but cause a crash effect when they wear off
Methamphetamine	Crank, crystal, glass, ice, speed	Injected, oral, smoked, sniffed	Central nervous system stimulant
LSD	Acid, microdot	Oral	Heightened perception, hallucinations, confusion
Phencyclidine and Analogs	PCP, angel dust, boat hog, love boat	Injected, oral, smoked	Numbness, incoordination, distinct changes in body awareness similar to those associated with alcohol intoxication
Psilocybin	Magic mushroom, purple passion, shrooms	Oral	Hallucinogen
Marijuana, Hashish	Blunt, grass, herb, pot, reefer, sinsemilla, smoke, weed, Mary Jane	Oral, smoked	Euphoria, mellowness, distortion in perception of time
Hashish	Hash	Oral, smoked	Euphoria and a sense of well-being, altered perception of distance and time
Anabolic Steroids	Testosterone, nandrolene	Oral, injected	Increase lean body mass, strength, and aggressiveness, cause hair loss, unexplained rage, body stops producing testosterone, testicles shrink, severe acne, depression, thoughts of suicide in some cases, tumors (liver in particular)
Heroin	Horse, smack	Injected, smoked, sniffed	Depression of the central nervous system, sense of euphoria
Opium	Dover's powder	Oral, smoked	Calm feeling, free of pain, irregular heartbeat
Barbiturates	Barbs	Injected, oral	Slurred speech, shallow breathing, sluggishness, fatigue, disorientation

Adapted from the National Institute of Drug Abuse

patients. The mixture can cause serious problems! "Doctors warn that combining the two drugs can cause heart problems or erections that don't subside for more than four hours, possibly leading to anatomical damage" (Leinwand, 2002).

Roofies and GHB are very common in the club scene and can be slipped into a drink (alcoholic or not) with little trouble. Because they are usually odorless and colorless and have a very quick effect on the body, they rapidly alter your alertness and ability to function.

OUT ON A BINGE

When Drinking Goes Awry

Binge drinking is classified as having more than five drinks at one time. Many people say, "I only drink once a week." However, if that one drinking spell includes drink after drink after drink, it can be extremely detrimental to your liver, your memory, your digestive system, and your health in general.

Most college students report that they do not mean to binge drink, but it is caused by the situation such as a ballgame, a party, a campus event, or a special occasion. A 2005 study by the Youth Leadership Institute found that 20% of male freshmen drank 10 or more drinks in a single party or event. This has actually become the number one public health problem of unintended health consequences, which means unintended sex, drunk driving, crashes, date rape, and violence.

In their breakthrough work, *Dying to Drink*, Harvard researcher Henry Wechsler and science writer Bernice Wuethrich explore the problem of binge drinking. They suggest, "Two out of every five college students regularly binge drink resulting in approximately 1,400 student deaths, a distressing number of assaults and rapes, a shameful amount of vandalism, and countless cases of academic suicide" (Wechsler and Wuethrich, 2002).

Controlling Binge Drinking

Trying to control your own binge drinking is a situation reminiscent of the old saying, "Letting the fox guard the henhouse." After a few drinks, it is hard to "self-police," meaning that you may not be able to control your actions once the drinking starts. If you plan to drink, think about the following beforehand:

- Ask a friend to go with you so that you can watch out for each other.
- Drink two bottles of water for each alcoholic beverage you consume.
- Try to eat before, during, and after you drink.
- Consider *not* drinking and see how it goes.
- Give yourself a time limit for arriving and departing the event where alcohol is served.
- If you plan to have *even one drink*, arrange for someone you know to take you home.
- Remember: A designated driver is *not* the person who has had the least amount to drink—it is the person who has had nothing to drink.

YES YOU CAN!

IDEAS FOR Success

Consider the following strategies for protecting yourself when partaking of any beverage in public:

- ▶ Be suspicious of taking drinks from anyone you do not know or have not known and trusted for a long time.
- ▶ If you plan to drink anything, the best plan is to go to the service area and get it yourself or at least be close enough to see your drink being prepared or opened.
- ▶ Accept only unopened canned and/or bottled drinks when possible.
- ▶ Do not leave any beverage unattended while dancing or socializing. If you do, get another drink upon your return.
- ▶ Make it a habit to cover your drink with your hand while around a crowd of people. This can lessen the possibility of someone dropping a powder or liquid into your drink.
- ▶ Try to socialize with people you trust.

Goin' Out of My Head over You

The Residual Damage of Drugs and Alcohol

Perhaps the greatest tragedy of drug and alcohol abuse is the residual damage of unplanned pregnancy, sexually transmitted diseases, traffic fatalities, and accidental death. You already know that drugs and alcohol lower your resistance and can cause you to do things that you would not normally do, such as drive drunk or have unprotected sex.

Surveys and research results suggest that students who participate in heavy episodic (HE) or binge drinking are more likely to participate in unprotected sex with multiple sex partners. One survey found that 61% of men who do binge drink participated in unprotected sex as compared to 23% of men who do not binge drink. The survey also found that 48% of women who do binge drink participated in unprotected sex as compared to only 8% of women who do not binge drink (Cooper, 2002).

These staggering statistics simply suggest one thing: Alcohol and drug consumption can cause people to act in ways in which they might never have acted without alcohol—and those actions can result in irreversible personal damage.

Sexually Transmitted Diseases

Sexually transmitted diseases (STDs) are diseases that are generally transmitted through vaginal or anal intercourse or oral sex. Although they are most commonly spread through sexual contact, some can be transmitted through related nonsexual activities. (For example, human immunodeficiency virus—HIV—can be contracted by using contaminated needles, and crabs can be contracted through contact with contaminated bed linens or towels.) It is estimated that one in every four college students has a sexually transmitted disease. Seven common STDs are described in the chart beginning on page 321.

New Worries about HIV and AIDS Transmission

There is good news and bad news. The good news, actually great news, is that there have been tremendous strides in the treatment of HIV and AIDS. In the past several years, a new generation of drugs called *protease inhibitors* have had a remarkable effect. They block reproduction of the HIV particles (Rathus, Nevid, and Fichner-Rathus, 1998). Used in connection with AZT and 3TC, these inhibitors have reduced HIV to below detectable levels in many people. The newest drug in trials, T-20, is called a fusion inhibitor. It blocks HIV from sticking to the blood cells that it attacks (Haney, 2003). For some, both HIV and AIDS have become more manageable illnesses.

That is the great news. *However,* the cocktail is not a cure. One of the most dangerous aspects of the new protease and fusion inhibitors is that people begin to think that HIV and AIDS are cured and that there is no longer a need to think about safe sex. Nothing could be further from the truth! While fantastic results have been shown in many people with HIV and AIDS, the cocktail is very expensive, and some people's bodies cannot tolerate the mixture.

Seven Sexually Transmitted Diseases

STD	TRANSMISSION	SYMPTOMS	DIAGNOSIS	CONSEQUENCES
AIDS/HIV	Sexual contact (vaginal, oral, and anal) Infusion with contaminated blood (sharing needles, etc.) From mother to fetus Breast feeding	People may go years without symptoms. When symptoms appear they may include flu-like symptoms, fever, weight loss, fatigue, diarrhea, and cancer.	Bodily fluids such as blood, urine, or saliva reveal HIV antibodies. Two tests include the Western Blot and the ELISA. A new "20 Minute Test" is now available at many doctors' offices.	Transmission to sexual partners Rapid progression if undiagnosed or untreated Cancer Pneumonia Death
Chlamydia	Sexual contact (vaginal, oral, and anal) By touching one's eye after touching infected genitals From mother to child	Women: Sometimes no symptoms; painful urination, occasional vaginal discharge, bleeding between periods Men: Discharge from penis, painful urination	A cervical smear for women Extract of fluid from the penis for men	Transmission to sexual partners Various inflammations Possible sterility in men and women
Gonorrhea	Sexual contact (vaginal, oral, and anal) From mother to child	Women: Vaginal discharge, painful urination, bleeding between periods Men: Discharge from penis, painful urination	Medical examination from discharge or culture	Transmission to sexual partners Pelvic inflammatory disease Sterility in men and women
Genital Warts	Sexual contact (vaginal, oral, and anal) Other types of contact such as infected towels or clothing	Women: Single or multiple soft, fleshy growths around anus, vulva, vagina, or urethra; itching or burning sensation around sexual organs Men: Burning around sexual organs; single or multiple soft, fleshy growths around anus or penis	Medical examination	Transmission to sexual and nonsexual partners Precancerous conditions Cannot be cured
Herpes (Simplex Virus Types I and II)	Sexual contact (vaginal, oral, and anal) Touching Kissing Sharing towels, toilet seats	Single or multiple blisters or sores on genitals; generally painful, but disappears without scarring, reappears	Medical examination Culture and fluid inspections	Transmission to sexual and nonsexual partners Cannot be cured
Hepatitis (Viral A, B, C, and D types)	Sexual contact, especially involving the anus Contact with infected fecal matter Transfusion of contaminated blood Severe alcoholism Exposure to toxic materials	Can be asymptomatic; mild flu-like symptoms, fever, abdominal pain, vomiting, and yellowish skin or eyes; loss of appetite; whitish bowel movements; brown urine	Medical examination of blood for hepatitis antibody; liver biopsy	Transmission to sexual and nonsexual partners Severe liver problems or failure Cancer of the liver Death

Seven Sexually Transmitted Diseases, *continued*

STD	TRANSMISSION	SYMPTOMS	DIAGNOSIS	CONSEQUENCES
Syphilis	Sexual contact (vaginal, oral, and anal) Touching an infected chancre	Four stages: (1) painless red spots later forming a sore; (2) skin rash or mucous patches; (3) latent stage, no symptoms; (4) complications leading to possible death	Primary stages by medical examination of fluid from a chancre Secondary stage by blood test, VDRL	Transmission to sexual and nonsexual partners Death (although seldom advances this far today)

Adapted from *Sex on Your Terms* by Elizabeth Powell, Allyn and Bacon, 1996, and *Access to Health*, 7th ed. by Rebecca J. Donatelle and Lorraine G. Davis, Allyn and Bacon, 2002.

Another worry comes from a study conducted at the University of California, San Diego. The results, reported in *The New England Journal of Medicine,* suggest that *one in five new HIV cases is a drug-resistant strain* (Lieberman, 2002). This means that the virus has mutated to a state where current drugs on the market take longer to work or do not work at all.

David Kirby, in his article "The Worst Is Yet to Come" (*The Advocate,* January 19, 1999), states, "Since the introduction of better AIDS treatments, researchers have been worried that safer-sex messages would lose their urgency. This year, those fears came true. One study after another, with depressing consistence, showed . . . alarming spikes in rates of HIV infection and ominously, of other sexually transmitted diseases as well." The Centers for Disease Control and Prevention, in their April 2006 report, stated that approximately 40,000 persons in the United States become infected with HIV each year.

Therefore, it is imperative that you know that HIV and AIDS have not been cured, and without considering your conduct and personal responsibility, you are as much at risk as you ever have been.

STDs and Birth Control

The following chart is provided to give you information about other serious sexually transmitted diseases and the most common birth control methods.

Birth Control

TYPE	USAGE	PREVENTION OF STDS		
		YES*	NO	NOT NECESSARILY
Abstinence	Refraining from *all sexual activity,* vaginal, anal, and oral. One hundred percent effective.	X		
Outercourse	Oral genital sex and mutual masturbation.			X
The Pill	Also called oral contraceptive. The most widely used form of birth control		X	
The Male Pill	Also called oral contraceptive. Newly developed for male usage.		X	
The Patch	Called the Ortho-Evra patch, it is a transdermal method of dispensing similar medicine as in the Pill. The patch lasts for one week.		X	
The NuvaRing	A clear, flexible vaginal ring that is self-inserted in the vagina and releases a low dose of hormones. It lasts for a month.		X	
Diaphragm	Round, flexible disk inserted into the vagina to cover the cervix.		X	
IUD	Also called intrauterine device. Must be inserted into the uterus by a physician.		X	
Male Condom	A sheath, generally latex, worn over the penis to prevent sperm from entering the vagina.	X		
Female Condom	A loose-fitting sheath inserted into the vagina to prevent sperm from entering the uterus.	X		
Spermicides	Inserted into the vagina to kill sperm. Comes in foams, jellies, suppositories, and creams.		X	
Withdrawal	Also called coitus interruptus. The penis is withdrawn from the vagina before ejaculation.		X	
Rhythm Method	Abstaining from sexual intercourse during the menstrual cycle when ovulation occurs.		X	
Norplant	Silicone tubes surgically embedded in a woman's upper arm to suppress fertilization.		X	
Sterilization	Male and female surgery. Male version is called vasectomy, and female versions are called tubal sterilization, tubal ligation, and hysterectomy.		X	
Cervical Cap	Much like the diaphragm, it is fitted into the vagina by a doctor. It is meant to be used with a spermicide and can provide up to 48 hours of protection.		X	

* Only total abstinence is 100% effective in preventing sexually transmitted diseases.

Think About It
Chapter Reflection

Your understanding of wellness and the gift that a healthy body is to you during your college education and beyond is a wonderful beginning to your college education. During this chapter you have been given the opportunity to think about the role the mind, body, and soul have in your overall approach to wellness. You've gotten to look at the importance of personal responsibility regarding your approach to relationships, alcohol, and drugs. College is a time when you have an opportunity to reflect on the great questions in life and enjoy wonderful relationships and conviviality, but this can only take place if your body, mind, and soul are healthy.

Remember these tips as you plan for your future of well living:

▶ Take time out to be with friends or family.

▶ Use the power of positive thinking.

▶ Keep yourself healthy with exercise.

▶ Take care of your spiritual health.

▶ Think before you drink.

▶ Develop a way to decompress after school or work.

▶ Understand that your choices have consequences.

▶ Eat a balanced and regular diet.

▶ Surround yourself with positive people.

▶ Protect yourself at clubs and parties.

Good luck to you as you begin developing your wellness plan and taking personal responsibility for your health and wellness.

To keep the body in good health is a duty . . . otherwise we shall not be able to keep our mind strong and clear.

—Buddha

Knowledge in Bloom

Each chapter-end assessment is based on *Bloom's Taxonomy of Learning.* See the inside front cover for a quick review.

Utilizes levels 1–6 of the taxonomy

Developing Your Personal Wellness Plan

Throughout this chapter, we have tried to give you information that will be useful to you as you think about your overall wellness. The following activity will ask you to look at your life in more detail. You will be asked to identify one area of wellness in the mind, soul, or body that you would like to improve.

The area of wellness I want to improve is _____.

Using the Change Implementation Model from Chapter 1, design a plan to bring this change in wellness into your life.

1. Determine what you need or want to change and why.
2. Research your options for making the desired change and seek advice and assistance from a variety of sources.
3. Identify the obstacles to change and determine how to overcome them.
4. Establish a plan by outlining several positive steps to bring about the change you identified.

5. Implement your plan for bringing about the desired change:
   a. Focus on the desired outcome.
   b. View problems as positive challenges.
   c. Turn your fears into energy by reducing anxiety through physical exercise, proper nutrition, and stress-management strategies.
   d. Associate with positive and motivated people.

Finally, think of a reward that you can give yourself once your wellness goal has been reached.

Preparing for Success

Refer to pages 308–309 of this chapter and answer the questions you developed from scanning this chapter's headings. You should also be able to answer the following questions if they were not on your list:

1. What is the difference between health and wellness? _____

   _____

2. What are some of the residual damages from drugs and alcohol? _____

   _____

3. Why are HIV and AIDS still a worry? _____

   _____

4. What is depression and how can you take steps to improve depression if you have it? _____

   _____

15

Plan

© Getty Images

No one can tell you what your life's work is, but it is important that you find it. There is a part of you that already knows; affirm that part.

Willis W. Harman

Why do I have to do this now when I have no idea what I really want to do when I get out of college? *Why* will a chapter on careers help me in college, at work, with my family, and beyond? *Why* is this information such a big deal right now?

C areers, like rockets, don't always take off on schedule. The key is to keep working on the engines.

—Gary Sinise

The major points in this chapter will guide you in making career choices and will assist you in learning to network and to find a mentor who can provide guidance. You will study steps to making career decisions and will have opportunities to apply them. You will understand how careers and jobs are changing and how you will need to adjust continuously throughout your career as jobs change and new work develops. The information in this chapter can help you assess the kind of person you are today and what kind of career you need to make you feel fulfilled and challenged. As you prepare today for a career that will last most of your life, *this chapter can help you:*

▶ Assess your career interests.
▶ Plan for a career instead of several jobs.

▶ Determine where the jobs are expected to be in the near future.
▶ Decide what kind of work best suits your aptitude and interests.
▶ Use a series of steps to make a career decision.
▶ Learn how to use a business network.
▶ Identify steps in finding a mentor.

We hope this chapter will provide eye-opening information that will help you make wise decisions about your future work. Our desire is that you will find a career that you love so much that going to work will seem like fun. It is important to remember that the decisions you make today will impact your career for the rest of your life.

Scan &

Take a few moments and **scan this chapter**. As you scan, **list five questions** you can expect to learn the answers to while reading and studying Chapter 15.

Example:
▶ What is meant by "plan for a career—not a series of jobs"? (from page 333)
▶ What are five of the steps in career decision making? (from page 337)

My Questions:

1. _____

_____ from page _____

2. _____

_____ from page _____

Name: Leon Nowlin
Institution: Indiana University Purdue University Indianapolis, Indianapolis, IN
Major: New Media—Visual Effects
Age: 20

the big WHY
. . . from another perspective

Jurassic Park changed my life. That's correct, animated dinosaurs on the rampage gave me the first glimpse of what I was going to do with the rest of my life. My excitement over movies like *X-Men* and *Titanic* solidified that I had made the right decision to major in New Media in the School of Informatics at IUPUI. I am studying to become a visual effects artist where I can use my vision and creativity to produce 2- and 3-D animation, movies, graphics, audio, video, and emerging forms of media.

Why is it important for you to know what you love and to have a goal in sight? Because if you are unsure about your future and what you want to do, college can quickly become another high school. By reading, researching, shadowing, questioning, and getting involved with your career decision, you can lay out a road map and have a clearer picture of where you are going. The information in this chapter can help you do that. Even if you know your major, some of the activities and questions in this chapter can help you refine your career decision and put you on the path to reaching your ultimate goal.

If you begin college and don't have a clear picture of what you want to do or where you are going, you can quickly become disillusioned and burned out. You can get sidetracked and before you know it, you've wasted a few years and thousands of dollars wandering toward a profession you don't even like.

By finding your passion early, you can begin to see how every test, every paper, and every class plays a role in what you are going to do with your life. You begin to see how biology and anatomy fit into animation. You begin to see how English and oral communication fit into movie making. You begin to see how history and geography classes give you the background to make a believable motion picture. You see how everything is connected.

Use the information in this chapter to help you find your passion or refine your career decisions. By doing so, your college experience will be much more rewarding.

3. _____

_____

from page _____

4. _____

_____

from page _____

5. _____

_____

from page _____

Question

PS   Reminder: At the end of the chapter, come back to this page and answer these questions in your notebook, text margins, or online chapter notes.

WHAT AM I GOING TO DO FOR THE REST OF MY LIFE?

"What am I going to do for the rest of my life?" is an overwhelming question for a beginning college student. You are having a hard enough time getting through classes, participating in extracurricular activities, dating, taking care of children, working part-time or full-time jobs, and meeting with teams to produce a project. How are you supposed to find time to make such an important decision in the midst of all this?

Well, first of all, you don't have to decide today. Of course, it's nice if you always knew you wanted to be an engineer or a broadcast major or a restaurateur or a teacher, but what if you just don't have a clue? Your advisor and your parents are pressuring you to make a decision, so what do you do?

Take your time. Research a variety of careers that you think might interest you. Talk to your advisor and to other professors. Read trade publications in a variety of work disciplines. Get a part-time job in a field that you think might interest you as a career. Shadow someone who is in a profession that appeals to you. Meanwhile, take general education courses that will apply to most majors until you can make up your mind. It's true that choosing a major and a career are very important decisions, but you don't have to rush into these decisions, and you must make your own choice.

In the next few years, the job market will change dramatically as we face sophisticated technology developments, expanding globalization, a shortfall of workers who are skilled and educated in areas where demand is growing, and a major shift in demographics worldwide. "During the past 30 years, the world has undergone accelerated technical and social change. Because of the bewildering combination of these and other cultural forces, many people now worry about their current jobs and the future of America in the world economy" (Gordon, 2005). Globalization and technology are driving dramatic changes in the world's job market. Because of technology, many jobs in this country are now being shipped overseas where these jobs can be performed at a much lower cost.

Despite major changes in technology, globalization, and a shifting and aging population, the future is bright for well-educated and skilled workers. According to the U.S. Bureau of Labor Statistics, in the year 2010 the U.S. economy should support about 167 million jobs, yet the labor force will only be able to fill about 157 million. You will be graduating at a time when demand should be excellent for college graduates.

THE COMING JOB BOOM FOR COLLEGE GRADUATES

Your Future Looks Bright If You Are a College Graduate

The job market is cyclical—up one day and down another. Some years, people are losing jobs all around you, while there are other years when companies are begging for employees and paying high salaries. Thanks to aging baby boomers, the job market is predicted to be outstanding for you in the coming years. There are 76 million baby boomers and only 46 million Gen Xers to take their places, says Eisenberg (2002). As the population ages, certain industries are already desperately seeking qualified employees.

According to the National Association of Colleges and Employers (NACE), "Employers are hiring 15% more college graduates this year. Baby boomers are retiring, and companies that have been holding back in recent years are now replacing tem-

Where Are You . . .

Before reading any further, take a moment and assess where you are at this moment with your knowledge about career development, mentors, and networking. Read each statement carefully and then respond accordingly.

1. I know the difference between a job and a career. YES NO

2. I know which major I want to declare. YES NO

3. I have a good idea about the courses I need to take to prepare me for my chosen career. YES NO

4. I understand how my personality traits relate to my career interests. YES NO

5. I understand the importance of finding a mentor in my chosen field. YES NO

6. I know the value of networking and feel that I am able to find a person or several people to guide me. YES NO

7. I know where I can go to take tests that will identify my interests and aptitude. YES NO

If you answered "Yes" to most of the questions (five or more), you have a very good idea of what you want to do with your life where jobs are concerned. You most likely have already had some experience or done some research on the career that you want. *If you answered* "No" to most of the questions, you will need to study this

you determine what careers might interest you.

porary positions with full-time jobs." The service sector reports the most aggressive hiring plans. "Nearly nine out of ten employers reported an increase in competition for new college hires," according to Marilyn Mackes, executive director of NACE. More than 20% are planning to raise their starting salaries to entice potential employees and to be successful in a very competitive job market.

Hospitals need more nurses and many pay starting bonuses to attract applicants. Pharmacies are paying very high salaries to attract new graduates. Large numbers of teachers, professors, and administrators are retiring over the next decade. According to Eisenberg, schools will need 2.2 million more teachers over the next decade, not to mention librarians, counselors, and administrators. Further, we need more electricians, plumbers, and contractors. Engineers and accountants are in great demand. The service industry in this country is exploding with great demand for excellent managers in the hospitality, retail, and entertainment industries.

College graduates who have the right skills, work attitudes, and habits will be in the driver's seat. All of this is very good news for your generation of college students! A good job should be there waiting for you.

The best jobs in America, according to CNNMoney.com, can be found in the medical professions, engineering, health care, and education. There is a current shortage of college professors, a profession that offers a very rewarding career for certain people.

The saddest words of tongue or pen are these four words: "*It might have been.*"

—Oliver Wendell Holmes

FIGURE 15.1   *The Ten Fastest-Growing Jobs*

Here are 10 occupations that are projected to see double-digit growth between now and 2014.

▶ Network systems and data communications analyst
▶ Physician's assistant
▶ Computer software engineer, applications
▶ Computer software engineer, systems software
▶ Network and computer systems
▶ Database administrator
▶ Physical therapist
▶ Medical scientist
▶ Occupational therapist
▶ College instructor

YOUR CAREER MAY CHANGE FREQUENTLY

Prepare for Flexibility

Regardless of your choice of careers, you may see your field change dramatically over the coming years. Technology is impacting everything we do. Since technology feeds on itself, computers and software are constantly doing tasks faster and better than ever before. Machines are taking over jobs that employees used to do. You might as well know this fact today: You have just begun to learn! As soon as you graduate and accept a job, the first thing you will probably have to do is go back to school in a corporate environment to learn how to do things their way.

Depending on the career you select, you might even see it totally disappear, making it necessary for you to retool and learn something new. Employment sources predict that today's young people will change jobs as often as seven times during a lifetime. The old days of going to work for a company and staying there forever are gone.

Your college career and all that you will learn during the next four years has to prepare you for the future. You need to take charge of your own destiny, seeking the right career, the professors who can teach you the most, the temporary jobs that can prepare you for the real career path, and the extracurricular activities that will give you leadership experience.

You have probably grown tired of hearing, "These are the best years of your life." In many ways they are, but the truth is, they don't have to be the last great years of your life. If you are in college to really learn, grow, mature, and prepare for a great future, the best years may lie ahead. Years when you can put what you have learned into practice, years when you can find new solutions and lead other people to success, years when you can just enjoy the experience of continuing to learn and grow.

So, how do you learn to be flexible? Drink up knowledge like a sponge. Read, read, read! Learn to follow directions and think for yourself. Practice thinking creatively to solve new problems.

> The four great questions: Why are you here? Where have you been? Where are you going? What difference will you make?
>
> —Hal Simon

Improve your writing and speaking skills. Become an expert with computer applications. Learn to work with a diverse population by making friends of different nationalities and ethnic backgrounds. Relate to people who are not just like you. Get comfortable with all age groups. Take risks and get out of your comfort zone. Study personal finance so you can manage your own personal affairs. Gain enough management skills to manage your own business, even if you plan to be a doctor. Getting an education is heavy stuff. After all, you are preparing for the rest of your life!

CAREER PLANNING

Where the Jobs Are

While it may be difficult to make a decision today regarding your career, you might be interested in studying projections regarding the growth industries. According to Tieger and Barron-Tieger (2001), the service industries, along with health, engineering, business management, and social services, will offer the best opportunities in the coming years. As shown in Figure 15.2, of the 10 fastest-growing industries, nine belong to one of these industry groups.

Other occupations expected to grow at a rapid rate include human service workers (55%); data processing equipment repairers (52%); medical records technicians (51%); speech pathologists and audiologists (51%); amusement and recreation atten-

gathering,

Barron-Tieger, 2001).

PLAN FOR A CAREER— NOT A SERIES OF JOBS

Everyone at some time faces the age-old question, "Should I be what others think I should be or should I be what I want to be?" Life's work for many people turns out to be what other people think it should be. Well into the latter half of the twentieth

FIGURE 15.2	*Industries Projected to Experience the Most Growth*
Computer and data processing services	108%
Health services	68%
Management and public relations	60%
Miscellaneous transportation services	60%
Residential care	59%
Personnel supply services	53%
Water and sanitation	51%
Individual social services	50%
Offices of health practitioners	47%
Amusement and recreation services	41%

century, women were expected to have traditional female careers, such as teaching, nursing, or homemaking. They had little opportunity to select a different profession that suited them; society selected their professions for them. It was uncommon for women to enter the fields of engineering, construction, management, public safety, or politics; the avenues to such choices were not open. Today men and women are pursuing careers that might be very different from the ones their parents or grandparents pursued.

College students, male and female, still face pressures to be what others want them to be. Parents actively guide their children toward professions that suit their ideas of what their children should do. Some students have little choice in deciding what they will do for the rest of their lives.

> The purpose of life is to discover your gift. The meaning of life is to give it away.
>
> —David Viscott

For nontraditional students, spouses, time, and finances may dictate a profession. Many choose courses of study that can be completed quickly because finances and family considerations pressure them in that direction. Money is often another consideration when choosing a profession. Regardless of the pressures you have in your life, be careful to research your choices, talk with people already in the profession you are considering, and consider the long-term effects of your decisions. You want your career decisions to be well thought out, well planned, and carefully *executed*.

You are the only person who will be able to answer the questions, "How do I want to spend my time?" and "What is my purpose in life?" No parent, teacher, partner, counselor, or therapist can fully answer these questions for you. Another person may be able to provide information that can help you make the decision, but ultimately, you will be the person in charge of your career path and your life's work.

An informational interview is a useful way to research job options. These interviews can help you figure out how a career path can fit with your life goals.

© PhotoDisc, Inc.

WHAT DO YOU WANT TO BE WHEN YOU GROW UP?

Your Career Self-Study

More people than you would imagine have trouble deciding what they want to be when they grow up. Studies indicate that more than 20 percent of all first-year college students do not know what their majors will be. That's all right for the time being, but before long you will need to make a decision.

The questions that follow are designed to help you make that decision regarding what you want to do with the rest of your life—your career.

What is your personality type? You can best answer this question by taking a personality inventory, such as the Myers-Briggs Type Indicator.® (An inventory based on the MBTI is located in Chapter 6 of this book.) This question is important, because your personality may very well indicate the type of work in which you will be successful and happy. If you are a real people person, you probably will not be very happy, for example, in a job with minimal human contact and interaction.

Describe your personality type.

How will your personality type affect your career path?

What are your interests? Understanding your specific interests may help you decide on a career. If you love working on cars, you might consider becoming a mechanical engineer. If you love to draw or build things, you might be interested in architecture or sculpting.

What are your major interests?

How can these interests be transferred to a career choice?

Do you enjoy physical or mental work? Many people would go crazy if they had to spend so much as one hour per day in an office. Others would be unhappy if they had to work in the sun all day or use a great deal of physical strength. The answer to this question will greatly narrow your list of potential career choices. For example, if you are an outdoor person who loves being outside in all kinds of weather, then you should probably avoid careers that are limited to indoor work. You should also consider whether you have any physical limitations that might affect your career choice.

Do you enjoy physical or mental work or both? Why?

What does this mean for your career path?

Do you want to make a lot of money? Most people, if asked, "Why do you work?" would respond, "For the money." There is nothing wrong with wanting to make money in your profession, but not all professions, regardless of their worth, pay well. Some of the hardest and most rewarding work pays the least. You have to decide whether to go for the money or do something that is personally challenging to you.

Is your major goal in choosing a profession money or something else? What?

What does your goal mean for your career path?

Where do you want to live? Although this question may sound strange, many careers are limited by geography. If you are interested in oceanography, you would be hard-pressed to live in Iowa; if you love farming, New York City would be an improbable place for you to live. If you like small towns, you might not be happy in Atlanta. Some people simply prefer certain parts of the United States (or the world) to others. You need to ask yourself, "Where do I eventually want to live?" "What climate do I really enjoy?" "In what size city or town do I want to work?" "Where would I be the happiest?" "Do I want to live near my family or away from them?" "Do I want to be close to the ocean?"

Where do you eventually want to live? Why?

What does your preference mean for your career path?

Do you want to travel? Some jobs require travel; some people love to travel, some hate it. Ask yourself whether you want to be away from your home and family four nights per week, or whether you want a job that does not require any travel.

Do you enjoy travel? Do you want to do a lot of traveling?

What does this mean for your career path?

How do you like to dress? Some people enjoy dressing up and welcome the opportunity to put on a new suit and go to work. Others prefer to throw on an old pair of blue jeans and head out the door. Jobs have different requirements in terms of dress, and you will be affected by them every workday, so you will want to consider your own preferences.

There is often a typical style of dress or attitude associated with different professions. Will dress codes or other personal-behavior requirements affect your career decisions? Do you think they should?

© Stockbyte

How do you like to dress?

What does this mean for your career path?

What motivates you? What are the one or two things in your life that motivate you? Money? Power? Helping other people? The answer to this question is an essential element in choosing a career. You have to find that certain something that gives you energy and then find a profession that allows you to pursue it with fervor and intensity.

What is your motivational force and why?

How could this help you in deciding on a career path?

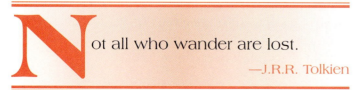

ot all who wander are lost.

—J.R.R. Tolkien

What do you value? Do you value relationships, possessions, money, love, security, challenges, or power? Once you have identified what you value in your life, you can identify careers that closely match your personal value system and eliminate careers that don't. If you have to constantly compromise your values just to get a paycheck, you may be unhappy.

What do you truly value in your life?

How might these values affect your career decisions?

What are your skills? Are you especially good at one or two things? Are you good with computers, a good manager of money, a good carpenter, a good communicator? Your skills will play a powerful part in selecting a career. If you are not good or skilled at manipulating numbers, then you will probably want to avoid careers that require their constant use. If you are not a good communicator, then you probably do not want a career that requires you to give daily presentations. Employers still stress the importance of three basic skills: writing, speaking, and listening. If you have these skills, you are ahead of the pack. If not, you need to enroll in a class that will help you to become better at all three.

What are your skills? What do you do well?

How could your strongest skills help you make a career decision?

Do you like routine? The answer to this question will narrow down your choices tremendously. If you like routine, you will want a career that is conducive to routine and provides structure. If you do not like routine and enjoy doing different things each day, certain careers will be unrealistic for you.

Do you like routine or do you prefer variety? Why?

How does this affect your career path?

Are you a leader? One of the most important questions you must ask yourself is, "Do I enjoy leading, teaching, or guiding people?" If you prefer to be part of the crowd and do not like to stand out as a leader or manager, some careers may not suit you. If you like to take charge and get things done when you are with other people, you will find certain careers better than others. How you relate to leadership will be a part of your personality inventory.

Do you consider yourself a leader? Are you comfortable in a leadership role? Why or why not?

How will your feelings about leadership affect your career path?

How do you feel about managing other people?

Dream Job

Using a variety of resources, write a description of your dream job—the job you would have if you could do anything you would like to do.

_____

_____

_____

_____

_____

Bloom Level 5 question

Help Me: I'm Undeclared

No, it isn't a fatal disease. Being undeclared is not a disgrace or a weakness. It is a temporary state of mind, and the best way to deal with it is to stop and think. You should not declare a major because you are ashamed to be undeclared, and you shouldn't allow yourself to be pressured into declaring a major. Instead, you can take measures to work toward declaring a major and being satisfied with your decision. It is better to be undeclared than to spend several semesters in a field that is wrong for you, wasting hours that won't count toward a degree. On the other hand, the sooner you declare a major, the less likely you are to take courses that don't count toward your eventual decision. While you need to take your time and make a good decision, you

© Reuters/Corbis

J.K. Rowling, the internationally known author of Harry Potter books, first studied to be a secretary, along with French, so she could be a bilingual secretary. Self-described as "the worst secretary ever, very unorganized," she really just wanted to write. She wrote her first book, Rabbit,

DID YOU KNOW

She was divorced and very poor shortly before the birth of her daughter, but she kept writing about wizards. At one time, she was so poor that she had to take her young daughter into restaurants where they could stay warm while she wrote the first Harry Potter novel, which she sold for only $4,000. It took her five years to bring her first book to publication.

Today Mrs. Rowling's name is a household word and her Harry Potter books are internationally famous. Her works rekindled many people's interest in reading, especially young Americans. Mrs. Rowling earned over $400 million on her first three books alone.

Nine Steps to Career Decision Making

Step 1—Dream! If money were not a problem or concern, what would you do for the rest of your life? If you could do anything in the world, what would you do? Where would you do it? These are the types of questions you must ask yourself as you try to select a major and career. Go outside, lie on the grass, and look up at the sky; think silently for a little while. Let your mind wander, and let the sky be the limit. Write your dreams down. These dreams may be closer to reality than you think. In the words of Don Quixote, "Let us dream, my soul, let us dream" (Miguel de Cervantes).

Step 2—Talk to your advisor. Academic advisors are there to help you. But don't be surprised if their doors are sometimes closed. They teach, conduct research, perform community service, and sometimes advise in excess of 100 students. Always call in advance; make an appointment to see an advisor. When you have that appointment, make your advisor work for you. Take your college catalog and ask questions, hard questions. Your advisor will not make a career decision for you, but if you ask the proper questions, he or she can be of monumental help to you and your career decisions. Use students in your program as advisors, too. They will be invaluable to you as you work your way through the daily routine of college. Experienced students can assist you in making decisions about your classes, electives, and work-study programs. They can even help you join and become an active member of a preprofessional program.

Step 3—Use electives. The accreditation agency that works with your school requires that you be allowed at least one free elective in your degree program. Some

> It's a sad day when you find out that it's not an accident—or time—or fortune, but just *yourself* that kept things from you.
>
> —Lillian Hellman

programs allow many more. Use your electives wisely! Do not take courses just to get the hours. The wisest students use their electives to delve into new areas of interest or take a block of courses in an area that might enhance their career opportunities.

Step 4—Go to the career center. Even the smallest colleges have some type of career center or a career counselor. Use them! Campus career centers usually provide free services. The same types of services in the community could cost from $200 to $2,000. The professionals in the career center can provide information on a variety of careers and fields, and they can administer interest and personality inventories that can help you make career and other major decisions.

Step 5—Read, read, read! Nothing will help you more than reading about careers and majors. Ask your advisor or counselor to help you locate information on your areas of interest. Gather information from colleges, agencies, associations, and places of employment. Then read it!

Step 6—Shadow. Shadowing describes the process of following someone around on the job. If you are wondering what engineers do on the job, try calling an engineering office to see whether you can sit with several of their engineers for a day over spring break. Shadowing is the very best way to get firsthand, honest information regarding a profession in which you might be interested.

Step 7—Join preprofessional organizations. One of the most important steps you can take as a college student is to become involved in campus organizations and clubs that offer educational opportunities, social interaction, and hands-on experience in your chosen field. Preprofessional organizations can open doors that will help you make a career decision, grow in your field, meet professionals already working in your field, and, eventually, get a job.

Step 8—Get a part-time job. Work in an area that you may be interested in pursuing as a career. Get a part-time job while you are in school or work in a related job in the summer.

Step 9—Try to get a summer practicum or internship. Work in your field of interest to gain practical experience and see if it really suits you. Some programs require a practicum or internship, and this experience often leads to your first full-time job.

NETWORKING: THE OVERLOOKED SOURCE FOR CAREER DEVELOPMENT

We are often so concerned with books, computerized databases, and interest inventories that we forget to look in our own backyards when thinking about careers. Networking is one of the most important aspects of career development. Look at the person sitting beside you in your orientation class. That person could be a future leader in your field of study. You might be thinking, "No way," but you'd be surprised at how many people lose out on networking opportunities because they do not think ahead. The person sitting beside you is

> Friends do business with friends.
>
> —J. W. Marriott

important. You never know where or when you may see this person again—he may be interviewing you for a job in 10 years, or she may be the person with whom you will start a business in 15 years. "Too far down the road," you say? Don't close your eyes—15 years will pass faster than you think.

You've all heard the expression, "It's not what you know, but who you know." Few statements could be more true, and college is the perfect place for making many personal and professional contacts. At this moment, you are building a network of people on whom you can call for the rest of your life. Your network may include people you know from a variety of areas:

High school and college   Student government
Clubs and professional organizations   Newspaper staff
Sporting teams and events   Family connections
Fraternities and sororities   College committees
Community organizations   Volunteer work

MENTORS

A mentor is someone who can help open doors for you, who will take a personal and professional interest in your development and success. Often a mentor will help you do something that you might have trouble doing on your own. It may be too soon for you to determine now whether you have found a mentor, and you may not find that person

...ent-mentor relationship is unique. You help each other. Your mentor may provide you with opportunities that you might not otherwise have. You may have to do some grunt work, but the experience will usually help you in the long run. While you are helping your mentor, your mentor is helping you by giving you experience and responsibility.

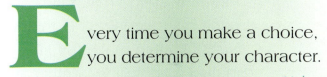

Every time you make a choice, you determine your character.

—Unknown

As a young, uncertain first-year college student, Derrick applied for and was awarded a work-study position with Professor Griffon. His job was to help Professor Griffon ready a semester calendar of events from plays to lectures to dances to speakers. One of his responsibilities was to prepare mailings and other advertising materials for the humanities series. The work was monumental, the pay minimal, and Professor Griffon was not always in the best of spirits. On some days, Derrick left the office swearing that he would never return. But he had little choice—the job paid more than unemployment. Derrick stayed with the job, and before too long, Professor Griffon began to give him more challenging work.

One day, an important member of the community came to the office. Derrick and the professor were both working at their desks. As the professor and the guest discussed a lucrative contract for an artist, Derrick overheard Professor Griffon tell the guest he could "bring the contract by tomorrow and leave it with Derrick, my assistant." "Assistant," Derrick thought, "that's interesting."

Before Derrick graduated with his two-year degree, he had a wealth of experience, knowledge, and, most important, contacts! He had learned how to run the lighting board in the theater, he had managed the box office, he had developed a marketing plan for one of the events, and he had been able to shadow many of the artists who came to the auditorium to perform. All this was possible because of his relationship with Professor Griffon. This student–mentor situation was rewarding for both of them. They helped each other, and both profited.

FIGURE 15.3   *Benefits of Having a Mentor*

- ☑ Mentors teach, advise, and coach.
- ☑ Mentors serve as a sounding board for ideas.
- ☑ Mentors serve as constructive critics.
- ☑ Mentors can promote you among their peers and contacts.
- ☑ Mentors provide information to help with career development.
- ☑ Mentors can increase your visibility on campus and in the work arena.
- ☑ Mentors introduce you to people who can advance your career.

How to Find a Mentor

You can't go shopping for a mentor; you don't advertise; you can't use someone else's mentor. You find a mentor through preparation, work, and a feeling of being comfortable. The following suggestions may help you find a mentor:

- ▶ Arrive at class early and work hard.
- ▶ Develop an outstanding work ethic.
- ▶ Seek advice from many professors and staff members.
- ▶ Ask intelligent, thoughtful questions.
- ▶ Offer to help with projects.
- ▶ Convey the impression that you are committed, competent, and hardworking.
- ▶ Look for opportunities to shadow.
- ▶ If a professor or staff member gives you an opportunity, take it.
- ▶ Look at grunt work as an opportunity for bigger things to come. You are learning!

> Many people worry so much about managing their careers, but rarely spend half that much energy managing their lives. I want to make my life, not just my job, the best it can be. The rest will work itself out.
>
> —Reese Witherspoon

BRINGING IT ALL TOGETHER

Throughout *Cornerstone,* we have tried to suggest that you can change your attitude, your behavior, your actions, and your life. If we did not believe this, we would not have spent 10 years of our lives writing and revising this book, nor would we have spent a collective 60-plus years teaching and working with students.

Change is possible and, in many instances, practical and necessary. However, change does not come without sacrifice, hard work, and much determination. But you already know that, don't you? You had to change to get this far in the text and in your college career. But change is not all that you face in the months, semesters, and years to come. You will also be faced with many hard, life-altering decisions that will affect you, your family, and your livelihood for many years.

One of the most important decisions that you will make, consciously or unconsciously, is deciding what type of person you want to be, what you plan to do in your life, and what contributions you plan to leave to this world when your time here is finished. The world in which we live is full of roadblocks that can potentially cause us to lose focus and fall out of balance. Consider the following facts: Americans reporting that they were "*very happy*" were no more numerous in the early 1990s than in 1957. In 1993, only 21% of 18- to 29-year-olds thought that they had a chance at the "*good life*" as compared to 41% in 1978. Today, Americans spend 40% *less time* with their children than they did in 1965. Employed Americans spend 163 *more hours* per year on the job than they did in 1969. Sixty-nine percent of Americans would like to *slow down* and live a more relaxed life (Sherfield, Montgomery, and Moody, 2001).

As a mature, rational, caring human being, you should realize that you are a part of a bigger picture. This world does not belong to us; we are only borrowing it for a while. Everything you do affects someone else in some way. You must realize that what you do—not just what you do for your career, but your daily actions—matters to someone. There is value in every job, and there is honor in all professions performed well and honestly. When making career and life decisions, you need to take into account the fact that other people, strangers and friends, will eventually be looking to you as a mentor and a role model. This is a major responsibility that you cannot avoid; rather, you should relish the opportunity to inspire and teach. Embrace the moment. Finally, you must realize that unless you are out there, daily, creating a better future for yourself, you have no right to complain about the one that is handed to you.

Think About It

Making a decision about your major or career can be difficult, but fortunately, you still have a few months before you have to make this choice. Use this time to explore all avenues that will expose you to different possibilities. This is a growing time for you and you might discover new interests and directions that you have never considered before. Follow your heart, and pursue your dreams. If there is something you have always wanted to do or be, chances are your desires will not change even after you study other options.

The most important thing for you to remember is that this is your one lifetime. You need to prepare to do something you love. No matter how much money you make, you won't be happy unless you are doing something that matters to you, something that allows you to keep learning and becoming, something that provides you opportunities to give back—perhaps the best gift of all.

As you reflect on this chapter, keep the following pointers in mind:

▶ Identify the assets you can offer a company.
▶ Make educated and researched decisions.
▶ Learn to promote and sell yourself in an interview.
▶ Discover your personality type.
▶ Shadow and do volunteer work.
▶ Realize life is more than money.
▶ Know your own value system.
▶ Identify what motivates you.
▶ Never be afraid to change.
▶ Make your own decisions. Pinpoint your interests.

If you follow your bliss, doors will open for you that wouldn't have opened for anyone else.

—Joseph Campbell

Knowledge in Bloom

Each chapter-end assessment is based on *Bloom's Taxonomy of Learning*. See the inside front cover for a quick review.

Utilizes level 4 of the taxonomy

Developing Skills and Knowledge to Make Wise Career Decisions

Explanation: This activity will ask you to examine the career path that you have chosen or a career path in which you may be interested. Using Bloom's level 4, Analysis, examine each question carefully and answer them related to what you want for yourself in the future.

Process: In order to select a career and then to pursue it, there are many things you need to think about. You will be asked a series of questions that will cause you to think about where you are going with your life. All the questions that follow are level 4 according to Bloom's Taxonomy.

What career do you think you want based on what you know now?

_____

_____

_____

Why do you think you want to do this? What appeals to you about this particular career?

_____

_____

_____

_____

What most interests you today? Can you relate a career to this interest?

_____

_____

_____

How important to you is prestige? Why?

_____

_____

_____

How important to you is feeling that you are making a difference? Explain.

_____

_____

_____

How important to you is making a lot of money?

_____

_____

Regardless of what you think about money, you have to have a certain amount to live. How much do you think that is? Does your career interest pay enough to support you and a family? Do you need to rethink your choice or modify it? Refer to the chapter on money matters and think about the section on budgeting as you answer this question.

_____

_____

_____

Does your career interest relate to your values? Do you see any conflicts with your values? If so, explain.

_____

_____

_____

For a good life, which values, people, places, and emotions do you feel you need?

_____

_____

_____

Is there something you want to be remembered for that can be related to a career? Write a statement about what you think the purpose of your life is.

_____

_____

_____

What is the difference between "making a living" and "living your life"?

_____

_____

_____

Who is the person in your life who has the career that you want? Why do you admire that person and his or her career?

_____

_____

_____

The answers to these questions hold some of the keys to deciding on the right major that would lead to the perfect career for you. You don't have to decide today, but you need to be closing in on what you want to do when you graduate.

Preparing for Success

Refer to pages 328–329 of this chapter and answer the questions you developed from scanning this chapter's headings. You should also be able to answer the following questions if they were not on your list:

1. What is shadowing? _____
_____

2. Why is networking important? _____
_____

3. Why is flexibility important? _____
_____

4. Discuss five of the nine steps to making a career decision. _____
_____

Glossary

Academic freedom   Professors in institutions of higher education are allowed to conduct research and to teach that research, regardless of controversial issues or subject matter. Academic freedom allows the professor the right to teach certain materials that might not have been allowed in high school.

Academic integrity   You have read, fully understand, and adhere to the policies, codes, and moral values of your institution. This implies that you will not cheat, plagiarize, or be unfair in your academic, social, cultural, or civic work.

Accreditation   Most high schools and colleges in the United States are accredited by a regional agency. This agency is responsible for ensuring that minimum standards are held at all institutions that are members in the accreditation agency. The Southern Association of Colleges and Schools is one example of an accreditation agency.

Adding   Adding a class during registration periods or during the first week of classes means that you will be taking an additional class in your schedule.

Administration   The administration of a college is usually made up of nonteaching personnel who handle all of the administrative aspects of the college. The administration is headed by the president and vice presidents. The structure of the administration at each college varies.

Advising   To make sure that you know what classes to take and in which order, you will be assigned an academic advisor—most often a faculty member in your discipline or major—when you arrive on campus. This advisor will usually be with you during your entire degree. She is responsible for guiding you through your academic work at the college.

African American studies   This curriculum deals with the major contributions by African Americans in art, literature, history, medicine, sciences, and architecture. Many colleges offer majors and minors in African American studies.

AIDS   This acronym stands for Acquired Immune Deficiency Syndrome, a disease that is transmitted sexually, intravenously, or from mother to child. Currently, no known cure for AIDS exists, but several medications, such as AZT and protease inhibitors, help to slow the deterioration of the immune system.

Alumna, Alumni, Alumnus   These terms are used to describe students who hold degrees from a college. The term *alumna* refers to a woman, *alumni* is plural, and *alumnus* refers to a man. The term *alumni* is used most often.

Anti-Semitism   Discrimination against people of Jewish descent.

Anxiety   This term refers to the way your body reacts when you are afraid, nervous, or overly stressed about an issue. Many times you will hear the term "test anxiety," indicating that a person is nervous or anxious about taking a test.

Articulation   An articulation agreement is a signed document between two or more institutions guaranteeing that the courses taken at one college will transfer to another college. For example, if Oak College has an articulation agreement with Maple College, it means that the course work taken at Oak College will be accepted toward a degree at Maple College.

Associate degree   The associate degree is a two-year degree that usually prepares the student to enter the workforce with a specific skill or trade. It is also offered to students as the first two years of their bachelor's, or four-year, degree. Not all colleges offer the associate degree.

Attendance   Each college has an attendance policy, such as "a student can miss no more than 10% of the total class hours or he will receive an F for the course." This policy is followed strictly by some professors and more leniently by others. You should always know the attendance policy of each professor with whom you are studying.

Auditing   Most colleges offer the choice either to enroll in a course or to audit a course. If you enroll in a course, you pay the entire fee, attend classes, take exams, and receive credit. If you audit a course, the fee is usually lower, you do not take exams, and you do not receive credit. Course auditing is usually done by people who are having trouble in a subject or by those who want to gain more knowledge about a particular subject. Some colleges charge full price for auditing a course.

Baccalaureate   The baccalaureate degree, more commonly called the bachelor's degree, is a four-year degree in a specific field. Although this degree can be completed in as few as three years or as many as six-plus years, traditionally the amount of academic work required is four years. This degree prepares students for such careers as teaching, social work, engineering, fine arts, and journalism, to name a few. Graduate work is also available in these fields.

Bankruptcy   Bankruptcy is when a person must file legal papers through a lawyer to declare that she cannot pay her bills. Filing bankruptcy destroys one's credit history and it takes 10 years for the bankruptcy to disappear from one's credit report.

Binge drinking   Binge drinking is defined as having five or more alcoholic beverages at one sitting.

Blackboard   Blackboard is a delivery platform for distance education courses taken over the Web. Several platforms exist, including WebCT and Course Compass.

Board of Trustees   The Board of Trustees is the governing body of the college. The board is appointed by government officials (usually the governor) of each state. The board hires the president and must approve any curriculum changes to degree programs. The board also sets policy for the college.

Campus   The campus is the physical plant of the university or college. The term refers to all buildings, fields, arenas, auditoriums, and other properties owned by the college.

Campus police   Each college and university has a campus police office or a security office. You will need to locate this office once you arrive on campus so that, in case of emergency, you will be able to find it quickly. Campus security can assist you with problems ranging from physical danger to car trouble.

Carrel   This is a booth or small room located in the library of the college. You can reserve a carrel for professional use throughout the semester or on a weekly basis. Many times, the carrel is large enough for only one person. Never leave any personal belongings or important academic materials in the carrel because they may be stolen.

Case study   A case study is a story based on real-life events. Cases are written with open-ended conclusions and somewhat vague details to allow the reader to critically examine the story and develop logical solutions to resolve issues.

Catalog   The college catalog is a book issued to you at the beginning of your college career. This book is one of the most important tools that you will use in developing your schedule and completing your degree. The catalog is a legally binding document stating what your degree requirements are for the duration of your study. You will need to obtain and keep the catalog of the year in which you entered college.

CD-ROM   A compact disk containing information, images, that carries supplemental information to support the material in the text.

Certificate   A certificate program is a series of courses, usually one year in length, designed to educate and train an individual in a certain area, such as welding, automotive repair, medical transcription, tool and die, early childhood, physical therapy assistance, and fashion merchandising. While these programs are certified and detailed, they are not degrees. Often, associate and bachelor's degrees are offered in these areas as well.

CLEP   The College Level Examination Program, or CLEP, is designed to allow students to "test" out of a course. CLEP exams are nationally normalized and often are more extensive than a course in the same area. If you CLEP a course, it means that you do not have to take the course in which you passed the CLEP exam. Some colleges have limits on the number of hours that can be earned by CLEP.

Club drugs   Club drugs are drugs taken at raves, parties, or dance clubs. Some of the most common club drugs are GHB (gamma hydroxybutyrate), Ecstasy, roofies, and meth.

Cognate   A cognate is a course (or set of courses) taken outside of your major. Some colleges call this a minor. For instance, if you are majoring in English, you may wish to take a cognate in history or drama. Cognates are usually chosen in a field close to the major. It would be unlikely for a student to major in English and take a cognate in pharmacy.

Commitment   A term that refers to a pledge or promise to do something in the future. It is also considered to be a personal contract for your own goals in life.

Communications   College curricula often state that a student must have nine hours of communications. This most commonly refers to English and speech (oral communication) courses. The mixture of these courses will usually be English 101 and 102 and Speech 101. This will vary from college to college.

Comprehensive exams   This term refers to exams that encompass materials from the entire course. If you are taking a history course and your instructor informs you that there will be a comprehensive exam, information from the first lecture through the last lecture will be included on the exam.

Continuing education   Almost every college in the nation offers courses in continuing education or community education. These courses are not offered for college credit, but continuing education units are awarded in many cases. These courses are usually designed to meet the needs of specific businesses and industries or to provide courses of interest to the community. Continuing education courses range from small engine repair to flower arranging, from stained glass making to small business management.

Co-op   This term is used to refer to a relationship between business/industry and the educational institution. During a co-op, the student spends a semester in college and the next semester on the job. Some co-ops may be structured differently, but the general idea behind a co-op is to gain on-the-job experience while still in college.

exploration, discovery, and results take place in a well-structured group. Cooperative learning teams are groups that work together on research, test preparation, project completion, and many other tasks.

Corequisite   A corequisite is a course that must be taken at the same time as another course. Many times, science courses carry a corequisite. If you are taking Biology 101, the lab course Biology 101L may be required as the corequisite.

Counseling   Most colleges have a counseling center on campus. Do not confuse counseling with advising. Trained counselors assist you with problems that might arise in your personal life, with your study skills, and with your career aspirations. Academic advisors are responsible for your academic progress. Some colleges do combine the two, but in many instances, the counselor and the advisor are two different people with two different job descriptions.

Course title   Every course offered at a college will have a course title. You may see something in your schedule of classes that reads: ENG 101, SPC 205, HIS 210, and so forth. Your college catalog will define what the abbreviations mean. ENG 101 usually stands for English 101, SPC could be the heading for speech, and HIS could mean history. Headings and course titles vary from college to college.

Credit   Credit is money or goods given to you on a reasonable amount of trust that you can and will repay the money or pay for the goods. Credit can come in several forms; credit cards and loans are the most common. Credit can be very dangerous to a person's future if he has too much or does not repay the debt in time.

Credit hour   A credit hour is the amount of credit offered for each class that you take. Usually, each class is worth three credit hours. Science courses, foreign languages, and some math courses are worth four credit hours because of required labs. If a class carries three credit hours, this usually means that the class meets for three hours per week. This formula may vary greatly in a summer session or mid-session.

Credit score   Your credit score is calculated by the amount of debt you have, your salary, your payment history, your length of residence in one place, and the number of inquires into your credit history, to name a few. Your credit score is used to determine if you will be extended future credit and the interest rate that you will be charged. A low score could mean that you cannot get credit or that you will pay a very high interest rate. Negative credit reports stay on your credit history for seven years.

Critical thinking   Critical thinking is thinking that is purposeful, reasoned, and goal directed. It is a type of thinking used to solve problems, make associations, connect relationships, formulate inferences, make decisions, and detect faulty arguments and persuasion.

Curriculum   The curriculum is the area of study in which you are engaged. It is a set of classes that you must take in order for a degree to be awarded.

Dean   The word *dean* is not a name, but a title. A dean is usually the head of a division or area of study. Some colleges might have a dean of arts and sciences, a dean of business, and a dean of mathematics. The dean is the policy maker and usually the business manager and final decision maker of an area of study. Deans usually report to vice presidents or provosts.

Dean's list   The dean's list is a listing of students who have achieved at least a 3.5 (B+) on a 4.0 scale (these numbers are defined under GPA). This achievement may vary from college to college, but generally speaking, the dean's list is comprised of students in the top 5% of students in that college.

Default   A default is when a person fails to repay a loan according to the terms provided in the original loan papers. A default on a Guaranteed Student Loan will result in the garnishment of wages and the inability to acquire a position with the government. Also, you will receive no federal or state income tax refunds until the loan is repaid. Further, a Guaranteed Student Loan cannot be written off under bankruptcy laws.

Degree   When a student completes an approved course of study, she is awarded a degree. The title of the degree depends on the college, the number of credit hours in the program, and the field of study. A two-year degree is called an associate degree, and a four-year degree is called a bachelor's degree. If a student attends graduate school, she may receive a master's degree (approximately 2 to 3 years) and sometimes a doctorate degree (anywhere from 3 to 10 years). Some colleges even offer postdoctorate degrees.

Diploma   A diploma is awarded when an approved course of study is completed. The diploma is not as detailed or comprehensive as an associate degree and usually consists of only 8 to 12 courses specific to a certain field.

Distance learning   Distance learning is learning that takes place away from the campus. Distance learning or distance education is usually offered by a computerized platform such as Blackboard, WebCT, or Course Compass. Chat sessions and Internet assignments are common in distance learning.

Dropping   When a student decides that he does not enjoy a class or will not be able to pass the class because of grades or absenteeism, he may elect to drop that class section. This means that the class will no longer appear on his schedule or be calculated in his GPA. Rules and regulations on dropping vary from college to college. All rules should be explained in the catalog.

Ecstasy   Ecstasy, or "X," is a club drug that is very common at raves and dance parties. It produces a relaxed, euphoric state, which makes the user experience warmth, heightened emotions, and self-acceptance. It can cause severe depression and even death among some users. Ecstasy is illegal to use or possess.

Elective   An elective is a course that a student chooses to take outside of her major field of study. It could be in an area of interest or an area that complements the chosen major. For example, an English major might choose an elective in the field of theatre or history because these fields complement each other. However, a student majoring in English might also elect to take a course in medical terminology because she is interested in that area.

Emeriti   This Latin term is assigned to retired personnel of the college who have performed exemplary duties during their professional careers. For example, a college president who obtained new buildings, added curriculum programs, and increased the endowment might be named president emeritus or emerita upon his or her retirement.

Ethnocentrism   Ethnocentrism is the practice of thinking that one's ethnic group is superior to others.

Evening college   The evening college program is designed to allow students who have full-time jobs to obtain a college degree by enrolling in classes that meet in the evening. Some colleges offer an entire degree program in the evening; others only offer some courses in the evening.

Faculty   The faculty of a college is the body of professionals who teach, do research, and perform community service. Faculty members have prepared for many years to hold the responsibilities carried by this title. Many have been to school for 20 or more years to obtain the knowledge and skill necessary to train students in specific fields.

Fallacy   A fallacy is a false notion. It is a statement based on false materials, invalid inferences, or incorrect reasoning.

Readmit   When a student has "stopped out" for a semester or two, he or she will usually have to be readmitted to the college. This term does not apply to a student who elects not to attend summer sessions. Usually, no application fee is required for a readmit student. He does not lose his previously earned academic credit unless that credit carries a time limit. For example, some courses in psychology carry a 5- or 10-year limit, meaning that if a degree is not awarded within that time, the course must be retaken.

Registrar   The registrar has one of the most difficult jobs on any college campus. She or he is responsible for all student academic records. The registrar is also responsible for entering all grades and all drops and adds, printing the schedule, and verifying all candidates for graduation. The Office of the Registrar is sometimes referred to as the Records Office.

Residence hall   A residence hall is a single-sex or coeducational facility on campus where students live. Many new students choose to live on campus because residence halls are conveniently located. They are also a good way to meet new friends and become involved in extracurricular activities. The college usually provides a full-time supervisor for each hall and a director of student housing. Each hall usually elects a student representative to be on the student council.

Residency requirement   Many colleges have a residency requirement, meaning that a certain number of hours must be earned at the "home" institution. For many two-year colleges, at least 50% of the credit used for graduation must be earned at the home college. For four-year colleges, many requirements state that the last 30 hours must be earned at the home college. All residence requirements are spelled out in the college catalog.

Room and board   If a student is going to live on campus, many times the fee charged for this service will be called "room and board." This basically means a place to stay and food to eat. Many students may opt to buy a meal plan along with their dorm room. These issues are usually discussed during orientation.

Root problem   The root problem is the main issue, the core of the situation at hand. Most troublesome situations have several problems, but usually one major "root" problem exists that causes all of the other problems.

Scholar   A scholar is usually someone who has performed exceptionally in a certain field of study.

Section code   At many larger colleges, many sections of the same course are offered. The section code tells the computer and the registrar which hour and instructor the student will have for a particular class. A typical schedule may look something like this:

English 101	01	MWF	8:00–8:50	Smith
English 101	02	MWF	8:00–8:50	Jones
English 101	03	T TH	8:00–9:15	McGee

The numbers 01, 02, and 03 refer to the section of English in which the student enrolls.

Senior   The term *senior* is used for students in their last year of study for a bachelor's degree. The student must have completed at least 90 credit hours to be a senior.

Sexism   Sexism is discrimination based on sex and social roles.

Sexual harassment   Sexual harassment is defined as any type of advance that is unwanted by the receiver, including touching another person, taunting a person verbally, denying promotions based on forced relationships, and so forth.

Shorthand   A system by which you create your own symbols and shortened words to take notes in your class or text. They may include symbols such as =, +, &, #, and so on.

Social sciences   The social sciences are courses that involve the study of or interface with society and people. Social science courses may include, but are not limited to, psychology, sociology, anthropology, political science, geography, economics, and international studies.

Sophomore   The term *sophomore* refers to students who are in their second year of study for a bachelor's degree. A student must have completed at least 30 credit hours to be a sophomore.

Sororities   Sororities are organizations of the Greek system in which females are members. Many sororities have on-campus housing complexes. Initiation into a sorority differs from organization to organization and campus to campus.

Staff   Personnel in the college setting are usually divided into three categories: administration, staff, and faculty. The staff is responsible for the day-to-day workings of the college. Usually people in admissions, financial aid, the bookstore, housing, student activities and personnel, and so forth hold staff titles. The people heading these departments are usually in administration.

Stereotype   This term refers to an opinion that a person might hold of another person based on a group of people. If one person wears a red cap you might stereotype that person in the same category as a gang member who wears a red cap. There is little basis for this judgment.

Student Government Association (SGA)   This is one of the most powerful and visible organizations on the college campus. Usually, the SGA comprises students from each of the four undergraduate classes. Annual elections are held to appoint officers. As the "student voice" on campus, the SGA represents the entire student body before the college administration.

Student loan   Unlike a grant, a student loan must be repaid. The loans are usually at a much lower rate of interest than a bank loan. For most student loans, the payment schedule does not begin until six months after graduation. This allows the graduate to find a job and become secure in his or her chosen profession. Students deciding to return to school can get the loan deferred, with additional interest, until completion of a graduate degree.

Summary   A short restatement of the material that you have studied or heard in class.

Suspension   Suspension may occur for a variety of reasons, but most institutions suspend students for academic

---

Fees   Fees refer to the amount of money charged by a college for specific items and services. Some fees may include tuition, meal plans, books, and health and activity fees. Fees vary from college to college and are usually printed in the catalog.

Financial aid   If a student is awarded money from the college, the state, the federal government, private sources, or places of employment, this is referred to as financial aid. Financial aid can be awarded on the basis of either need or merit or both. Any grant, loan, or scholarship is formally called financial aid.

Fine arts   Many people tend to think of fine arts as drawing or painting, but in actuality, the fine arts encompass a variety of artistic forms. Theatre, dance, architecture, drawing, painting, sculpture, and music are considered part of the fine arts. Some colleges also include literature in this category.

Foreign language   Almost every college offers at least one course in foreign languages. Many colleges offer degrees in this area. For schools in America, foreign languages consist of Spanish, French, Russian, Latin, German, Portuguese, Swahili, Arabic, Japanese, Chinese, and Korean, to name a few.

Formula   A general rule of how something is done, usually expressed in mathematical symbols.

Fraternities   A fraternity is an organization of the Greek system, which has members who are men. Initiation for each is different. Honorary fraternities, such as Phi Kappa Phi, also exist. These are academic in nature and are open to males and females.

Freshman   This is a term used by high schools and colleges. The term *first-year student* is also used. This term refers to a student in his or her first year of college. Traditionally, a freshman is someone who has not yet completed 30 semester hours of college-level work.

Gay studies   This curriculum deals with the major contributions by homosexuals and lesbians in art, literature, history, medicine, sciences, and architecture. Many colleges offer classes and/or minors in gay, lesbian, bisexual, or transgendered studies.

GHB, or gamma hydroxybutyrate   GHB is a club drug that comes most often in an odorless, liquid form but can also come as a powdery substance. At lower doses, GHB has a euphoric effect and can make the user feel relaxed, happy, and sociable. Higher doses can lead to dizziness, sleepiness, vomiting, spasms, and loss of consciousness. GHB and alcohol used together can be deadly.

GPA, or grade point average   The grade point average is the numerical grading system used by almost every college in the nation. GPAs determine if a student is eligible for continued enrollment, financial aid, or honors. Most colleges operate under a 4.0 system. This means that all As earned are worth 4 quality points; Bs, 3 points; Cs, 2 points; Ds, 1 point; and Fs, 0 points. To calculate a GPA, multiply the number of quality points by the number of credit hours carried by the course and then divide by the total number of hours carried. For example: If a student is taking English 101, Speech 101, History 201, and Psychology 101, these courses usually carry 3 credit hours each. If a student made all As, she would have a GPA of 4.0. If the student made all Bs, she would have a 3.0. However, if she had a variety of grades, the GPA would be calculated as follows:

	Grade	Credit		Q. Points		Total Points
ENG 101	A	3 hours	×	4	=	12 points
SPC 101	C	3 hours	×	2	=	6 points
HIS 201	B	3 hours	×	3	=	9 points
PSY 101	D	3 hours	×	1	=	3 points

30 points divided by 12 hours would equal a GPA of 2.5 (or a C+ average).

Grace period   A grace period is usually 10 days after the due date of a loan payment. For example: If your car payment is due on the first of the month, many companies will give you a 10-day grace period (until the 11th) to pay the bill before they report your delinquent payment to a credit scoring company.

Graduate teaching assistant   You may encounter a teaching assistant as a freshman or sophomore. In some larger colleges and universities, students working toward master's and doctorate degrees teach undergraduate, lower-level classes un-

Grant   A grant is usually money that goes toward tuition and books that does not have to be repaid. Grants are most often awarded by state and federal governments.

Hate crime   A hate crime is categorized as a violent act toward a certain group of people motivated by the hatred of that group of people.

Hepatitis   Hepatitis has three forms: A, B, and C. Hepatitis A comes from drinking contaminated water. Hepatitis B is more prevalent than HIV and can be transmitted sexually, through unsterile needles, and through unsterile tattoo equipment. Left untreated, hepatitis B can cause serious liver damage. Hepatitis C develops into a chronic condition in over 85% of the people who have it. Hepatitis C is the leading cause of liver transplants. Hepatitis B and C can be transmitted by sharing toothbrushes, nail clippers, or any item contaminated with blood. Hepatitis B and C have no recognizable signs or symptoms. Some people, however, do get flulike symptoms, loss of appetite, nausea, vomiting, or fever.

Higher education   This term is used to describe any level of education beyond high school. All colleges are called institutions of higher education.

Homophobia   Homophobia is the fear of homosexuals or homosexuality.

Honor code   Many colleges operate under an honor code. This system demands that students perform all work without cheating, plagiarism, or any other dishonest actions. In many cases, a student can be removed from the institution for breaking the honor code. In other cases, if students do not turn in fellow students who they know have broken the code, they, too, can be removed from the institution.

Honors   Academic honors are based on the GPA of a student. Each college usually has many academic honors, including the dean's list, the president's list, and departmental honors. The three highest honors awarded are summa cum laude, magna cum laude, and cum laude. These are awarded at graduation for students who have maintained a GPA of 3.5 or better. The GPA requirement for these honors varies from college to college. Usually, they are awarded as follows:

3.5 to 3.7 cum laude
3.7 to 3.9 magna cum laude
4.0 summa cum laude

Honors college   The honors college is usually a degree or a set of classes offered for students who performed exceptionally well in high school.

Humanities   The humanities are sometimes as misunderstood as the fine arts. Courses in the humanities include history, philosophy, religion, and cultural studies; some colleges also include literature, government, and foreign languages. The college catalog will define what your college has designated as humanities.

Identification cards   An identification card is essential for any college student. Some colleges issue them free, while some charge a small fee. The ID card allows the student to use the college library, participate in activities, use physical fitness facilities, and many times attend college events for free. They also come in handy in the community. Movie theatres, museums, zoos, and other cultural events usually charge less, or nothing, if a student has an ID. The card will also allow the student to use most area library facilities with special privileges. ID cards are usually validated each semester.

Identity theft   Identity theft is when another person assumes your identity and uses your credit, your name, and your Social Security number. Identity theft can't always be prevented, but to reduce the risk, always guard your credit cards, your address history, and most importantly, your Social Security number and driver's license number.

Independent study   Many colleges offer courses through independent study, meaning that no formal classes and no classroom teacher are involved. The student works independently to complete the course under the general guidelines of a department and with the assistance of an instructor. Many colleges require that a student maintain a minimum GPA before enrolling in independent study classes.

Internship   An internship involves working in a business or industry to gain experience in one's field of interest. Many colleges require internships for graduation.

Journal   Many classes, such as English, freshman orientation, literature, history and psychology, require

students to keep a journal of thoughts, opinions, research, and class discussions. Many times, the journal is a communication link between the students and their professors.

Junior   The term refers to a student who is enrolled in his or her third year of college or a student who has completed at least 60 credit hours of study.

Late fee   A late fee is an "administrative" charge that lenders assess if a loan payment is late.

Learning style   A learning style is the way an individual learns best. Three learning styles exist: visual, auditory, and tactile. Visual means that one learns best by seeing; auditory means that one learns best by hearing; and tactile means that one learns best by touching.

Lecture   A lecture is the "lesson" given by an instructor in a class. The term usually refers to the style in which material is presented. Some instructors have group discussions, peer tutoring, or multimedia presentations. The lecture format means that the professor presents most of the information.

Liberal arts   The liberal arts consist of a series of courses that go beyond training for a certain vocation or occupation. For instance, a student at a liberal arts college might be majoring in biology, but he or she will also have to take courses in fine arts, history, social sciences, math, "hard" sciences, and other related courses. The liberal arts curriculum ensures that the student has been exposed to a variety of information and cultural experiences.

Load   A load refers to the amount of credit or the number of classes that a student is taking. The normal load for a student is between 15 and 18 hours, or five to six classes. For most colleges, 12 hours is considered a full-time load, but a student can take up to 18 or 21 hours for the same amount of tuition.

Major   A major is the intended field of study for a student. The major simply refers to the amount of work completed in one field; in other words, the majority of courses have been in one related field, such as English, engineering, medicine, nursing, art, history, or political science. A student is usually required to declare a major by the end of the sophomore (or second) year.

Meal plan   A meal plan is usually bought at the beginning of the semester and allows a student to eat a variety of meals by using a computer card or punch system. Meal plans can be purchased for three meals a day, breakfast only, lunch only, or any combination of meals.

Media   This term refers to a collection of communication devices such as television, Webcasting, podcasting, print journalism (magazines, newspapers), books, and the Internet.

Mentor   A mentor is someone whom a student can call on to help through troubled times, assist in decision making, and give advice. Mentors can be teachers, staff members, outstanding fellow classmates, or higher-level students. Mentors seldom volunteer to be a mentor; they usually fall into the role of mentoring because they are easy to talk with,

knowledgeable about the college and the community, and willing to lend a helping hand. A student may, however, be assigned a mentor when she or he arrives on campus.

Methamphetamine   Crystal meth, as it is commonly called, is an illegal drug sold in pills, capsules, powder, or rock forms. It stimulates the central nervous system and breaks down the user's inhibitions. It can cause memory loss, aggression, violence, and psychotic behavior.

Minor   The minor of a student is the set of courses that he or she takes that usually complements the major. The minor commonly consists of six to eight courses in a specific field. If a student is majoring in engineering, she might minor in math or electronics, something that would assist her in the workplace.

Mnemonic   A memory trick that helps you retrieve information that is stored in long-term memory. It helps you associate new information with information you already know.

Multiple intelligences   Multiple intelligences are the eight intelligences with which we are born. Howard Gardner, who believes that we all have one of eight intelligences as our primary strength, introduced the theory. The intelligences include Music/Rhythm, Logic/Math, Visual/Spatial, Naturalistic, Interpersonal, Intrapersonal, Verbal/Linguistic, and Body/Kinesthetic.

Natural and physical sciences   The natural and physical sciences refer to a select group of courses from biology, chemistry, physical science, physics, anatomy, zoology, botany, geology, genetics, microbiology, physiology, and astronomy.

Networking   Networking refers to meeting people who can help you (or whom you can help) find careers, meet other people, make connections, and "get ahead."

Online classes   Used in conjunction with distance learning or distance education, online classes use the Internet as a means of delivery, instead of a traditional classroom.

Orientation   Every student is requested, and many are required, to attend an orientation session. This is one of the most important steps that a student can take when beginning college. Important information and details concerning individual colleges and their rules and regulations will be discussed.

Podcasting   This term refers to information that is recorded verbally for downloading and use with a personal MP3 player.

Plagiarism   This term refers to the act of using someone's words or works as your own without citing the original author. Penalties for plagiarism vary from college to college, but most institutions have strict guidelines for dealing with students who plagiarize. Some institutions force the student to withdraw from the institution. Your student handbook should list the penalties for plagiarism.

Prefix   A prefix is a code used by the Office of the Registrar to designate a certain area of study. The prefix for English is usually ENG; for Religion, REL; for Theatre, THE; for History, HIS; and so forth. Prefix lettering varies from college to college.

Preprofessional programs   Preprofessional programs usually refer to majors that require advanced study to the master's or doctoral level to be able to practice in the field. Such programs include, but are not limited to, law, medicine, dentistry, psychiatry, nursing, veterinary studies, and theology.

Prerequisite   A prerequisite is a course that must be taken before another course. For example, most colleges require that English 101 and 102 (Composition I and II) be completed before any literature course is taken. Therefore, English 101 and 102 are prerequisites to literature. Prerequisites are always spelled out in the college catalog.

President   A college president is the visionary leader of an institution. She or he is usually hired by the Board of Trustees of a college. Primary responsibilities involve financial planning, fundraising, community relations, and the academic integrity of the curriculum. Every employee at the college is responsible to the president.

Priority   A priority is something that you have chosen to put in the forefront of your life, your time schedule, and/or your budget.

Probation   Many times, a student who has below a 2.0 in any given semester or quarter will be placed on academic probation for one semester. If that student continues to perform below 2.0, suspension may be in order. The rules for probation and suspension must be displayed in the college catalog.

Procrastination   The practice of putting things off until the last minute or even until it is too late to complete the task. Procrastination is a habit that can be broken with practice and dedication.

Professor   Many people believe that all teachers on the college level are professors. This is not true. A full professor is someone who may have been in the profession for a long time and someone who usually holds a doctoral degree. The system of promotion among college teachers is as follows: adjunct instructor, instructor, lecturer, assistant professor, associate professor, full professor (professor).

Protease inhibitors   Protease inhibitors are a series, or "cocktail," of drugs used to fight HIV/AIDS and slow the destruction of the immune system. They have been instrumental in extending the lives of people living with HIV and AIDS. However, a new strain of HIV has arisen that is immune to the protease inhibitors presently used.

Provost   The provost is the primary policy maker at the college with regard to academic standards. He or she usually reports directly to the president. Many colleges do not have a provost but have a vice president for academic affairs or a dean of instruction.

Racism   Racism occurs when a person or group of people believes that their race is superior to another race.

knowledgeable about the college and the community, and willing to lend a helping hand. A student may, however, be assigned a mentor when she or he arrives on campus.

Methamphetamine   Crystal meth, as it is commonly called, is an illegal drug sold in pills, capsules, powder, or rock forms. It stimulates the central nervous system and breaks down the user's inhibitions. It can cause memory loss, aggression, violence, and psychotic behavior.

Minor   The minor of a student is the set of courses that he or she takes that usually complements the major. The minor commonly consists of six to eight courses in a specific field. If a student is majoring in engineering, she might minor in math or electronics, something that would assist her in the workplace.

Mnemonic   A memory trick that helps you retrieve information that is stored in long-term memory. It helps you associate new information with information you already know.

Multiple intelligences   Multiple intelligences are the eight intelligences with which we are born. Howard Gardner, who believes that we all have one of eight intelligences as our primary strength, introduced the theory. The intelligences include Music/Rhythm, Logic/Math, Visual/Spatial, Naturalistic, Interpersonal, Intrapersonal, Verbal/Linguistic, and Body/Kinesthetic.

Natural and physical sciences   The natural and physical sciences refer to a select group of courses from biology, chemistry, physical science, physics, anatomy, zoology, botany, geology, genetics, microbiology, physiology, and astronomy.

Networking   Networking refers to meeting people who can help you (or whom you can help) find careers, meet other people, make connections, and "get ahead."

Online classes   Used in conjunction with distance learning or distance education, online classes use the Internet as a means of delivery, instead of a traditional classroom.

Orientation   Every student is requested, and many are required, to attend an orientation session. This is one of the most important steps that a student can take when beginning college. Important information and details concerning individual colleges and their rules and regulations will be discussed.

Podcasting   This term refers to information that is recorded verbally for downloading and use with a personal MP3 player.

Plagiarism   This term refers to the act of using someone's words or works as your own without citing the original author. Penalties for plagiarism vary from college to college, but most institutions have strict guidelines for dealing with students who plagiarize. Some institutions force the student to withdraw from the institution. Your student handbook should list the penalties for plagiarism.

Prefix   A prefix is a code used by the Office of the Registrar to designate a certain area of study. The prefix for English is usually ENG; for Religion, REL; for Theatre, THE; for History, HIS; and so forth. Prefix lettering varies from college to college.

Preprofessional programs   Preprofessional programs usually refer to majors that require advanced study to the master's or doctoral level to be able to practice in the field. Such programs include, but are not limited to, law, medicine, dentistry, psychiatry, nursing, veterinary studies, and theology.

Prerequisite   A prerequisite is a course that must be taken before another course. For example, most colleges require that English 101 and 102 (Composition I and II) be completed before any literature course is taken. Therefore, English 101 and 102 are prerequisites to literature. Prerequisites are always spelled out in the college catalog.

President   A college president is the visionary leader of an institution. She or he is usually hired by the Board of Trustees of a college. Primary responsibilities involve financial planning, fundraising, community relations, and the academic integrity of the curriculum. Every employee at the college is responsible to the president.

Priority   A priority is something that you have chosen to put in the forefront of your life, your time schedule, and/or your budget.

Probation   Many times, a student who has below a 2.0 in any given semester or quarter will be placed on academic probation for one semester. If that student continues to perform below 2.0, suspension may be in order. The rules for probation and suspension must be displayed in the college catalog.

Procrastination   The practice of putting things off until the last minute or even until it is too late to complete the task. Procrastination is a habit that can be broken with practice and dedication.

Professor   Many people believe that all teachers on the college level are professors. This is not true. A full professor is someone who may have been in the profession for a long time and someone who usually holds a doctoral degree. The system of promotion among college teachers is as follows: adjunct instructor, instructor, lecturer, assistant professor, associate professor, full professor (professor).

Protease inhibitors   Protease inhibitors are a series, or "cocktail," of drugs used to fight HIV/AIDS and slow the destruction of the immune system. They have been instrumental in extending the lives of people living with HIV and AIDS. However, a new strain of HIV has arisen that is immune to the protease inhibitors presently used.

Provost   The provost is the primary policy maker at the college with regard to academic standards. He or she usually reports directly to the president. Many colleges do not have a provost but have a vice president for academic affairs or a dean of instruction.

Racism   Racism occurs when a person or group of people believes that their race is superior to another race.

Readmit   When a student has "stopped out" for a semester or two, he or she will usually have to be readmitted to the college. This term does not apply to a student who elects not to attend summer sessions. Usually, no application fee is required for a readmit student. He does not lose his previously earned academic credit unless that credit carries a time limit. For example, some courses in psychology carry a 5- or 10-year limit, meaning that if a degree is not awarded within that time, the course must be retaken.

Registrar   The registrar has one of the most difficult jobs on any college campus. She or he is responsible for all student academic records. The registrar is also responsible for entering all grades and all drops and adds, printing the schedule, and verifying all candidates for graduation. The Office of the Registrar is sometimes referred to as the Records Office.

Residence hall   A residence hall is a single-sex or coeducational facility on campus where students live. Many new students choose to live on campus because residence halls are conveniently located. They are also a good way to meet new friends and become involved in extracurricular activities. The college usually provides a full-time supervisor for each hall and a director of student housing. Each hall usually elects a student representative to be on the student council.

Residency requirement   Many colleges have a residency requirement, meaning that a certain number of hours must be earned at the "home" institution. For many two-year colleges, at least 50% of the credit used for graduation must be earned at the home college. For four-year colleges, many requirements state that the last 30 hours must be earned at the home college. All residence requirements are spelled out in the college catalog.

Room and board   If a student is going to live on campus, many times the fee charged for this service will be called "room and board." This basically means a place to stay and food to eat. Many students may opt to buy a meal plan along with their dorm room. These issues are usually discussed during orientation.

Root problem   The root problem is the main issue, the core of the situation at hand. Most troublesome situations have several problems, but usually one major "root" problem exists that causes all of the other problems.

Scholar   A scholar is usually someone who has performed exceptionally in a certain field of study.

Section code   At many larger colleges, many sections of the same course are offered. The section code tells the computer and the registrar which hour and instructor the student will have for a particular class. A typical schedule may look something like this:

English 101	01	MWF	8:00–8:50	Smith
English 101	02	MWF	8:00–8:50	Jones
English 101	03	T TH	8:00–9:15	McGee

The numbers 01, 02, and 03 refer to the section of English in which the student enrolls.

Senior   The term *senior* is used for students in their last year of study for a bachelor's degree. The student must have completed at least 90 credit hours to be a senior.

Sexism   Sexism is discrimination based on sex and social roles.

Sexual harassment   Sexual harassment is defined as any type of advance that is unwanted by the receiver, including touching another person, taunting a person verbally, denying promotions based on forced relationships, and so forth.

Shorthand   A system by which you create your own symbols and shortened words to take notes in your class or text. They may include symbols such as =, +, &, #, and so on.

Social sciences   The social sciences are courses that involve the study of or interface with society and people. Social science courses may include, but are not limited to, psychology, sociology, anthropology, political science, geography, economics, and international studies.

Sophomore   The term *sophomore* refers to students who are in their second year of study for a bachelor's degree. A student must have completed at least 30 credit hours to be a sophomore.

Sororities   Sororities are organizations of the Greek system in which females are members. Many sororities have on-campus housing complexes. Initiation into a sorority differs from organization to organization and campus to campus.

Staff   Personnel in the college setting are usually divided into three categories: administration, staff, and faculty. The staff is responsible for the day-to-day workings of the college. Usually people in admissions, financial aid, the bookstore, housing, student activities and personnel, and so forth hold staff titles. The people heading these departments are usually in administration.

Stereotype   This term refers to an opinion that a person might hold of another person based on a group of people. If one person wears a red cap you might stereotype that person in the same category as a gang member who wears a red cap. There is little basis for this judgment.

Student Government Association (SGA)   This is one of the most powerful and visible organizations on the college campus. Usually, the SGA comprises students from each of the four undergraduate classes. Annual elections are held to appoint officers. As the "student voice" on campus, the SGA represents the entire student body before the college administration.

Student loan   Unlike a grant, a student loan must be repaid. The loans are usually at a much lower rate of interest than a bank loan. For most student loans, the payment schedule does not begin until six months after graduation. This allows the graduate to find a job and become secure in his or her chosen profession. Students deciding to return to school can get the loan deferred, with additional interest, until completion of a graduate degree.

Summary   A short restatement of the material that you have studied or heard in class.

Suspension   Suspension may occur for a variety of reasons, but most institutions suspend students for academic

many cases, a student can be removed from the institution for breaking the honor code. In other cases, if students do not turn in fellow students who they know have broken the code, they, too, can be removed from the institution.

Honors   Academic honors are based on the GPA of a student. Each college usually has many academic honors, including the dean's list, the president's list, and departmental honors. The three highest honors awarded are summa cum laude, magna cum laude, and cum laude. These are awarded at graduation for students who have maintained a GPA of 3.5 or better. The GPA requirement for these honors varies from college to college. Usually, they are awarded as follows:

3.5 to 3.7 cum laude
3.7 to 3.9 magna cum laude
4.0 summa cum laude

Honors college   The honors college is usually a degree or a set of classes offered for students who performed exceptionally well in high school.

Humanities   The humanities are sometimes as misunderstood as the fine arts. Courses in the humanities include history, philosophy, religion, and cultural studies; some colleges also include literature, government, and foreign languages. The college catalog will define what your college has designated as humanities.

Identification cards   An identification card is essential for any college student. Some colleges issue them free, while some charge a small fee. The ID card allows the student to use the college library, participate in activities, use physical fitness facilities, and many times attend college events for free. They also come in handy in the community. Movie theatres, museums, zoos, and other cultural events usually charge less, or nothing, if a student has an ID. The card will also allow the student to use most area library facilities with special privileges. ID cards are usually validated each semester.

Identity theft   Identity theft is when another person assumes your identity and uses your credit, your name, and your Social Security number. Identity theft can't always be prevented, but to reduce the risk, always guard your credit cards, your address history, and most importantly, your Social Security number and driver's license number.

Independent study   Many colleges offer courses through independent study, meaning that no formal classes and no classroom teacher are involved. The student works independently to complete the course under the general guidelines of a department and with the assistance of an instructor. Many colleges require that a student maintain a minimum GPA before enrolling in independent study classes.

Internship   An internship involves working in a business or industry to gain experience in one's field of interest. Many colleges require internships for graduation.

Journal   Many classes, such as English, freshman orientation, literature, history and psychology, require

students to keep a journal of thoughts, opinions, research, and class discussions. Many times, the journal is a communication link between the students and their professors.

Junior   The term refers to a student who is enrolled in his or her third year of college or a student who has completed at least 60 credit hours of study.

Late fee   A late fee is an "administrative" charge that lenders assess if a loan payment is late.

Learning style   A learning style is the way an individual learns best. Three learning styles exist: visual, auditory, and tactile. Visual means that one learns best by seeing; auditory means that one learns best by hearing; and tactile means that one learns best by touching.

Lecture   A lecture is the "lesson" given by an instructor in a class. The term usually refers to the style in which material is presented. Some instructors have group discussions, peer tutoring, or multimedia presentations. The lecture format means that the professor presents most of the information.

Liberal arts   The liberal arts consist of a series of courses that go beyond training for a certain vocation or occupation. For instance, a student at a liberal arts college might be majoring in biology, but he or she will also have to take courses in fine arts, history, social sciences, math, "hard" sciences, and other related courses. The liberal arts curriculum ensures that the student has been exposed to a variety of information and cultural experiences.

Load   A load refers to the amount of credit or the number of classes that a student is taking. The normal load for a student is between 15 and 18 hours, or five to six classes. For most colleges, 12 hours is considered a full-time load, but a student can take up to 18 or 21 hours for the same amount of tuition.

Major   A major is the intended field of study for a student. The major simply refers to the amount of work completed in one field; in other words, the majority of courses have been in one related field, such as English, engineering, medicine, nursing, art, history, or political science. A student is usually required to declare a major by the end of the sophomore (or second) year.

Meal plan   A meal plan is usually bought at the beginning of the semester and allows a student to eat a variety of meals by using a computer card or punch system. Meal plans can be purchased for three meals a day, breakfast only, lunch only, or any combination of meals.

Media   This term refers to a collection of communication devices such as television, Webcasting, podcasting, print journalism (magazines, newspapers), books, and the Internet.

Mentor   A mentor is someone whom a student can call on to help through troubled times, assist in decision making, and give advice. Mentors can be teachers, staff members, outstanding fellow classmates, or higher-level students. Mentors seldom volunteer to be a mentor; they usually fall into the role of mentoring because they are easy to talk with,

Fees   Fees refer to the amount of money charged by a college for specific items and services. Some fees may include tuition, meal plans, books, and health and activity fees. Fees vary from college to college and are usually printed in the catalog.

Financial aid   If a student is awarded money from the college, the state, the federal government, private sources, or places of employment, this is referred to as financial aid. Financial aid can be awarded on the basis of either need or merit or both. Any grant, loan, or scholarship is formally called financial aid.

Fine arts   Many people tend to think of fine arts as drawing or painting, but in actuality, the fine arts encompass a variety of artistic forms. Theatre, dance, architecture, drawing, painting, sculpture, and music are considered part of the fine arts. Some colleges also include literature in this category.

Foreign language   Almost every college offers at least one course in foreign languages. Many colleges offer degrees in this area. For schools in America, foreign languages consist of Spanish, French, Russian, Latin, German, Portuguese, Swahili, Arabic, Japanese, Chinese, and Korean, to name a few.

Formula   A general rule of how something is done, usually expressed in mathematical symbols.

Fraternities   A fraternity is an organization of the Greek system in which a male student is a member. Many fraternities have their own housing complexes on campus. Induction for each is different. Honorary fraternities, such as Phi Kappa Phi, also exist. These are academic in nature and are open to males and females.

Freshman   This is a term used by high schools and colleges. The term *first-year student* is also used. This term refers to a student in his or her first year of college. Traditionally, a freshman is someone who has not yet completed 30 semester hours of college-level work.

Gay studies   This curriculum deals with the major contributions by homosexuals and lesbians in art, literature, history, medicine, sciences, and architecture. Many colleges offer classes and/or minors in gay, lesbian, bisexual, or transgendered studies.

GHB, or gamma hydroxybutyrate   GHB is a club drug that comes most often in an odorless, liquid form but can also come as a powdery substance. At lower doses, GHB has a euphoric effect and can make the user feel relaxed, happy, and sociable. Higher doses can lead to dizziness, sleepiness, vomiting, spasms, and loss of consciousness. GHB and alcohol used together can be deadly.

GPA, or grade point average   The grade point average is the numerical grading system used by almost every college in the nation. GPAs determine if a student is eligible for continued enrollment, financial aid, or honors. Most colleges operate under a 4.0 system. This means that all As earned are worth 4 quality points; Bs, 3 points; Cs, 2 points; Ds, 1 point; and Fs, 0 points. To calculate a GPA, multiply the number of quality points by the number of credit hours carried by the course and then divide by the total number of hours carried. For example: If a student is taking English 101, Speech 101, History 201, and Psychology 101, these courses usually carry 3 credit hours each. If a student made all As, she would have a GPA of 4.0. If the student made all Bs, she would have a 3.0. However, if she had a variety of grades, the GPA would be calculated as follows:

	Grade	Credit		Q. Points		Total Points
ENG 101	A	3 hours	×	4	=	12 points
SPC 101	C	3 hours	×	2	=	6 points
HIS 201	B	3 hours	×	3	=	9 points
PSY 101	D	3 hours	×	1	=	3 points

30 points divided by 12 hours would equal a GPA of 2.5 (or a C+ average).

Grace period   A grace period is usually 10 days after the due date of a loan payment. For example: If your car payment is due on the first of the month, many companies will give you a 10-day grace period (until the 11th) to pay the bill before they report your delinquent payment to a credit scoring company.

Graduate teaching assistant   You may encounter a teaching assistant as a freshman or sophomore. In some larger colleges and universities, students working toward master's and doctorate degrees teach undergraduate, lower-level classes under the direction of a major professor in the department.

Grant   A grant is usually money that goes toward tuition and books that does not have to be repaid. Grants are most often awarded by state and federal governments.

Hate crime   A hate crime is categorized as a violent act toward a certain group of people motivated by the hatred of that group of people.

Hepatitis   Hepatitis has three forms: A, B, and C. Hepatitis A comes from drinking contaminated water. Hepatitis B is more prevalent than HIV and can be transmitted sexually, through unsterile needles, and through unsterile tattoo equipment. Left untreated, hepatitis B can cause serious liver damage. Hepatitis C develops into a chronic condition in over 85% of the people who have it. Hepatitis C is the leading cause of liver transplants. Hepatitis B and C can be transmitted by sharing toothbrushes, nail clippers, or any item contaminated with blood. Hepatitis B and C have no recognizable signs or symptoms. Some people, however, do get flulike symptoms, loss of appetite, nausea, vomiting, or fever.

Higher education   This term is used to describe any level of education beyond high school. All colleges are called institutions of higher education.

Homophobia   Homophobia is the fear of homosexuals or homosexuality.

Honor code   Many colleges operate under an honor code. This system demands that students perform all work without cheating, plagiarism, or any other dishonest actions. In

reasons. While GPA requirements vary from college to college, usually a student is suspended when his grade point average falls below a 1.5 for two consecutive semesters. The college catalog contains the rules regarding suspension.

Syllabus   In high school, you may have been given a class outline, but in college, you are given a syllabus. This is a legally binding contract between the student and the professor. This document contains the attendance policy, the grading scale, the required text, the professor's office hours and phone number(s), and important information regarding the course. Most professors also include the class operational calendar as a part of the syllabus. This is one of the most important documents that you will be issued in a class. You should take it to class with you daily and keep it at least until the semester is over.

Tenure   You may hear someone call a college teacher a "tenured professor." This usually means that the professor has been with the college for many years and has been awarded tenure due to his successful efforts in research, publication of books and articles, and community service. Usually, tenure ensures the professor lifelong employment.

TOEFL   TOEFL is an acronym for the Test of English as a Foreign Language. This test is used to certify that international students have the English skills needed to succeed at the institution or to become a teaching assistant. Some colleges allow international students to use TOEFL to satisfy their foreign language requirement.

Tolerance   Tolerance is the ability to recognize and respect the opinions, practices, religions, race, sex, sexual orientation, ethnicity, and age of other people.

Transcript   A transcript is a formal record of all work attempted and completed at a college. If a student attends more than one college, he will have a transcript for each college. Many colleges have a policy in which all classes, completed or not, remain on the transcript. Some colleges allow Ds and Fs to be removed if the student repeats the course with a better grade. Many colleges, however, leave the old grade and continue to count the D or F in the GPA. Rules regarding transcripts vary from college to college. Many employers now require that a prospective employee furnish a transcript from college.

Transfer   This term may refer to course work or to a student. If a student enrolls in one college and then wants to go to another, she is classified as a *transfer student*. The course work completed is called *transfer work*. Many colleges have rules regarding the number of credit hours that may be transferred from one college to another. Most colleges will not accept credit from another college if the grade on the course is below a C.

Transient   A transient student is someone who is attending another college to take one or two courses. If a student comes home for the summer and wants to enroll in a college near his home and maintain himself as a student at his chosen college, he is a transient student.

Transitional studies   Many colleges have an open admission policy, meaning that the door is open to any student. In these cases, the college usually runs a transitional studies program to assist the student in reaching her educational goal. If a student has not performed well in English, math, or reading, she may be required to attend a transitional studies class to upgrade basic skills in certain areas.

Value   This word has many meanings, but it can refer to your personal set of morals that you consider important. It can also refer to the amount of credit assigned to a course at your college.

Veteran's Affairs   Many colleges have an Office of Veteran's Affairs to assist those students who have served in the military. Many times, a college will accept credit earned by a veteran while in the service. Most of the time, a veteran's financial packages will differ because of the GI Bill.

Vice president   Many colleges have several vice presidents who serve under the president. They are senior-level administrators who assist with the daily operations of the college. Most colleges have vice presidents of academic affairs, financial affairs, and student affairs, to name a few.

Volumes   This term is used by most libraries in the nation. A volume is a book or a piece of nonprinted material used to assist the student in his studies. You may read that a college library has 70,000 volumes. This means that it has 70,000 books and other pieces of media. Many college libraries have collections that range in the millions of volumes.

WebCT   WebCT is a delivery platform for distance education courses taken over the Web.

Who's Who   This is a shortened title for *Who's Who in American Colleges and Universities,* a nationally recognized grouping. Students are nominated by the college because of their academic standing and their achievements in cocurricular activities and community service.

Women's Studies   Some colleges offer majors and minors in women's studies. The curriculum is centered around the major contributions of women to art, literature, medicine, history, law, architecture, and sciences.

References

ACT, Inc. *National Dropout Rates, Freshman to Sophomore Years by Type of Institution.* Iowa City, IA: ACT, 2000.

Adler, R., Rosenfeld, L., and Towne, N. *Interplay. The Process of Interpersonal Communication*, 2nd ed. New York: Holt, Rinehart and Winston, 2001.

Advanced Public Speaking Institute. "Public Speaking: Why Use Humor?" Virginia Beach, VA: Author, *www.public-speaking.org/public-speaking-humor-article.htm.*

American College Testing Program. *National Drop Out Rates.* Iowa City, IA: ACT Institutional Data File, 1995.

Amnesty International. Death penalty information. *www.web.amnesty.org.*

Anderson, D. *The Death Penalty—A Defence.* Sweden, 1998. Translated into English in 2001 at *http://w1.155.telia.com/~u15509119/ny_sida_1.htm.*

Armstrong, T. *Multiple Intelligences in the Classroom.* Alexandria, VA: Association for Supervision and Curriculum Development, 1994.

Astin, A. *Achieving Educational Excellence.* San Francisco: Jossey-Bass, 1985.

Bach, D. *The Finish Rich Notebook.* New York: Broadway Books, 2003.

Barnes & Noble and the Anti-Defamation League. *Close the Book on Hate: 101 Ways to Combat Prejudice*, 2000. Available online at *www.adl.org/prejudice/closethebook.pdf.*

Beebe, S. A., and Beebe, S. J. *Interpersonal Communication: Relating to Others,* 3rd ed. Boston: Allyn & Bacon, 2002.

Benson, H. *The Relaxation Response.* New York: Caral Publishing Group, 1992.

Benson, H., and Stuart, E. *The Wellness Book.* New York: Fireside, 1992.

Benson, H., and Stuart, E. *The Wellness Book: The Comprehensive Guide to Maintaining Health and Treating Stress-Related Illness.* New York: Birch Lane Press, 1992.

Benson, H., and Stuart, E. *Wellness Encyclopedia.* Boston: Houghton Mifflin, 1991.

Berenblatt, M., and Berenblatt, A. *Make an Appointment with Yourself: Simple Steps to Positive Self-Esteem.* Deerfield Beach, FL: Health Communication, 1994.

Best Jobs in America. CNNMoney.com. May 28, 2006. *http://money.cnn.com/magazines/moneymag/bestjobs/top50/index.html.*

Beyer, B. *Developing a Thinking Skills Program.* Boston: Allyn and Bacon, 1998.

Boldt, L. *How to Be, Do, or Have Anything.* Berkeley, CA: Ten Speed Press, 2001.

Bosak, J. *Fallacies.* Dubuque, IA: Educulture Publishers, 1976.

Boyle, M., and Zyla, G. *Personal Nutrition.* St. Paul, MN: West Publishing, 1992.

Bozzi, V. "A Healthy Dose of Religion." *Psychology Today,* November, 1988.

Brightman, H. Georgia State University Master Teacher Program: On Learning Styles. *www.gsu.edu/~dschjb/wwwmbti.html.*

Broderick, C. "Why Care About Your Credit Score?" InCharge Education Foundation, Inc., 2003.

Bucher, R. D. *Diversity Consciousness: Opening Our Minds to People, Cultures, and Opportunities.* Upper Saddle River, NJ: Prentice Hall, 2000.

Buscaglia, L. *Living, Loving, and Learning.* New York: Ballantine, 1982.

Business and Legal Reports, Inc. *Staying Safe on Campus.* Madison, CT: Author, 1995.

Cameron, J. *The Artist's Way: A Spiritual Path to Higher Creativity.* New York: Penguin Putnam, 1992.

Cardinal, F. "Sleep Is Important When Stress and Anxiety Increase." The National Sleep Foundation, April 10, 2003.

Cetron, F. "What Students Must Know to Succeed in the 21st Century." *The Futurist, 30,* no. 4, July–Aug. 1996, p. 7.

Checkley, K. "The First Seven . . . and the Eighth." *Educational Leadership, 55,* no. 1, September 1997.

Chickering, A., and Schlossberg, N. *Getting the Most Out of College.* Boston: Allyn and Bacon, 1995.

Chopra, D. *The Seven Spiritual Laws of Success.* San Rafael, CA: New World Library, 1994.

Christian, J., and Greger, J. *Nutrition for Living.* Redwood City, CA: Benjamin/Cummings Publishing, 1994.

Chronicle of Higher Education, The. 49(1), August 30, 2002.

Clegg, R. "The Color of Death." *National Review Online,* June 11, 2001, *www.nationalreview.com/contributors/clegg061101.shtml.*

Cloud, J. "The Pioneer Harvey Milk." Accessed at *www.time.com.*

CNN Money. "More Credit Late Fees Paid." May 12, 2002. Accessed at *http://money.cnn.com/2002/05/21/pf/banking/cardfees/.*

Cohen, L. *Conducting Research on the Internet.* University of Albany Libraries, 1996a, *www.albany.edu.*

Cohen, L. *Evaluating Internet Resources.* University of Albany Libraries, 1996b, *www.albany.edu.*

Cojonet (City of Jacksonville, FL). "Consumer Affairs Gets New Tough Law on Car Title Businesses." Accessed at *www.coj.net/Departments/Regulatory + and + Environmental + Services/Consumer + Affairs/TITLE + LOANS.htm.*

Coldewey, J., and Streitberger, W. *Drama, Classical to Contemporary,* rev. ed. Upper Saddle River, NJ: Prentice Hall, 2001.

"College Credit Cards." September 15, 2006. Accessed at *http://www.credit-card-articles.com.*

"Commonly Abused Drugs." National Institute on Drug Abuse. Accessed at *www.nida.nih.gov/DrugsofAbuse.html.*

Cooper, A. *Time Management for Unmanageable People.* New York: Bantam Books, 1993.

Cooper, M. "Alcohol Use and Risky Sexual Behavior among College Students and Youth." *Journal of Studies on Alcohol, 63*(2), 2002, p. S101.

Cooper-Arnold, Amy L. "Credit Card Debt: A Survival Guide for Students." *www.youngmoney.com/credit_debt/credit_basics/050804-02,* 2006.

Daly, J., and Engleberg, I. *Presentations in Everyday Life: Strategies for Effective Speaking.* Boston: Houghton Mifflin, 2002.

"Dan White." Accessed at *www.findagrave.com/php/famous.php?page=name&firstName=Dan&lastName=White.*

Daniels, P., and Bright, W. *The World's Writing Systems.* Oxford, England: Oxford University Press, 1996.

Debtsteps.com. "Learn About Credit Card Debt." September 15, 2006. Accessed at *http://www.debtsteps.com./credit-card-debt-facts.html*

de Cervantes, M. S. *Don Quijote de la Mancha.* Translation by John Rutherford. New York: Penguin, 2000.

Donatelle, R., and Davis, L. *Health: The Basics.* Upper Saddle River, NJ: Prentice Hall, 2002.

Dunn, R., and Griggs, S. *Practical Approaches to Using Learning Styles in Higher Education.* New York: Bergin & Garvey, 2000.

Eddlem, T. "Ten Anti–Death Penalty Fallacies." *The New American, 18*(3), June 3, 2002.

Eisenberg, D. "The Coming Job Boom." *Time Online Edition,* April 29, 2002, *www.time.com/time/business/article/0,8599,233967,00.html.*

Ellis, D., Lankowitz, S., Stupka, D., and Toft, D. *Career Planning.* Rapid City, SD: College Survival, Inc., 1990.

Elrich, M. "The Stereotype Within." *Educational Leadership,* April 1994, p. 12.

Equifax.com. "Glossary of Terms." Accessed at *www.econsumer.equifax.com/consumer/forward.ehtml?forward=credu_glossaryterms.*

Equifax.com. "Identity Theft and Fraud." Accessed at *www.econsumer.equifax.com/consumer/forward.ehtml?forward=idtheft_howitstrikes.*

Equifax.com. "Teaching Students about Money and Credit." Accessed at *www.equifax.com/CoolOnCredit/parent1.html.*

Facione, P. *Critical Thinking: What It Is and Why It Counts.* Santa Clara: California University Press, 1998.

Freshman Survey Data Report. Cooperative Institutional Research Program Sponsored by the Higher Education Research Institute (HERI). University of California, Los Angeles, 1999.

Fulghum, R. *All I Really Need to Know, I Learned in Kindergarten.* New York: Ivy Books, 1988.

Gardenswartz, L., and Rowe, A. *Managing Diversity: A Complete Desk Reference and Planning Guide.* New York: Irwin/Pfeiffer, 1993.

Gardner, H. *Frames of Mind: The Theory of Multiple Intelligences.* New York: Basic Books, 1983.

Gardner, H. "Reflections on Multiple Intelligences: Myths and Messages." *Phi Delta Kappan, 77,* no. 3, November, 1995, p. 200.

Gardner, J., and Jewler, J. *Your College Experience.* Belmont, CA: Wadsworth, 2000.

Gay, Lesbian and Straight Education Network. "Just the Facts." New York: GLSE, 2000. Synopsis found online at *http://msn.planetout.com/people/teens/features/2000/08/facts.html.*

Gonyea, J. C. "Discover the Work You Were Born to Do." MSN.com Careers, 2002, *http://editorial.careers.msn.com/articles/born.*

Gordon, Edward E. *The 2010 Meltdown: Solving the Impending Jobs Crisis.* Westport, CT: Praeger, 2005.

Grilly, D. *Drugs and Human Behavior.* Boston: Allyn and Bacon, 1994.

Gunthrie, H., and Picciano, M. *Human Nutrition.* Salem, MA: Mosby, 1995.

Hales, D. *Your Health.* Redwood City, CA: Benjamin/Cummings Publishing, 1991.

Haney, D. "New AIDS Drugs Bring Optimism." *The Las Vegas Review Journal,* February 12, 2003.

Hanna, S. L. *Person to Person.* Upper Saddle River, NJ: Prentice Hall, 2003.

Hickman, R., and Quinley, J. *A Synthesis of Local, State, and National Studies in Workforce Education and Training.* Washington, DC: The American Association of Community Colleges, 1997.

Hidden Menace: Drowsy Drivers. *www.sleepdisorders.about.com/library/weekly/aa062902a.htm.*

"Identity Theft and Fraud." *Money Matters 101,* p. 9, 2005.

Jerome, R., and Grout, P. "Cheat Wave." *People Magazine,* June 17, 2002, p. 84.

Kaihla, Paul. (2003) "The Coming Job Boom." *www.business2.com/b/2/subscribers/articles/print/0,17925,516005,00.html.*

Kanar, C. *The Confident Reader.* New York: Houghton Mifflin, 2000.

Kirby, D. "The Worst Is Yet to Come." *The Advocate,* January 19, 1999, p. 57.

Kleiman, C. *The 100 Best Jobs for the 90's and Beyond.* New York: Berkley Books, 1992.

Konowalow, S. *Cornerstones for Money Management.* Upper Saddle River, NJ: Prentice Hall, 1997.

Konowalow, S. *Planning Your Future: Keys to Financial Freedom.* Columbus, OH: Prentice Hall, 2003.

Lecky, P. *Self-Consistency: A Theory of Personality.* Garden City, NY: Anchor, 1951.

Leinwood, D. "Ecstasy-Viagra Mix Alarms Doctors." *USA Today,* Sept. 23, 2002.

Lieberman, B. "1 in 5 New HIV Cases Is a Drug-Resistant Strain, Study Finds." *The San Diego Tribune,* August 8, 2002.

Mackes, M. *Report on College Graduates' Prospects.* National Association of Colleges and Employers, 2006.

Maker, J., and Lenier, M. *College Reading,* 5th ed. Belmont, CA: Thompson Learning, 2000.

Managing and Resolving Conflict, http://hr2.hr.arizona.edu/06_jcl/jobdesc/groundrules.htm.

Manisses Communications Group. *Alcoholism & Drug Abuse Weekly, 13*(36), September 2001, p. 7.

Mass, J. cited in Kates, W. "America Is Not Getting Enough Sleep." *The San Francisco Chronicle,* March 30, 1990, p. B3.

McGraw, P. C. *Life Strategies Workbook.* New York: Hyperion, 2000.

McKay, M., and Fanning, P. *Self-Esteem.* Oakland, CA: New Harbinger, 2000.

Motley Fool, The. "How to Get Out of Debt." Accessed at *www.fool.com/seminars/sp/index.htm? sid=0001&lid=000&ref=.*

National Association of Colleges and Employers. "Top Ten Personal Qualities Employers Seek." *Job Outlook,* NACE, 2000.

National Foundation for Credit Counseling. "National Foundation for Credit Counseling Announces Study Results on the Impact of Credit Counseling on Consumer Credit and Debt Payment Behavior." Press release, March 21, 2002. Accessed at *www.nfcc.org/newsroom/shownews.Cfm?newsid=257.*

"Nellie Mae Study." *Credit Cards 101,* p. 1, 2005.

Nelson, D., and Low, G. *Emotional Intelligence: Achieving Academic and Career Excellence.* Upper Saddle River, NJ: Prentice Hall, 2003.

Nevid, J., Fichner-Rathus, L., and Rathus, S. *Human Sexuality in a World of Diversity.* Boston: Allyn and Bacon, 1995.

Okula, S. "Protect Yourself from Identity Theft." Accessed at *http://moneycentral.msn.com/articles/banking/credit/1342.asp.*

Ormondroyd, J., Engle, M., and Cosgrave, T. *How to Critically Analyze Information Sources.* Cornell University Libraries, 2001, *www.library.cornell. edu.*

Ormrod, J. E. *Educational Psychology: Developing Learners.* Upper Saddle River, NJ: Prentice Hall, 2003.

Pauk, W. *How to Study in College,* 8th ed. New York: Houghton Mifflin, 2005.

Paul, R. *What Every Person Needs to Survive in a Rapidly Changing World.* Santa Rosa, CA: The Foundation for Critical Thinking, 1992.

"Poll: What Is the Biggest Problem Facing College Students?" September 15, 2006. Accessed at *http://www.youngmoney.com/aboutus.*

Popenoe, D. *Sociology,* 9th ed. Englewood Cliffs, NJ: Prentice Hall, 1993.

Powell, E. *Sex on Your Terms.* Boston: Allyn and Bacon, 1996.

Radelet, M. "Post-Furman Botched Executions." Accessed at *www.deathpenaltyinfo.org/botched.html.*

Rathus, S., and Fichner-Rathus, L. *Making the Most Out of College.* Englewood Cliffs, NJ: Prentice Hall, 1994.

Rathus, S., Nevid, J., and Fichner-Rathus, L. *Essentials of Human Sexuality.* Boston: Allyn and Bacon, 1998.

"Retention Rates by Institutional Type." Los Angeles, CA: Higher Education Research Institute, UCLA, 1989.

Rogers, C. *On Becoming Partners: Marriage and Its Alternatives.* New York: Delacorte Press, 1972.

Romas, J., and Sharma, M. *Practical Stress Management.* Boston: Allyn and Bacon, 1995.

Rooney, M. "Freshmen Show Rising Political Awareness and Changing Social Views." *The Chronicle of Higher Education,* January 31, 2003.

Salmela-Aro, K., and Nurmi, J. E. "Uncertainty and Confidence in Interpersonal Projects. Consequences for Social Relationships and Well-Being." *Journal of Social and Personal Relationships,* 13(1), 1996, pp. 109–122.

Schacter, D. *The Seven Sins of Memory: How the Mind Forgets and Remembers.* New York: Houghton Mifflin, 2001.

Sciolino, E. "World Drug Crop Up Sharply in 1989 Despite U.S. Effort." *New York Times,* March 2, 1990.

Seyler, D. *Steps to College Reading,* 2nd ed. Boston: Allyn & Bacon, 2001.

Shaffer, C., and Amundsen, K. *Creating Community Anywhere.* Los Angeles: Jeremy P. Tarcher Publishing, 1994.

Sherfield, R. *The Everything Self-Esteem Book.* Avon, MA: Adams Media, 2004.

Sherfield, R., Montgomery, R., and Moody, P. *Capstone: Succeeding Beyond College.* Upper Saddle River, NJ: Prentice Hall, 2001.

Silver, H., Strong, R., and Perini, M. "Integrating Learning Styles and Multiple Intelligences." *Educational Leadership,* 55, no. 1, September, 1997, p. 22.

Smith, B. *Breaking Through: College Reading,* 7th ed. Upper Saddle River, NJ: Pearson Education, 2004.

Southern Poverty Law Center. *Ten Ways to Fight Hate.* Montgomery, AL: Author, 2000.

Syemore, R., and O'Connell, D. "Did You Know?" *Chatelaine,* 73(8), August 2000, p. 30.

"Ten Credit Card Management Tips." Accessed at *www.aol1.bankrate.com/AOL/news/cc/20021218a. asp.*

Texas A&M University. "Improve Your Memory." Accessed at *www.scs.tamu.edu/selfhelp/elibrary/memory.asp.*

Tieger, P., and Barron-Tieger, B. *Do What You Are: Discover the Perfect Career for You Through the Secrets of Personality Type,* 3rd ed. Boston: Little, Brown, 2001.

Uncle Donald's Castro Street. "Dan White: He Got Away with Murder." Accessed at *http://thecastro.net/milk/whitepage.html.*

U.S. Bank. *Paying for College: A Guide to Financial Aid.* Minneapolis, MN: Author, 2002.

U.S. Department of Commerce. *2000 U.S. Census.* Washington, DC: U.S. Government Printing Office, 2001.

UC Berkeley—Teaching Library Internet Workshop. "Evaluating Web Pages: Techniques to Apply and Questions to Ask." *www.lib.berkeley.edu/TeachingLib/Guides/Internet/Evaluate.htr* (2005).

Copyright by the Regents of the University of California.

Warner, J. "Celebratory Drinking Culture on Campus: Dangerous Drinking Style Popular among College Students." *Parenting and Pregnancy,* November 5, 2002.

Warnick, B., and Inch, E. *Critical Thinking and Communication—The Use of Reason in Argument.* New York: Macmillan, 1994.

Watson, N. "Generation Wrecked." *Fortune,* October 14, 2002, pp. 183–190.

Wechsler, H., and Wuethrich, B. *Dying to Drink: Confronting Binge Drinking on College Campuses.* New York: Rodale Press, 2002.

Werner, R. *Understanding.* Newport, RI: TED Conferences, 1999.

Whitfield, C. *Healing the Child Within.* Deerfield Beach, FL: Health Communication, 1987.

Woolfolk, A. *Educational Psychology,* 8th ed. Boston: Allyn and Bacon, 2001.

World Almanac and Book of Facts, The, 2002. New York: World Almanac Books, 2003.

Wurman, R. *Understanding.* New York: Donnelley & Sons, 1999.

Yale Study of Graduating Seniors. New Haven, CT: Yale University, 1953.

Young, J. "Homework? What Homework?" *The Chronicle of Higher Education,* December 6, 2003.

Zarefsky, D. *Public Speaking: Strategies for Success,* 3rd ed. Boston: Pearson/Allyn & Bacon, 2001.

Zimring, F. *Capital Punishment and the American Agenda.* Cambridge, MA: Cambridge University Press, 1987.

Index